Leaving India

Leaving India

MY FAMILY'S JOURNEY FROM
FIVE VILLAGES TO FIVE CONTINENTS

minal hajratwala

Houghton Mifflin Harcourt · *Boston New York*
2009

For information about permission to reproduce selections from this book,
write to Permissions, Houghton Mifflin Harcourt Publishing Company,
215 Park Avenue South, New York, New York 10003.

www.hmhbooks.com

Library of Congress Cataloging-in-Publication Data
Hajratwala, Minal.
Leaving India : my family's journey from five villages to five continents /
Minal Hajratwala.
p. cm.
Includes bibliographical references and index.
ISBN 978-0-618-25129-2 (alk. paper)
1. Hajratwala, Minal. 2. Hajratwala, Minal—Family. 3. Gujarati
Americans—Biography. 4. Children of immigrants—United States—
Biography. 5. Immigrants—United States—Biography. 6. Gujaratis
(Indic people)—Biography. 7. Immigrants—Biography. 8. India—
Emigration and immigration—Psychological aspects. 9. East Indians—
Migrations—Case studies. 10. Emigration and immigration—
Psychological aspects—Case studies. I. Title.
E184.G84H35 2009
973'.049140092—dc22 [B] 2008036079

Printed in the United States of America

Book design by Lisa Diercks
Typeset in Minion

Map by Jacques Chazaud

DOC 10 9 8 7 6 5 4 3 2 1

Photographs on spine: TOP: The author at Disneyland in 1978,
after her family moved from New Zealand to the United States.
BOTTOM: Kaashi R. Narsey, the author's grandmother,
with her middle son, Ranchhod, ca. 1936.

for my family
past, present, future
given & chosen

CONTENTS

ACKNOWLEDGMENTS

This project benefited deeply from the contributions of my parents: translators, guides, fans, and storytellers. I am grateful for their ongoing and unconditional love.

To write a first book is to pay off many debts. I give thanks to the myriad beings of many realms who helped me grow into my voice:

Almost every member of my extended family hosted, fed, or chauffeured me during the course of eight months of travel and research; they are in my hearts, and I hope they will forgive me for not naming them all individually. (Similarly, my deepest apologies to those whose names do not appear in the accompanying family tree. As it is meant to clarify relationships for the reader, the tree includes only those who appear by name in the book. Absolutely no slight or offense is intended!) A list of those who graciously submitted to interviews appears in the bibliography.

I would be remiss not to thank personally Mukesh V. Khatri and his family in London, with whom I stayed an entire month; Dinesh and Kokila Kalidas, members of the motel diaspora, who arranged accommodations for me around the world; and Kiran C. Narsey, who generously allowed me to draw from his unpublished history of the Narseys firm. In the category of virtual family, Ahalya and Sarosh Katrak (Mumbai) and Swapna and Sanjeev Roy (Kolkata) hosted me for many research days and made necessary introductions.

Many thanks to the scholars and sources who generously shared their expertise and pointed me toward resources I would not have discovered otherwise: Brij V. Lal and Padma Narsee, Australian National University,

Canberra; Kanti Jinna, Canberra; Kalpana Hiralal, University of Durban-Westville; and Joy and Peter Brain, Durban. Radha Patel lent me a substantial portion of her desi diaspora library. Falu Bakrania allowed me to audit her "South Asian Diasporas" course at Stanford University, bringing me up to date on academic work in this area. Paul Tichmann assisted me in accessing the Kapitan file in the archives of Durban's local history museum housed in the Old City Courthouse. Additionally, librarians and library staffs around the world have my greatest appreciation, particularly at the National Archives of Fiji, National Archives of South Africa in Cape Town, Gandhi-Luthuli Documentation Centre at the University of Durban-Westville in South Africa, National Library of India in Kolkata, University of Pune, University of Mumbai at Kalina, British Library in London, Columbia University in New York, Stanford University in California, San Francisco Public Library, University of Michigan libraries including the Bentley Historical Library, Canton Public Library in Michigan, and Azaadville Public Library outside Johannesburg, South Africa.

In India, research often seems possible only through acts of grace. In Mumbai, Sadanarth Bhatkal made it possible for me to conduct research at the Asiatic Society. In Ahmedabad, Rashmikant and Meghlata Mehta made the needed calls of introduction. Varsha Jani of the L. D. Institute of Indology in Ahmedabad kindly shared her thesis on the Solanki dynasty. Bhartiben Shelat and her staff at the Bhojai Library in Ahmedabad photocopied rare books and made it possible for me to view Solanki-era sculptures in the collection. V. P. Trivedi at the Gujarat Vishwakosh Trust gave me access to that encyclopedia publishing house's private library. At the Vadodara Central Library, Chandrakant P. Toraskar assisted me in finding Gujarati texts.

When at last I let go of my geekish love of research in order to actually write, I was blessed to have the most capable of research assistants, Ahmad Musaddequr Rahman, who worked tirelessly for a year to track down government documents, articles, and elusive facts. Hedgebrook writer's colony provided me with the space, solitude, and support necessary for plumbing the mystical depths.

My route to publishing was seamless and enjoyable, thanks to Sam Freedman, proposal midwife, and Anna Ghosh, agent extraordinaire. At Houghton Mifflin, I was blessed with an amazing team of editors. Eamon

Dolan, Anjali Singh, Beth Burleigh Fuller, and Katya Rice each played a crucial role in championing and shaping the manuscript. I am so grateful for their kind, incisive encouragement and care.

Personal thanks go to the members of my writing group, Pueng Vongs, Sandip Roy, and Daisy Hernandez, whose gentle, incisive critiques were a steady source of inspiration and improvement. Linda Gonzalez, Canyon Sam, Sunita Dhurandhar, and others wrote with me in community, easing the isolation of our writing lives. Lisa Margonelli, Nancy Netherland, Soo Mee Kwon, and Raoul V. Mowatt generously provided feedback on the manuscript. Coaches and teachers, formal and informal, offered wise counsel that guided me through every aspect of the process: Susan Griffin, Liu Hoi-Man, Kate Reber, Ryumon (Hilda Gutiérrez Baldoquín), and Little Clarence. Extra-special gratitude goes to Shaily Matani, who did all of the above and more; to Miriam Kronberg; and to Parijat Desai. Finally, George "Daddi G" Ophelia endured the trials of being a writer's partner with the compassionate patience of a Zen monk, and even served as research assistant from time to time; I was sustained throughout by her steady support. Of love, one can never say enough.

A NOTE ON THE TEXT

As a reader, I find it most inconvenient to be forever flipping to a glossary in the back of a book. When I find it necessary to use non-English words, therefore, I define them nearby, preferably in the very same sentence. A few basic terms recur throughout this book and are worth explaining at the outset:

Gujarat is an old name for a region that has been apportioned many times over the last few centuries; I use it to refer to the area now within the modern state of Gujarat. I use *southern Gujarat* to refer to the southern portion of the modern state of Gujarat, from Vadodara to the Maharashtra border. Navsari and the other villages of my family fall in the southernmost part of this area. Prior to independence, one district of this region was named "South Gujarat," but I have avoided that capitalized term, as it is confusing in the modern context. I use the term *British Gujarat* to refer to the portion of modern Gujarat that fell within the British-ruled region called the Bombay Presidency, and which included the city of Surat.

Gujarati refers to the language, people, and things of the Gujarat region. It can be used as either adjective or noun. Thus, my family is originally from Gujarat; we are Gujaratis, we eat Gujarati food, and the language we speak is Gujarati.

Khatri refers to the clan—a subgroup of a caste, and the people and customs related to it—to which my family belongs. Other groups in other places throughout India also use the same word. In this book, it refers to the members of this group who originate in five particular villages in southern Gujarat.

Politics has a tendency to muddle geography; unless otherwise noted, place names in India and elsewhere refer to modern boundaries, though the territories may have gone by other names during the period discussed. However, I use the variant of the name that is relevant for the time period in question; for example, for the modern city of Vadodara, previously known as Baroda, my spelling varies with the context.

By *Indian diaspora,* I mean people who trace their roots to India, however that locale was defined *at the time of emigration.* Although certain early emigrants came from what is now Pakistan or Bangladesh, the task of statistically winnowing them from those who came from modern "India" seems both impossible and unnecessary, for in their own eyes they too came from India. After 1947, my *Indian diaspora* refers to these earlier emigrants, their descendants, and emigrants from independent India. It does not include, however, Pakistanis and Bangladeshis who emigrated after independence; their stories must be considered in the light of their homelands' own divergent histories, a project that is beyond the scope of this book.

Occasionally, when it is necessary to speak more broadly, I use the terms *South Asia* and *South Asian diaspora.* South Asia encompasses the land that falls in the modern nations of Afghanistan, Pakistan, India, Nepal, Bangladesh, Burma (Myanmar), Sri Lanka, and the Maldives. *South Asian diaspora* is thus an umbrella term for emigrants from this region and their descendants. I use it sparingly, aware of the tendency for the Indian experience to overshadow those of smaller groups.

Finally, although sizable migrations have taken place *within* South Asia at various times (notably from India to Burma and Sri Lanka), I restrict my definition of the Indian diaspora to those who traveled *outside* South Asia. Re-migration from neighboring nations is frequent and difficult to track; to include these migrants might artificially inflate the diaspora figures, and I have chosen a conservative, if somewhat arbitrary, approach.

When rendering Indian languages in English script, scholars use diacritical marks to distinguish a hard *t* from a soft *t,* a long *i* from a short *i,* and so on. I find these marks minimally helpful for pronunciation, maximally confusing to the casual reader, and most bothersome to the noble typesetter and copyeditor, in whose good graces it is always wise to remain. So I prefer a phonetic approach. There is one significant vowel distinction, which I render as follows: *aa* for the long *a* (pronounced as in *father*), and *a* for the short, neutral *a* (as in *elephant*). For proper names, however, I follow common or traditional usage. Thus I write *Navsari, Gujarat, Hajratwala*, although these are pronounced *Navsaari, Gujaraat, Hajratwaalaa*. (For the very curious, *Minal* is pronounced *MEE-nalr*; it rhymes, roughly, with *venal*, not *banal*.)

My family speaks a village form of Gujarati, particular to our region and caste. Many of my interviews took place entirely or largely in this Gujarati. (Translations are mine, except as noted.) Speakers of a more formal version of the language may thus find "errors," as I have tried to render our folk speech faithfully, rather than "correctly."

Similarly, all beliefs, rituals, and superstitions described herein are particular to my people and, in some cases, only to my family. Despite the efforts of various sorts of charlatans, don't let anyone tell you they have the "correct" version of Hinduism. Hinduism is a vast, diverse religion; nothing depicted here (or anywhere) should be taken as a universal Hindu or Indian principle, for there is no such thing.

Finally, the reader should know that this is a work of nonfiction. I have been asked frequently whether I am fictionalizing, and the answer is no; whether I have changed people's names, and the answer is—except in one case, noted in the text—no; whether I am breaking or am tempted to break confidences, and the answer is no. The journalist in me is scrupulous about such matters, and no "poetic license" has been taken. Those family members who are main subjects and were alive at the time of the completion of the manuscript have had an opportunity to read their sections in advance and to correct matters of fact. All remaining errors are, of course, mine.

In rendering dialogue, I use quotation marks for words I have heard personally; some are translated by me. For bits of conversation that were related to me by one or more people who were present, I use the European system of dashes to introduce speech; the reader should take these words as conveying the sense, but perhaps not the exact text, of the conversation, which was sometimes being recalled many decades afterward. In this category, too, are the family letters rendered in Chapter 6 (Brains); the letters themselves, alas, no longer exist. For conversations described to me by someone who was not present, I do not attempt to quote directly. For internal thoughts or very lengthy anecdotes that were voiced in an interview with me, I use the person's exact words (sometimes in translation) in italics; otherwise, I do not attempt to reconstruct internal dialogue.

This book was eight years in the making, and to write it I interviewed nearly one hundred family members, friends, and community sources. I would not intentionally compromise their truth. Where their memories contradict one another, I have either made the differences transparent, or I have not included the incidents in question. In my heart the journalist and the poet hold hands and walk into the dark, each with her own methods, her own sticks and tools. It is for others to say how "literary" or "creative" they find this text; for myself, I am comfortable with the knowledge that it is, to the best of my capacity, simply nonfiction.

> And inasmuch as the house of history is, like the house of dreams and other things of that sort, ruinous, apologies must be made for discrepancies.
>
> —Abdul Qadir Badauni

*On the sixth night Vidhaataa, Goddess of
Destiny, takes up what she finds below the
sleeping infant: awl and palm leaf under a string
hammock, or ballpoint pen and blue-lined paper
under a crib from the baby superstore.*

*She eats the offering: sweets, coins.
She writes.*

*Reviewing the accumulated karma of past lives,
enumerating the star-given obstacles of this one,
she writes.*

*And what Destiny writes, neither human nor god
may put asunder.*

1. WATER

The remnants of the Solanki dynasty were scattered over the land.
— James Tod, *Annals and Antiquities of Rajasthan,* 1829

The god/dess Ardhanaarishvara
Lake of Nails, Mount Abu, Rajasthan, India
.
?
.
↓
The Solanki dynasty
Rajasthan and Gujarat, India
ca. 961–1242
.
?
.
↓
The Khatris of the five villages
Gujarat, India
ca. 1765
.

.
↓
Narsai and Ratan
The village of Navsari, Gujarat, India
ca. 1870s

"*t*HE LAKE OF NAILS is where your history begins," Bimal Barot tells us.

Dust filters through the half-light of afternoon. I am slightly nauseated, two days of traveler's sickness and a journey through winding alleyways—not to mention several countries, by now—having taken their toll. After interviewing relatives at half a dozen stops on my forty-thousand-mile-plus air ticket, piecing together the story of our family's migrations, I have come to India: to find whatever fragments remain here, to trace the shape of our past and learn how it shadows or illuminates our present.

Written records about private lives, though, are sparse. In English they come only from encounters with the colonial bureaucracy, usually at or after the moment of emigration. Before that, any information is kept in Gujarati, the language of our region, and in the Indian manner—which is to say haphazardly. Historical property records are inaccessible, but a date engraved on a house tells when it was built. Birth certificates may not exist, but an old lady's memory links a child's birth with a cousin's wedding with an eclipse of the moon.

But there is one objective Gujarati source, a collection of books filled with personal data. In the time before widespread literacy, one caste had access to the written word. Others, if they could afford it, paid these learned men to keep track of—or spruce up, if need be—their personal histories.

So I find myself sitting, with my parents, in the home of our clan's genealogist.

. . .

In a way it is astonishing that we have arrived here at all, on the strength of a name and a vague address given to me in Fiji weeks earlier by a distant uncle, who last used the information several decades ago:

Behind the Temple of Justice
Vadodara
Gujarat
INDIA

Vadodara is busy and industrial; home to 1.4 million, it is the third largest city in the state of Gujarat. Its air, which these days is a soup of diesel and factory fumes, was once so fragrant that it drew vacationers of the highest rank. The Prince of Wales, visiting in 1876, enjoyed the flowered breezes of the Garden Palace as a guest of the local maharaja — a kept man of the British Empire, who despite liberal inclinations squandered his people's money on luxuries and on making a good impression. For the English prince's visit, the maharaja ordered an honorary parade of soldiers, elephants with parasols, drums, spears, flowing robes, and horses kicking up dust. In this manner also, more pomp than substance, the maharaja ruled over the five villages where my ancestors lived.

The Temple of Justice turns out to be another of his old palaces, now repurposed as a courthouse. "Behind" means a neighborhood of gullies too narrow for our taxi to navigate. We transfer to a motorized ricksha to enter the maze, then stop and ask directions.

"The house is closed," someone calls out. One old woman sitting on a porch directs us left; her companion, equally wizened, points right. A boy hops into our ricksha and takes us to a house where after some time a man comes out. The boy runs off, the man hops in, we go back past the old ladies, one shouts a friendly, "Told ya so, this way," and so it goes till we reach a low-ceilinged house where a girl opens the door and, hearing the name we ask for, nods.

Inviting us in, she tells us the power has just gone out. Her father is not home right now, and he has the books. Still, she gestures for us to sit and wait, then withdraws behind a cotton curtain. We sit in the dim living room for several minutes, breathing deeply — a relief, after the ricksha's diesel fumes.

When the girl returns from the back of the house, she brings her uncle:

4

a slim man with a full mustache and a few days' growth of beard, wearing a short-sleeved cotton shirt and a blue satin dhoti wrapped around his legs. He greets us and introduces himself. The name we came with is his grandfather's; his father is also dead by now; but he and his cousin, the girl's father, are keepers of the tradition.

To keep the records up to date, he explains, they—like their male ancestors before them—make their livelihood by traveling from town to town, recording new births, deaths, marriages, and sometimes emigrations, all for a fee. What they know of our community alone fills ten great books. He takes out another family's to show us what a book looks like: a huge, loose-bound sheaf twice as wide as an open newspaper, stained red at the edges. Upon closer examination, the stain turns out to be rows of red fingerprints, left by the powdery paste known as *kanku* with which the genealogists consecrate the pages during prayer. The oldest books are kept on bark.

I have already seen some of the names in the books.

In 1962, my father, a twenty-year-old amateur artist, drew a curving, flowering family tree. He was given the information by his father, who most likely purchased it from one of this genealogist's forefathers.

At the top of my father's drawing are a few pieces of data from antiquity. Some are obsolete: a word that identifies us with one of the seven original branches of humanity at the time of Creation, the name of our family physician in ancient days. Others continue to have ritual or practical use:

Kshatriya, our caste, places us among the warrior-kings who are generally considered to be second of four in the hierarchical Hindu caste system: lower than the priests, higher than the merchants and the laborers. No relative in living memory was actually a warrior or a king, yet this caste identity persists, and continues to be held with pride.

Solanki is our branch or clan. This is a kind of subcaste or lineage: the group of people we think of as our close relatives, a cluster of Kshatriyas who live in certain villages—five villages, to be precise—and with whom we share rituals and sacraments. It is this group for whom Bimal Barot and his family serve as record-keepers.

Our family goddess is *Chaamundaa.* To her we make offerings at weddings and births, that she might bring good fortune to all. Western books on Hinduism describe her as gory and gruesome: "emaciated body and

shrunken belly showing the protruding ribs and veins, skull-garland . . .
bare teeth and sunken eyes with round projecting eye-balls, bald head
with flames issuing from it . . ." But our goddess, at least the version represented by a statue in the village temple, is marble-skinned and rosy-
cheeked, slightly plump and curvaceous in the manner of a maternal
Marilyn Monroe. The benevolent smile she wears is, admittedly, at odds
with the fearful scimitar and dagger she wields and the bloodied demon
corpse at her feet.

Below these basic bits of information, in the neat, curling letters of
our language, my father has inked thirteen generations of male names.
Naanji, at the tree's root, rises thickly into his lineage of sons who begat
sons. Halfway up the page, the tree begins to branch. The most prolific
limb is that of Narsai, my great-great-grandfather.

I am interested in whether the genealogist has any further information
about these ancestors. Any birth or death dates? Any tidbits on occupation, place of residence, fees paid? And—might the charts list the names
of the women?

"Possibly," he says politely, which also means possibly not. He regrets
that our books are traveling with his cousin just now; but for three thousand rupees, or sixty dollars, they will hand-copy our genealogies and
mail them to us.

The price is steep in Indian terms, the result uncertain; but he knows
we are from America. We will pay. Meanwhile, we sit in the half-dark of
the power outage as he tells us older tales—muddled, mysterious, mythic.

Once upon a time, he begins, the god Vishnu became furious.

I am familiar with Vishnu; when I was thirteen, I impersonated him
for a school presentation. Coached by my father and dressed by my
mother, I arrived at my suburban Michigan high school festooned in blue,
red, and gold silk, with thick bands of bells around my ankles. In the
school library I sat cross-legged and explained "my" role as preserver of
the universe, the member of the trinity who keeps everything going, main-
tains the status quo. I described, in some detail, "my" ten incarnations on
earth—the giant fish who saved the world from the floods, the turtle, the
boar, the lion-man, the strong dwarf, and so on—and fielded questions
from white classmates who did not know the first thing about "me."

The genealogist is speaking of Vishnu's sixth incarnation, a holy warrior whose mission was to eliminate all the other warriors on earth. Enraged by mankind's endless warfare and the arrogance of kings, this divine warrior slaughtered all of the world's Kshatriyas. When they sprang up again on the battlefield by means of miracles, he kept going. In the end he killed them off twenty-one times; apparently the twenty-first genocide did the trick. Then he turned their lands over to the priests and returned to his heavenly abode.

But as any good Hindu knows, by the laws of karma you can never end killing by killing. After the slaughter, the priests had no way of defending their realms against either the demons who roamed the earth or the corruption in their own ranks. Without warriors, the earth was overtaken by sin. And the Earth herself, a goddess, begged for relief.

The great sages decided to do what they could: pray. With their fingernails they dug a giant pit in which they lit a sacrificial fire. They begged the gods for new warriors to destroy the forces of evil, including a demonic she-buffalo who was terrorizing the land. By the power of their prayer, from the fire arose a fearsome divine being, never before seen on earth: Ardhanaarishvara.

Here my father raises his hand for a pause, to translate the word.

But I already know it. *Ardhanaa,* meaning half. *Ishvara,* meaning god or goddess—or, in this case, both. Divided down the middle, Ardhanaarishvara is half god and half goddess, portrayed in the full glory of divine femininity (one round breast, one curvy hip) and divine masculinity (half of a flat, muscular torso, one arm bearing a weapon). She/he is a sort of patron saint for India's eunuchs and has been claimed in recent years by gays and lesbians as well. Spiritually, Ardhanaarishvara symbolizes the union of opposites: male and female, certainly, but also effort and surrender, reason and faith, worldly joys and spiritual liberation. I have incarnated this deity as well, in a rather scandalous performance-art piece in front of hundreds—not suspecting that, if the genealogist is correct, she/he is my direct ancestor.

In order to destroy the demons, Ardhanaarishvara created four great warriors to help. After the victory, these four propagated a new race of warriors and kings, repopulating the Kshatriya caste. One of the four, named Solanki, became a great king, head of his own tribe—our tribe.

· · ·

Listening, struggling to follow the complex narrative twists with an imperfect understanding of the language, I feel the nausea of my recent illness and the skepticism of my journalist self fade away. The poet-mystic in me is captivated. Even as I enjoy the childlike comfort of storytime, I begin to sense that these odd, otherworldly stories may indeed be the ones I have come to find.

The girl goes into the back room and brings out glasses of water, which we accept but dare not drink; our American stomachs are sensitive to anything but bottled water. The genealogist takes a sip, then continues.

"The Solankis ruled for many years," he says. "And then, seventy-one generations ago, they were defeated."

My father asks, "How many years is a generation?"

The storyteller looks puzzled, shrugs. In those days people lived to be a hundred years old, so maybe three generations per century? Or four, five, six? He has never thought about it.

In any case, our ancestors fled south. They took refuge at a hill fort named Champaner, not far from where we sit, a few hours by car. There they remained for some time—a generation, several?—until one Mahmud Saahib Begada attacked the town with a fierce and powerful army. At the most desperate moment of battle, our ancestors uttered prayers. Divine intervention came once again, in an odd form. The Goddess of Asafoetida—a spice—appeared before them.

"Please help us," they begged her. The nature of her powers was unclear, but asafoetida is certainly an acquired taste and smell; perhaps they hoped she might smoke out their enemies with its pungent aroma.

"Stop this fighting," she said.

"But we are warriors," said they, who had sprung from the palm of a previous deity in order to do battle, and knew nothing else. "How will we live? What should we do?"

The Goddess of Asafoetida replied in keeping with her domestic concerns. "Take up the craft of weaving," she said. "The sages have no cloth; they are forced to wear skins and leather, which is a sin. You must weave for them."

And so the warriors became weavers: they laid down their arms and retreated farther south. The five royal Solanki brothers each settled in a different village, so our people became the Kshatriyas of the five villages. They retained a separate caste identity. Over generations, only the pronunciation changed slightly, to match the local dialect: instead of Kshatriyas, *Khatris.*

For hundreds of years, nothing happened. Living quiet lives as weavers, they would wait out the centuries until the next great scattering—recorded in the genealogists' books not as myth or legend, but only as a series of emigrations, guided by forces nearly as mysterious as gods and demons.

I spent the next few days trying to readjust to solid food, and to reconcile these stories with history. At first glance they resisted being placed in historical time; then again, the seventy-one generations and the place names seemed like tantalizing clues. My father and I visited the library for a history lesson.

From the fragile pages of an old Gujarati text, my father read and translated aloud the history of the Solanki dynasty and the story of their origin in the sacrificial fire at the Lake of Nails. They were indeed great kings, reigning over a large swath of western India for almost three centuries, from 961 until 1242, when a rival tribe ousted them from their northern capital.

I found no book, then or afterward, that told where the Solankis went next. But Fort Champaner was at the southern reaches of their realm, perhaps a logical place to retreat. And it was indeed sacked by one Mahmud Begada, in the year 1484.

Two days later we visited Champaner, where we found nothing but a row of huts and stalls built along the ruins of an old fortress. Swarms of monkeys leapt about, chattering their own sharp-toothed explanations.

I continued to research the dynasties and the fire-pit tribes, trying different timelines to see if "seventy-one generations ago" could be matched with any known dates involving the Solankis' loss of their kingdom. It couldn't, but my preoccupation with this math problem was curious. Surely it was a trivial item, a distraction from the overall story I was researching: that of how millions of Indians, including my relatives, had been leaving India and settling all over the world for the better part of two centuries.

Indeed, the story of our diaspora sprawled around me. Every village we visited in Gujarat seemed to overflow with overseas visitors, who took up bed space in their relatives' homes, purchased heaps of fabric in the sari shops, and carried bottles of water with them everywhere. 'Twas the season of the NRI: the Non-Resident Indian, as we are known in India's bureaucratese. We NRIs tend to visit in December and January, when Western school holidays coincide with India's temperate season.

Cloistered in libraries while my family joined the transcontinental shopping spree, I found to my pleasure that one of the Solanki queens had been named Minal-devi (Minal the goddess). Although I knew that my mother had named me after a friend, I felt a glimmer of—could it be?—pride, as if royal blood might indeed be flowing through my American veins.

And immediately, also, shame. The caste system with its dirty logic and visible oppression was all too clear around me. How could I write the story of my family, whose very origin myth was grounded in caste pride and purity, without being complicit in this system of oppression?

Months later, back home in California, a parcel came in the mail: a large pink piece of paper, poster-size, onto which had been copied a lineage. There were no female names, no birth or death dates. Indeed, only one date appeared on the whole page, at the very beginning of the family tree. It was the date that the first ancestor's name, Naanji, had been written in the books: A.D. 1765.

It still didn't solve the math problem.

There is no hard link between the medieval Solanki dynasty and my family. Between the last Solanki king's demise in the thirteenth century and our modern family tree's beginning is a gap of five centuries. Any vagabond tribe might have adopted the names and legends of its former rulers and over time created for itself a royal past.

Colonial scholars, trying like me to make sense of such tales, speculated that just such a process was at the root of the fire-pit myth itself. Certain invaders or upstart clans, people whose caste origins were suspect, might have invented lineages for credibility's sake. By shoring up military victories with convenient links to ancient myth, their genealogists collaborated in investing might with a kind of divine right. Various British scholars guess the medieval Solankis to have been invaders from Bombay or modern Pakistan, or even "Scythian mercenaries." If so, it may be that the tradition of migration runs deeper in our blood than I had imagined.

· · ·

But as my father and I studied the histories that first afternoon in the Vadodara library, one name leapt from the brittle pages: Mulraaj, the first Solanki king.

In every wedding in our clan, two small figures are shaped from soft clay—men on horseback, armed with swords—and placed on the altar. They are worshipped in a set of ceremonies whose details have traditionally been a closely guarded secret, shared only with immediate family members; even servants are typically sent out of the room. The small soldiers guard a tiny fortlike structure, also made of clay. And this diorama is known as Mulraaj.

Until now, Mulraaj has been only a name, its origins lost in a fog of ritual, stripped—as ritual often is—of its root meanings. Perhaps, my father surmised, this is the old Solanki ancestor come to inhabit, briefly, our lives; to join the celebration and offer his blessings.

If so, King Mulraaj must wonder at traveling so far from his realm. The miniature kings formed of village mud who blessed my great-grandparents' arranged marriages more than a century ago are kin to the ones formed of craft-store clay who blessed my cousin's love marriage to a Vietnamese American woman in the year 2001 in Ames, Iowa. And the progeny of Mulraaj, if that is who we are, are now spread around the world. Though we trace our roots to a tiny region in northwestern India, only one of my thirty-six cousins lives there today.

The rest of us have spread out over five continents, in nine countries, to almost every time zone on the planet. The story of this scattering, and how it happened, is what I have set out to tell—not only for my family's sake, but as a window into the extraordinary narrative of India's diaspora, which is perhaps the fastest-growing dispersal of people in the world today.

The Indian government, eager to market to our nostalgia via business investments, shopping, and tourism, has tried to estimate the numbers of Indians living abroad. The most recent approximate count is 11.5 million. And how many of us are seeking, studying, or shopping for some myth of our origins?

The Lake of Nails, where Bimal Barot said our history began, has a real geographical location: in the modern state of Rajasthan, on the peak called Mount Abu. The lake is said to be the gigantic fire pit dug by the sages with their hands and filled in by rain after the supernatural battle. Nearby are two breathtaking marble temples, with room after room of carved deities and intricate archways, built during the long and architecturally prolific Solanki reign. Wandering the temples, I have trailed my fingers over the white marble goddesses carved into every nook from floor to ceiling. Walking the lake's shores, I have gazed into its murky, polluted waters, and wondered.

Every dry season, I am told, the bottom of the lake shows the curving scoop marks of the sages' giant fingernails.

Diaspora: a people dispersed. From the Greek *dia,* asunder, and *speiren,* to sow. A scattering of lives.

The Jews were the original diaspora, and for centuries they held near-exclusive claim to the word. My old Webster's, 1940, extends the word to "Christians living among the heathen." Today the world is globalized, and the heathen have their own diasporas—Chinese, African, Arab, Indian, each growing and multiplying at phenomenal rates. Among these are my family and I, sown asunder, trailing our threads of culture and nostalgia around the globe.

In the psychology of diaspora many pathologies have been defined: disorientation, alienation, difficulty in assimilating. Studying deaths among early Indian indentured laborers in South Africa, the scholars Joy and Peter Brain note that nostalgia was a diagnosed condition, often described as the reason for suicide, a leading cause of death among the immigrants. Is the grief I have felt, sometimes, in this writing, a kind of transmitted nostalgia—a mourning for what was lost, against the narrative of progress and accomplishment that characterizes most contemporary stories of our diaspora? I think sometimes of the villages where my ancestors lived, which I have visited for only a few days in my life. And I wonder what it would be like to know that out of legendary time, your fathers and forefathers lived and died on the same patch of soil where you yourself would live and die.

In such a life, I imagine, the circular nature of time must be clearer, less bound to a narrative of motion through space. No dispersal; no progress. Lifetime upon lifetime must unfold in much the same manner, personalities changing, circumstances remaining the same. And perhaps because of this it would be easier to see around the bend of Time's corner, as my great-great-grandfather Narsai did.

Narsai was a poor man, but he was intimate with destiny. In a pan of water, Narsai could find a lost child, a stolen gold ring. In the half-moon of your thumbnail, he could forecast the clouds on your horizon. The villagers referred to him by this skill, *hazrat-waalaa:* one who prophesies. When the fashion of surnames took hold, generations later, ours became Hajratwala—but that is getting ahead of the story.

If I had his second sight, perhaps I could scry to find out where we have been and what we have lost. Instead I must trace the story of my family and our travels using imperfect methods: documents, memories, legends. No dates or details of Narsai's biography are recorded, only the legend of his ability to water-gaze.

Of his wife, Ratan, we know little more, except that she lived to see the dawn of 1928—long enough to coddle her first grandchild and to have her memory committed to paper, captured in black and white. A single photograph of her survives. It is a studio portrait, taken at a point in history when her sons had attained some prosperity, by perhaps the town's only photographer.

At first glance my great-great-grandmother looks stern, because of the rigid posture that she has been instructed to hold, or that she herself feels is appropriate for such a moment. She wears a sari, its border draped stiffly across a cotton blouse and drawn over her head. She appears to be in her late thirties or forties, though it is hard to tell exactly. She is already the mother of a daughter and six sons. Widowed, her forehead lacks the red dot that is the mark of a married woman in our community; in its place is a slight furrow. Her hair is pulled back severely from her face, whose features contain, however, a softness. It was not the fashion of the time to smile for the camera, but one senses that, given permission, she might.

Narsai and Ratan remain to me mythical beings, partially veiled. On the edge of history, they are the first to emerge from its mists. Do they sense, somehow, that theirs is the moment just before everything changes forever? Can they guess that on the plot of land where they live, their sons' sons will build houses several stories high and populate them with their own families, then watch them go vacant and even crumble as the children migrate overseas?

Of their six sons, the fourth was my great-grandfather, Motiram. Family legend has it that his father taught him the art of soothsaying.

But every Hindu fortuneteller knows the ancient curse: As long as you prophesy you will always be poor. So Motiram, in a season of drought, plague, and migration, decided the art would die with him. Forsaking the tiny, clear pools of water that were his father's domain, Motiram set out to master a greater sea.

part one: "coolies"

1900

Estimated size of the Indian diaspora: 373,609
Countries with more than 10,000 people of Indian origin: 6

1. British Guiana
2. Trinidad and Tobago
3. Mauritius
4. Natal
5. Jamaica
6. Fiji

2. CLOtH

What is Fiji? It is heaven! . . . You will eat a lot of bananas and a
stomach-full of sugar cane, and play flutes in relaxation.
  —Recruiter of Indian indentured workers, 1893

Narsai and Ratan
Navsari, India
↓

Raghnath ⎤
Daahyaa ⎬ *Africa*
Gopaal ⎦ *and Aden*

Jamnadas ⎤
MOTIRAM ⎬ *Fiji Islands*
Jiwan ⎦

Nandi   *India*

*Y*OUR GREAT-GRANDFATHER *wanted to go to Fiji, so he went.*

In our families, migration stories are told like this—the motives purely personal, almost arbitrary. In the books, the recovered histories, I find other origin myths: not desire but economics, politics, the needs of colonial powers. I have set out to find the meeting place, where character intersects with history.

What we know for sure about Motiram is this:

He was born late in the nineteenth century in the village of Navsari, near the great port of Surat, in southern Gujarat, in the far western elbow of India.

In 1909, he went to the Fiji Islands.

In 1911, he established a small tailoring shop, later to become one of the largest department stores in the South Pacific isles.

He was not a prophet.

He made it possible for two of his brothers, their children, and all of their descendants to exit India.

History helped. As the nineteenth century slipped into the twentieth, young men from all over India were converging on the great ports of Calcutta and Madras. There they boarded ships to seek their fortunes, or at least a respite from chronic poverty.

A century later, I will never know how Motiram weathered his first days at sea, if he was afraid; nor can I calculate the precise combination of ambition, wanderlust, and desperation which led him to cross two oceans.

But I know what pulled Motiram across the seas: an empire in need.

August 1, 1834, was Emancipation Day in the British Empire. After centuries of moral and political wrangling, abolitionists won the great victory. All slaves were to be freed.

For a few hundred years, Africans in chains had supplied the labor necessary for rapid imperial expansion. Without them, the plantation economies of the colonies verged on collapse. Panicked memos traveled back and forth to London; a scheme to keep former slaves as "apprentices" failed when the slaves learned of their liberation. The Crown compensated owners for the loss of "property," but money alone could not harvest the crops.

Casting about for a practical solution, the imperial eye landed on India. There, legions of peasants were languishing in idle poverty, eager for work, if only they could afford the sea passage. So it was decided: they would mortgage the trip with their years.

Abolitionists cried foul, but over the next several decades an old system of travel and bondage was reincarnated and implemented on a grand scale: indenture. Weeks after Emancipation Day, the process of replacing slave labor began at the docks of Calcutta. It was the beginning of the modern Indian diaspora.

White colonists found the scheme nearly as cost-effective as slavery. The Indians signed up for five years' bonded labor, six days a week, nine hours a day. In return, they received round-trip passage on a converted slave ship plus a small wage, with deductions for food and illness. Those who enlisted called it the *girmit* system, a mispronunciation of the word *agreement*.

Perhaps the phonetic abridgment was appropriate—for as an agreement the system left much to be desired. Poor Indians were lured, tricked, or kidnapped outright by profit-hungry agents, who received a commission for each worker they managed to deliver. Largely illiterate, the new recruits relied on these agents to translate the English contracts. The agents often promised work elsewhere in India, or nearby, with the freedom to return home at any time. But the papers—most of them "signed" with thumbprints and X's—committed people to field labor, thousands of miles and oceans away. And those who tried to leave their jobs were beaten, whipped, or imprisoned.

By their sweat Queen Victoria's realm continued to swell. Sugar sprawled over the Pacific and Caribbean; trains steamed across continents; mines tunneled deep into Africa. Eventually 1.5 million Indian men, women, and children would cross the seas as what they called *girmityas*—or what the whites called "coolies."

Thousands more boarded the same ships as free agents. Some were recruited for special skills; others learned of opportunities and took a leap. By a quirk of economics and tradition and groupthink, many hundreds of these travelers came from Gujarat, from the region where my ancestors lived. They were ineligible for indenture, since bonded workers could be recruited only from provinces the British determined to be teeming with excess population. So they went as paying passengers: traders, entrepreneurs, skilled workers.

Motiram would become one of these, riding the crest of the first wave of the modern Indian diaspora.

In the Export Trade Gallery of the Calico Museum of Textiles in Gujarat's commercial capital, Ahmedabad, one walks amid walls draped with gorgeous cottons and silks, each behind a layer of glass. Occasionally the harsh cry of a peacock from the gardens outside punctuates the silence. Otherwise, the few visible staff members and even fewer visitors move about quietly, perhaps squinting a bit.

The light is dim to protect the fragile textiles, many of which are already faded. Some are centuries old; all are remnants of a craft dating back millennia, and of a trade so vast and impressive that writers from Ptolemy to Marco Polo praised Gujarat as a lush, fertile region whose woven cloth was among the finest in the world. Today's diaspora is grafted onto these older patterns of trade and travel, like a tapestry unraveled and reshaped by the world's ever-changing needs.

I pause before one of the museum's oldest pieces, a large square on which plump geese waddle in rings of eight. Their eyes are nested circles of green, yellow, cream, and antique red fading to pink. One goose looks forward, one back, so that they appear coupled, lustily chasing each other amid an orgy of flowers and cornices. Here and there the tapestry is torn, frayed, so that hardly a goose remains intact. Still, they are in good shape for a flock six hundred years old.

Excavated from a medieval Coptic fort along the caravan routes outside Babylonia, this sample was originally woven and block-printed by hand in Gujarat. How exactly the geese reached what is now Egypt is a mystery; perhaps a trader took them on a pilgrimage ship to Mecca, then up the coast of North Africa to the mouth of the Nile. The design on the cloth is found also in Indian caves from the sixth century, in a painting that shows someone wearing a shirt made of such cloth. The image on the cave wall, too, is patchy with age, its paint faded as if the cloth it depicts has worn thin.

I am sure these ragged medieval holes would tell a story, if only we could read it.

Since before the land was named India, people have been migrating across the Himalayas and the seas. Four millennia ago, traders from the Indus Valley left intricately carved seals in ancient Mesopotamia (now Iraq). A thousand years ago the Gypsies trekked north from India, carrying their linguistic roots in *water, hair, drink, see, man.* For centuries Hindu and Buddhist monks have spread their gods across Asia, while Muslim traders built boats to transport precious cargoes of pilgrims, spice, and cloth to Arabia and Africa.

Tales of these wonders stirred the yearning of foreigners, from Alexander the Great to Christopher Columbus, who set out for India with, in some cases, whole armies. Motiram and his family lived in a region bordered by the Arabian Sea and the Deccan Plain, swept through by various waves of invaders and conquerors—empires rising and yielding way since time immemorial, working their subtle changes on a seemingly eternal pastoral landscape.

In the nineteenth century, the greatest of these powers was the British Empire, whose reach was so broad that one lord famously bragged, "The sun never sets upon the interests of this country." It was a quirk of geography and timing that those interests reached into the tiny village of Navsari and swept up Motiram and all of his brothers.

Ten miles or half a day's journey north of the village on rough roads, one may enter the thousand-year-old metropolis of Surat through the Navsari

Gate. The history of Surat is intertwined with the story of our diaspora: place of first contact, place of opportunity and decline and opportunity again. A point of departure; of many departures.

Founded as a minor port by the Solanki kings, Surat was made a great one by their Muslim successors. While some orthodox Hindus believed that crossing the ocean's "black waters" would result in loss of caste, Muslims faced no restrictions and, indeed, were enjoined to make a pilgrimage to Mecca. Under Muslim rule, Surat became the "blessed port" of the Mughal Empire, India's gateway to the Holy Land. Each March, four ships laden with a thousand pilgrims each departed from Surat to Mecca, returning in September.

These religious voyages were opportunities to carry on a vibrant trade. Muslims from Gujarat traversed the entire Indian Ocean—from the Arabian Sea down the long coastline of Africa to the South China Sea—setting up permanent settlements as far afield as Japan. By the 1600s, Surat was the main trading center of the great Mughal Empire, and its reputation was international. It was a must-see port of the Orient.

Three centuries before my great-grandfather's time, when the British East India Company formed for the purpose of trading in India, Surat was the logical place to begin. Company ships made several attempts to reach India by sea around the perilous Cape of Africa, succeeding at last in 1607. The Portuguese and the Dutch were already in Surat, both established enough to try to blockade and fire upon the English ships. But the English persisted, and set up a trading post. Surat was their first toehold in the land that would become "the jewel in the crown" of the British Empire.

John Ovington, chaplain of the English trading post from 1689 to 1692, said the city was "reckon'd the most fam'd Emporium of the *Indian empire*," its streets and bazaars "more populous than any part of *London*." Cotton, indigo, and opium were the main draws, but the list of items traded at Surat was long: Copper, tin, quicksilver (mercury). Carpets, linens, yarns. Vermilion, sandalwood, lead. Elephants' teeth, tortoiseshell, cowries, coral, amber, ebony, diamonds, agates. Soap, sealing wax, rosin, borax, ammonia, saltpeter (for gunpowder), camphor, turpentine, enamel, gum. Tea, sugar, wheat, rice. Cloves, cinnamon, ginger, tamarind, pepper, saffron, cumin, myrrh, musk. Gold and silver, in the form of coins, ornaments, bars, and threads woven into exquisite silks. And cloth, in varieties unimaginable, a riot of colors, textures, and designs.

John Ogilby, His Majesty's cosmographer, writing in 1673, found "Portugefes, Arabians, Perfians, Armenians, Turks, and Jews" doing brisk business in Surat. Demand for the goods traded in Surat was so fierce, he wrote, that the city "fwallows all the Gold and Silver which comes from the Perfian Gulph and Arabia, as alfo a great part of the Riches of India, and the Gold of China."

Soon, Surat was swallowing the riches of England as well. In London the craze was for calico, muslin, chintz—varieties of cotton cloth from India. Parliamentarians fretted: Asian luxuries pouring in meant Britain's gold bullion was pouring out, creating a drastic trade imbalance. And textile makers took notice as well: homegrown British cloth could not compete with cheaper, higher-quality cottons and silks from India. British weavers marched and rioted. By 1701, as one historian writes, "the clamour reached [such] a climax that the English Parliament had to pass an Act forbidding the import of cloth from Surat and banning the use of Indian silk in England."

Slowly Surat's fortunes—and those of the countryside surrounding it—began to fade. The river port was capricious, flooding the town each monsoon and at other times silting over, becoming impassable. The city was plagued by chronic conflict among various European and Muslim rulers, as well as attacks by pirates and marauders lusting after its treasure houses. Soon the British, impatient for stability and greater control, decided to establish a port of their own. They took their business 160 miles down the coast, where they made a new island city they called Bombay. From there, through a combination of strategic alliances and military battles, they consolidated power in India. Eventually they drove out their rivals, and India—once a trading partner so wealthy it seemed to threaten the economy of London—became a colony of the British Empire.

In and around Surat, where it had all begun, the transformation was dramatic. The city was reduced from a great international port to a strictly local one. The region's thriving and diversified economy became dependent almost entirely on cloth.

There is a sense in which village life seems unchanging, so that I feel I might intuit, just under the surface of the Navsari of today, the Navsari of my great-grandfather's time.

Motiram's people occupied a small neighborhood on the western side of town, and would have socialized only with their own kind. Neither wealthy nor poor, the Khatris followed the hereditary occupation, weaving. "As a class they are said to be thriftless and idle, and . . . excessively fond of strong drinks," commented an 1877 British survey of castes in the area. "Their features are regular and complexion fair." Few were educated or even literate.

A street over from Khatri lane was the neighborhood of shoemakers. Beyond that lay the fishmongers' ghetto, where one could buy bushels of the pungent dried fish that the British dubbed "Bombay duck." For fresh groceries Motiram's mother could go to the market, or simply wait for the day's catch to come through the streets in a basket on the head of a woman who called out, "Fresh fish! Ohhhh, fish! Beautiful fresh fish!" Cows wandered the streets freely, in a kind of symbiosis: women put out leftover food for the sacred animals, and in exchange the cattle dropped their dung to be collected and smeared on the walls, where it dried into a smooth, odor-free plaster. At dawn Hindu women consecrated their doorsteps with red dye, a few grains of rice, and a few flowers. At dusk, the flames of prayer and cooking glowed from each home, as they had for generations. When people died, their ashes were scattered in the local river, which poured, a few miles west, into the Arabian Sea.

The sea had shaped the village since its origins. Because of its strategic coastal location, Navsari was more cosmopolitan than many other Indian hamlets. Temples and shrines of four faiths dotted its streets: Hindu, Muslim, Jain, and Zoroastrian. It was the Zoroastrians who, fleeing persecution in Persia, had founded the town in 1142.

In Motiram's time, the region that encompassed Navsari was divided so that it looked, on the map, like a pastiche of jerry-rigged dots and shapes. Most areas were under the direct rule of the British. The rest belonged to a local ruling family entirely beholden to the British, and as rapacious. Their territory was disconnected; Motiram's hometown of Navsari fell in one of the larger chunks, at the tip of a free-floating amoeba just four miles long. As hub of its subdistrict, Navsari had modern conveniences: post office, train station, library, and a new town hall complete with clock tower.

Despite these innovations, colonization and corruption were taking their toll.

In 1909, for example—the year that Motiram left home—the kingdom's major sources of income were sales of cotton, indigo, and opium, supplemented by heavy taxes on land, salt, and liquor. Navsari, a town of 21,000, had more than six hundred liquor shops and a single high school, which graduated five students in 1909. The maharaja, whose stated objective for his regime was to be "like the English," spent twice as much on his palace as on the entire school system. His annual report devoted a paragraph each to hospitals, plague relief, and the problem of child marriages—but several pages described a twenty-city world tour undertaken "for the benefit of his health," the royal youngsters' progress at Harvard and Oxford, and the fireworks exploded to entertain the visiting British viceroy.

For centuries, weaving the plain cotton saris worn by working-class Indian women had provided an adequate living for Motiram's clan. In a typical home, a loom sat in a pit in the floor of the house. For each garment the weaver first set up the warp, the regularly spaced vertical threads that dictated the width and length of the cloth. Then, sitting on the floor, legs resting down in the pit, he or she threw the threaded shuttle from one hand to the other and back again. This horizontal motion created the weft. Gradually, over perhaps four days, a complete sari would grow from the loom.

Every few weeks a broker went from house to house to collect the completed saris, which he would sell in the markets at Surat and elsewhere. The broker would bring a few rupees to pay for the work and a batch of soft raw cotton for the next order. This cotton was the training ground for children as young as five, who learned to spin sitting at floor level above their weaving parents. Using a simple wooden wheel, they could stretch and twist the soft clouds into thread.

Generations of our ancestors had worked in the same way. And until the eighteenth century, textile workers in England competed on an equal basis. The level of artistry varied, but in both places cloth-making was a home-based industry. One weaver could keep up with the output of four spinners; a whole family working together could earn a living wage.

Then came the machines, the push for speed.

The flying shuttle, in 1733, quadrupled the pace; now one English weaver needed sixteen spinners to keep up. And for the first time a weaver could make cloth wider than the span of his or her arms. The family was no longer sufficient; the product had outgrown the human.

The spinning jenny, of 1765, allowed English spinners to make thread more quickly, to keep up with their weavers. Faster and better machines followed. Giant looms were powered by river water flowing through wooden mills; from these origins, all future cloth factories would be known as mills. Spinning and weaving, in England, became mill—or factory—work. In 1785 a steam engine powered a cloth-making factory for the first time, a priest invented the power loom, a Frenchman introduced chlorine bleaching of cotton, and a hot-air balloon crossed the English Channel. The world was growing smaller. The great change that would become known as the Industrial Revolution was well under way.

In village India these developments were felt as distant murmurs. There were rumors of great machines that did the work of a hundred men, of massive boats that ran on fire and water. But Britain, concerned with competition, did not allow the export of textile machines until 1843. Ten years later, India opened its first cotton mill, in Bombay.

Still, for a time the damage was limited. Thread from Europe's spinning machines was weaker and looser than that spun by hand. As late as 1866 the textile scholar Forbes Watson called European muslins "practically useless" compared with the Indian product, because they fell apart after several washings.

Inevitably the technology improved, and price overtook the desire for quality in the marketplace. By 1875, when Motiram's parents were perhaps starting their young family, nearly three-quarters of the cloth consumed in Gujarat was made by machine.

In rural Gujarat, the shift was evident as farmers turned their fields to cotton to feed the mills. In 1900, three million acres were devoted to cotton; seven years later, cotton took up four million acres. By 1918, the figure was 4.75 million, or 13 percent of the entire region's occupied land. In certain districts, cotton accounted for more than half the cultivated area.

The cotton boom, along with an aggressive tax policy, made Gujarat— renowned for centuries as one of the most fertile provinces of the world —unable to feed itself. The British-controlled portion of Gujarat was importing half a million tons of grain in a normal year, two million in a famine year.

The new cotton farmers saw little profit. Instead they struggled to keep up with a tax structure designed to ensure that, whether the crops thrived or failed, London would get its due. Small cotton farmers were taxed now not only on their harvests but on the land itself, so they bore all of the losses caused by Nature's fluctuations. In a good year, farmers could sell their cotton, pay current and back taxes, and have enough left over to buy food. In a drought year, they had neither a food crop nor cash profits. Many people simply starved.

It would have taken far greater power than a soothsayer's to stave off the seven years of drought that marked Motiram's childhood. Season after season, the skies remained empty, as if the gods of wind and rain had fallen into a deep, careless slumber.

Even in relatively prosperous Navsari, hard times were evident. Hungry refugees from the rural areas poured into town at the rate of a thousand per day. Rice and millet doubled in price. The Milky Lake at Navsari's edge dropped to the lowest levels in recorded history; the Purna River slowed like the last trickle of blood from a dying man. Thousands in the region starved to death, and many more died of poverty-related disease.

It was the worst famine in sixty years. For Motiram's generation, the calamity of 1899 was a milestone used for decades afterward to reckon dates, births, and fateful decisions.

Historians used to speak of "push" and "pull" as the main factors in migration, principles as basic to human motivation as warp and weft are to cloth. Push begins at home; it is what makes you leave your motherland. Pull is the force drawing you elsewhere; it is what makes the foreign destination appealing. Though recently this mechanistic model has been replaced by more subtle theories of human motivation, the simple version retains a ring of truth. Despite the complexities involved in Motiram's story, perhaps a strong push was required after all. If so, the famine of 1899 might have been the spark that led Motiram and his kin to look, for the first time in more than four centuries, beyond their town's borders.

As weaving became less and less sustainable, among the Khatris it was more and more the province of women, who could stay home and weave while still cooking the meals, watching the children, and sweeping the floors. By the turn of the century, it was common for men to branch out, seeking related work as tailors in Surat, Bombay, and other cities.

Perhaps, for a young Khatri man in such times, the move to Fiji seemed like just another step.

The remote archipelago once known as the Cannibal Islands was an unlikely choice. Early Hindu travelers from Gujarat were likely to follow the westward routes to Africa and the Middle East that had been established by their Muslim countrymen. Three of Motiram's brothers tried those routes, traveling overseas to Africa and to Aden, at the mouth of the Red Sea. Of them, only their passport photos remain, and their names: Raghnath, Daahyaa, Gopaal. Eventually they would die or disappear abroad, leaving no children, only their child-brides at home—stunted limbs on the family tree.

The Fiji Islands, much farther and in the other direction, were not on anyone's lips. Until, in 1901, the Colonial Sugar Refining Company of Fiji recruited twenty Gujaratis with needed skills. Soon a couple of Gujarati jewelers followed; they found themselves in great demand as the indentured laborers, the girmityas, chose to preserve their savings in gold and silver. Fiji gained a reputation as a place where it was easy for men with talent to thrive.

In 1908, a member of Motiram's caste went to ply his skills as a tailor.

A year later, Motiram followed.

To pay for his passage, he mortgaged the ancestral land. He left two brothers, his mother, his wife, and two sons at home. The year was 1909, and he was not afraid.

Or: He was desperate. His father and three of his brothers had already died; he was the man of the house; he had to do something.

Or: They had not yet died; he was carefree. He was young and did not think of his own death.

Or: He thought of dying far from home. When he took his family's leave, none of them dared hope to see each other again.

Or: They planned to meet in two years. He would work and make some money and come home.

Or: He might never come home.
He would come home only once.

From the dirt roads of lower Gujarat, Motiram would have crossed the
subcontinent by train, a three-day journey to the great eastern seaport.
Once in Calcutta, perhaps he sought out the ancient shrine of Kali, the
fierce goddess for whom the city was named, to pray for safekeeping.
Waiting for a ship, he might have stayed a few days in "Black Town" —
the Indian section of the city, described by one visiting reporter as "anxiously thrust away from sight by the aristocratic and splendid metropolis, like a dirty garment under a gaudy silk robe." Eventually he would
have made his way to the "coolie" depots and docks.

There, throngs of men and some women gathered under the watch-
ful eyes of recruiters. Ships laden with hundreds of emigrants each were
sailing for Malaysia, Mauritius, Guyana, Surinam, South Africa, Trinidad,
Jamaica — and Fiji.

With his life savings and a bundle of spare clothes, Motiram climbed
aboard and joined the great migration.

Shipside, conditions had improved since indenture's dawn, when
"coolies" were accommodated scarcely better than the slaves who had
occupied their berths only a few years before. Public outcry in Britain
and India had led to reforms in the terms and conditions of travel. Still,
abolitionists continued to decry the "new system of slavery," while cap-
italists sought to paint a picture of opportunity and prosperity. Both sides
had a portion of the truth.

By the winter of 1909, when Motiram boarded a ship, a typical cargo
to Fiji consisted of 750 to 1,200 indentured Indians. A contemporary contract shows the British government of Fiji paying the firm of James
Nourse Ltd. five pounds and fifteen shillings sterling "for each adult
Indian (male or female) of the age of ten years and over landed alive."

The final condition was necessary; the journey took eleven to eighteen weeks by steamer, long enough for at least a few of the indentured
to die of suicide or meningitis, the fiercest of the diseases that spread on
the crowded ship. The paying Indian passengers — rare — were accommodated no differently from other "coolies"; everyone shared the same

floor space for their bedrolls, the same communally cooked food, the same rationed water.

Steaming in toward Fiji, perhaps the sojourners glimpsed the Union Jack hoisted at their arrival. But the ship veered to the outlying island of Nukulau, white quarantine buildings stark against green jungle. From there they could catch a first leisurely view of the mainland curving around the bay where a famous Fijian king had killed his first man in a fierce canoe battle and where, in mythical times, the Fijian shark god slew the great sea serpent. In the harbor, the masts of ships from Sydney, London, Auckland rose like anachronistic telephone poles, triangle sails slicing upward against the flat sea and sky.

The quarantine island was a temporary holding site for those entering Fiji, as Ellis Island and Angel Island were for newcomers to the United States. Immigrants to Fiji—the vast majority of them Indians—spent a week or two in what amounted to a large barn as they were processed and deemed disease-free. One contemporary arrival complained, "When we arrived in Fiji we were herded into a punt like pigs and taken to Nukulau where we stayed for a fortnight. We were given rice that was full of worms. We were kept and fed like animals . . ."

At last, several months after leaving home, Motiram disembarked at Fiji's harbor capital, Suva.

Suva was all water, a revelation of blues and greens. The blue of distance; the green of abundance. The wharf was a long tongue lapping toward the opposite shore, whose dramatic volcanic peaks framed the bay. Turning toward land, Motiram would have passed under the palm trees that graced the waterfront, and walked uphill. The city was edged by jungle, sea, and swamp. If the day was dry, his feet tramped on red soil padded over coral that had been harvested from nearby reefs. If it was rainy, he slogged through streams of red mud.

For Motiram the difference between the old and new lands was also in the tongue. Of the three thousand free Indians who lived in Suva in 1911, two dozen, at most, spoke Gujarati. The rest spoke a local version of Hindustani, quite distinct from any known in India. This linguistic innovation—and its sister tongues that were developing in Trinidad,

Guyana, and other indenture colonies—was a uniquely diasporic phenomenon, born of necessity. Flung together in these foreign lands, people
from various parts of India blended their languages and invented a new
way of communicating across regional barriers.

Among the colonies, Fiji had been a latecomer both to the indenture
scheme and to the British Empire itself. Its fierce coral reefs and fiercer
inhabitants, with their reputation for eating missionaries, had staved off
colonialism for decades. Not until the 1850s did American and British
enclaves become well established; in 1870 Australians moved in. Conflicts
ensued, with rogue pirates and official navies duking it out at sea. Each
colonial power also demanded, tricked, or forced the native Fijians to
yield more and more of their land.

After one skirmish, the Americans claimed that the Fijian king owed
them compensation for damages. But Fiji was rich in tropical beauty, not
in cash. As the "debt" mounted, the Americans threatened war if the king
did not pay.

Unwilling to tax his people into starvation, the king gazed at the war-
ships in the harbor and begged Britain to take over his lands and debts.
This "tragic episode," as Leo Tolstoy called it in an essay against imperialism, ended in 1874 with Britain taking possession of the more than three
hundred islands of Fiji.

It was an early British governor of Fiji who brought Indians to his tiny
colony. He needed to show a profit quickly; empires are not built of char-
ity, and every outpost had to be self-supporting. He would not conscript
the native Fijians, who after all had voluntarily given their country to the
Crown. Besides, the Fijians were considered poor workers: they were
under the illusion that the land would provide, as it had for generations.

Fresh from postings in Trinidad and Mauritius, where Indian labor
had converted tropical jungle to lucrative plantations, the governor decided to apply once again the magic formula of sugar plus indenture. In
1879, the first girmityas arrived in Fiji.

Thirty years later, Motiram arrived to an established Indian community.
Despite the language barrier, its familiar sights and smells must have been
a comfort. Parts of Suva resembled any Indian city: women in saris hag-

gling over vegetables at the market, men in turbans and dhotis walking the streets, whites in their official ghettos sweating in the attire of the colonist. An English guidebook of the times advised visitors to wear knickerbocker suits with leather leggings as a protection against mosquitoes. Swamps, snakes, and the heat troubled the English, who believed that their Indian workers had an easier time laboring in the savage conditions.

By 1909, enough Indians had served out their indenture terms that they were settling where they wished, farming and building, transforming the colony. Along a pockmarked road that ringed the island's black mountain, Indian towns were rising. As always in the economy of plantations, workers outnumbered their masters. Indians made up nearly a third of the islands' population in 1911, owing both to continued immigration and to the fact that the native Fijian population was shrinking from measles and other new ailments. One in four Indians was Fiji-born.

In Suva, free Indian workers were busy at the docks, loading ships with crops grown by indentured Indians on the plantations. Sugar was the main commodity, with coconuts and bananas also profitable; exports had tripled since the first girmityas' arrival. Indian hawkers filled the city's markets with fresh vegetables and fruit, grown on their own patches of land in the countryside.

The year that Motiram arrived, Fiji opened its first library in Suva, a gift from Andrew Carnegie, stocked with 4,200 books. The Grand Hotel was under construction, soon to become one of the finest establishments in the Pacific, where European guests could take saltwater baths and be "served in truly oriental style by white-turbaned waiters," as one guidebook promised. Government buildings stood white and majestic on the site of the old native village. Suva boasted a grand town hall, a museum, and streetlamps lit each evening by "coolies" bearing ladders and kerosene. The governor's plan was working.

Motiram would have settled in town among the free Indians, perhaps renting a room or a bed in a house with other men. He took his meals at one of the "lodges," cafeteria-style establishments where men without wives could buy cheap, hot plates of curry and rice. The commercial district contained everything to serve the needs of a small urban population: grocers, chemists, tailoring enterprises. Walter Horne & Co. Ltd. advertised:

OUR
TAILORING DEPARTMENT
WITH EXPERT CUTTERS and DESIGNERS
GUARANTEES <u>GOOD TAILORING</u> FOR
EVERY ORDER.
Those who are unable to attend personally may rely on
GOOD FIT by filling in one of our SPECIAL
MEASUREMENT FORMS, which will be supplied with
patterns on application.
STYLES—SMART
PRICES—LIGHT
SMART CLOTHS makes the MAN
<u>IF</u>
HORNE & Co. makes the CLOTHES.

Behind the scenes, Horne & Co. was a small factory, rows of treadle machines set up in a warehouse. It was here that Motiram learned the subtle dance of feet and hands, machine and cloth, that would give him —and his community—a foothold in Fiji. He became a tailor.

At home his ancestors were only weavers. "Only": those who made order from the chaos of clouds, the rough, soft bundles of raw cotton. Some-one spun. Someone wove. To buy rice and grain, they wove every free hour of the day, men and women both, while there was light or while the fingers could feel the design.

That was in the old country.

In the new country the cloth came to him, woven elsewhere, by ma-chine; he did not have to think about the weaving. About the weavers. Instead he learned to measure, to stitch. To kneel at the customer's feet, to raise one hand to the waist, to keep his eyes low, to remember the number: in inches, fractions of inches. To translate, silently, the English numerals to Gujarati in his mind.

To trace the patterns; to cut the fabric. To stitch. To thread the ma-chine, to break the thread with his teeth, to pump the machine with his foot. To finish the seam. To cut the last thread.

To fit the customer. To kneel again. To adjust the hem.

. . .

He could not think about his ancestors the kings. He thought of his sons who would eat; who would come to the new country and learn to feed themselves; who would feed their wives and sons, and marry off their daughters.

Motiram sent some money home to his family, lived cheaply, and tried to save as much as he could. Horne & Co. offered a decent job, but wage labor was never the goal. His people believed that working for oneself, or in a family enterprise, was the only way to ensure long-term security. Taking a job in the white-run factory was only a means to learning the business, so that someday he could start his own tailoring shop.

Bent over a sewing machine ten hours a day, dreaming of a future when he could be his own boss, surely Motiram did not have hours to spend in sea-gazing. Still, from time to time he must have glanced out across the water, which in those days washed up to the center of town. The swells of ocean and river, the lush greens of taro, ferns, cane, palms, could not have been more different from the land Motiram had left behind.

Despite its natural abundance, though, Fiji presented obstacles: not only language but caste, culture, and perhaps simple homesickness. When Motiram strode a Navsari lane, everyone he met would know not only his thin frame but the weave of his clothing, his father's second sight, the genealogy he wore in his face, the waft of his mother's meat and spices, whatever family quarrels raged and were quelled.

In Fiji these were private knowings, comforts he carried only in his own body, mingling with the sweat of the wet tropics, the hot and daily rainfall. He had to learn to exist among strangers. At the factory he stitched and hemmed, and men knew only what they saw on him, a "coolie" body, or what he told them as he learned a smattering of English. If he spoke and worked carefully, if he measured his words and deeds as precisely as inseam, waist, waist-to-hem, then he would go back to mother, brothers, wife, sons, home, land—someday.

Someday was meant to be two years, but in two years he had saved just enough to start a shop. Adopting his father's first name as his own last name, using the spelling someone gave him, he became Motiram Narsey. His tailoring shop, M. Narsey & Co., opened in 1911.

In a rented portion of a wooden building at the corner of Renwick Road and Ellery Street, in the main business section of town, Motiram began his new life as an entrepreneur. A hitching post stood just out front, for customers' horses; nearby were the post office, banks, and white-owned businesses. A few yards away ran a creek, and on its far side Chinese and Indian shops crowded together in congested alleyways. Down the street was the shop started by another Khatri, the one in whose footsteps Motiram had followed.

Competition was gentle and work plentiful, enough for each man to call others to help. Motiram wrote home, sent for his brother Jamnadas. The whites sold them machines, thread, cloth. He sent for his sister's husband, Govind.

The shop grew crowded with sewing machines, lined up in a neat row. At night they spread bedrolls on countertops and floors, strung mosquito nets over jerry-rigged sleeping spaces. The workday started at dawn and ended at dark, long tropical days well suited to men who wished to turn a profit. Slowly M. Narsey & Co. began to pull customers: Indians who were more comfortable buying clothes from their own kind, and those of any stripe who sought the lowest price.

Seven years after landing, and five years after starting his shop, business was good enough that Motiram could leave his brother and brother-in-law in charge and make the long-delayed visit home. It was 1916 — coincidentally, also the last year that girmityas could sign up for indenture. The system was ended by imperial decree, as neo-abolitionists had finally managed to draw sufficient attention to its outrages. It did not hurt that by this time most of the labor needs of British colonies could be met by Indian workers already in place. From now on, the Indian diaspora would have to grow on its own.

Was it a pleasant visit? Seven years away: he must have grown slimmer, or plumper. He had acquired Western clothes, the habit of shoes. Did his mother, his wife, start as they recognized him? As he touched his mother's feet, surely there were tears in her eyes, and perhaps his.

He paid off the mortgage on the ancestral land. He spent time with his two young sons, who did not know him; he fathered a third.

The wild island was no place for a wife; he did not try to bring her back to Fiji, though she wanted to come.

Or: She did not want to come. Her name was Kaashi, she was a village girl, and to all of her descendants she would be known as Maaji: respected mother. He wanted her to come, but she refused.

For fifty more years, she would refuse to leave India.

He left her again.

Motiram must have felt, on that visit, like a big man in the small town of his ancestors. Strolling Navsari's unchanged streets, he was recognized not only as his father's son but also as a prodigal son, returned from the wilderness. And was there a new quality in his eyes, the eyes he turned now on his home?

For *home* was a landscape in decline. Though Navsari was an oasis of relative stability, the surrounding areas remained in profound depression. A historian, perusing famine records for the area, notes grimly, "Conditions were bad again in 1911–12, 1915–16, 1918–19 and 1920–21."

By contrast, opportunity in Fiji was plentiful. Rather than a homecoming, Motiram's trip became a recruiting mission. He turned evangelist, encouraging others of his caste to make the transition he had made. His youngest brother, Jiwan, accompanied him back; the next year, eleven more Khatris made the trip. Most of them worked, at least at first, for the pioneering tailor shops.

Kamal Kant Prasad, a historian who in the 1970s interviewed sources now deceased to research the rise of Gujaratis in Fiji, pieced together this portrait of Motiram's shop:

> The Narsey business was well organized . . . Motiram Narsey
> relied upon his large family network to provide the necessary
> manpower. His own immediate family served in managerial
> capacities, whereas other Khatris performed much of the
> menial tasks. Managerial duties embraced a wide range of activities, and largely entailed the careful supervision of the
> everyday activities of the concern — meeting the customers,
> measuring them, delegating the sewing tasks, undertaking the
> fitting, and finally consolidating the sales. In the shop there
> was an actual barrier separating the owner or supervisor from
> his workers. The owner worked on a long counter where he
> supervised the cutting. In front of him, or to either side of

him, were placed rows of machines where his workers performed the sewing tasks. His machine was normally set apart from the rest, in a position from where he could constantly supervise his workers. Only he had access to the area behind the counter where the money was kept.

In the Fiji census of 1911, taken while Motiram was at Walter Horne & Co., the government had counted twelve Indian tailors in all the country. By the early 1920s, so many Khatris had opened their own shops that they monopolized the trade, driving even the big European houses to focus on importing and retailing and to leave the tailoring to the Khatris. Within another fifteen years, Gujaratis would dominate Suva's retail economy. Motiram's was one of three tailoring shops that brought in dozens of Khatris over the next decade and, Prasad writes, "dictated the pattern of Khatri emigration from Gujarat."

In the vast ocean of the Indian diaspora, the migration of Khatris to Fiji constitutes a tiny trickle, significant as perhaps a brief squall of rain. Yet an ocean does not form from nothing; it is entirely composed of such currents, all swirling together to make a massive, powerful force. The many microcultures of India give rise to a Gujarati diaspora, a Bengali diaspora, a Punjabi diaspora; and within each of these we can distinguish castes and subcastes, regions and subregions. Ours is one of these subdiasporas, famous only to ourselves, approaching and associating with these others where the Indian population is small, otherwise retreating and coalescing, jelling back into itself when it reaches a critical mass.

In Fiji, Motiram must have had social and business intercourse with others of his countrymen, Indians of many castes and states, as well as the often mixed-caste "Hindustanis" of Fiji. Yet he and his descendants structured their lives around language and caste, Gujarati, Khatri, specific and recognizable, so tightly that his granddaughters, for example, to this day have only Khatri associates, their social lives almost exclusively composed of relatives, even though they live in Toronto, London, and other metropolises. This clannishness is, to some extent, a factor in our community's economic success.

Still, we are undeniably part of a larger picture—a worldwide network of Indians outside India, bonded by historical circumstance. Ours is but one small undercurrent in an ocean: a diaspora that was and is being built one journey, one family, one economic niche at a time.

Could Motiram read the newspapers? Never mind; he could hear. Someone read to him, or he heard the radio news. Or he talked with other men in the places where men talked: at the market, in the lodges, near the seaport watching the ships, in the back rooms behind the shop where they slept and, breaking Fiji's prohibition laws for nonwhites, drank.

The things that circled the globe began to touch him. A prospering businessman, he wore shoes every day, and European suits. He grew a mustache, and combed it; it balanced his thick, serious eyebrows. He followed the news: Ships coming in. Prices of goods. War. The world had become round, interconnected, and many things were circumnavigating it, traveling from place to place: ideas, fashions, patterns of mercantilism. And a new epidemic.

In the *Fiji Times and Herald,* advice for staving off the disease was plentiful. A local chemist recommended "eucalyptus oil sprinkled around dwelling rooms, camphor carried about the person, and some Antiseptic Lozenge, such as eumenthol jujubes, for the mouth and throat." The New Zealand Board of Health prescribed a few drops of quinine every four hours, plus gargling with baking soda. Quarantines held up ships for weeks as panic swept the world.

In 1918, a ship named the *Talune* docked in the port of Apia, in Western Samoa. The New Zealand officers and crew knew that some of their passengers were ill, with symptoms that resembled the deadly disease known variously as influenza, Spanish influenza, and the flu. Yet they told the harbormaster there were "only sniffles, but nothing serious." One passenger called out a warning—"There is sickness in this boat!" —but was not understood, or was ignored. People disembarked; people embarked.

Then the *Talune* carried on to nearby Tonga and to Fiji.

Within two weeks, 7,500 Samoans—22 percent of the island's population—were dead. It was the world's worst single case of the epidemic.

In Fiji, the disaster lasted through the end of the year, when the colony's chief medical officer reported a total mortality of about 8,000.

In the capital alone, 469 people died of the flu. Around the world, the epidemic would claim 20 million to 100 million lives.

Motiram, at perhaps thirty-five years old, was one of its casualties.

In bed with the flu, armed with Tylenol and cough drops, I wake in a sweat, the covers tossed about me like seas. *Imagine dying this way,* I tell myself. Who knows how many days and nights feverish chills racked my great-grandfather's body, what dreams and delusions filled his last hours? Growing weaker, confined at last to bed, his body would have been less and less able to fight the quick-moving virus replicating itself in every cell. Was he alone in a cot strung behind the shop, or in one of the makeshift quarantine clinics set up around town? Did his kinsmen tend him, or stay away from fear? Whose name did he call out in delirium? No records survive; no one is alive who remembers, who can offer more than this threadbare witnessing.

What was left: an unfinished story.

What was left: Motiram's two brothers, a brother-in-law, a shop full of workers. A storefront with treadle machines and customers. The knowledge of how to run a tailoring shop in Suva. And a path for his sons to rise out of poverty.

What was left: a wife and three sons in India. The eldest, Ratanji, was only eleven when Motiram died. Three years later he would come to Fiji and work for his uncles, eventually taking over the shop. By the end of Ratanji's forty-five years in the business, M. Narsey & Co. would become Narseys Limited—one of the largest department stores in the islands.

What was left: the beginnings of a new home for his people. When does an outpost become a settlement, a group of sojourners turn into a community? Births, weddings, deaths: the reenactment of ritual on foreign shores is one thread in the tapestry.

Motiram was not the first of our people in Fiji, but he holds a place in history nevertheless. He was the first of our tribe to die there, the first whose ashes might have graced the South Pacific—dissipated in the warm blue waters of shark gods, cannibals, pirates, and tragic bargains.

3. BREAD

To deny yourself the pleasure of a good bunny chow is to deny an integral part of South Africa's culinary heritage.
— *Sunday Times*, Johannesburg, 2001

Dayaram and wife (name unknown)
Village of Gandevi, India

Kaashi (Maaji) and Motiram Narsey
GANDA and Amba

IN THE PHOTOGRAPH, Maaji, as we always called her, is well into her eighties, squatting waist-high in shiny leaves. She was born in India around 1886, married Motiram Narsey sometime before 1909, and lived a few more years after this photograph was taken in the 1960s, in Fiji. Her hair is sparse and very white, bright as sun on the leaves, thick eyeglasses rejecting the light, painted beams of the bungalow behind her. Through its wooden shutters, one can see into the house: a sofa, aluminum barrels and trays, black coil of hose or wire, part of a ladder, a frame, doorways within doorways. Her head hunches forward over her collarbone; her shoulder blades almost touch her heart. She does not smile. Her back aches, perhaps, but harvesting betel leaves from the yard is a job she will let no one else do. *Paan,* our people call it; it is eaten after meals, and stains the teeth and tongue red. As she squats, one hand rests on a knee; the other, long and wasting, reaches into the vines, disappears. She seems all bone, skin thrown over it like a carelessly wrapped sari. Her sari itself is white, cotton, draped loosely and without adornment, the garb of widows.

In a season of migration, women like Maaji watched their neighborhoods empty out like villages in wartime, left populated only by the female, the aged, the feeble, and the young. While Maaji's husband traveled east to the wide-open opportunities of Fiji, those who boarded westbound ships to what the colonizers called "the dark continent" found a more complicated welcome. One of these was her younger brother, my great-great-uncle Ganda, who was only a boy when he went to the land that would become South Africa.

Brother and sister did not meet again for decades, yet they maintained a warm connection. The photograph of Maaji crouching in the leaves was taken sometime after she finally consented to join her sons in Fiji in the 1960s. On the back, my grandfather wrote a note about how his mother was settling in: *In our yard a lot of paan is growing and Maaji is collecting paan and the wedding was also performed in the yard.*

He sent the photo to her brother in South Africa, whose granddaughter—herself now white-haired and kindly—gave it to me in 2001.

On December 9, 1904, Ganda turned eleven years old in Navsari, India. An orphan, perhaps he had stayed with relatives a while after his sister's marriage. But most of his uncles and male cousins were already in South Africa. He decided, or it was decided for him, that he would join them in a land rumored to be rich with opportunity.

Of the three-week journey, his grandchildren know only that he traveled illegally. They like to think he was a stowaway; it lends a certain romance and swashbuckle to the tale. Nostalgia, a soothing gloss upon history.

Aboard ship, conditions were most unromantic. Who cared for him, who fed him? The details are lost—but fortuitously, an Indian professor visiting South Africa the same year, 1905, wrote of his own sea voyage. From his account we can catch a flavor of the times, a glimpse perhaps of Ganda's world.

"There were, say, a hundred Indians, traveling as deck-passengers," the professor noted. "I could not see any place where they could sit, put their luggage and take undisturbed rest for a while." In fierce rains and winds, they "had to stand or lie down exposed even at night"; cooking equipment was so scarce that some fasted for days, waiting their turn.

But the journey was perhaps the easier hurdle, compared to the arrival. For the world was divided into places that welcomed Indians, like Fiji; places that did not, like Europe; and places that were deeply ambivalent—like South Africa. Did the emigrants feel the currents of history swirling around them? Surely Ganda, a mere child, knew nothing of the greater forces of empire and conquest that were at play. He did not intuit the heart of his new country, nor could he have foreseen how it would invent, over his lifetime, the world's most thorough and systematic net of anti-Indian restrictions; how it would grow more and more hostile to all its dark citizens, against the flow of human progress, till it became a world pariah; or how fiercely his people would have to fight, in that golden land, for the right to earn their daily bread.

Grain, sugar, cattle, diamonds, gold: the riches of southern Africa were abundant. The saga of how they came to be concentrated in the hands of a white minority, at the expense of a vast African majority, is too long and tragic to be given justice here. But the bare outlines can be sketched out, for they are the shape into which Ganda's story must be poured.

The first whites settled at the tip of Africa in 1652, charged with setting up a rest stop for the ships of the Dutch East India Company, the world's greatest trading corporation of its time. The Cape was well situated midway on the route between the Netherlands and the Indies. To supply the company's ships with fresh grain, fruit, vegetables, and meat, the Dutch built a fort, orchards, and farms, using the labor of slaves — most from India, Sri Lanka, and Indonesia. Over time, the rest station of eighty-one people became a settlement of nearly thirty thousand whites and slaves, sprawling north over a vast territory.

Once the Dutch were well established, the British swooped in for the spoils — drawn again by the strategic location, halfway to India. Over centuries of warfare, the two European groups managed to subdue, by brute and near-genocidal force, the Africans who inhabited the land.

They also established an edgy truce with each other. The British, the official rulers, installed a semi-democracy in which all white men had a vote. The Dutch descendants formed the numeric majority and therefore could control most local policy through their elected legislators. Between them, they divided southernmost Africa into four colonies, one of which possessed a climate suitable for sugar: the Colony of Natal.

Named for the day it came into view of Vasco da Gama's ships — Christmas — Natal had a coastline blessed by the warm winds of the Indian Ocean. But its Africans, recently conquered, were seen as neither docile nor industrious enough to plant and work sugar. "The fate of the Colony hangs on a thread and that thread is Labour," one newspaper editorialized in 1859. In 1860, by a now well-refined formula, the first indentured Indians arrived in Natal.

As workers bound by contract, the Indians were welcomed. Once their contracts expired, however, a backlash began.

"The ordinary Coolie . . . is introduced for the same reason as mules might be introduced from Monte Video, oxen from Madagascar or sugar machinery from Glasgow," editorialized the *Natal Witness,* the newspaper of the planters, in 1875. "He is not one of us, he is in every respect an alien; he only comes to perform a certain amount of work, and return to India."

But the "ordinary Coolie" did not wish, most of the time, to return to poverty in India, choosing instead to try his or her luck in the new land. The whites found themselves unable to force the Indians to go home, for back in India, the British government was still trying to relieve population pressure. Britain insisted that its colonies had to allow Indians to travel freely, to buy land, and to settle at will—or it would cut off the labor supply.

Under the provision that Indians must be allowed to travel freely, Gujaratis entered South Africa as free, or "passenger," Indians. Among them were Ganda's uncles, the first of whom arrived in 1887. Soon free Indians were carrying on a thriving trade throughout Natal, and spreading to neighboring colonies as well.

But the whites of South Africa never resigned themselves to this situation. Unlike colonial administrators in Fiji and other indenture colonies, they were not mere sojourners, content to stuff their pockets with profits and go home to Britain. Indeed, the majority were so many generations removed from the Netherlands that South Africa was their only home. They formed a hardscrabble tribe with a distinct language that came to be known as Afrikaans, called themselves Afrikaners, and possessed a mythology and single-mindedness to rival any others in Africa. According to their own Bible, they were a chosen people; a core of their theology was the superiority of the white race to the black and brown. They had fought wars and spent two and a half centuries making sure that Africans did not own their own land. The idea of sharing their God-given territory with mere "coolies" was shocking, offensive, and nearly heretical.

Yet they were caught in a bind. "There is probably not a single person in Natal who does not, if spoken to on the subject deplore the Asiatic invasion," wrote the *Witness,* in 1890, "but . . . We want labour, is the cry; the Government will not force the native to work; and so we must take what offers and what is cheap."

So they continued to bring in Indian workers, who continued to ex-

ercise their right to stay after their contracts expired; and they continued, reluctantly, to admit passenger Indians. Ganda's uncles soon called
over their sons and cousins, establishing themselves in Johannesburg and
in Durban, the main city of the colony of Natal.

By 1904, more than a hundred thousand Indians were living in Natal
—outpacing, for the first time, the white population. The census taker
warned, "To any one knowing the rapidity with which these Eastern Races
increase, through early marriages, etc., this question should form matter
for serious consideration . . . It is appalling to consider what the Indian
figures may be in the near future."

"Appalling" was, in the rhetoric of the day, an understatement. Afrikaner
politicians and newspapers were railing against what they called the "invasion." Keeping within the letter of the British Empire's requirements,
each of the four South African colonies began to apply its own legislative thumbscrews. Natal forced indentured Indians to pay a hefty annual
tax at the end of their terms, in the hope that they would either go home
or re-indenture. The Transvaal forbade Indians to own land in certain
areas, particularly its gold-rich terrain, and tried to close its borders to
Indians seeking to move north from Natal. The Cape Colony also restricted immigration and trade, while the Orange Free State barred Indians altogether and expelled the few already present, declaring it did
not need indentured workers. Some cities required Indians, as members
of an "uncivilised race," to register if they entered the town limits. Others
compelled free-roaming Indians to carry "passes" to prove that they were
not runaway indenturees, and forced Indian shops and homes into segregated "bazaars" or "locations." Towns barred Indians as well as Africans
from using taxis and trams, owning guns, drinking liquor, even walking
on certain sidewalks.

Of the dozens of laws aimed at Indians decorating the legal gazettes
of the South African colonies, perhaps the most urgently debated and
carefully crafted were the ones on immigration. Although Ganda's uncles
had entered South Africa freely, by the time he made his own journey in
1905, the net had tightened.

"As the steamers sailed on towards the South," wrote the professor, "the
constant talk among the poor passengers was about the restrictions of

landing." At the port leading to South Africa's gold country, where Ganda might have hoped to find his uncles, four passengers were denied permission to land. Among them were a barber who had borrowed 300 rupees for the journey, an "aged man" who wept as his landing permit was taken away, and "a boy under his teens":

> He was brought on board the ship in the promise of getting down on land by his relative. At the place, being fearful of himself, the relative got down quite heedless of the boy.
> The boy wept aloud, the tears running from his eyes.

The boy, the barber, the aged man, and thousands of other Indians of that era, seeking to migrate for economic opportunity, were trapped in the gap between the British Empire's rhetoric and its practice. South Africa was not even the world's most extreme case as it wrestled with the common problem of what to do about the "coolies."

"The whole subject is perhaps the most difficult we have had to deal with," fretted an internal London bureaucratic memo, 1897. "The Colonies wish to exclude the Indians from spreading themselves all over the Empire. If we agree, we are liable to forfeit the loyalty of the Indians. If we do not agree we forfeit the loyalty of the Colonists."

What had seemed an elegant solution to two problems—relieving population pressure in India and providing cheap labor to the farthest reaches of the growing empire—was now a headache in itself. For the Indians were part of a larger British strategy and could not be as easily maltreated as, say, Aboriginals or native Africans. The Indians had certain rights, a certain degree of clout. Trade with India made up a hefty portion of the British economy, accounting for a fifth of British exports. By 1901, when King Edward VII inherited the throne from his mother, Victoria, four in five of his subjects—300 million—were Indian. They made the empire an empire; they had to be kept, if not happy, at least placid.

Already in Bombay a self-styled Indian National Congress was calling mass meetings and petitioning for rights; its leaders were making dangerous, fiery speeches. The "Sepoy Rebellion" or Mutiny of 1857, when Indian soldiers rioted and had to be violently suppressed, was within the political memory of the bureaucrats in London. Acts that fostered ill will in India, acts that provided fodder for the nascent independence movement's outrage, were not fiscally sound.

Because of this, London could not allow the colonies to adopt blatant racial discrimination. Subtle discrimination was, however, a different matter. To satisfy imperial politics, the legislators of Natal were forced into creativity. They could not, for example, limit *Indian* immigration; British subjects possessed the right to travel freely, and this right could not be taken away—at least, not on overtly racial grounds. So Natal imposed a "literacy" test. The immigration officer could require any prospective immigrant to answer, in writing, *in a European language,* certain questions. If the would-be immigrant was white but illiterate, the officer waived the test. But if he was swarthy, or otherwise undesirable, the test was given; and even if he was educated to the highest degree in his native language, he would not pass if he could not write his answers in a European tongue.

This creativity did not go unnoticed. In a 1900 speech to the heads of the colonies, their boss, Joseph Chamberlain, praised Natal for its "entirely satisfactory" solution. Soon Australia, which was having a problem with the Chinese (it wanted railroad labor, and received aspiring human beings), refined the solution further. It barred anyone who, "when an officer dictates to him not less than fifty words in any prescribed language, fails to write them out in that language in the presence of the officer."

Any prescribed language. Asian immigrants were asked at the docks to take dictation in Dutch, in German, in Portuguese, by officers who laughed at their confusion. Similar nondiscriminatory discriminations spread to New Zealand, Canada, other parts of Africa. The United States considered a literacy test in 1917, but—unbound by British civility and economic interests—opted to simply exclude all Asians.

In 1913 Natal's legislators would adopt what was then known as the Australian system; they knew it as their own, and welcomed it home like a prodigal son. It allowed them to bar virtually every Indian immigrant. In the news reports of the day, one senses glee, pride, the thrill and relief of a hurdle overcome.

At Ganda's arrival in 1905, the system was not yet airtight. Even so, every Indian immigrant had to fill out a simple standard form, take dictation of words of the officer's choice in English, and give prints of his fingers and thumb. Permits were being demanded from women and from boys under sixteen, who had previously been left unmolested. In some cases even infants were required to take out and pay for permits. Shipping companies who carried illegal immigrants were fined if they allowed "undesirables" off the ship. One shipmaster locked seventy-five passengers into the hold for three days, without food or water, because their papers were questionable; only a lawyer's intervention freed them.

Unwanted, harassed, deterred, the Indians kept coming—exhibiting their own creativity. The man in charge of keeping them out complained that "Asiatic cunning" made his mission impossible. Indians slithered through his fingers, entered through neighboring countries, claimed distant relatives as their own siblings and children.

His officers were kept busy. The Bombay–Durban steamer made one trip a month. Other ships came from Calcutta and Madras. And there were land routes, from elsewhere in South Africa, from Portuguese East Africa (now Mozambique), and from German South-West Africa (now Namibia). It was not easy to police so many borders.

Ganda could have traveled by any of these routes. In the year of his journey, the main port of entry for Indians, Port Durban in the Colony of Natal, turned away half of the Indians arriving: 1,526 men, 18 women, and 49 children. And officials confiscated 225 forged documents, purchased on the black market in India. The crackdown would grow even more severe; in 1908, nearly six thousand Indians would be turned away.

But by then Ganda was settled in Durban—having somehow given the authorities the slip.

Durban: "a second-rate Bombay," one contemporary called it. Although Indians made up less than three percent of South Africa's population, segregation and internal travel restrictions confined them largely to the city of Durban and its outskirts. This unnatural concentration created what over Ganda's lifetime would become the largest "Little India" in the world: the Grey Street neighborhood.

Here stood the largest mosque in the Southern Hemisphere, built from the profits of Gujarati traders. Colorful mounds of vegetables and spices —chili, cumin, coriander—filled the market stalls. Scribes stood ready to write letters home for the illiterate; Indian tailors made suits to measure; Indian jewelers offered real and faux gold trinkets for any budget. Many of the staples were imported from India: cooking oil, basmati rice, burlap sacks filled with the special flour for making *rotli,* the traditional round Gujarati flatbread. Luxury goods, too—insurance or waistcoats, Egyptian cigars, Turkish caps, Chinese silks, Persian rugs, tickets for trips on European steamers—could be bought within a block or two of Ganda's new domicile.

Grey Street was named for Sir George Grey, onetime governor of the Cape. The neighborhood was developed during Queen Victoria's reign, its streets named for members of the royal family: Queen Street and Albert Street (for her husband); Victoria, Alice, Beatrice, and Lorne Streets (for her daughters); Prince Edward and Leopold Streets (for her sons); and even Louise Lane and Maud Lane (for her granddaughters). Once, it had been a white residential area.

The land was marshy, though, and difficult for wagons to navigate. Gradually the whites moved on to more desirable neighborhoods. A group of Muslim storekeepers bought a portion of the now-cheap marshland, reclaimed the swamps, and erected a mosque in 1881. By Ganda's time, the cobblestone streets around the mosque were the city's main hub of Indian social and commercial activity.

But Grey Street was more than a colorful clustering of an ethnic minority. It was also a product of the Indian "problem" and white South Africa's response to it—a ghetto enforced by law.

Beginning in 1885, the first Gujaratis in Durban had set up shop several blocks away, in the city's main commercial district, on West Street. A steady stream of other Indians, both former indentured workers and new Gujarati "passengers," had followed suit.

This set off a small panic among the white merchants downtown, who did not want to have their shops next to "coolies"—or to compete with their cheaper prices. All over the colony, a similar pattern was developing in the towns as Indians set up small stores wherever they could buy or rent space.

Many of these first Gujaratis were Muslims who, in an effort to distinguish themselves from the poor Hindu masses and fall to the whiter side of the rigid racial line, styled themselves "Arabs." But the whites knew a "coolie" when they saw one. Variously the traders were also called Bombay-wallahs, Banias (for the Hindu merchant caste), and, in the unforgettable phrase of Natal's governor, "black matter in the wrong place." Like most of his subjects, the governor would have liked to keep out passenger Indians altogether—though he was still importing three thousand indentured Indians a year, at the request of Natal's sugar planters, rail companies, and coal mines.

Indian shopkeepers, it was widely held, undercut "legitimate" businesses. At rallies and town-hall meetings throughout Natal, the complaint rose: Indians kept their stores open on Sundays, when good Christians must rest. They worked late into the nights, when family men should be with their wives and children. They had minimal requirements of clothing, food, and luxury, subsisting "on the smell of an oil rag," their white competitors complained. How could a white man raise his family if he must match these conditions?

In 1897, the Natal colony gave its town councils the power to deny trade licenses to anyone, with minimal cause and no right of appeal. Neutral in language, the law was aimed at and deployed against Indians.

Some towns used their new powers to expel all of their Indian shopkeepers. In Durban, the town council was content to drive Indians out of long-established business locations downtown, on specious charges of sanitation or bookkeeping irregularities. By 1908, the licensing bureau was proud to report, Durban had succeeded in cutting back the number of Indian licenses by a third. Virtually all remaining businesses were in the Grey Street area.

For Ganda, eleven years old, it would have been easy enough to disappear into the ghetto. An uncle and cousins lived in the neighborhood, and they must have taken him in. They would have known that, sooner or later, he would need an official identity: he could be stopped on the street at any time and asked to show his documents; he could be arrested for breaking the 9 P.M. curfew or walking on a sidewalk reserved for whites; he could be deported.

So his relatives—being, after all, wily Asiatics—hatched a scheme.

In Johannesburg, cousin Chhiba reported to the police that his son had gone missing. He gave a description, a name. Perhaps he said that the boy might have run away, to Durban.

Meanwhile, in Durban, Ganda filed for his identity papers. He had no birth certificate, but that was not unusual. He gave his "father's" name, Chhiba of Johannesburg.

As for his last name, the uncles and cousins used "Kapitan." Most rural

Indians never use a surname until they encounter a Western authority, and so it was with Ganda's predecessors, who had to invent one upon landing in South Africa. Kapitan is a unique choice among our people, and the stories of its origin vary widely. Three brothers jumped around like monkeys and were nicknamed "three monkeys," or *kappi tran*. Or, it comes from the first port where they landed in South Africa: Cape Town, pronounced according to the principles of Indian-English phonetics. Or, the first family member in South Africa came on a ship steered by a man called *el capitán*, which the sojourner thought to be a fine surname and so adopted as his own.

In any case, armed with these names, young Ganda submitted his papers and his references. Crosschecking, the officials found the missing-persons report. They verified his identity.

Ganda's middle name, by tradition, should have been his father's name, Dayaram. He would have become known as G. D. Kapitan; the Durban institution he founded would have been G. D. Kapitan & Son Vegetarian Restaurant. His father would have lived forever, almost, in that single initial recognizing his paternity.

But now his name reflected his new "father." And somehow in the transcription process, Chhiba became Chhagan. He became Ganda Chhagan Kapitan, a self-made man—G.C., for short.

Despite the concentration of Indians in Durban, few schools were open to Indian children. In any case, schools cost money, and Ganda had none. He apprenticed as a tailor instead. At fifteen he opened his own tailoring stall, becoming one of thousands whose entrepreneurial spirit was considered part of the "Indian problem" in South Africa. When he could afford it, he moved out on his own, living in a rented room in the mosque building. All around were apartments housing Indian families and bachelors and, at street level, their shops and curry houses.

His cousin Fakir owned one of these food shacks, in an arcade across the street from the mosque, at 154 Grey Street. And this became, for Ganda, an unlikely opportunity. Fakir was caught unexpectedly in the net of South Africa's immigration laws. He needed to leave his shop in the care of someone trustworthy. But most of his other relatives lived far away or had their own businesses to run.

Ganda was young, just a teenager, but he had several years of work experience under his belt; more importantly, he was, as Gujaratis say, *ghar-no maanas:* a man from home, a kinsman. He could be trusted. Fakir traveled to Fiji, where he had other relatives, until the paperwork could be sorted out. He left his eatery in Ganda's charge—temporarily, they believed.

As it turned out, Fakir could not come back. The year was 1912, and Ganda hung his own name on the shingle. He was seventeen years old. For the rest of his life, he would feed the people of Grey Street.

Vegetable curries, rice, the thick lentil soup called *daal.* Sweet, milky tea and deep-fried samosas. Food was a basic, and as the community grew, so did Ganda's business. Strictly vegetarian, he cultivated a loyal clientele who came for curries and rice at lunch and dinner, tea and snacks all day long. At some point it must have seemed like a good idea to have a helpmeet; perhaps he realized he was no longer a sojourner but an immigrant. Now that he was settled in business, the natural step would be to settle down with a wife.

Few Khatri women were in South Africa, fewer still of marriageable age. In any case, a girl raised in India was more likely to possess the proper domestic skill set and temperament. So he took a vacation: a trip to India to get married.

The match was arranged, of course; the girl's name was Amba, and she had lived her entire life in the village of Gandevi. They walked around the marriage fire four times, and soon afterward they were on an ocean liner—this time, as paying passengers.

Plunged into the hustle and bustle of Durban, Amba had no trouble keeping busy. The Grey Street shop where Ganda spent his hours was a small wooden shack with an outdoor kitchen; barely screened from the busy street, it was no place for a woman of their caste. But in their apartment, just around the corner on Pine Street, attached to the mosque building, she sewed shirts for extra money, and she made snack foods in her own kitchen for sale in the restaurant. Durban's climate was just like home in a year when the rains were good—warm, neither dry nor humid, a solid seventy to eighty degrees most of the time. The hills and farms surrounding the city were verdant, and Indian farmers from the countryside kept the city well supplied with all of the proper Indian vegetables. Among Amba's specialties were two types of thin lentil-flour wafers known as *paapad* and *paapadi,* which she rolled out on a round wooden board, then arranged to dry in the sun so they could be stored indefinitely and deep-fried whenever needed.

Their neighbors included many Gujaratis, shopkeepers of one kind or another. Devout Hindus, Ganda and Amba formed ties with the small Hindu community while keeping good relations with their mostly Muslim neighbors, worshipping their own pantheon in an altar at home while living under the archways and minarets of the mosque. Each dawn a holy man climbed to its highest point to broadcast the call: *Allah u Akbar,* God is great, Hasten to prayer . . . At nightfall Ganda watched as most of the street's merchants locked up their shops and, along with many of their customers, disappeared through the main archway of the mosque, pausing at a courtyard fountain to wash their hands and feet before entering the inner chamber to kneel and pray: *Allah u Akbar . . .* Closing up, he too went home to his devotions, to practice a religion and way of life that seemed, to the men who ran his country, both outlandish and barbaric.

In March 1913, a high court of South Africa declared invalid the marriage of two Hindus—and, by extension, invalidated the marriages of Ganda and Amba Kapitan and every other Hindu and Muslim couple in South Africa. A stroke of the judicial pen rendered illegitimate any marriage conducted by rites of "a religion that recognizes polygamy," even if the marriage was itself monogamous.

Aside from the indignity, many Indian spouses were in danger of being stripped of citizenship and deported. The outcry was immediate. Large crowds of Indian men and women took to the streets in protest. The ruling crystallized the community's outrage over decades of mistreatment and ignited a fire that Indian advocates had been carefully stoking for years.

Seeds of this organizing had been planted on Grey Street, where a shopkeeper had hired, in 1893, a young lawyer from his hometown in Gujarat. Upon arrival, the Oxford-educated lawyer was kicked off trains, insulted in courts, and beaten in the streets for his color—and soon realized the pervasive injustices facing Indians in South Africa. "I then awoke," Mohandas Gandhi would later write, "to a sense of my duty."

Although Gandhi had moved to Johannesburg, he had left his mark on the Durban neighborhood. At 113 Grey Street was the office from which he first published his weekly newspaper, *Indian Opinion,* in 1903. Down the block was Congress Hall, home to South Africa's first Indian civil rights organization, founded by Gandhi and a group of merchants in 1894.

And he had graduated from his early protest tactics, filing petitions and writing pointed letters to the editor, to taking the initiative—by staging mass actions. In one dramatic moment in 1906, Gandhi had gathered hundreds of Indians who together vowed, before God, to resist draconian regulations that required all Indians to be registered and fingerprinted like criminals and that allowed police officers to search houses and demand domicile certificates at any time, on punishment of deportation. They burned their certificates on a massive pyre. It became "shameful," Gandhi wrote, to refer to such nonviolent resistance using English words. His newspaper held a contest, and the technique was renamed *satyagraha,* "force which is born of Truth and Love," or "soul force."

South Africa's Indians were trying out and developing the strategies that would become Gandhi's legacy to the world: peaceful defiance of unjust laws, long marches on foot, mass meetings, fasting, political oaths before God, and deliberate courting of arrest. They won small victories, suffered greater defeats; time and again, Gandhi turned to his core supporters, the Gujarati merchants of Durban's Grey Street and of Johannesburg, to help bankroll the movement.

Three generations later, every Gujarati in Durban claims a Gandhi connection, swears that the Great Soul once patronized his ancestor's family establishment. It is likely that Ganda saw and even met Gandhi, but unlikely that the restaurant fed him; by this time Gandhi was subsisting mainly on a diet of fruit and nuts, eschewing cooked foods. Whether or not the two men ever exchanged words or broke bread, what is certain is that all of the major events of the community passed by Ganda's front door. And because South Africa's was no ordinary Indian community, with no ordinary leader, Ganda's small fast-food stall turned out to be a front seat to history.

The marriage ruling led to two years of a massive satyagraha campaign. After thousands of arrests, strikes, police crackdowns, and even some deaths, the government and the protesters reached a compromise: the Indian Relief Act of 1914, which restored some rights. Gandhi sailed back to India on the winds of victory, carrying with him a new methodology of passive resistance. In Durban he was a homegrown hero; in India he was not yet the Mahatma, the Great One, but a young lawyer who, having spent twenty-one years fighting for justice in the diaspora, had managed to cause the empire some embarrassment.

But the price of victory for Indians in South Africa was high: an absolutely closed door to Indians outside. There would be no new immigration for any reason: no siblings or ailing parents; no entrepreneurs or laborers or students; no grooms, no brides. South Africa's Indian sons and daughters would marry, from now on, within South Africa. As it turned out, Amba was one of the last brides from India.

The closed door created an unintended side effect, entrenching the Indian population even more and solidifying its position as a population not of immigrants but of South Africans born and bred. By the 1920s, Indians in South Africa were no longer an expatriate population. Three in five were born in the new country. Among these were two new Kapitans: Ganda and Amba's daughter, Parvati, born in 1918, and their son, Dalpat, six years later.

As the family grew, the neighborhood was changing. A few blocks from the mosque, a flourishing nightlife district pulsated with jazz joints, billiards clubs, and ballrooms for dancing. Men of all races brushed elbows to bet on boxing and horses, and by the time Parvati and Dalpat were in primary school, at least a dozen Indian-owned cinemas were showing Hollywood films. Grey Street was no longer the swampy outskirts of the city; it was a busy sector in its own right, its shacks and horse stalls slowly giving way to modern buildings, paved roads, motorcars. In keeping with the times, the façade enclosing the mosque was completely rebuilt in 1930. A two-story structure rose up all around like a fortress: shops on the ground floor, apartments upstairs, the mosque itself hidden mostly within, like a secret treasure. Amid the material pursuits of streetside, its minarets were the only sign of its reaching toward the heavens.

Soon the owner of 154 Grey Street decided to remake his side of the block, too. Ganda was on good terms with his landlord, who agreed to renovate the humble thirty-year-old eatery with its outdoor kitchen into a wholly modern structure—part of the new, grand Aboobaker Mansions, named for the very first Gujarati in Durban, whose son owned the property.

For longtime tenants, units were built to specification. Ganda worked out a design for his ideal shop, then watched it take shape: a front room with glass windows for displaying wares and letting in sunlight, and long tables and wooden chairs for seating a few dozen customers. A full indoor kitchen with industrial-size stoves and ovens. A courtyard out back where firewood for the ovens could be piled neatly along a wall. Two storage rooms downstairs: a cold room for vegetables and perishables, and a granary filled with flour, rice, and daals. Two more storage rooms upstairs, for stocks of Chiclets, candy, cigarettes, and other easy over-the-counter sales. Also upstairs was a two-bedroom apartment where Ganda moved his family, reducing his commute by a block.

After their one-room existence, the apartment in Aboobaker Mansions was, if not a mansion in the modern sense, expansive. Inside, it opened onto an Indian-style courtyard where children played in the stairways and adults called across the railings, women visiting to borrow a cup of flour, to swap recipes and news, to catch up on the latest gossip. Inside, Ganda and Amba had their own room for the first time since Parvati's birth seventeen years before. The two teenagers shared another room, and the hallway in between led to a balcony that faced the mosque, where Amba hung her laundry. An inner courtyard led to a kitchen, toilet, and bath. Just below was the newly renovated store. The year was 1935, and Dalpat was eleven years old, the age that his father had been when he came to South Africa. The new sign proudly proclaimed the boy's inheritance and destiny: G. C. Kapitan & Son Vegetarian Restaurant.

Around Grey Street, factories were springing up: shoes, clothing, leather. The owners were mostly white and Indian; the workers, mostly African. As black Africans entered the city in larger numbers, Grey Street shop windows took to displaying traditional African clothing and modern Western clothes alongside saris and salwar kameez. In such a stratified society even food had a color, yet the colors were beginning to blend; Indians could be seen eating "mealies," or boiled corn, and Africans developed a taste for curry.

. . .

The whites might have liked some of the new flavors, but the large populations of black and brown people who produced them were a grave problem. Seeking always to keep the races as separate as possible, and to keep crowds of black or brown South Africans from "swamping" the white cities, they produced a series of racial zoning proposals; a 1944 planning map, for example, shows an ideal Durban divided into zones for "Europeans," "Asiatics," "Natives," and "Coloureds." As officials considered the feasibility of various versions of such plans, they also enforced a steady stream of race-restrictive regulations. Some targeted business, that old sticking point between Gujaratis and whites. Others targeted black Africans, who were barred from entering the cities without passes, being on the streets after certain hours, and — most significantly for Ganda — eating in restaurants.

The date of this change is uncertain; it may have been a strictly local ordinance, or an old regulation being freshly enforced during one of many periodic attempts at shepherding the unwieldy mix of populations. Whenever it occurred, its impact was significant, for by this time a substantial portion of the curry houses' clientele was African.

Ganda and other restaurateurs, thinking quickly, realized they must begin to sell "take-aways." In search of a cheap container, in the age before Styrofoam, they hit upon the humble bread loaf. They invented what became known as the bunny chow.

To make a bunny chow, you need a loaf of bread and a scoopful of vegetable, meat, or bean curry. Cut off the end of the bread and hollow it out, reserving the soft innards. Fill it with curry. Serve.

To eat it is another trick altogether. If you just bite in, everything spills out — a steaming, spicy mess, dripping all over your lap. With experience, you learn to nibble gently at the outer crust; to cradle the loaf in one hand and gently scoop out curry with the other, using the extra bread that was pulled out earlier, or your fingers, so that nothing spills; to savor the complementary tastes of rich spices and soothing, yeasty bread. When the loaf is no longer overflowing, you grasp it with both hands and lift it to your mouth. Bite carefully, taking both curry and bread in each bite. Continue eating until entire loaf and all curry is consumed. Lick fingers and wipe mouth, chin, et cetera.

At a modern bunny chow joint, Africans of all colors can be seen chowing down. Watching them, black, brown, and white, it is easy to forget that the bunny chow was born of segregation—South Africa's extreme and relentless version of it.

The etymology of "bunny chow" is as uncertain as the identity of its inventor. Descendants of the pioneering Grey Street restaurateurs battle it out valiantly on both counts, without any expectation of settling the question at this late date. Ganda, a lifelong vegetarian, does seem to be the undisputed creator of the "beans bunny," the version in which the loaf is stuffed with a rich, spicy stew of tomatoes and fava beans.

As for the mysterious name, some see, Rorschach-like, the shape of a rabbit in the steaming loaf. Others hear it as a combination of *bun* and *aachaar,* a kind of Indian pickle that is not actually part of the dish. Ganda's grandchildren say "bunny" comes from *bania,* the British pronunciation of *vaaniyaa,* the name of the merchant caste in Gujarat— which in South Africa came to mean any Indian shopkeeper, regardless of caste or language. And "chow," they say, means simply food.

The precise date of the bunny chow's explosion onto the culinary scene was not, alas, recorded by any of its inventors or consumers. But a clue lies in the story of bread itself.

For even as the South African government was harassing Indian entrepreneurs and African customers, it was propping up other segments of the economy. To aid white family farms, the government had been heavily subsidizing local wheat and controlling wheat imports since 1917. Over the next few decades, the effort intensified so that, during the worldwide Great Depression, wheat growing was the most profitable branch of farming in South Africa. During World War II, to keep the consumption of wheat steady despite higher wartime production costs, the South African government began subsidizing bread. In 1941 the "standard loaf," a regulation-size loaf of brown bread, was introduced.

Subsidized and sold at the low, uniform price of five shillings a loaf, bread soon became a staple for all classes of South Africans. And this subsidy may well have been the tipping point that made loaves cheaper than rotli, cheap enough to be used on a large scale.

Rice, eaten mostly by Indians, and corn, eaten mostly by black Africans, were not subsidized. Shortages of other commodities persisted. But bread became cheap, dirt cheap. As cheap as rhetoric.

"Vote for white bread and a white South Africa," urged the campaign signs of South Africa's newly formed National Party. The year was 1948, and the party's candidate for prime minister was a man named D. F. Malan, a seventy-four-year-old Afrikaner. Back in 1912, when Ganda was stirring his first pots of curry for the masses, Malan had made the pages of the *Indian Opinion* as a young politician representing South Africa at an imperial conference. The treatment of Indians throughout the British Empire was the conference's central issue. Restricting Indians, he had told the assembled leaders frankly, was simply "self-preservation for the Europeans."

More than three decades later, Malan was the leader of a party espousing a new policy that it claimed would solve South Africa's racial problem once and for all: *apartheid,* or total segregation. To keep South Africa as a white man's land, it was necessary to banish Africans to "homelands," except those who were needed to work for whites, and to send the Indians back to India.

Malan was a statesman, able to read his constituency's desires. The ultimate aim of all anti-Indian legislation over the years had remained consistent: to induce Indians to leave South Africa altogether. Although more than eighty percent of the Indian population was by this time born in South Africa, Afrikaners and their elected representatives continued to speak wistfully of repatriation, not peaceful cohabitation, as the final solution to the "Indian problem." Various governments had introduced schemes offering free passage and cash bonuses to those who agreed to go back to India and stay there.

A few went back for other reasons, like Ganda's daughter, Parvati; her marriage was arranged in India, where she had never lived but would stay the rest of her life. But for most of South Africa's Indians, established for generations—especially the shopkeepers and small landowners, those whom the whites most wanted to get rid of—life in India held little appeal. Ganda's business was thriving; his son had married, joined the family business, and made Ganda a grandfather. Three generations lived together in the Grey Street apartment. It was a good life—better than the one he could have had in impoverished India.

White South African propaganda made much of this. One brochure published by the Durban City Council in 1947 proclaimed that Natal was an "economic paradise" for Indians. The glossy twenty-eight-page mini-magazine featured photographs of large Indian mansions, Indian children in art class, Indian men playing golf. "Is there any country in the world where Indians are better treated than they are in South Africa?" it asked. "Why was it that so few of them were willing to accept a free passage back to their own country?"

The audience for such arguments was an international one, particularly around and after 1947.

On August 15 of that year, the British colony of India was split into the two free nations of India and Pakistan. All over the world, Indians held independence parades. Grey Street was festooned with the colors of the new national flags, the sidewalks filled with celebrants who came to hear patriotic speeches, to cheer, and to feast. The new Indian prime minister sent his daughter, Indira, to visit South Africa; on Grey Street she met local leaders and ate a bunny chow.

By this time, approximately 1.2 million people of Indian origin were living outside the Indian subcontinent. As the Narseys were putting down roots in Fiji and the Kapitans in South Africa, so the great world-tree of the diaspora had put down roots. And the Natal census writer's fears of a rapidly multiplying race had come true. South Africa, with its 266,000 Indians, was second on the list of countries with a substantial Indian population.

As the list of countries had grown, so had the backlash. Back in London, the India Office, the vast apparatus that managed not only India but all issues relating to Indians throughout the British Empire, found its in-box cluttered with dispatches from "Her Majesty's Subjects" in distress. *Indians in Madagascar: discrimination in the matter of taxation. Indians in California: decision of US Supreme Court regarding eligibility of Hindus for American citizenship. Racial discrimination against Indian passengers in Lake Kioga in Uganda. Restrictions placed on Indians in the Belgian and French Congo . . . in South Africa . . . in Canada . . . Entry of Indians into the USA: protest of Mr Prag Narayan against the treatment of his relative*

Mr B N Gupta by American immigration authorities at Ellis Island. Laws were passed against Indian traders in Gibraltar and "coloured alien" seamen in Glasgow; Indians in Kenya were assaulted. Canada introduced voting discrimination; in Fiji, segregation was proposed in the mining town of Tavua. Indians faced sanctions, violence, or discrimination in Guatemala, Guadeloupe, Martinique, Réunion, Kenya, Iraq, Trinidad, Panama, Rhodesia, Indochina, Malaya, Morocco, Zanzibar, Hong Kong, New Caledonia, and places whose names seem to come out of antiquity: Abyssinia, Arabistan, Jabaland, Sarawak, Somaliland, Mesopotamia, Palestine. The map of the world shifted, and as it did, India's diaspora shifted and expanded to cover it. The tree branched and branched again, grew gnarled and complex, and found everywhere the fierce competition for survival.

Because of empire, impoverished Indians left home; because of empire, they had somewhere to go. And when the backlash came, it was empire to which they turned for redress. The battle that the Indians of Grey Street were fighting in South Africa was not unique but an inherent part of a worldwide phenomenon that had developed alongside the sudden, rapid growth of the diaspora.

The Indians, especially the mercantile Gujaratis, found themselves caught in what academics call "pariah capitalism." In this particular incarnation of the "free market," members of one group—typically Asians or Jews—occupy a middle or "pariah" position between the true but invisible ruling class and the truly oppressed. Over and over, this multilevel hierarchy would lead to a dangerous backlash against Indians in nations as far-flung as Uganda, Burma, the United States, Fiji—and South Africa.

Gandhi, arguing for the rights of South African Indians, had counted upon his status as a subject of the British Empire. He based each of his petitions on a few lines in the proclamation that Queen Victoria had made in taking possession of India from the British East India Company in 1857: "We hold ourselves bound to the natives of our Indian territories by the same obligations of duty which bind us to all our other subjects," the queen asserted, adding, "We declare it to be our royal will and pleasure that none be in any wise favoured, none molested or disquieted, by reason of their religious faith or observances, but that all shall alike enjoy the equal and impartial protection of the law." On the strength of this promise, Gandhi and those who came just after him had attempted to argue for equal rights.

But Gandhi's great work was India's independence. In South Africa, the festive atmosphere masked, for a day, a grim situation—for Gandhi's fragile compromise of 1914 had come to seem a trick. The bargain had been no new immigration in exchange for equitable treatment of Indians already in South Africa. Instead, the inequities had multiplied.

Every pretext was used, from "unhygienic" conditions to the "unassimilable" nature of Indians. Indian activists pointed out that their people, at only 3.5 percent of the population, might have assimilated if they had been allowed to spread out across South Africa, instead of being forced into certain areas. But "unassimilable" became a self-fulfilling prophecy; ghettos were used to justify further ghettoization. The Pegging Act of 1943, passed in a hysteria over supposed Indian "penetration" into the white areas of Durban, temporarily halted all property sales from one race to another. The Asiatic Land Tenure Act of 1946 strengthened it and made it permanent. Dubbed by Indians "the Ghetto Act," the 1946 legislation allowed the government to assign racial designations to areas and to forcibly relocate Indians.

For decades, Grey Street's Indians had organized, rallied, and filled up government files in London with urgent blue-and-white telegrams, rows of capital letters with undertones of panic and outrage. Atop them, undersecretaries of this and that attached coolly worded memoranda that recommended no response.

Now the once-powerful British Empire had softened into a weak thing called the Commonwealth, with virtually no sway over its independent members' actions. Instead, the Indians of South Africa placed their hope in a brand-new invention: the United Nations. To the first sessions of this new world body, born of the promise of worldwide peace and justice, they brought their case, their petitions and their erudite arguments. Eventually they would win a precedent-setting resolution requiring the government of South Africa to meet with the government of India and then report back to the council of nations about its treatment of Indian residents.

Even this victory, achieved by a long passive-resistance campaign and years of organizing, was not effective in changing conditions on the ground. South Africa's politicians insisted, as they would for the next forty-five years, that racial politics were a strictly internal matter. And internally, a major shift to the right was taking place.

In a postwar South Africa struggling to find its economic footing, Malan's platform struck a chord. Pogroms to banish Indians to India and black Africans to the margins would improve the economy for white South Africans, he vowed; the country's leadership had gotten away from what mattered to the common man. Bread was a potent symbol of the problem. Brown bread was a reminder of wartime rationing and hardship. Although the price of the "standard loaf" was steady at five shillings, the size of the loaf had been reduced. And white bread was dear: manufactured only by permit, it was both scarce and, at six shillings and two pennies, expensive.

So Malan and his party promised to bring back the luxury of white bread for all. It was a move of populist genius, a classic "chicken in every pot" electioneering tactic. Linking white bread with "a white South Africa" made the message memorable and crystal-clear.

For good measure Malan vowed to break with Britain once and for all. No longer would Afrikaners have to abide by British policies. And if the other members of the Commonwealth did not like what South Africa did with its brown and black people, well, who needed the Commonwealth?

Malan's rhetoric was not only populist but also calculated. It masked the insidious side of the National Party's politics, which included a fascist agenda of restricting press and civil liberties even for white citizens, concentrating power under a strong central government, and enforcing that power by use of a secret police. A small cohort of thinkers had been formulating this agenda for years; for inspiration they had looked to Hitler, who rode into office by popular election on a tide of economic depression. In South Africa, as elsewhere, racial politics were a ready distraction from the underlying agenda. And although black Africans would be the main targets of apartheid, it was the Indians who, in election season, made an ideal rhetorical scapegoat.

The Indians sensed that they were being set up as South Africa's Jews, and they were afraid. In panic, they tried to organize. "The dark shadow of Fascism is moving swiftly over South Africa," warned one activist,

Yusuf Dadoo, who was known to enjoy a bunny chow now and then at Ganda's place, in a pamphlet prepared for circulation at the United Nations as well as within South Africa.

But on election day in May 1948, the Indians were armed only with pamphlets and endless, carefully composed petitions and pleas and delegations. The whites were armed with the vote.

AT LAST WE HAVE GOT OUR COUNTRY BACK, blared one headline declaring victory for Malan's party.

For hard-line Afrikaners, the election was a victory of epic proportions. It was vengeance for the political battles with London they had lost in the century and a half that they had been subjects of the British Empire, vengeance for all the small compromises to sovereignty and dignity. The truce between British and Afrikaner was over. No longer would they bow, even symbolically, to the foreign king or queen. No longer would they share the illusion of equality with the black and brown savages who had somehow been allowed, for far too long, to have their way in South Africa. It would at last be a country properly run, for the benefit of its rightful rulers. The white man was about to have his day.

For all others, it was to be a long day indeed.

The morning after the election, of course, nothing had really changed. It took some time for the machinery of fascism to be built, the newspapers to be censored, the new policies to be discussed and implemented.

One campaign promise was kept quickly. On November 1, 1948, a new bread policy was introduced. White bread was liberated, so that any baker could make it without a permit; and it was subsidized, set to sell at five shillings and eight pennies. The change was a boon for bakers and millers, and made white bread widely available for the first time in six years.

It made little difference to the Indians of Grey Street, who kept serving up bunny chows in the "standard" brown loaf, still four pennies cheaper — or to their customers, working Indians and Africans for whom every penny mattered.

From the front door of G.C. Kapitan & Son Vegetarian Restaurant, the view consisted of the wide gray boulevards named for South Africa's old rulers, the imposing mosque built by Indians where five times a day the faithful were called to prayer, and, arching over them both, the great blue

African sky. Africans themselves were present in numbers that ebbed and flowed according to the jobs available in the city and the laws permitting or prohibiting freedom of travel.

To Ganda they must have appeared as they did to most of the Indian trading class—useful as customers, but otherwise alien and even frightening. One Indian wrote that black South Africans

> are the descendants of some of the slaves in America who managed to escape from their cruel bondage and migrated to Africa. They are divided into various tribes such as the Zulus, the Swazis . . .

Such startling ignorance might be humorous were its author not one of Natal's most learned Indians and civil rights activists: Gandhi. That Gandhi could make such a statement in a memoir of his twenty-one years in South Africa shows how small a role actual Africans played in the imagination of his class of Indians at the time.

In fact, the black Africans who were Ganda's customers and countrymen—the great majority of South Africans—fell into several groups, with long and complicated histories. The main groups in Durban were the Xhosa, traditionally cattle farmers but now mostly wage laborers, since the whites had taken over their grazing lands; and the Zulu, who had fought fiercely but found that in the end their spears and swords were no match for cannonballs and guns. All in all, eight wars of dispossession (the "Kaffir Wars," in British histories of the period) and dozens of minor skirmishes had been fought before southern Africa came under the rule of white men. The land was soaked with blood by the time the first indentured Indians arrived in 1860. In Ganda's time, defeated men of all these tribes and others could be seen in the streets of Durban.

But few Indians knew or cared to know their story, past or present. When Indians did think of Africans, it was to object to being lumped together with them. The Natal Indian Congress, the group founded by Gandhi and his posse of Gujarati merchants, wrote in one of its first petitions that it was "most humiliating for their dignity to be classified and as it were to be equalled with the coloureds." In 1912, the year Ganda became a restaurateur, the *Indian Opinion* published an appeal to the government by the Johannesburg Indians:

As some of our Indian children are by force of circumstances receiving their education in Coloured Schools . . . [and] as our numbers are large enough to fill a good-sized school, such as the present proposed building, we feel we are justified in asking for our children to be educated by themselves, under one roof.

By the end of the year, a Gujarati school had sprung up in Johannesburg, built by Indians and subsidized by the white government. Segregation per se was not a point of contention. Gujaratis and many other Indians, accustomed as they were to a caste system back home, objected to neither racial separation nor racial hierarchy—only to economic inequality and the indignity of being assigned to a place near the bottom, near the Africans.

So in the first half of the century, no major Indian leader sought any coalition with Africans or spoke of them as brothers and sisters in the fight against racism. When the Natal Native Congress, later to become the African National Congress, was inaugurated in 1912 with a gathering of seven hundred people in Durban to agitate for equality, most of the Indians remained distant. In 1939, answering a black South African leader's question about the wisdom of forming an "Indo-African non-white united front," Gandhi wrote publicly that it would be a mistake: "The Indians are a microscopic minority . . . You, on the other hand, are the sons of the soil who are being robbed of your inheritance. You are bound to resist that. Yours is a far bigger issue. It ought not to be mixed up with that of the Indian."

By contrast, Jawaharlal Nehru, using a situation in Ceylon in the same year to discuss the diaspora as a whole, counseled Indians abroad to forget their separate identity. They must commit to bettering their new countries, he said, and ally with the local people in their struggles.

Nehru was ahead of his time; in South Africa, Gandhi's message had the stronger pull. During Gandhi's years as a South African, there were no joint meetings, joint protests, or joint statements. This suited his people well, though years after his departure it would come back to haunt them.

For if Indians were reared in misinformation about Africans, Africans experienced a steady stream of negative information about Indians. In a mixed working class the two groups might have interacted, developed the beginnings of a camaraderie based on economic oppression. But the whites were careful to segregate their factories and mines. With the entrepreneurial class of Indians, the Gujaratis, those who wistfully thought of themselves as near-white, black Africans neither felt nor had any opportunity to feel a kinship. The Indians deserved to be treated as pariahs, to be cast out, for they were milking the country of its wealth, the propagandists accused; most of all they were exploiting the black man.

Indeed, when the black man looked up, he did not see the white man, who was if anything a distant shadow in government and superstructure. When poor and working-class black Durbanites looked around, they could see that it was Indians who employed their women at less than subsistence wages for domestic work, Indians who ran the shoddy bus lines into the city, Indians on whose land squatters erected shacks and paid for the privilege, Indians at whose stores they must shop for goods that always seemed too high in price, too low in quality.

It did not matter that these Indians were in many cases scarcely better off than their customers, nor that the deep causes of inequality lay in the pale hands of power that manipulated them both like puppet strings. *Back to India* was the whites' rallying cry and deepest hope; and it came to seem a solution to some portion of the masses of black Africans as well.

The Indians, campaigning as they did in the halls of power with declarations and petitions, with logic and outrage and appeals to human rights, neglected to wage any kind of campaign at all among their neighbors, or to build a solid coalition. And while or because Africans had no official power, they had the power all men have, which Gandhi had harnessed so effectively in a peaceful way but which, whipped up by white rhetoric, might easily turn violent. For even the desperate, without resources, have one last resort: the power latent in the human body to resist, to struggle, to rage.

All that was needed to explode this tinderbox of racial tension and economic oppression was a spark. It came at five o'clock on a Thursday evening, January 13, 1949, on Victoria Street, two blocks from G. C. Kapitan & Son Vegetarian Restaurant.

In the afternoon, something started a fight between a fourteen-year-old African boy and a sixteen-year-old Indian shop assistant in Durban's vegetable market. The African slapped the Indian, who complained to his boss—an older Indian man who retaliated by thrashing the African boy in the street.

It was rush hour, crowds surging from Grey Street and from downtown toward the bus terminal—"masses of irritable human beings," a white commission would later write. Human beings, black and brown, made more irritable by long suffering: poverty, ill treatment, injustice, despair.

And rage; surely there was rage.

"In the tussle the Native's head accidentally crashed through glass of a shop window," said the report, "and in withdrawing it the boy received cuts behind the ears, which caused the blood to flow."

For Africans passing by, it was as if the grim blur of their daily reality came into sudden, gruesome focus: here was an Indian man beating a bleeding African child.

That single tableau contained every Indian shopkeeper contemptuously calling out *kaffir* or *boy* or the generic *Jim;* every Indian housewife treating a servant worse than a slave; every Indian bus driver arrogantly refusing to give change; every Indian slumlord charging exorbitant rent for a few square feet of tin and tarp, shacks with no floors and holes in the walls. Held in that moment, as if in a freeze-frame, was the utter helplessness of the Africans' situation: kept on impoverished reserves; allowed into the cities only with passes and then only for the precise period of their workday; crowded into rickety buses and comfortless housing; robbed of any hope for protest or redress; and constantly at the mercy of oppressors—not whites, who were out of reach and in any case against whom rebellion was impossible, an act of suicide, but of these lowly intermediaries, these men and women with skins nearly as dark as theirs, raised for some inscrutable reason above black Africans, given a bevy of privileges they themselves did not have. Indians had shops, homes, jobs, sit-down meals; Africans, when they were allowed into the city at all, crouched on the sidewalk eating curry and bread with their hands.

For three days the blood flowed: African, Indian, and even a little white blood—the worst riots in Durban's history. Rioters terrorized Durban's central Indian district and the outlying areas, where poor Indians lived in shacks. Unchecked by police, they moved from looting and beating to arson, rape, killing. A white woman drove by in a car shouting, —The Government is with you, see, the police are not shooting you! White men watched from office windows and balconies, with something like glee. —Serves the coolies right, says one. —Too bad they got the wrong Indians, says another; for most of the dead were poor Indians, not shopkeepers.

Arun Gandhi, the Mahatma's grandson, was sixteen years old, born and raised in Durban; he witnessed police "rounding up the African gangs only to let them off at a quieter spot to loot, kill and pillage. Policemen and gangs of white youth also robbed the Indian shops of what they could get after the rioters had broken the windows."

On Grey Street, rioters threw brickbats into shop windows. Above, Indian families cowered in the flats, listened to the mayhem, prayed. The majestic mosque was spared. So was the small restaurant at 154 Grey Street; perhaps its DRINK COCA-COLA and JALEBI, PICKLES, CHILLI BITES signs did not tempt as strongly as the goods in nearby stores. And flames did not swallow the apartment where Ganda was living with his wife, son, two granddaughters, and his daughter-in-law, eight months pregnant. They were surviving another of South Africa's trials.

At last, the police and the military started shooting. By the time it was over, armored cars were rolling through Durban's streets. Two hundred Africans and Indians were dead, more than a thousand injured, including women and children raped. Three factories, 710 stores, and 1,532 homes were damaged or destroyed. Hundreds of families, both Indian and African, were suddenly homeless. Many would languish in makeshift refugee camps for months. The Grey Street merchants did their part for disaster relief; the Surat Hindu Association, in which Ganda was active, housed three hundred Indian refugees in its hall. And the city shut down. Among the disruptions, deliveries of newspapers and bread were suspended.

A contemporary report called the unrest the worst violence ever seen in the heart of a "civilized," Western city in peacetime. That assessment may still hold true; certainly the Durban riots had a higher death toll than the worst twentieth-century race riots in the United States: Watts, Detroit, South-Central Los Angeles. As with those uprisings, the Durban violence was so sudden and fierce that it seemed to rise out of nowhere. In fact, it had been a long time in the making.

In the dominant imagination, the riots served to confirm a vision of Africans as volatile, savage, animal. Above all, they were proof of the new government's thesis: that the races needed to be separated.

The logic of apartheid is difficult to follow, for it seems from our vantage point a strange kind of illogic. Liberal multiculturalism takes for granted that the route to racial harmony is mutual understanding, and the route to understanding is contact, exposure, conversation. So our modern studies show that those who know actual black people, or gay people, or whatever minority is being studied, are more likely to hold positive impressions of that minority group as a whole. To turn a stereotype into a human being requires, we now believe, some form of human connection.

This is a relatively new idea, perhaps only a generation or two old. In the Age of Imperialism, when the definition of *human* was "man" and the definition of *man* was "white," none of this was obvious. Various theories and catechisms explained the presence of "lesser" races; they were the white man's burden, for example, his to educate and convert, much as he was to tame the beasts of the wild and use them for his own needs; or they were descended from Cain, the killer, in a kind of doubling of original sin. Perhaps segregation began with the essential prejudice of colonialism. The invading powers took their desire to avoid the primitive, unclean, heathen, and made of it a theory, or several. There was *safety and sanitation* in the fortified white ghettos that the British built at the core of their colonial capitals; there was *separate but equal* in the American South. Behind it all was a powerfully primitive perception of race, ethnicity, or tribe as a human being's defining characteristic. Hindus and Muslims would be better off if each group had its own state; Native American tribes could be divided and ruled. It was a simple premise: that the races would get along better if completely separate. But this is to ascribe to it a kind of innocence—for "the races" did not begin on equal terms, nor did they have an equal capacity to assert their desires. In South Africa, as perhaps elsewhere, "get along better" was code for "serve white interests better." And "separate" was a euphemism for cruelly, desperately unequal.

To be fair, though, the idea of absolute equality was just as unimaginable to many Indians. Certainly my ancestors, who came with their caste pride, grafted it onto the social hierarchies of their adopted lands.

"Kaffirs" and "coloureds," *goriyaas* (whites) and *kariyaas* (blacks), *chinaas* and *jewtkaas* were all slotted into a mindset already accustomed to order. Perhaps the fact that Khatris considered themselves second from the top back home, below the priestly caste and above the merchants and laborers, made them comfortable being so in South Africa—below the whites, above the blacks. They might even have seen it as an extension of the caste ideology, millennia-old, that one's place in the hierarchy is based on karma accrued in previous lives. Regardless of actual occupation, caste status offered a sense of secure identity in relation to others, which coincided comfortably with South Africa's racial system. As long as our people were comfortably near the status to which they felt their karma entitled them, left unmolested in business and not consigned to the bottom of the pecking order, they did not protest too much.

Apartheid respected that status to a certain extent; it gave the Indians and "coloureds," as mixed-race people were known, a higher status than it accorded to the native Africans. Taking inspiration from Hitler's comprehensive racial registration system, the government in 1950 passed the Population Registration Act. In South Africa no such obscenity as yellow stars was necessary; most people wore their designations on their skin. But in cases where skin was insufficient, the registration system provided backup, measuring ethnicity by parental and grandparental blood and, in some cases, by the kink of the hair.

If South Africa's Indians had experienced life before apartheid as a patchwork of restrictions to be dodged and negotiated, afterward this would come to seem a blessing. The patchwork became a straitjacket. Racial registration was the basis for comprehensive legislation that viewed everything—residence, work, voting, property ownership, taxes—through a racial lens. The strictest laws from each region were adopted and nationalized. And where the law was open to interpretation, the most restrictive interpretations were taken. Loopholes closed and covert justifications such as sanitation fell by the wayside. Now the reasons were overtly what they always had been covertly: the desire to make South Africa a white man's country, and the belief that whites were superior, so that nonwhites should be accommodated only insofar as they met white needs.

Like other nonwhites in South Africa, the people of Grey Street chafed against apartheid's restrictions. The new tactics of repression demanded a new response. Suddenly the war was being fought on all fronts: internationally, at the United Nations and in the world press; nationally and provincially, at the ballot box and in the courts; and in the streets, where organizers traveled among the people, rallying and bringing what relief they could to South Africa's vast disenfranchised masses. As the regime cracked down on dissent as well, some of these strategies began to seem dangerous. Certain natural gathering places became known as safe meeting grounds.

In the back room of G.C. Kapitan & Son Vegetarian Restaurant, from time to time a clandestine political meeting took place. To an outsider, it looked like a group of "coolie" traders slurping curry in a "coolie" eatery. Only a select few knew their real business: perhaps discussing the latest disappearances and arrests, perhaps formulating a strategy for joint action with other nonwhite communities.

Among the Indians, these men and others continued to organize themselves racially. But alongside and even within the old Gandhian institutions, a new vision was coming into focus. Gandhi had pushed the Indians to have pride in themselves as *subjects* of the empire, entitled to equal rights on that basis. Apartheid radicalized a generation of activists who began to conceive of themselves as, at last, *citizens*.

Some were outspoken, such as Monty Naicker and Yusuf Dadoo, leaders of the Natal Indian Congress. Dadoo was the author of such seditious pamphlets as "Facts About the Ghetto Act" (1946) and "South Africa —On the Road to Fascism" (1948), and an organizer of massive Indian protests against apartheid. He, Naicker, and other activists could be seen at G.C. Kapitan's from time to time, though never in large enough numbers to draw too much attention.

Unlike their predecessors, these activists did not see themselves as Indians who merely lived in South Africa. Instead, they were South Africans who happened to be Indian: sons of the soil, as much as any other. The distinction between noun and adjective was crucial. They initiated coalitions with black Africans—casting their lot at last, as Nehru had recommended, with the natives of their land. Solidarity was perhaps the Indians' best hope for escaping the pitfalls of pariah capitalism.

In Durban, I stayed with Ganda's grandson's family in the old Grey Street apartment with its sunny courtyard, balcony, and close-up view of the mosque. One day I ventured to the city's local-history museum. In the United States such museums are filled with busts of the city's founding fathers, early baby carriages and wagon wheels, fragments of newspaper. But here, the local history is apartheid. If I was lucky, I thought, I might discover some useful facts about Durban that would put my great-great-uncle's story in a larger context.

The museum is housed in an elegant old building that was once the city's Native Affairs Department. Here, black and brown South Africans stood in endless queues to appeal to white bureaucrats for passes, permits, all the bits of paper that upheld the apartheid regime. Wandering through the rooms, I ended up in what had been the segregated post office, next to the old ricksha licensing department. Several displays detailed the rise of the city's segregated neighborhoods. In a back corner I began reading about Durban's "Little India," the Grey Street area. Photographs showed Indian cinema halls, markets, and evidence that this ethnic clustering was not consensual: three white men in suits, squinting against the sun, were identified by a caption as the "three-man committee of the Group Areas Board," charged with implementing complete segregation of the city in 1969.

As I scanned the photos, I saw a face I recognized: my host, standing in front of the restaurant his grandfather had started. Others showed Ganda himself; there he was in the restaurant in 1947, celebrating India's independence. A glass case nearby displayed receipts and stationery from his restaurant, and a plaque on the wall gave a brief history of Ganda's professional life.

He had opened the restaurant in 1912, and counted among his customers "working class people as well as prominent figures . . . Indira Gandhi, Yusuf Dadoo and Monty Naicker, Ahmed Deldat and footballer, Bruce Grobelaar." The eatery was notable for its strict vegetarianism and was known as "a place where one could get a good meal at a reasonable price." The plaque credited Ganda with inventing the "beans bunny."

At home, over a meal and a pile of old photographs, I asked my cousins about their grandfather's life. The eldest daughter insisted again and again, "Grandfather was a real rags-to-riches story, you must say it: *rags to riches.*" Crowding around with their memories, they told me what they knew, recalling a routine that seems almost mythic:

At 2 A.M. Ganda rose to start the wood fires.

At 4 A.M. the staff arrived, quietly making their way upstairs to change into uniforms and aprons before going downstairs where the stoves and ovens were hot and ready for work.

At 5 A.M. Ganda presided over prayer hour, when the family and staff greeted the day by gathering around a sacred fire to chant ancient Hindu hymns, including the auspicious *gayatri* mantra: "O Giver of Life, Remover of pain and sorrow, Bestower of happiness, O Creator of the Universe: May we receive Thy supreme sin-destroying light, may Thou guide our intellect in the right direction." Together they offered food and flowers to the gods, along with an appeal for blessings to begin the day.

At 6 A.M. Ganda opened the shop, and let the staff take over as he went to bathe and have his own morning tea. Soon the workday began in earnest, the shop filling with tea drinkers and then emptying again just in time for the lunch crowd. After lunch he took off his apron and lay down for a nap, then at 3 P.M. called it a day in order to do what he termed his community work. By the 1960s he served in leadership roles in several community institutions: the social Gujarati Mandal, the religious Divine Life Society of South Africa, and the Surat Hindu Association, of which he was vice chairman for ten years. Many of the Khatris belonged to this latter organization; they were social and civic-minded, and raised money for the occasional disaster in India. They did not engage in politics, and they had nothing to do with Africans. Their main activities were holiday feasts and a year-round Gujarati school, where the community's children gathered in the late afternoons and weekends to study the mother tongue and the religion of their ancestors.

At 6 P.M. came evening prayer, then dinner; unlike other shopkeepers, who sometimes ate in family shifts (men first, women later), Ganda had a policy that the family must sit together at dinnertime. Each meal was preceded by the gayatri mantra again, chanted three times.

At 7 P.M. the shop closed, and he made his after-dinner rounds, traveling to West Street to place orders for the next day or two, perhaps buying a toy now and then for his grandchildren. Then he went to bed, only to start again in a few hours.

On another day, Ganda's grandchildren took me to visit a Kapitan cousin who, they said, had been active in the anti-apartheid movement. I was eager to meet him, since most of the Khatri community members I had encountered were decidedly ambivalent about the onset of black majority rule, as Ganda would have been.

The cousin greeted us from behind the counter of a small video-rental store that he was running with his wife, in what was once a working-class Indian neighborhood but was becoming, post-segregation, racially mixed. One of his eyes was slightly off-center, out of sync with the other, as if he were seeing something else entirely. And indeed, his perspective was different from that of other Gujaratis, many of whom continue to view black Africans as a savage threat.

"I have seen our own people shoot a man for stealing a loaf of bread —I have seen it," he told me, grief written in the lines of his face. From a long habit of secrecy, he declined to be referred to by name; let us call him, then, Raman.

As a child in the 1950s, Raman kicked a soccer ball around with a racially mixed group of teenagers in his neighborhood, which was not yet strictly segregated. In the volatile protest years that followed, many young people were radicalized; some of the older boys joined up with the activist African National Congress and brought him along to meetings. As a teenager he too enlisted, and by his twenties he was traveling regularly into the townships, the immense, semi-urban ghettos to which most Africans were confined, to organize and bring relief.

As Ganda was serving up bunny chows and endless cups of tea to the Indian community and its leaders, Raman and other activists were walking the muddy alleys of the townships, their feet learning the textures of the bitter red soil. As Ganda raised funds for and organized functions at the Gujarati school, Raman and his comrades were organizing student walkouts and protests and dreaming of a new South Africa.

By the late 1970s, the ANC was a banned organization, with most of its leaders in prison or in exile; it began to organize a military wing decamped just outside South Africa's borders. In this environment, everyone was a potential government spy or collaborator. Raman married, kept up appearances, and hid his activities even from his wife. Many of his comrades were arrested; some were killed. It was simply safer for her not to know. Maintaining a low profile, he managed both to resist and to survive.

· · ·

Survival and resistance, in those years, meant something different to everyone. Ganda's grandchildren see his entire bearing, his posture and immaculate attire, as resistance: a statement that whatever laws were passed, he carried his dignity with him. He wore pressed shirts, carefully creased pants, suspenders, and, often, a topcoat and smart black Nehru cap. He was rotund but never sloppy, his mustache neatly combed, his shoes shined. And amidst the uncertainty of his times, he cooked.

One grandson recalls the bakery delivering a thousand loaves of bread on peak days. During festivals marking the Hindu and Muslim holy days, business was so brisk that the family and staff did not have time to sort coins into the cash register but instead stuffed them into large garbage sacks and weighed them, to estimate the take. Hundreds or thousands of sweets, samosas, and of course bunny chows left the kitchen each week. Everyone in the family worked in shifts, girls and boys alike. The upstairs flat, with its open courtyard, became an annex to the restaurant: Amba and her daughter-in-law and granddaughters chopped onions and tomatoes, washed buckets of beans, shaped thousands of sweets with hands that knew the exact weight and size of a *laddoo* or a *pendo*.

With the consolidation of the apartheid government's power, from the 1950s onward, Indian and African neighborhoods were bulldozed, raided, terrorized; thousands and then hundreds of thousands were forced to move to new "locations," residential areas without running water, plumbing, sewage, or electricity. Thousands more were denied licenses to trade, even where they had been running businesses for generations. Grey Street was "frozen," with no new property acquisition or building allowed after 1957. Then in 1971 it was designated a strictly residential area, and all existing businesses were threatened with removal.

Ganda must have been glad he was only a tenant, that he had never taken the step of owning property; his potential losses were limited. Protests were filed. Nothing changed. In the end perhaps two things saved Ganda and his neighbors from displacement. First, Grey Street was already segregated as an Indian area, thanks to the white merchants of Natal early in the century. Second, to stop Indians from coming to Grey Street, the mosque would have had to be demolished, an act that surely would have caused an international outcry. It dominated the skyline, solid, a mass that even a white infidel could not raze. Perhaps some things were sacred after all.

As we drove through Durban one day, one of Ganda's grandsons pointed out the market areas: the African herb market, and the Indian "squatters" market where fruits and vegetables were sold by farmers from the countryside (who squatted next to their goods). The stalls were lined up on a steep concrete ramp that seemed to arc into nowhere.

It was not an architectural illusion. The markets had once been at ground level, but the apartheid government wanted to keep Africans and Indians out of the city center. The stalls were evacuated, then demolished; the demolition was to make way for a highway, the government said. But only the ramp was built, climbing from nowhere to nowhere. And there it remained, evidence of race hate in massive concrete, a scar on the landscape; a memory.

Perhaps it was during this time, through the years of struggle, that Ganda began to feel like a South African: to think, to act, to breathe as a South African.

Motiram's roots in Fiji were scarcely a decade old when he died; Maaji, surely, felt Indian to the end. But Ganda lived sixty-seven of his seventy-eight years in Durban. Perhaps there was no precise moment, only a feeling that grew over time—when he first held the papers bearing his new name, when he hung this new name over the storefront, when he created his own version of the bunny chow, when he watched his grandchildren begin to toddle. Despite the white perceptions, despite even the habits of his own people, surely he was not a foreigner all that time. His hometown ties were strong, and when he made enough money, he donated some of it for a clinic in the village in India, then a school in his wife's name. But India became a foreign land, and he a visitor and tourist when he went there, always returning home to the segregated airports of South Africa, with their WHITES ONLY and NON WHITES ONLY signs.

In 1972, at age seventy-eight, surrounded by his family in the apartment on Grey Street, Ganda died peacefully, of simple old age. His obituary was published in both of the city's white-run newspapers. In the *Natal*

Mercury, it appeared on page 7 along with other ethno-specific items: an Indian wedding announcement, ads for Indian-only apartments, a Dale Carnegie course for Indians, an update on the squatters' market controversy that was then raging, and the doublespeak news that "Indian areas to the north of the city will be transformed into beautiful residential suburbs through town planning."

His son, and then his son's children, would keep the restaurant open for twenty more years, serving up hundreds of thousands of beans bunnies. And the bunny chow itself would outlive apartheid, migrating to restaurants all over South Africa and then—as South African Indians migrated overseas—to Canada, England, and the World Wide Web.

Was the bunny chow a subversive response to repression? Or was it accommodation, compliance, opportunism? A cynic would say its Indian inventors were merely ensuring their profits; a loyalist might argue they did the best they could under trying circumstances, and that they too were just struggling to survive. And perhaps a poet would find it a potent metaphor for how the first generation of our diaspora views itself: essentially Indian at the core, packaged in and adapted to the local mores only as much as is conducive to economic survival. Without quite knowing it, however, this melding of tastes and textures becomes our lives—neither wholly "authentic" from the Indian perspective, nor fully assimilated from the vantage point of a white-bread culture, but a new creation in itself.

Long after Ganda's death, and a couple of years after the restaurant closed its doors—victim to a change of lease—the long, harsh day of apartheid came to a close. Overnight the revolutionaries became officials in charge of, among other things, writing a new history. And someone called cousin Raman.

A local-history museum was being erected, telling the stories of all the peoples of Durban. Would Raman contribute his family's items for the section on Grey Street? Your family was important, and you were on our side, he was told; and so he gathered photographs and memorabilia. Among his prized possessions was a letter from Nelson Mandela to the family member who owned a restaurant in Johannesburg, thanking him for providing a safe place for anti-apartheid leaders to meet. One of

Ganda's grandsons, a photography hobbyist, contributed several images. Raman's father, grandfather, and several of his uncles were restaurateurs; he turned their papers over to the museum, which made them part of the permanent display. And so the businessmen of the Kapitan family were given a tiny piece of immortality.

Ganda's restaurant stood in a row of Indian businesses, any of which might have been chosen to represent the story of Grey Street. But history is never neutral, nor perhaps should it be. All histories are intimate, constructed by those with an interest in the stories they choose to tell— shaped, like bread, by the human hand.

At the southernmost tip of Africa, a lighthouse rises from the shoals where two oceans meet. I have clambered among the rocks and sand, waded into the waves. One sea is browner, the other bluer, and it is not a trick of the light.

To the west, the cool Atlantic swells up toward London, New York, and South Africa's most picturesque city, Cape Town. To the east, the Indian Ocean is several degrees warmer; it gives the coast of Africa from Durban to Mombasa a tropical climate profitable for sugar and tourism, almost homelike for the more than a million Indians who have lived there for generations. This confluence of oceans is a rare coincidence of political and natural geography, where the act of naming does not create an arbitrary border, but gives voice to a natural one.

And yet it is the most fluid, the most porous of borders. East and west meet with a great force, a terrible frothing and crashing of waves. The whitecaps swirl, and as much as one tries to follow a dark wave, it curls under a paler one from the other side; as far as I can track a blue wave, it does not, of course, hold. Like the several great civilizations that have clashed and coexisted in southern Africa over the last two centuries, the waters cannot be segregated.

And who can tell which wave is resisting, which collaborating? The sea reveals no moral; what moves the whole is a greater tide. Perhaps the currents of history are what they are, and we only choose—or think we choose—which side to view them from, and where to take a stand.

part two: subjects

1945

Estimated size of the Indian diaspora: 1,157,728
Countries with more than 10,000 people of Indian origin: 10

1. Mauritius
2. South Africa
3. Trinidad and Tobago
4. British Guiana
5. Fiji
6. Kenya
7. Tanganyika
8. Uganda
9. Jamaica
10. Zanzibar

4. salt

Instead of a common riot confined to one class of persons it was
of the nature of a wide spread insurrection.
—Account of the salt-tax riots of 1844, Surat, India

Chhagan and Jamnaa
Village of Gandevi, India

↓

Dullabh
Maanek
NAROTAM and Benkor
Mani
Kalyaan

*M*Y MOTHER'S FAMILY is considered "small," meaning that it has had a scarcity of sons. Unlike my father's family tree, which branches again and again — seven sons, five sons — my mother's family tree is a straighter line: only a few boys per generation. From this slim history, her father, Narotam, emerged.

The only grandparent I remember was my Aaji, his widow. We met for the first time when I was seven, shy and reeling from the shock of migration. My family had just moved from New Zealand, the only home I remembered, back to the United States. After stops in Fiji to visit too many relatives (my only memory is of a fish bone getting painfully stuck in my foot) and in California, we landed in Iowa to visit my mother's brother and his family. He had brought Aaji to live with him a few years earlier. When I was enjoined to hug her, I obeyed — and promptly broke into tears, at the strangeness of it all.

From then on we saw her once or twice a year in Iowa. I learned to embrace her without sobbing, leaning into the softness of her sari and comfortable rolls of fat. But the combination of infrequent visits, strange old-lady smells, and the fact that she could never seem to pronounce my name correctly kept us strangers. I was distracted too, I suppose, by her odd habits. She sniffed something from a small tin that she kept hidden in her bosom, and when I asked my mother what it was, she said *tamkhil* — tobacco. I had never heard of snuff before, and filed this away in my mental folder of things old Indian ladies do. She was quiet, never saying much except to moan *Raam, Raam*, invoking the name of the Hindu god-king whenever she had to stand up or sit down, arthritic knees creaking. She drank, before dinner and sometimes before lunch, a shot of whiskey mixed with water, chased by a Guinness. My parents being teetotalers, I found this alarming as well. It never occurred to me to ask her about history—not even about my grandfather, my Aajaa.

Aajaa. The word feels strange in my mouth, for I never had occasion to use it, missing him by six years and two continents. Growing up in New Zealand and then Michigan, away from other relatives, I knew little about Narotam Chhagan: that he died when my mother was still in school; that his death and the collapse of the family business left my mother and grandmother very poor; that he had met the prince of Tonga; and that he and his friends drank so much that my mother fled the house on weekends, seeking a few hours' respite at double-feature matinees, which is why even today she hates alcohol and adores Burt Reynolds.

When I was eleven years old, it was a movie that showed me another side of my Aajaa's life: Richard Attenborough's *Gandhi.* Today, I can critique the film for its historical distortions and Hollywood lens. But back in 1982, in suburban Michigan, it was a precious opportunity to see India and Indians on the big screen.

First, however, we had to find a screen. In the conservative, middle-class suburb of Detroit where we lived, *Gandhi* was not a big release. The town's sole movie house, the Penn Theater, was an old-fashioned hall with red plush seats that showed such classics as *Casablanca* and *Gone with the Wind.* My family never went there, opting instead for James Bond flicks and *E.T.* at the sixplex in a nearby suburb's mall. I did not see the Hollywood classics until years later, in a university class on the history of film. By then, in the 1990s, the Penn Theater had changed; an enterprising Indo-American was renting the theater on Saturday mornings, showing Bombay musicals to packed houses, selling samosas and chai along with popcorn at the concession stand.

But during my childhood, the Indian community in Michigan was still tiny, so we had to drive half an hour to the progressive university town of Ann Arbor to see *Gandhi.* It was screened in one of the university's auditoriums. We sat near the front, next to the center aisle, craning our necks throughout the three-hour epic.

Halfway through, a pivotal scene occurs. Gandhi's followers have marched to the sea to protest a tax on salt. As they approach the saltworks, a row of police armed with *lathis*—five-foot clubs tipped with steel—stand ready to stop them. Gandhi's men, though, keep walking. When they are just a few inches away, the police officers strike: heads crack, faces split, ribs are smashed.

But more men take their place, row after row advancing—peacefully, calmly, with determination but not violence. And as the police keep beating them down, the camera dissolves to "Walker," an American reporter played by Martin Sheen. He is at the phone, calling in his story. From the script:

> "They walked, with heads up, without music, or cheering,
> or any hope of escape from injury or death." (His voice is taut,
> harshly professional.) "It went on and on and on. Women
> carried the wounded bodies from the ditch until they dropped
> from exhaustion. But still it went on . . .
> "Whatever moral ascendance the West held was lost today.
> India is free, for she has taken all that steel and cruelty can
> give, and she has neither cringed nor retreated."
> (On Walker close. His sweating, blood- and dirt-stained
> face near tears.) "In the words of his followers, 'Long live
> Mahatma Gandhi.'"

Then the word INTERMISSION filled the screen, and the lights went on in the Ann Arbor auditorium, and my mother turned to me in the light and said with some surprise, "You're crying."

After a moment she added, quietly, "You know, my dad was in that march."

According to his first passport, now yellowed and crumbling, Narotam was born in the village of Gandevi, Surat District, in 1908. A later passport gives a birth date, December 12, which he must have invented for a government bureaucrat. In a village where the passing of time is measured by religious festivals and natural or personal disasters, where birthday celebrations are reserved for the incarnations of the gods on earth, no one would have memorialized the exact moment of arrival of the second son of a family so humble they were known as the Chaliawalas, people of the sparrow.

Against the blur of history, one episode of my grandfather's life stands out in sharp relief. Luckily, a photograph was taken at precisely this moment. He stands young, intense, dressed like a saint all in white. The way the silver has faded over seven decades creates a halo around his body, a pale, pure cocoon of light. It is July 1930, and he has emerged from three months of hard labor in prison, for joining Gandhi's nonviolent revolution.

In front of a backdrop painted to look like a courtyard, my grandfather's robes beam purity and defiance: *khaadi* cotton, not from Great Britain's mills but made in India, in the villages, on the spinning wheels of revolution. It might have been my grandmother who wove the spun thread into three yards of cloth for him on a rickety hand loom.

Gandhi predicted the simple wooden spinning wheel would overturn the British Raj. *Chakra:* the word is the same as for the mythical wheels of fire deployed by the Hindu gods in battle. And in what became the world's greatest nonviolent war, the domestic version proved a powerful weapon, sending the flames of revolution into every household, every hut.

For India's poor, spinning made not only political but also economic sense, freeing them from the expense of foreign cloth and offering a dignified means of making a living. For the wealthy, the rough, homespun saris and dhotis became a symbol of what today we might call, with the cynicism of our age, political correctness.

But for Gandhi's true believers, there was no cynicism. Many were not political or urban elites but villagers from humble families and of even humbler means. In that era of great hope and great uncertainty, some dreamed of new possibilities, others cowered in fear, and a handful put their bodies on the line. Their general was a slim, soft-spoken man in a loincloth, and one of his foot soldiers was my Aajaa.

For at least four thousand years, Hindus of the "upper" castes have divided human life into four stages: student, householder, retiree, renunciate. In trying to write about my Aajaa's life, I am reminded again of how little I know about most of my ancestors; how little anybody knows. They were peasants, after all, the details of their lives sketchy from the very beginning. But Narotam would have known about these phases, and hoped his life would follow the ideal pattern of millennia.

He could not have had much of a carefree childhood, coming from a family where he, his parents, and his siblings—two brothers and two sisters—had to work hard and constantly. School was a luxury in which they could not indulge. Child marriage was routine, a way to guarantee a young person's future and strengthen the web of relationships between families. Narotam's parents matched him with a girl of the same caste, Benkor, who lived just blocks away in the same village and whose father had died. They were perhaps ten years old when they circled the marriage fire.

After the wedding, Benkor went back home, as was the custom; tradition held that the girl could not go to her in-laws until she reached puberty and her in-laws paid a bride price. But years passed, and Narotam's family had no money, not even for the customary pair of thick silver anklets. Benkor waited.

The village of Gandevi had been, in earlier centuries, a prominent weaving center. But by the time Narotam was a young man, the town was emptying out. The decline of Gandevi's weaving class was of such concern that the kingdom's census bureau conducted a special report in 1931. A typical weaver, the report said, "ekes out a miserable existence," making barely eight rupees a month because of competition from machine-made cloth. One finished sari—a labor of three to five days—was worth only a rupee or two. My mother and her siblings remember their parents' tales of hard times, when the family lived from payment to payment—buying food only when a sari was finished, nearly running out by the time the next one came off the loom and was rushed to the middleman. Despite government efforts at forming cooperatives and encouraging new designs, the census report said, the village's weavers had "an air of being completely beaten."

Eighty-eight Khatri families, and about a hundred of various other castes, were still weaving in Gandevi, the report said, making for "466 workers" supporting themselves and "434 dependents." But most families were bowing to reality. Economic conditions had "forced many a weaver out of his occupation and even out of the country . . . They took to other avocations like tailoring or migrated to foreign countries like Africa and the Fiji Islands." Twenty years earlier, when the census began measuring emigration, about 2,500 people from the region had gone overseas; by 1931, the figure had more than doubled, to 6,687. Africa was the primary destination; a group of two hundred Muslims left for Spain; and nearly two hundred people went to Fiji.

Narotam's family, initially, took the less expensive step of sending its sons to Bombay, as thousands of poorer families were doing. By the time Narotam was nineteen, he was working as a street tailor in the great metropolis of British India. He spent his days sitting at a manual sewing machine in a twelve-by-five-foot room that doubled as his bedroom at night. It faced the street, and he sewed blouses and trousers to order.

While jobs in the villages were scarce and poorly paid, work in the city was abundant. Thousands of peasants like Narotam joined the great migration to the new metropolises, swelling Bombay's population to one million, making it one of the largest cities in the world. The new laborers and traders came from all over northern and western India, crowding into tenements and shacks, speaking English if they could but otherwise mainly Hindi, Marathi, and Gujarati.

A hundred sixty miles from home, Narotam lived with an older cousin and other working-class Gujaratis, with whom he could share language and food. Their talk would have centered around money and, increasingly in those days, politics.

India's political news after World War I was driven largely by Gandhi, whom the poet Rabindranath Tagore had christened "Mahatma," the Great One. Since leaving South Africa, Gandhi had become, through his various campaigns for *swaraj,* or self-rule—independence from Britain—a household name in India. Gujaratis took inordinate pride in seeing one of their own emerge as the nation's political and spiritual leader.

In 1929, when Narotam was a twenty-year-old street tailor, Gandhi was a sixty-year-old activist who was facing a delicate choice. Some of his fellow leaders in the Indian National Congress were urging a war for independence. Gandhi, too, wanted swaraj, but only by nonviolent means. He believed that India could gain freedom by appealing to the noblest part of the British soul—if and only if Indians held firm to the moral high ground.

In January 1930, Gandhi wrote that he was "furiously thinking" night and day. The country was ripe for a mass movement, he believed, and he was seeking an issue that could unify all Indians. It would have to be something that affected all, without regard to privilege or region or religion; it would assert a right that was so obvious and natural as to be incontestable; and it would provide a way for every Indian to break the law with little effort.

He settled on salt.

"History has no instance of a tax as cruel as the salt tax," Gandhi declared; through it, "the State can reach even the starving millions, the sick, the maimed and the utterly helpless." The issue was not only taxation, though the tax was heavy, working out by his account to 2,400 percent over the sale price. Indians were also forbidden to harvest or sell it on their own, those privileges being reserved for the government monopoly that produced it in India or imported it from Britain. A massive infrastructure of tax and customs officials enforced the law, which was one of the oldest sources of revenue; at one point in the mid-1800s, an immense barrier consisting mostly of a thorny hedge ran down the center of the country for 1,500 miles, patrolled by twelve thousand officers whose job was to prevent illicit salt from traveling between parts of India. In a nation surrounded on three sides by sea, restricting salt was not only difficult but seemed, to Gandhi, ludicrous. In an open letter to the viceroy, Gandhi wrote, "The illegality is in a Government that steals the people's salt and makes them pay heavily for the stolen article."

He closed by politely informing the viceroy that unless the tax was repealed, civil disobedience would begin March 11, 1930. Gandhi and a group of followers would walk west from their ashram to the Arabian Sea, where they would "steal" salt from the British-owned saltworks and from the ocean itself. The route of 241 miles would take twenty-four days, passing through the rural districts of Gujarat—just a few miles from Narotam's hometown.

In the traditional Hindu view of life, adolescence is not about raging hormones, wild haircuts, or bad attitudes. It is a serious time, built on celibacy and spiritual learning. Out of childhood, a young man becomes a *brahmachaarin:* literally, student of the soul, of god, and of ultimate reality.

Narotam had spent his teenage years not in such study but in work, saving what he could to send back to his parents in the village. His father had finally taken out a loan for Benkor's dowry and brought her home, at the shockingly old age of twenty. Narotam went back to Gandevi to settle down. The villages, like Bombay, were astir with news of the salt march, in local dailies and in Gandhi's own Gujarati weekly, *Navajivan,* or "new life."

Thousands of villagers gathered along the route to see the Mahatma and support the movement. Walking ten to twelve miles a day, Gandhi gave rousing speeches and recruited volunteers. He urged village headmen to resign their posts and cease cooperating with the British government. He promoted other elements of his agenda: spin khaadi and boycott foreign cloth; include "untouchables" in all aspects of society; close down the liquor stores. He told Gujaratis to seize the moment to lead their nation into freedom. He asked the warrior caste to take up its age-old profession, this time on the battlefield of nonviolent struggle. And he told young men like Narotam to spend their brahmachaarin period in the movement, rather than in the schools and industries run by the British. They were to examine their souls as they fought for the soul of their country.

"What student is he who will continue to study at such a time?" Gandhi asked a crowd on March 17, two weeks before the march passed by Narotam's hometown. "Today I ask them to leave schools and come out on the battlefield and become mendicants for the sake of the country . . . The final battle has to be waged."

On April 3, the marchers spent the night in Navsari—just twelve miles north of Narotam's village. Nine thousand gathered to hear Gandhi speak, according to the police; fifty thousand, said the pro-independence newspaper. Navsari's population was less than twenty-five thousand, but people came from all the villages around. The speech was given in the dry reservoir bed, the Milky Lake, the only open place in town large enough for such a crowd.

And perhaps it was here, a day's walk from the coast, that Narotam joined the movement. In a family of weavers descended from warriors, what did it take for one young man to leave the tiny hamlet of Gandevi, where even today cow-dung dust rises from the unpaved streets, and begin walking toward the sea? He left behind a disapproving father, a worried mother and wife, and an infant daughter they had named Sarasvati, after the goddess of wisdom and learning.

. . .

The marchers were prepared to be arrested, beaten, even killed; as a grim reminder, their pilgrimage was timed to coincide with the anniversary of the Jallianwala massacre in Calcutta. There, a British general had ordered his soldiers to fire on a stadium full of unarmed men, women, and children, killing hundreds. The debacle made the general a sort of populist hero in the British press, and he was never convicted of any crime.

Now, Gandhi expected to be arrested at any moment. To ensure that the volunteers would remain nonviolent even in his absence, and as part of their spiritual training, he insisted on strict discipline throughout the march. The rules were many. They would start walking at 6:30 A.M., break at 8 A.M. for prayer and a meal, walk several miles before dinner, then walk again until nightfall. They would sleep outdoors. They would not drink alcohol. They would wear homespun khaadi at all times—an order that resulted in shortages, to which enterprising factory owners responded with counterfeit, machine-made versions of the rough cloth.

They would eat food supplied by local people, which was to be "the simplest possible," Gandhi wrote in his instructions to the villages along the route. "Sweets, even if prepared, will be declined. Vegetables should be merely boiled, and no oil, spices, and chillies, whether green or dry, whole or crushed, should be added or used in the cooking . . . The people should incur no expense on account of betel leaves, betel-nuts or tea for the party."

As they neared Dandi, conditions became even more ascetic. The size of the march was growing, and supplies were scarce. Gandhi gathered the volunteers for prayer at 4 A.M. on April 3 and told them, "We shall have to use water as if it was milk." Food, too, was to be rationed, with each meal consisting of a small amount of puffed rice, gram flour, and boiled water with a spoonful of butter and sugar. He added, "Another piece of information I have received is that the Government intends to use fire-engines to stop us. We have prepared ourselves for death from cannons and guns, compared to which this is nothing . . . You must bear in mind that not one of us will retreat. I do not think the Government will be so cruel, but we must be prepared."

All the while, volunteers were expected to follow the nineteen-point code of nonviolent behavior: "1. A Satyagrahi, i.e., a civil resister will harbour no anger. 2. He will suffer the anger of the opponent. 3. In so doing he will put up with assaults from the opponent, never retaliate . . ."

. . .

Upon arriving at the coast on April 5, Gandhi walked along the beach. "Dandi itself has a tragic history," he wrote. "As I walk about the otherwise beautiful peace-giving shore and listen for the heavenly music of the gentle waves, I see about me wasted human effort in the shape of dilapidated embanked fields without a patch of vegetation. These very fields, immediately the hateful salt monopoly is gone, will be valuable salt pans from which villagers will extract fresh, white sparkling salt without much labour, and it will give them a living as it did their ancestors."

The Arabian Sea lapping up against Dandi's shore is so saline that the satyagrahis of 1930, in order to make salt, had only to pick up the natural deposits that lay drying in tide pools. On the morning of April 6, Gandhi bent over, seized a fistful of muddy salt from the ground, and declared the beginning of "the war against salt tax." All over India, people began gathering and making illegal salt.

The government's response was muted at first, so Gandhi set his sights on a bigger target: the Dharasana Salt Works, with its piles of salt shining behind barbed wire. The press had begun calling him "the salt robber," but he told his followers, "Real robbery will consist only in plundering yonder heaps of salt."

And then he was arrested.

With that, the nation was aflame. At mass demonstrations all over India, people lit bonfires of foreign-made cloth. Students walked out of classrooms, whole villages refused to pay taxes, women picketed liquor stores, and officials quit their government posts. In Bombay and Karachi, tens of thousands of people rallied around symbolic pans of drying saltwater. And a steady stream of patriots was rushing toward the sea.

Gandhi's arrest did not stop the marchers from moving ahead to Dharasana. New leaders stepped up and led the raid on the saltworks.

Narotam was one of the first to jump the barricades.

UPI reporter Webb Miller, witnessing one of the confrontations, filed the real version of the news report that had brought me, as an eleven-year-old watching the Hollywood version, to tears:

> Suddenly, at a word of command, scores of native police
> rushed upon the advancing marchers and rained blows on

their heads with their steel-shod lathis [heavy wooden sticks with iron bands on them]. Not one of the marchers even raised an arm to fend off the blows. They went down like ten-pins. From where I stood I heard the sickening whacks of the clubs on unprotected skulls . . . There was no fight, no strug-gle; the marchers simply walked forward until struck down.

Those not hospitalized went to jail. The salt march—with its strict daily routine of predawn prayer, measured walking, and spiritual speeches by Gandhi—may have been Narotam's first exposure to the con-centrated religious study befitting a brahmachaarin. Jail was the next.

For Gandhi, who had spent nearly two years in prison on sedition charges from 1922 to 1924, a cell was a place for meditation. Kept in iso-lation in a prison named Yeravda, he was writing dozens of letters date-lined "Yeravda Palace," "Yeravda Pleasure House," and, most often, "Yer-avda Mandir" (temple).

Narotam, too, might have found jail restful, a time to meditate. It is doubtful he had many visitors, ninety miles from home in the big city of Baroda. Nor were there many letters, surely, for no one in his family could write much, and he could not read much. For company, he had the guards and his fellow prisoners. Living two to a cell, the satyagrahis —except for leaders like Gandhi—were mixed in with the regular prison population, and were allowed to see one another freely. It was the only extended period of solitude, even leisure, in Narotam's life.

Although the satyagrahis were in prison for breaking laws, once behind bars they were among the most disciplined inmates. Gandhi en-couraged them to follow the rules, except when those rules were "con-trary to human dignity"; if the food was rotten, for example, they were to refuse it, but if it was merely tasteless, they were not to complain. They were to insist on what they needed to fulfill religious vows, such as spin-ning khaadi; but otherwise they were not to seek special privileges, such as books and newspapers.

Free of the obligations of family and finances, in the company of other civil resisters, Narotam learned to knit, crochet, meditate, and practice yoga. Needles and other implements might pose a danger in the hands of a violent prisoner, but in the hands of one sworn to nonviolence, they were strictly domestic. It was a time he would look back on with pride, telling his children decades later, "See, I wouldn't know how to knit if I hadn't gone to jail."

During the three months Narotam spent behind bars, the salt campaign intensified dangerously. Eventually all of the movement's leaders were imprisoned, spinning khaadi several hours a day and forbidden to write on political matters; but new leaders and new followers arose. And the government did not fail to respond. By one estimate, sixty thousand people were jailed across India for gathering, making, or rallying around salt.

Gujarat remained the campaign's epicenter. Waves of spontaneously organized, resolutely nonviolent volunteers from all over India traveled to the coast of Gujarat to make salt from the ocean or take it from the British company's salt pans. Government police, frustrated by the volunteers' unvarying tactic of walking forward unarmed, shifted from clubbing their heads to storming them with horses to "rendering . . . unconscious by squeezing their privates," according to a report by the freedom movement's secretary in Gujarat. Over one three-week period, the secretary counted 1,333 wounded, out of 2,640 volunteers. Four men died.

As Gandhi had hoped, the salt campaign was a turning point in swaying international opinion in favor of the Indian cause. Bertrand Russell, for example, wrote, "This sort of thing filled every decent English person with a sense of intolerable shame, far greater than would have been felt if the Indian resistance had been of a military character."

At home, the brutality helped make the volunteers into heroes. When Narotam was released, the whole town of Gandevi turned out for a parade in his honor. Such celebrations were held all over Gujarat; the satyagrahis were treated like soldiers returning from a just war. The salt movement had shaken the Raj, and many Indians believed independence was imminent, thanks to men like Narotam who had sacrificed for the good of all.

To Narotam's father, however, his son was not so much a hero as a young rebel about to go astray. The movement's dangers had become all too clear, and Narotam's father had a plan.

Narotam's older brother and a cousin were already working as tailors in Fiji. To finance the trip, the women of the family had had to pawn all of their meager jewelry. Even Benkor, who had waited so long for her silver dowry anklets, had sold them.

Now, the eldest son had sent some money back, and Narotam's father wanted to use it to send his second son to the colony as well—away from the dangers of radical politics, and where he could help support the family.

Narotam could no longer indulge in his brahmachaarin stage; he was launched, according to tradition, into the "householder" stage of life. Here the spiritual lessons learned in youth are not abandoned. Rather, a householder must learn to apply them in a more complicated environment. He must learn his *dharma*.

Dharma has a dual meaning: religion and duty. In the second stage of life, a Hindu confronts this duality, learning to reconcile his spiritual life with familial duties.

For Narotam it must have been a difficult transition. He had just experienced his first chance to study his own soul. Then, just as quickly, he was forced to become a man of responsibility. Did his obligations to a network of kin—parents, brothers, sisters with wedding expenses, a wife and child—weigh heavily on him? Surely he must have felt some sorrow at leaving his comrades in the movement. Yet perhaps it was tempered by the stoicism that is the nature of our people. We are not ones to rail against the gods—or, as in Narotam's case, against our fathers' wishes. Narotam began to make preparations. He would leave Benkor and baby Sarasvati with his parents, and set out alone.

For my grandmother Benkor, it was another separation from the husband she had barely had time to know. She understood the need; the men of her own family were also on the move, following the trend noted that year by the special census of Gandevi. Benkor's uncle had traveled to Kenya to try his luck. Within a few years, her brother and cousins would follow him and settle there. By 1933, so many Indian entrepreneurs were living abroad that the most ambitious of them formed the Imperial Indian Citizenship Association, whose published directory estimated a total of 2.5 million Indians living abroad in the British colonies and Commonwealth countries.

Among these were all of Benkor's male relatives. She would not see them again until she was an old woman, after each of them had lived a whole lifetime in the colonies. Now her husband, too, would join the great tide of emigration. His destination, tiny Fiji, with 77,000 Indians, was fifth on the list of countries with a substantial Indian population.

In the passport office of the empire, in Bombay, Narotam had his picture taken for the second time in his life. His national status was listed as "British subject by birth," his occupation as "tailor," his height as five feet. On August 8, 1931, he boarded a ship called the *Ganges* in Calcutta. On September 3, Fiji's afternoon newspaper reported its arrival at Suva harbor.

The same newspaper carried ads for goods imported by the ship (mustard oil, Rangoon rice, Genuine Indian Brassware), an advertisement for M. Narsey & Co. (Printed Chiffons, Numerous Patterns to Choose From, Absolute Bedrock Prices — Call Early), and a news item: "Mahatma Gandhi, Dressed in Loincloth, Sailed for England." Gandhi had been released from prison in order to attend an imperial conference, where he hoped to raise for the first time in London the formal prospect of India's independence. As Narotam reached Fiji, Gandhi was aboard the S.S. *Rajputana*, telling the Associated Press that he was "hoping against hope" for freedom.

In Fiji, Narotam found a country far different from the land of opportunity that had welcomed Motiram Narsey. Because of the worldwide depression, the capital was no longer a bustling port. Three years earlier, Suva had shipped 121,000 tons of sugar around the world; in 1931, the market could support only 68,000 tons.

Narotam worked for a while as a tailor with his brother, who eventually retired to India because his health was poor. Once on his own, Narotam decided to risk moving to the only section of the island that was thriving: the town of Tavua, on the northern coast, where surveyors had recently discovered gold. He went north, setting up a tailoring shop to serve those rushing to exploit the gold and, soon, silver buried in the island. He sewed women's clothes and saved money to send home.

The Gujaratis of Fiji mostly kept apart from native people, except as business demanded. Many of my relatives say they were afraid at first of the tall, strong people who seemed as fierce as their historical reputation for cannibalism suggested. Natives and whites tended to see the Indians as clannish and separatist—but the Indians were in fact divided among themselves. While indentured Indian immigrants had quickly dropped many distinctions of caste and region, the Gujaratis who came later had the money to travel home frequently. They maintained strong ties to home and rarely married outside their castes. They owned a large proportion of the retail stores and generally imported relatives as assistants, rather than hiring local Indians. Some Gujaratis even acted as loan sharks, extending credit at unfavorable terms against future paychecks. In 1937, two hundred Indo-Fijians signed a petition urging limits on further immigration:

> There are certain undesirable types of Immigrants; Fiji is full with such. These men refuse to admit in their social circle which in itself creates bad feeling; there is nothing but these traders refuse to employ local borns in services; they refuse to teach them any form of trade; they refuse to spend in Fiji; their God is money.

They were talking about the Gujaratis.

In the decade of Narotam's arrival, Fiji took a series of steps to discourage young Gujarati men from coming and going strictly for the purpose of making money. It began charging the hefty fee of £50 for each immigration permit and giving preference to those who were accompanied by wives. M. Narsey & Co. spearheaded a protest letter, which received a courteous but unyielding reply from the colonial secretary in London. He acknowledged the contributions of the "Bombay community" but encouraged the Gujaratis to promote family migration.

Narotam sent for his wife in 1937. Benkor left behind their six-year-old daughter to be raised by Narotam's parents in India. Narotam's younger brother, Kalyaan, also came to Fiji with a young wife. Together the brothers expanded from tailoring to retail, opening a ready-made clothing shop in Tavua. They sold T-shirts and dress shirts, trousers, dresses, and the native attire, a kind of wraparound skirt called the *sulu,* to Fijians and local Indians.

The shop had a small room in the back where they kept their files and, when business was slow, retired to drink tea. A shady path led to the kitchen, and down another path was the single bedroom. Just beyond that was the outhouse. For bathing, water had to be brought from the river; a bucket sat in a small tiled area next to the store, with ropes strung around it so that temporary walls of cloth could be drawn for privacy. In the yard, chickens clucked and pecked at the dry soil, and sometimes a goat grazed, waiting to grace the family's dinner table. Benkor bore a second girl in 1939, and a third in 1942.

After his adventures in the movement, the life of an entrepreneur and family man in Fiji would have been quite a contrast for Narotam. His days were filled with practical details, far from the continuing and dramatic battles of the independence movement and the ideals he cherished. But perhaps he took solace in the Bhagavad Geeta, a religious text whose passages on dharma Gandhi urged his followers to memorize. "Better is one's own duty, though devoid of merit, than the duty of another well performed," the god Krishna tells the hero Arjuna in the Geeta. "Therefore, always perform your work, without attachment, which has to be done; for a man who works without attachment attains the Supreme."

Narotam earned a reputation for helping others in the tightly knit Khatri community of Fiji. In a typical instance, a young man knocked on his door well after midnight. He owed so much money, he said, that his creditors were coming to beat him the next morning. Would Narotam hide him for the night?

Narotam did, and in the morning he negotiated with the merchants, buying the man some time by paying a percentage of the loans. Through such acts Narotam found his role in the community, reconciling the obligations of a businessman with the Gandhian philosophy of service.

World War II sharpened the division between the native Fijians and the Indians, who were by now about half and half on the island. One out of every three native Fijian men between the ages of eighteen and sixty volunteered to fight on behalf of the empire. But the Fiji Indians balked. First they demanded the same rate of pay as white soldiers, and were refused; then they argued that growing sugar and other economic activity was their contribution to the war effort. Then, in 1943, a strike by Indian cane workers over low prices left most of the harvest to rot in Fiji's fields.

The Indians were labeled disloyal, and their status as citizens of Fiji was further diminished.

July 24, 1945, was the day my grandmother had been waiting for, in some ways her whole life long. Fiji's internal politics were volatile, and World War II was about to end, but neither of these was the reason for her prayers or sighs of *Raam, Raam.* She was going into labor.

More than fifteen years had passed since Benkor had put on silver anklets and a modest but freshly pressed sari and walked to her in-laws' house. The daughter she had left there was nearly grown. In the new land, Benkor had borne two more girls. She was married to a good man, and though they were working hard, they were no longer at the edge of poverty. Her days were filled with raising the children, tending chickens and goats, cooking three meals a day on a woodstove, grinding her own grain in a hand-cranked mill, carrying clothes and dishes to the river to wash them, and filling the kerosene lamps at dusk.

What she wanted now was what, twice, had eluded her. Twice, a son had slipped from her womb and failed to survive: one a miscarriage, one stillborn. Narotam's brothers had no sons, either; the family name could die out in one generation. Though Benkor lived far from her in-laws and the land where she grew up, she had brought with her at least some of the old ways. Her deepest desire now was for a baby boy.

So she prayed to the family goddess. Benkor made a vow, a kind of bargain that is common among our people: If You grant me a son, I will not indulge in new clothes for him for one year.

The goddess responded. Narotam and Benkor named their only son Champak, after the frangipani tree with its fragrant yellow flowers that grew in both the soil of Gujarat and the soil of Fiji. Though he was the child of a tailor, nursed to the clickety-clack of sewing machines, Champak did not wear new clothes until his first birthday.

Narotam and Benkor's last child, Bhanu, my mother, was born in 1946. A year later, the independence for which my grandparents and millions of other Indians had struggled and prayed came to India at last.

On the subcontinent, two nations were being carved from the empire, and the parturition was bloody. Riots, mass rapes, and mob murders took place as Hindus and Muslims crossed the lines—Hindus into the new India, Muslims into the new Pakistan—that had looked so neat and tidy on the maps approved in England. Independence and the trauma of partition would launch a new wave of diaspora, as people from the new borderlands fled to third countries as refugees.

News of the violence did not reach the colonies until a day or two later. So the mood among overseas Indians on Independence Day— August 15, 1947—was one of pure celebration. In South Africa, Grey Street was festooned with ribbons and banners; restaurants hosted parties or put up sales on sweets, while activists looked hopefully toward a new strategy that involved negotiations between two sovereign nations. The final British count of their Indian subjects' diaspora showed 1,157,728 Indians living throughout the empire. One in four was in South Africa; one in ten lived in Fiji.

In Tavua, Narotam sewed satin dresses in the new country's colors for his middle daughters. They marched proudly down Tavua's main street, a parade of shopkeepers and farmhands and children chanting "Jai Hind!" ("Long live India!"), waving the three-striped flag of the new nation: saffron for courage and sacrifice, white for peace and truth, and green for faith and chivalry. In the center of the white stripe, in dark blue, symbolizing the hope of the masses, was the spinning wheel.

Within months, Narotam took his family home.

In Gandevi the family settled, like most villagers, into a house made of mud and reinforced with cow dung. In January 1948, Sarasvati's marriage was arranged—and Gandhi was assassinated. Relatives remember Narotam listening to the radio news at his daughter's wedding, and weeping.

Independence alone could not fix the problems of rural India's economy: poverty, drought, chronic unemployment. The forces sweeping the sons of Gujarat out to the colonies were as strong as ever, and in 1951 Narotam returned to Fiji with his young son, Champak.

Narotam's younger brother, Kalyaan, and his wife, Rukhmani, were still there, without children of their own. Rukhmani took care of the boy, who was a handful. Soon business was good enough that Narotam gave up the clapboard house in Tavua and bought half of a British-style bungalow in the big city, Suva. They all moved in, and he sent for his wife and three younger daughters. And his fortunes began to change.

The new house was uphill from the main part of town, across the street from a Catholic church. It had hardwood floors and luxuries unknown in either Tavua or Gandevi: indoor plumbing, electricity, a refrigerator. Narotam's family kept one bedroom, Kalyaan and Rukhmani — still childless — the other. The house was divided, like a modern duplex; the other half was owned by a fellow Gujarati, who was also the landlord of their business space downtown. There, Kalyaan minded a new retail shop while Narotam started a wholesale business. From Britain, Australia, and New Zealand, samples of cloth and clothing came to Suva. Narotam carried them to Gujarati tailors and retailers throughout Fiji, taking and filling orders. He learned enough English to befriend useful contacts in the government import and licensing offices, banks, and other commercial concerns.

When he was home, the house became a center for parties; the whiskey started flowing on Saturday afternoon and did not stop until early Monday, with breaks in between for barbecued lamb, garlicky chicken, rice and daal. His friend Ratanji Narsey, one of Motiram's sons, was a regular guest. At Khatri community events, several times a year, the two men often took charge of cooking giant pots of curried goat stew outdoors. For a special treat, they skimmed the fat from the top of the goat stew and mixed it with Johnnie Walker, their favorite brand of whiskey. With a twist of lime, the strong soup served as a perfect appetizer-cocktail.

In 1956 and 1957, Narotam's two middle daughters married. Their weddings were lavish affairs; hundreds of guests drank and dined in the house and the large adjoining yard. A whole room was set aside for the white guests — bankers, government officials, and their families — who sat at tables instead of the floor, and ate from ceramic plates instead of paper. Fans circulated the hot tropical air, glass ashtrays collected their cigarettes, and young nephews were dispatched to keep their plates and glasses full. Narotam shook their hands awkwardly, used his self-taught English to thank them for coming, to accept their congratulations and compliments on the food. Their presence was a sign that his family had truly arrived.

Soon Narotam expanded his wholesale business to other islands. Visa stamps from Western Samoa, American Samoa, and Tonga filled his passport from 1959 to 1964. Prince Tungi of Tonga became a friend, staying in the Suva bungalow when he visited Fiji. Benkor and Rukhmani would cook massive quantities of food for the prince, who was so large that he could not sit on the floor and dine with the rest of the family. After some searching, they found a chair he would not break.

From his travels, Narotam brought back not only orders but also luxury items: frozen lamb chops and lamb brains from New Zealand, American delicacies that his children adored—Planters peanuts, Double-mint chewing gum, shoestring potato chips. Despite his newfound prosperity, he continued to use the skills he had learned in jail, knitting and crocheting, to relax. In the cool air of morning he would practice yoga on the veranda, concluding with a ten-minute headstand; one friend from the time describes him as a "health freak." Then he would sit in his chair on the porch and drink a cup of chaa, perhaps reading the English newspaper slowly, line by line. Grandchildren came, and he practiced nonviolence on them; "Give him a drink of water," he would say of a misbehaving youngster, calming him down in a time when strappings were a more common form of discipline.

After one's children are grown, a Hindu can enter the final two phases of life: retirement and renunciation. In retirement, a man has a chance to enjoy the fruits of his labor and the knowledge that his children are self-sufficient. Next comes renunciation, when he sheds the world's pleasures and obligations for a concentrated period of spiritual study. Sometimes this means making a pilgrimage, sometimes merely devoting more time to praying, singing hymns, studying scriptures, practicing yoga, or simply meditating. In the old days, it might have meant retreating into a forest ashram to pursue a wholly meditative life.

But just as Narotam's brahmachaarin period was abbreviated by poverty, financial worries plagued his retirement as well. His high-cholesterol weekends caught up with him; he suffered two heart attacks and by 1964 was no longer able to travel. Kalyaan, his brother, was more interested in the retail store than the import-export business, so they hired a partner to take up the traveling. But the partner turned out to be either a swindler or an extraordinarily poor salesman; he returned from his travels with copious expenses and few orders.

Then disaster struck. They were leasing the retail space, and the landlord was a competitor. When the lease expired, he refused to renew it. Their shop closed, opening again in a few days with the other man's goods.

Suddenly the cash flow to the household stopped. Narotam and Kalyaan tried to keep the business running in a smaller store, renting space in the Narsey's building, but the income was not enough to meet two families' expenses. The brothers began to quarrel.

Alcohol, by releasing one from inhibitions, makes a man more who he is. Narotam was a quiet man and a quieter drunk; after several rounds of whiskey and beer, he preferred to stumble home and into bed, where he would not stir till morning. But Kalyaan was hardheaded and abrasive. Drunk, he was loud, argumentative, even abusive.

Walking home with Narotam from the club, Kalyaan shouted at his elder brother over how they were dividing the proceeds or who had failed to pay the bills on time. Bitter about not having children of his own, he accused Narotam of draining the business to spend money on his children and their families.

Indeed, Narotam's children did need his help. He had sent his only son, Champak, to study in America in 1963. At the time, business had been good; now, only a couple of years later, it was difficult to keep up with the tuition. As for his daughters, two of them had husbands who seemed unable to provide enough to feed and clothe the children. Narotam slipped them cash when he could, but the last time one of them had asked for money, he had had to refuse. Furious, she had stopped speaking to him.

One morning in 1965, Narotam rose from his mattress on the open-air, slatted veranda where he preferred to sleep, and stumbled. Bhanu, who was seventeen and the only child still at home, heard the noise and woke her mother. It was about 2 A.M., and raining. From their own bedroom the women could make out his silhouette, staggering and weaving from his cot toward the steps. Thinking he was still drunk and disoriented, Benkor rose to help him toward the bathroom, which required a few yards' journey around the outside of the house.

As they reached the bottom step, Narotam could not hold back. He vomited into the rain, a large pool that Benkor would have to clean up in the morning. Then suddenly he squatted on the lawn. Benkor went back inside, retrieved an umbrella, and held it over him as he created a second large pool, this one diarrheal. She helped him back to his bed on the veranda, then slept a few more precious hours till dawn.

. . .

A Fiji morning is loud with roosters and dogs, a household's ablutions, cacophony of steel and aluminum pots as women prepare tea, breakfast, and lunch. Benkor rose, made tea, and woke her daughter for school, asking her to wake Narotam as well. When Bhanu went out to the veranda, though, she let out a shout—then raced to telephone the doctor.

Narotam's tongue lolled from the corner of his open mouth. His daughter had just learned cardiopulmonary resuscitation, so after calling the doctor she tried the only thing she could think of that might help. Stripping away the bedcovers, she placed her hands on either side of his sternum, and put her lips over his mouth. As she blew air into his lungs, she pressed down on his ribs, hoping to restart the rhythm of his heart.

In a few minutes the doctor arrived, and the women had to step back as he pulled a long needle from his bag, then thrust it into Narotam's chest: Adrenalin, a last-ditch effort to make the heart kick alive.

Then there was nothing more to do.

Narotam's immediate cause of death was a massive 2 A.M. heart attack, accompanied in the typical manner by a sudden loss of bowel control and a slow ticking down of his heartbeat. Among the possible larger causes were financial stress, genetics, karma, and a lifetime of whiskey, cigarettes, and high-cholesterol meals. He never reached the final period of spiritual study, renunciation. A day later, they scattered his ashes in the Pacific Ocean.

At the funeral, his friends drank and drank.

Today, Dandi, where Narotam and Gandhi picked up their first fistfuls of salt, is barely a town—so unremarkable that on at least one modern map of Gujarat, it is mislocated some fifty kilometers north up the coast. Named for an ancient lighthouse (*diva daandi* in Gujarati means "stick of light"), it is the dusty endpoint of a main road, with a few ramshackle buildings: restaurant, corner store, and several shacks selling liquor to tourists from the neighboring "dry" districts of Gujarat, where Gandhi's prohibition campaign enjoys enduring legal success. In the main plaza, just before the beach, a man sells juice from freshly cut sugar cane, squeezing each long stalk through the teeth of a large steel machine set on the cobblestones. A memorial and museum are decaying near the town, showing Gandhi bending over in the famous salt-robbing pose.

On the beach itself, racks of fish are strung to dry in the sun, filling the air with their pungent aroma. The day we visited in 1997, my brother and I dipped our toes in the sea and took pictures on the beach, and I thought about my Aajaa.

His life is a complicated example for me, its moments of shining idealism and sad compromise illustrating the relentless ironies of diaspora. Born a British subject, he helped his countrymen gain their freedom, only to die a British subject in yet another colony. Born poor, he became wealthy but died poor again. A man of strong principles, by the time of my mother's memory he was weak, often drunk, patriarch of a clan of merchants and traders, plagued by swindlers and cheats.

And yet that is not the whole story. One step out of India, he made the next possible. In Fiji his children went to missionary schools, where they studied the Bible and learned English. At home, they might sit on the floor and eat with their hands, but in school, they memorized how to set a table with two forks to the left, knife and spoon to the right. Decades later, armed with this knowledge, the two youngest would come to America. And their own children would treasure that jailbird photograph taken decades ago, the one that hints at another kind of man: a young revolutionary infused with the light of belief.

At the water's edge I stood alone for a few minutes, gazing at the orange sun sinking into the sea, trying to feel my Aajaa's spirit in the salt air. But spirits rarely come when called, and after a while, I turned back toward the darkening land.

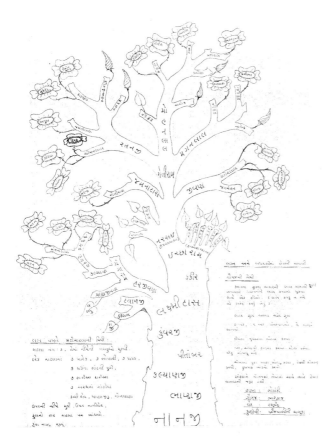

The family tree drawn by my father ca. 1962 or 1963, with male names in Gujarati.

RIGHT: *Ratan Narsai, my great-great-grandmother. No picture exists of her husband, Narsai, the seer.*

LEFT: *Motiram, my great-grandfather.*

Kaashi Motiram Narsey, my great-grandmother, whom everyone called Maaji (respected mother), with paan leaves, 1960s.

G. C. Kapitan in front of his restaurant in Durban, South Africa.

G. C. Kapitan (center) visiting Fiji in January 1965; left, Ratanji Narsey, G. C.'s nephew, my father's father.

G. C.'s son Dalpat and family at the height of "petty apartheid" in South Africa, when all public places were being segregated; they are at the international airport en route to a family vacation in India, ca. 1960s.

Narotam after his release from prison for participating in Gandhi's salt march, July 1930.

Ratanji, Kalyaan, and Narotam (third, fourth, and fifth from left), and others drinking in the backyard—a typical Sunday activity in Suva, Fiji, in the 1960s.

Ratanji Narsey, my grandfather, who migrated to Fiji at age 14 after the death of his father, Motiram, and then headed the Narseys enterprise. This is a hand-painted colorization of a photograph, ca. 1940s.

Thakor ("Tom"), standing, with his father, Ratanji, in the Narseys office in Fiji, ca. 1960s.

The Narsey family in Suva, 1962 or 1963. The unmarried sons are wearing printed Fijian "bula" shirts (back row: Bhupendra, second from left, and Manhar, third from right). The married sons and the sons-in-law are wearing suits (back row: Ranchhod, third from left, holding baby, next to his wife, Manjula; second row: Chiman, third from right). Ratanji and Kaashi are at center.

The Narseys Building in 2001: still a downtown Suva landmark, but the family business has been shuttered for two decades.

My mother, Bhanu (left), with school friends in Fiji, ca. 1960.

My father, Bhupendra, being seen off by his mother at the docks, 1963.

ABOVE: *Bhupendra and Champak sightseeing upon their arrival in San Francisco, 1963.*

RIGHT: *Bhupendra graduated with a master's degree in 1965. His father made multiple copies of this photo and sent it to all the family.*

5. STORY

It is almost impossible to like the Indians of Fiji. They are suspicious, vengeful, whining, unassimilated, provocative . . . Above all, they are surly and unpleasant.
— James Michener, *Return to Paradise,* 1951

Narsai and Ratan
↓
Motiram and Kaashi ("Maaji")
↓
Ratanji and Kaashi
Magan |
Mohan |
↓

Kamu
Chiman
Kanchan
Jayanti
RANCHHOD and Manjula
Bhupendra
Manhar
Lila

*I*F MY MOTHER'S PEOPLE are quiet and humble, my father's are loud and brash—a clan of taletellers. For most of my life, the other descendants of Motiram Narsey have been strangers to me, with familiar faces (their resemblance to my father is strong) but unfamiliar temperaments. Far away in Fiji, they presided over the rise of a business that made our family's name so well known that even now it carries currency there, though all but a few have emigrated and more than a decade has passed since the Narseys department store shuttered its doors. Of the Narsey clan, the one I came to know best, through a few extended visits, was my uncle Ranchhod: my father's brother, and one of Motiram Narsey's grandsons.

He had a story for any occasion. *Speaking of spirits,* he might start up, *one time on a deserted jungle road in Papua New Guinea, we met two men. We were staying at the army base—they didn't have any hotels for non-whites then—and we were just walking back from town. It was almost night. My friend had decided we should take the shortcut. I didn't want to, but he insisted. Suddenly two men appeared on the road. They were dressed all in white.*

Here he would pause, just long enough to let the listener absorb the significance of this detail: they were dressed all in white.

Then one of them asked for a cigarette. I knew what he was, so I gave him my whole pack! And my matches, too.

—Where are you going? the ghost asked us.

—Just to the base.

—Go back the other way.

— But this is a shortcut.

— Sometime — here my uncle's voice would drop ominously, the ghost still speaking in his own Indian-English accent *— shortcut never make it.*

We were so scared! We turned around and went back the long way. It was dark now. When we finally got to our room, I stopped my friend from going in. I got some water and I said a prayer over it, and I sprinkled it on us. Like this.

And only then did I let him go in, and I went in myself, and thanked god for saving us from who knows what.

It is business that gives diasporas their strength and vibrancy, according to some economists: tight networks of kin across several continents are uniquely qualified to move goods and ideas, allowing ethnic diasporas to thrive in a global economy. But as any grandmother knows, it is story that truly holds a people together. When I asked my uncle Ranchhod what exactly his business entailed, he gave me a story.

It was hard to keep five thousand cartons of tinned salmon a secret, but Ranchhod was trying. The tins sat on the main dock of the Fiji Islands with his name on them, the key to his future success. The year was 1957, and the middle son of the Narsey family was embarking on an age-old Gujarati tradition called "middling": serving at the junction between producer and customer.

He had never tasted the pink fish from Canada. But he had come to know that Fijians savored it, so Gujarati shopkeepers all over the islands stocked it, each year importing the maximum allowed under the rules of the British Commonwealth — that final shadow of empire, whose regulations were carefully designed to maintain a delicate balance of trade between its nations and territories. A single white-owned company held a monopoly on importing salmon into the colony of Fiji. Now, Ranchhod was planning to ambush it and capture the trade. He was twenty-two years old, and motivated by debt.

He owed £150 to the family firm, which had just paid for his wedding trip back home to India and for his and his bride's passage to Fiji. He had a newly outfitted office with his name on the door: Hazrat Trading Co. Its ledger opened with £500 in its "Debts" column, start-up capital from the parent company, which he was required to pay back within

a year. His salary was £30 a month. It did not take an accounting certificate, which he had, to calculate that he needed to make money quickly.

His assets were these: Business skills he had picked up during a prior
six-year sojourn in Fiji, where he had arrived from India at the age of fifteen. A friend who suggested the salmon deal and told him which government official to bribe. Ambition. Youthful arrogance, perhaps even
recklessness. A certain capacity to charm. And the five thousand cartons,
which, he hoped, would pay off his debts, prove his mettle as a businessman, and earn him the praise of his father and uncles.

What he did not have was a truck to transport the salmon or a warehouse in which to store it. His conversational English, the lingua franca
of business in Fiji, was minimal; on principle, he had refused to learn
the language of India's oppressors. He had no financial reserves. And because this was not exactly the sort of business his elders had in mind—
he was supposed to be a salesman, not an importer—he could not go to
them for help. He wanted the deal to be a surprise. Once the profits were
in, he reasoned, no one would carp over the details.

So he learned to wheel and deal. In exchange for a bottle of fine whiskey,
a petty government official handed over the list of shopkeepers who had
applied to buy salmon for the year. Ranchhod went to visit them one by
one, persuading them to sign over their licenses to him as their receiving
agent—a fellow Indian rather than a *goriyaa,* a white man. He wheedled
a bank manager into advancing payment to the Canadians. He paid a
white-owned agency to deliver the cartons to each shopkeeper and, though
the agents did not normally do so, to collect payments as they went.

When the salmon reached its various destinations around Fiji and the
checks started to come in, Ranchhod did not tally or record them; he
took them directly to the bank. After some days, the bank manager called
him: —What would you like me to do with the money?

—It's yours, said Ranchhod, —you take it.

—No, I took mine already. Your loan is paid, this is your profit.

—Oh!

He ordered the profit put into the Hazrat Trading Co. account, and
went to report back to his uncle. —On five thousand cartons, he said,
explaining the deal, —I have made a profit of £2,000.

—Impossible, said Uncle Magan. —Bullshit!

· · ·

By the time Ranchhod told me the story almost fifty years later, it had been refined and perfected. The important thing was not the salmon and profits but the bragging rights: the *story* of the salmon and profits, the staging of the secret and its revelation for maximum effect and drama, both in the moment and ever after. The anecdote had become a *kathaa:* story, epic, ritual.

In its most formal incarnation, a kathaa is a ritualized recitation of a religious tale, extolling the feats or virtues of a particular god or goddess before an audience of the devout. But *kathaa* is also the everyday word for story, of various sorts: *panchaati,* gossip; *samaachaar,* news; *raavan-kathaa,* complaints of epic proportions; and *raam-kathaa,* a tale of heroic deeds. My uncle was a prodigious and entertaining storyteller, and in almost every story he told, he was the hero—which says something about either his character or his capacity for embellishment, or both.

The kathaa of the Narseys business, of which Ranchhod's tale was but a small piece, had been mostly a success story despite the death of its founder, Motiram, in 1918. Motiram's brothers had run M. Narsey & Company ably. They opened a grocery section briefly, then closed it to focus on the growing demand for their tailoring skills. They won a major government contract to sew police and military uniforms. Their biggest competitor, Walter Horne & Co., where the founder had gotten his start, closed down. And they brought their sons and nephews over from India to work for them.

Motiram's eldest son, Ratanji, had been just eleven years old when his father died, leaving his widowed mother, our Maaji, to manage the household. Maaji sent Ratanji to Fiji to work for his uncles when he turned fourteen. His two brothers soon followed. Upon coming of age, each of the boys went back to India to marry and then sojourned to Fiji again to work, leaving his bride in Maaji's care. In 1928, Ratanji's wife bore their first child. By the end of the decade, the company's profits were sustaining several households back in India.

By 1936, Gujaratis, who had started arriving in Fiji only three decades earlier, numbered 2,500, or three percent of the islands' total Indian population. As the Narseys and other Khatris came to dominate tailoring in Suva, a few men began bringing their wives and children to Fiji. They were making the shift from a bachelor society to one that included families, caste-based societies, and regular social and religious gatherings. In 1931, Ratanji's wife, Kaashi, came to Fiji, leaving their daughter at home in India with Maaji.

More children followed. Ranchhod, his parents' fifth child, was born in Suva on New Year's Day, 1935. His father, at twenty-eight years old, had already spent half his life in Fiji. But Kaashi never took to island life; four childbirths later, she wanted to go home. And Ratanji agreed, perhaps swayed by the fact that his earnings would go further in India, with its lower cost of living and the favorable exchange rate. Ranchhod was still in diapers when mother and children moved back to the village of Navsari.

They lived in a new four-story house of brick and cement, built with the Fiji money. Carved above the third-floor balcony, in the architectural fashion of the time, is the date of construction in two languages: the Gujarati year, 1993, and the English year, 1937. Three similar houses, built by Ratanji's brothers and uncles, stood nearby. They towered above the rest of the neighborhood with its single-story homes of wood, tin, and cow-dung plaster.

Ranchhod grew used to seeing his father once every few years, visits that were characterized by treats, arguments, and, afterward, the births of more children. His brother Jayanti cried and screamed each time their father left, so Ratanji sometimes departed in the middle of the night to avoid a scene. By the time Ranchhod was ten, he had two more brothers and a sister; his mother had also borne a son who died as an infant. The children split naturally into two groups, and Ranchhod was the youngest of the older set.

As World War II began, the Narsey brood enrolled in Public School No. 4. Before its end, thousands of Indians had died fighting for the Allies, a fact used by activists to bolster the moral argument for India's independence. Gandhi was more determined than ever to promote nonviolent struggle, but others were impatient with his methods. In the spirit of the times, Ranchhod and Jayanti joined a militant nationalist youth gang.

At ten and eleven, the boys were too young to be involved in the real action. But they made good, unobtrusive moles: They would go into the town's police station to beg a pencil or a newspaper or a piece of carbon paper, and as they hung around they would eavesdrop to find out whether the officers had any plans for, say, reacting to a demonstration the next day. Or they would be given mysterious parcels and told to tie them to the railroad tracks, small attempts at disrupting the British-run railroads. Whatever they understood of the politics, the gang's rebellious spirit excited them. And it fit Ranchhod's mischievous streak—one that frequently tested his mother's shallow reservoir of patience.

Kaashi raised eight children almost as a single parent, saddled with all of the responsibility but little authority. Nor did she have companion-ship from her own kin; her three brothers had all migrated to South Africa. Her mother-in-law, Maaji, lived just around the corner, close enough to criticize and to claim the privilege of making all significant family decisions. When it came to power, Kaashi could exercise it only over her own children—and not always then.

Jayanti and Ranchhod were hellions, prone to practical jokes. Walk-ing behind a fisherwoman with a basket on her head, fish mouths and tails wagging from its brim calling to be liberated, Ranchhod would sneak up behind her and knock it down. As the shiny fish were sent slipping and swimming through the dirt, he would run away, laughing. Navsari was small enough that everyone knew whose child he was, and within a half-hour the woman came complaining: —See what your son did! Kaashi had to pay for the ruined basket of fish and, worse, endure the humiliation of being berated by a lower-caste fishwife. To rein in her troublesome middle sons, she felt her only recourse was the belt.

In a narrow street with open windows, people could hear her children screaming. More than once, a beating went on so long that a neighbor had to come to Ranchhod's rescue, urging calm while counseling Kaashi not to hit the children so much. "She was a child abuser," one of her chil-dren would say later, without judgment or sorrow, but perhaps a bit of pity for the frustration that drove her to such ends.

Despite his antics, Ranchhod was a good student. His math scores were so high that he was chosen for a special program in which four boys from the local secondary school were sent during school hours to earn an ac-counting certificate in the nearby city of Surat. But because he and Jayanti were militantly anti-British throughout the 1940s, they refused to learn English.

Against their protests, an uncle—who in their father's absence served as guardian and decision maker—placed them in a school where the education was reputed to be better. There, English was a required subject. In the end-of-year exams, Ranchhod passed history, geography, Gujarati, science, and mathematics—and failed English, turning in a blank paper.

The headmaster understood the nature of the protest, and promoted Ranchhod to the next year anyway. Jayanti eventually consented to learn a little English, but Ranchhod would not yield. In the second year he failed English again, but was promoted again. He realized that if he did not want to attend an English school, he would have to take more drastic measures. In the third year, he made sure to fail not only English but also history, geography, and—most painfully—math.

The headmaster called him into the office.

—I understand why you are failing English, he said. —But math is your top subject. Why fail?

—I just don't want to study here, Ranchhod said. He was fourteen years old, unable to articulate more. The independence battle was over, and India had won. All official boycotts and protests were finished. Still, Ranchhod could not wrap his tongue around the foreign language.

At that, the headmaster hit him with a cane, again and again. Every few strokes he paused: —Are you going to study or not?

—No, Ranchhod said.

The caning went on, but Ranchhod's will did not break. Stubbornness was a family trait. The headmaster gave up, and reported him to his uncle.

At home, Ranchhod showed the uncle his accounting certificate and said he would practice that trade. But the uncle, furious at the boy's disobedience, ripped up the certificate, suspended Ranchhod by his wrists from a hook in the ceiling, and administered another beating with a belt. Again, it was to no avail. At last the uncle threw up his hands, and wrote to Ranchhod's father in Fiji.

It seemed to Ranchhod that he had won the battle.

Years later, Ranchhod's beatings were transformed into funny stories, nostalgic tales of the wild old days. He believed he had survived his father's absence and his elders' discipline unscathed. He grew ever more willful, his spirit more fiery, apparently impervious to their efforts.

Could this toughness itself have been a form of scarring, a kind of thickening over the wound? Such a question could not have been raised within the narrative of his childhood. Instead he was said to have inherited the family temperament, the stubborn streak of the Narsey clan.

The Narsey temper, alive to this day, is legendary, dramatic, and public. One of the last Narsey weddings I attended erupted in a shouting match, complete with people storming out of the wedding dinner, over a series of conflicts obliquely related to a decade-old unpaid debt and a lifetime's worth of perceived slights. From time to time this fury seems to possess us all, men and women, boys and girls, old and young alike.

Once when Ranchhod was a child, his mother asked him to retrieve some mangoes from the storage area, on the top floor of the house. He whined about having to climb so many stairs. One of his uncles, overhearing, was seized by a fit of anger so terrible he climbed the three flights himself, picked up the mangoes that lay spread all over the floor, and hurled them out the open window one by one.

The upper balcony provided one of Ranchhod's sisters with a place to scream and threaten to throw *herself* over the railing after one of her regular arguments with their mother, Kaashi. She was stopped only when Kaashi came up and shouted, — Do it, go ahead! Kaashi half pushed her, which called the bluff.

When Ratanji was home, he and Kaashi also feuded, seemingly at any provocation. Once he brought back from his travels an expensive bar of extra-dark chocolate. He shared it among the children, but they spat it out, unaccustomed to the bitter aftertaste. Then they cringed as he shouted at Kaashi, — What useless children you've raised!

What is remembered, what is passed on? Some of my cousins and I have wondered aloud why our parents, the eight Narsey siblings, have continued to argue fiercely all their lives. Neither age nor geographical dispersal seems to have dimmed their capacity for drama, which continues by fax and cell phone and e-mail, in broken English and transliterated Gujarati, sometimes unto the next generations. Is it nurture, nature, destiny? One cousin shared with me his theory: as children they had suffered, he thought, from being part of such a large, dispersed family. The boys were taken to Fiji at a young age, the girls married off, so that brothers and sisters did not grow up together, nor did they ever have the full attention of either parent. And as a result, none of them had been loved enough as children, or developed a solid bond with one another; they had virtually from birth entered into a fierce rivalry over their parents' attention, which somehow then continued on, decades after the parents were scattered ash, and which survived the further scatterings of geography, time, and migration.

It is, of course, just a theory; just one possible meta-story attempting to explain all the others.

When Ranchhod flunked out of school, Kaashi arranged an apprenticeship for him at a local tailoring shop. He worked for several months without pay, learning the trade. He was aware of the unofficial family policy: every boy who "finished" his education, in whatever manner, went to Fiji to join the family business. He did not know what exactly was in his uncle's letter to his father in Fiji, but he hoped Ratanji would make an exception.

But when his father's reply came, it did not praise Ranchhod's political stance or encourage his accounting ambitions. —Send the boy to Fiji, Ratanji wrote; —we can always use another pair of hands in the shop.

On August 15, 1950, India's third Independence Day, a ship landed in Fiji with one reluctant fifteen-year-old aboard. Early the next morning, Ranchhod was put to work as a salesclerk. *My father gave me a B.S.C. degree,* he would say later, with bitter humor: *Behind the Sales Counter.*

The sales counter had improved since the early days, when Motiram Narsey had set up shop with a couple of sewing machines and a few bolts of trouser cloth. Now his descendants presided over a department store of sorts, with three divisions: an up-to-date tailoring shop with several sewing machines and a full staff; a menswear store selling ready-made clothes; and a haberdashery stocked with accessories such as handkerchiefs, ribbons, and undergarments. The customers were a broad mix of Indians, Fijians, and whites in search of affordable prices and high-quality brands. For a time, Narseys was proud to be the exclusive seller of Maidenform brassieres in Fiji.

But Ranchhod's English boycott was still going strong. When customers came in, whatever their race, he would greet them with the friendliest *How are you, how may I help you?*—in Gujarati. Most of them, of course, looked at him blankly.

A morning of this and Ranchhod was sent to the back room, to assemble coat hangers while the elders debated his future. The hangers came in two parts, the triangle and the hook; the two had to be united before they could be sold. After a few days of this mind-numbing work, Ranchhod was summoned for a reckoning with his father.

—What do *you* want to do? asked Ratanji.

By now Ranchhod had a clear enough picture of life in Fiji. All the men lived behind the store, and every morning he was wakened at 5 A.M.; if he lollygagged, an uncle kicked him till he got up. The workday ran from 6 A.M. to 9 P.M., except on Sundays, when they worked a "half-day," 7 A.M. to 4 P.M. Meals were communal, cooked by a kitchen servant from India, on an unvarying weekly rotation of dishes; no individual choice was entertained. Ranchhod's desire was clear.

—I want to go back to India, he said.

That, however, was not an option, and Ratanji's anger flared. It seemed he and his son were too much alike to get along. With Ranchhod refusing to learn English and Ratanji refusing to send him home, they were at an impasse.

Finally Uncle Magan, known for his cool head, intervened and agreed to handle the youth. He arranged for Ranchhod to apprentice at a local Gujarati tailoring shop, where he would not have to deal with English customers.

Among Ranchhod's duties, the most pleasant was that each evening he was sent to see if the draft beer was flowing at the bar next door. There, the proprietress took a friendly interest in Ranchhod. Though he was only fifteen, she served him a daily half glass of beer. Fiji was still not home, but it began to have its benefits.

Two years later, a tidal wave hit Suva. It washed through the downtown, filling buildings with seawater, tearing rooftops off stores and homes, and completely destroying the shop where Ranchhod worked. He switched to another, where he worked several months, until an owner wrongly accused him of stealing from the till.

Furious— *boiling mad,* as he later described it—Ranchhod went after the man with a pair of scissors, cursing and shouting, —I'll kill you! After that it was difficult to find a place for him in town. Eighteen years old, he could no longer evade his destiny. He ended up back at Narseys.

The family company was in a phase of expansion under Ratanji, who as Motiram's eldest son had inherited leadership of the firm. He had taken over from his uncles in 1946, and in the 1950s he set out to grow the company, with the help of brothers and cousins and, as they came of age, sons and nephews.

His greatest advantage was the abundance of sons born to the Narsey clan. More sons meant more hands at the rainmaking, less need for outsiders or even sons-in-law to have their hands in the till, to meddle in family affairs. Motiram and his two brothers had produced among them six sons, who looked to Ratanji as their leader by virtue of seniority; the next generation, Ranchhod's, was twenty sons strong. All but a handful eventually entered the family business. Most spent their entire working lives at Narseys, as Ratanji wanted.

And so nearly every year in the 1950s saw a milestone of growth. In 1952, Ratanji entered a joint venture to distribute and sell shoes. In 1953, he applied for and received a liquor license, on one condition: legally, the license had to be held by a limited partnership. On July 31, 1953, Narseys Ltd. was formed, with five partners holding five hundred shares apiece: Ratanji, his brother Magan, a senior cousin, and their two uncles, who were retired in India. It was the first Indian firm allowed to sell liquor in Fiji, starting in 1954. That year Narseys also opened a radio and electrical goods department, under the leadership of Ranchhod's eldest brother, Chiman. Ratanji's empire was growing.

But if the extended family was a strength, it was also a major source of headaches—as Ranchhod seemed determined to prove.

Still refusing to speak English, Ranchhod was put to work in the wholesale department, supervised by his uncle Thakor.

Thakor, a younger cousin of Ratanji's, had first arrived in Fiji at age twelve. Now thirty, he was short, jolly, disproportionately proud of his typing skills, and so accommodating that he allowed Fijians and whites to call him Tom. Making things easy for the customer was his first rule of business, and he began to train Ranchhod as assistant salesman.

Uncle Tom's business was wholesaling to small stores in the countryside. Together he and Ranchhod circled Fiji's main island by bus, carrying six large suitcases filled with samples of cloth, clothing, and accessories. On the first trip Ranchhod couldn't bear the pit toilets, which were rank and far filthier than even the ones in rural India. But he loved the adventure of travel, and by his second trip he had adjusted.

Most of the shopkeepers were Gujarati, so Ranchhod's language preference was not much of a barrier. Still, Thakor tried to get him to learn English, mentioning it daily till Ranchhod felt his temper rise. Not wanting it to erupt, he quietly replied one day, —Remember how I went after that man with a pair of scissors? I wish to respect you, Uncle, so please don't speak of this to me again.

Where Uncle Thakor failed, Uncle Magan, with his steady temperament and his gift for really listening to his juniors, finally began to tame the headstrong young man. Telling Ranchhod that the warehouse staff were having problems because of his insistence on writing Gujarati numerals, Magan wrote out the ten English digits on a sheet of paper. He added a few key words: *doz.* for dozen, *yd.* for yard, and the entire alphabet for good measure.

When Ranchhod submitted to learning these, Magan introduced a few phrases that would be handy for dealing with Chinese shopkeepers: *This is good. Very cheap. Shirt, pants.* In this manner Ranchhod picked up a smattering of English, for it seemed to him he was not learning the hated language; he was only learning business.

One afternoon Ranchhod picked up the telephone at work and heard his father's voice telling him to get to his office *right now.* He rushed up the street to Narseys, wondering what could be wrong. When he entered the office, his father started yelling and gesturing at him, so fiercely that Ranchhod feared he would be hit. The object of his anger was, apparently, a letter with a photograph of a white girl.

The letter was meant for Ranchhod, as Magan had signed him up for an international pen-pal program to practice English. Ranchhod's name had appeared on a list. This letter had been addressed simply to R. Narsey, so it landed on Ratanji's desk. The father opened it, saw it was for Ranchhod, and did not pause to read it; his own English might be painstakingly slow, but his temper was quick.

Ranchhod swore he had no idea who the girl was. Ratanji said he must be lying—what kind of girl would send her photograph to a stranger? Finally Magan read the letter and explained to Ratanji that the girl, an American, had sent a photograph by way of introduction. Ranchhod said he'd never wanted a pen pal anyway.

When the air cleared, Ratanji said, —Look, this is confusing, one of us must change our name.

—Why should you change, Ranchhod said, —you've had your name so many years. I'll change.

Among our people, first names are bestowed according to a sort of divine lottery. When a child is born, an astrologer checks the stars and specifies the two or three letters of the Gujarati alphabet with which the child's name may begin. The *raasi*, as this aspect of the child's horoscope is called, is intricately linked with destiny, personality, mood, future mate, luck with money, and so on; to deviate from it is to tempt fate. By chance, Ranchhod and Ratanji had drawn the same initial letter. They might change their first names, but only at their peril.

Last names, though, are held more lightly. My relatives, when confronted with the need for passports and business licenses, resort to various solutions. Some, like the Kapitans in South Africa, invent their own; some use their caste identity, Khatri; others whose names have two parts split them, so Manilal goes by Mr. Lal. Some put down their father's name, as Motiram did; and in this way a last name can become a marker of the moment of encounter, the moment of migration. Narsai the prophet became Narsey the business, and then Narsey the surname, for generations to come. Indeed, Ranchhod's passport listed him as Ranchhod Ratanji; but since the object was to avoid confusion with his father, he decided against Ratanji as a last name.

A surname might also carry a story. While the Fiji relatives used the business name, Narsai's descendants in India were known by his ability to see the future: to *hazrat bhartaa*, in the local idiom. *Hazrat* is an Islamic word for a holy man or prophet; one who glimpsed the future was said to fulfill or flesh out a prophecy, or the spirit of a prophet. It was this name, weighted with destiny and history, that Ranchhod chose for his own.

But Ranchhod Hazrat enjoyed no greater autonomy than had Ranchhod Narsey. The family in those days was a true patriarchy; the fathers ruled, and everyone else obeyed.

Those who lived under Ratanji's reign remember, above all, his strictness. No one went to the movies, to the swimming hole, to the ice cream shop without permission—and permission was usually denied. Well into their twenties, Ranchhod and his brothers and cousins had to sneak alcohol if they wanted to drink.

Some, like Jayanti, now in Fiji as well, took this authoritarianism in stride. Some rebelled outright: one of Ranchhod's uncles left the company with all of his sons, amid a storm of ill will. Ranchhod, watching the drama, must have seen that there was no easy way for him to strike out on his own. Though he chafed under the restrictions, he contented himself with minor acts of subversion: bribing the cook to buy oranges at the Saturday market, then hiding the rare treats till after 10 P.M., when the older men were safely asleep and would not catch a whiff.

Their eldest brother, Chiman, seemed to step easily into his natural slot as their father's protégé. In 1954 the company issued new shares, and all three brothers were given one hundred each.

—Does this mean I can come to the meetings? Ranchhod asked his father.

—Come, but don't say anything, Ratanji told him.

It was Chiman who was learning the inner workings of the company's management at their father's right hand: Chiman whom their father had sent to bookkeeping classes, Chiman who had been allowed to start his own division dealing in electronic goods, and Chiman who had just been made secretary of the company, his father's obvious heir.

In truth Ranchhod did not mind the wholesale work, and had even come to enjoy the travel. But he was restless. Would he forever be a junior member of the company, bound to bow to the will of others? Fiji was a *damn jungle*, he thought, and he didn't like being in a British colony, whites strutting around as if they owned the place, which they did. Work was constant. If he put in just as much labor in his beloved India, he reasoned, he would get ahead on his own and be out from under the thumb of the family. He resolved that if he ever found himself home, he would not come back.

When he turned twenty-one, his chance came. His father had decided it was time to take Ranchhod home to get married. Ratanji went ahead on a bride-scouting mission.

Before undertaking the journey himself, Ranchhod wrote his father a letter spelling out his conditions: First, the girl should be more than twenty years old. Second, she would live wherever he lived, not be left to stay with his mother for months or years on end, as was the common practice. Third, he wrote, *Selection is yours, choice mine.* He had seen his elder brothers and sisters marry young without any say in the matter, and the troubles that had resulted. His mother was constantly fighting with her two daughters-in-law, both teenagers, one of whom was "running away from home" every other week — which meant going down the street to her relative's house crying and tearing at her hair, embarrassing both families. One of his sisters, scandalously, had fled her marriage and was living at home; eventually, hers would be one of the few divorces approved by the community's five-member council of elders in India. Though Ranchhod knew his marriage would be arranged, he wanted at least to have veto power.

Ratanji agreed. He had a few girls from good families in mind and had already ordered their horoscopes; all that remained was for the groom to arrive.

Ranchhod traveled by boat to Australia and then Sri Lanka, caught a plane to Bombay, and took the Flying Rani train with his father back to their home village, Navsari. On the train Ratanji struck up a conversation with a Khatri man from a neighboring town, who learned of their purpose and asked them to promise to visit him once before making a decision. He would, he said, show them some girls from good families.

They arrived in Navsari, and within a few days Ratanji went to meet the man. He returned with the horoscopes of two sisters, both of whose charts turned out to be compatible with Ranchhod's. Kaashi went to visit the girls and their family; then Ranchhod's eldest sister, Kamu, went. Ranchhod inquired, — All of you have seen the girls; perhaps I should go see them and choose?

— Absolutely not, came Ratanji's reply.

— Well then, at least tell me what are the names?

— Manjula and Lalita.

— I like Manjula, Ranchhod decided, and his father looked at him suspiciously. Had he somehow met the girl, or heard some gossip? Manjula was also the choice of Kaashi and Kamu, and Ratanji thought they had told. But Ranchhod was simply remembering a childhood playmate, a sweet girl who lived near his grandmother's house, who had the same name. On the strength of that association he chose a wife.

Ranchhod was told that he could see Manjula once, to fulfill the terms of his letter and give his consent, before the engagement was made final.

So he found himself one morning sitting on a bench in a stranger's house, feeling awkward in his best set of clothes and dusty from the long bus ride into town, his hair oiled neatly back from his face. On one side sat his father, on the other the matchmaker from the train; across the way were an uncle and an aunt. Nervously Ranchhod took tea, barely noticing who offered it, and waited. The men talked casually as they drank the milky chaa, aromatic with cardamom, black pepper, cloves. They finished, and stood.

—OK, said the matchmaker, —let's go, what do you think?

—What? Ranchhod was confused.

—Well, did you see her or not?

—No, I didn't see anyone.

—That girl who brought tea, didn't you see?

He had thought they would be introduced, sit, perhaps talk a little. Instead, he was meant to glimpse her out of the corner of one eye, and get to know her by the gesture of her hand as she lifted each cup from the tray. Even this minimal meeting was a liberalization, a nod toward changing times, and Ranchhod knew he was pressing his luck; but truly, he said, he did not see the girl.

Exasperated, the matchmaker agreed to set it up again, that very afternoon. This time he sat next to Ranchhod and nudged him when the girl appeared in the doorway.

She came in with the tea.

She kept her eyes to the floor.

She wore a sari, modestly wrapped, in a modest color.

She walked around the room. She set a cup down near each man.

She did not speak, and no one spoke to her.

She left.

There was nothing wrong with her that he could see in such a short encounter. It was a formality, in any case, his elders having already approved the match; for him to back out now would be a matter of shame.

When they reached home, Ranchhod's father wrote a postcard to the matchmaker: —Everything is all right. Let's plan the wedding.

Even in a culture rich with stories, not everything can be said. Underlying the network of *gupshup* and legend is another skin, a myofascia of silence—and it is this, as much as the spoken word, that holds the society together. A shared notion of what can be spoken and what cannot, and in what context, gives each story and each storyteller a framework, a set of rules under which to function. A generation ago, on that day and place, and in that family, this layer of silence encompassed not only sexuality but everything near to it: women's health and illness, pregnancy, marriage itself.

So it was that Manjula did not know to whom she served tea twice that day. Guests were frequent, and if they came with an agenda, it was not for her to know or ask. Modesty demanded that she not look up, for curiosity or any other reason, and certainly not at a strange young man — whether or not she sensed his intensity, whether or not she felt the hands of destiny rubbing together. One day she was a girl in her parents' house, serving tea. And the next she was to be married; would travel to another village, then abroad. Serving tea, staying out of things, was a skill that would serve her well in her in-laws' home.

A few months after the wedding, Manjula was pregnant, and Ranchhod was scheming about how to avoid going back to Fiji. The whole family went on holiday to Pune, a pleasant hill town about a day's journey from Navsari. Far enough that a man could live independently, but close enough to stay in touch, it seemed to Ranchhod a perfect place to look for work.

Discreetly he began making inquiries. A distant relative told him about a large wholesaler of household goods that was hiring. Ranchhod met with the owner, who explained the job. A train compartment would be his home for two years. The train would travel throughout India delivering and picking up goods, everything from spoons to tablecloths. In each town it would rest a few days. A cook would travel with him, and he could either take his wife along or visit her with a free train ticket every few months. The pay was five hundred rupees a month, a large sum, especially when he would have no rent or food expenses.

Ranchhod decided to take the job. He expected resistance: his father always wanted all hands in the family firm.

But instead of a tongue-lashing from Ratanji, Ranchhod was surprised to receive a letter from Uncle Magan, accompanied by a bank draft of £150: Come back to Fiji, we are opening a business in your name.

Hazrat Trading Company. His own firm. It had a nice ring to it. Once again, Uncle Magan had figured out how to persuade him, gently, that what the family wanted was also in Ranchhod's own interests.

Ranchhod turned down the train job, and prepared to sail back to Fiji with his wife.

His parents, still in India, wanted Ranchhod to leave his wife in Navsari to bring her child to term. Ranchhod refused; he didn't want to subject her to his mother's erratic temper, to the drama of mother-in-law and daughter-in-law that he had observed taking place with his brothers' wives. He and his father began another war of wills.

When Ranchhod went to the local travel agency, he found that Ratanji had forbidden the agent to sell him a ticket. No one in Navsari would help him procure passports and passage, for fear of his father's wrath. At length he and Manjula traveled to Bombay, applied directly to the passport and visa offices, and took the £150 bank draft to the P&O Shipping Co. As a result of the ad-hoc nature of the arrangements, they were given separate spaces on the same boat, one in first class and one in second class.

As they prepared to sail, Ratanji realized that his son had won a round. He came to see the young couple off, and even gave Ranchhod five pounds for the journey.

On board they managed to trade roommates so that husband and wife could share a cabin. In Sydney, Australia, the five pounds paid for a couple of nights in a room, with shared bathroom, at a place known as the People Palace, where passengers from India stayed in transit while waiting for a connection to New Zealand or Fiji. The outfit was run by a father-and-son team who treated the Indians well, lent money to those who needed it until they reached their destination, and even spoke a little Hindi. Ranchhod and Manjula caught the flight to Fiji and began their new life. It was 1957, and Ranchhod launched Hazrat Trading Co. with the great salmon caper.

Once Magan recovered from the shock of his nephew's salmon profit, he set about calling the bank and the collection agency, verifying the amount. It checked out. Ranchhod smiled.

—My debt is paid, right?

—Yes, Hazrat Trading Co.'s £500 is paid.

—And the £150?

—No, said Magan, —that is your personal debt to Narseys.

—No problem, Ranchhod said, —take it out of my company's account and pay it to Narseys.

Magan shook his head. —This company is not yours, it belongs to Narseys Limited. And you also work for Narseys.

That was how Ranchhod realized he was still a servant of the company, one who owed five months' salary.

Despite that disappointment, Ranchhod threw himself into business with a passion. While the salmon deal did not erase his debts, it did give him more clout within the family. He became a signatory on Narseys bank accounts and was given freer rein to run Hazrat Trading Co. as he saw fit.

And it gave him a chance to compete for his elders' respect, love, and attention. To be taken seriously, he vowed to make money—serious money, not for himself but for the company. He went about this in the systematic manner of a driven man.

First he went to the bank manager who had been so kind, and asked to learn everything about the business of money. For several months, two hours each afternoon, Ranchhod sat with the man as he closed out the day's accounts and imparted whatever practical knowledge he could to a student who knew very little English but had a head for numbers and a hunger for knowledge.

Second, Ranchhod set about making Hazrat Trading Co. a cash cow. Its opening represented another step of expansion for Narseys, into a business known as "indenting."

From the same root as "indenture," the word referred to an ancient method of writing contracts in duplicate, then laying the two papers or parchments together and cutting a notched line (*in-dentis,* Latin, "to make jagged like a row of teeth") so that they would match if reunited. *To indent* became the formal business term for "to request or order goods from, to make an order for (goods)." In other words, Ranchhod was a manufacturers' agent.

No longer did he live behind the store; now that he had a wife, he needed proper accommodations. They lived with Chiman and his wife, in a new complex just built by the family: sixteen apartments around a central courtyard. Ratanji's dream was that all of his relations would live there as one big happy family, a mini-Khatriville in the heart of Suva. Color-ful laundry hung from the railings, women called to one another with the day's news, children ran up and down the central staircase shouting and playing—and squabbles broke out regularly, with great displays of shouting and door slamming.

Settling into this new milieu, Manjula experienced the physical changes of pregnancy and motherhood, as well as the emotional changes of being in a new place and in a new family. And she faced them largely alone, for Ranchhod's mind and time were fully occupied by business.

Late one night in 1961, Ranchhod sat in his office with the day's corre-spondence spread before him. He was twenty-six years old, married, a father of two—their first child was a girl, the second a boy—and a man of business. His office light often burned late, like the Fiji night sounds bright around him, dogs barking, jungle insects rubbing their wings. With him was a distant cousin, Kanti, whom he counted as a close friend. Ranchhod was an established presence within Fiji's Gujarati business community, though he remained small fry within the family: not the company director that his father and uncle were, nor the secretary that his eldest brother was. Now he had a problem, and he and Kanti were going to figure it out.

On his desk were the day's letters, typed in English and ready to be mailed out: orders, payments, instructions for merchandise delivery. Kanti picked up the first one and read the company name aloud, and Ranchhod told him what the letter inside should say.

—But it doesn't say that at all, Kanti said. Letter after letter, the whole stack was wrong.

In the morning Ranchhod summoned his secretary, fired him, and determined—after a lifetime of resistance—to learn English. What the British Raj, his father and uncles and teachers, and his own ambition could not accomplish, his temper did. He wrote to Uncle Magan, tem-porarily in India, who gladly sent a book two inches thick: *The Univer-sal Eng.-Guj. Practical Dictionary (containing many useful hints for study and for business).* The dictionary makers knew their market. Ranchhod began to read it, one page at a time. "A: The first letter of the English al-phabet. One of the tunes in the European music. An indefinite article which means one or any one . . ."

In this choice of pedagogical method, he followed in the footsteps of his father. Ratanji had studied only a couple of grades in India; when he went to Fiji at age fourteen, he could barely read Gujarati. But business required dealings in English, so his uncle Jiwan gave him an English–Gujarati dictionary, the only book they had that could bridge the two languages. — Study this, Ratanji was told. The men lived behind the store in those days; there was no desk, no table lamp. Young Ratanji went out under the streetlight after the day's work was done and memorized the dictionary, one word at a time.

Now Ranchhod was doing the same, although he had the luxury of studying indoors. As he progressed, he started reading daily headlines in the *Fiji Times,* dictionary by his side.

To encourage him, Uncle Magan wrote to two British companies with whom Narseys had dealings, explaining that his nephew was learning English and would be writing the correspondence to them from now on, as practice, and that he would appreciate their help in his nephew's education. For the letters, Ranchhod painstakingly arranged English sentences using the dictionary, a process that guaranteed errors of grammar and syntax. His typist was under instructions to type the letters exactly as written, in duplicate: one for the British traders to keep, the other double-spaced for them to correct and send back.

After a few months Ranchhod also began working with a Hong Kong company run by Gujaratis. He told them about his informal lessons, and they offered to help by sending him not only a corrected version of his English letters but also a Gujarati translation of what he had written, so that he could better understand where his mistakes lay.

As his English improved, the company's lawyer — a family friend — suggested a next level: that Ranchhod read the *Royal Gazette,* in which Fiji's new laws and regulations were published, and explain them to Magan to the best of his understanding. His banker then suggested a book, building on their earlier lessons together: *How to Beat the Bank.* In this way Ranchhod slowly gained a practical education in business, banking, and law as he learned English.

His studies enabled him to work independently and to expand his ambition to the English-speaking world — or at least as much of it as could be accessed from Fiji. Armed with samples, typewriter, and carbon paper (the modern version of notching), he began traveling the South Pacific, hawking the wares of the world to Indian, Chinese, white, and indigenous shopkeepers. He brought back profits, and stories: braving ghosts and malaria in Papua New Guinea, swallowing terrible food (*only nuts and pig meat*) in Samoa, overcoming racism to get served a beer in Australia. His passport filled up with exotic stamps: Tonga, the Cook Islands, Tahiti, the Solomon Islands, Vanuatu, Wallis and Futuna, Hong Kong, New Zealand.

The world began coming to Fiji, too. Long a favorite destination of cruise ships from Australia and New Zealand, Suva was the most developed among the tropical ports of the South Pacific—and the one that afforded tourists the most shopping opportunities, thanks largely to its Gujarati storekeepers. In 1963, Fiji hosted the South Pacific Games and launched a campaign to market itself as a "duty-free" shopping destination. When the government published a directory to guide visitors to the Games around Suva, Narseys purchased full-page advertisements on the inside front and back covers ("Now available in Fiji—Olympus Pen Range Cameras—Sole Distributor"). That year, 24,246 tourists came to Fiji. By the end of the decade, the annual number would more than quadruple.

Suddenly Chiman's pet project, importing electronics to Fiji, was paying off; it positioned Narseys to exploit the new trend. In addition to cameras, transistor radios had recently been invented, replacing the large, valve-style radios of previous years. Hi-fi sound systems, electric shavers and fans, and similar gadgets were just becoming affordable. Soon, consumer electronics became the cornerstone of an expanding economic bubble in Fiji. Virtually every Khatri shopkeeper posted blazing DUTY FREE banners in the windows and began stocking cassette players, radios, watches, pens, cigarette lighters, and other goods for the tourist market. Two or three times a week, a cruise ship would pull into the harbor at 6:30 A.M. The brass band of the Fiji Royal Military Force welcomed the boatload of tourists, then led a two-block parade up to the main shopping area. Storefronts that had once featured clothing and household goods now sported the latest gadgets, each proclaiming with loud signs and sidewalk solicitors that its prices were the best. Even the owner of the eating lodge, whose family had served up meals to working Indian men since early in the century, converted his prime downtown space to a duty-free shop. Most tourists were from New Zealand and Australia, where taxes on electronics were high. Seduced by the low prices into a kind of consumerist trance, they carted away several radios each, half a dozen cassette recorders or cameras, as much as they could carry for themselves and to give away as gifts.

For the shopkeepers, retail was no longer a subsistence economy—it was a booming business. Narseys entered a partnership with another Khatri family firm to import Matsushita transistor radios from Japan on an exclusive basis for the entire South Pacific. The first year, Narhari Electronics sold more than one hundred thousand transistor radios. In another sign of boom times, the Bank of Baroda, Gujarat, set up a branch in downtown Suva. Many Gujaratis moved their business there, where they could obtain loans more easily than at a white bank and deposit money directly into accounts for families back home.

The boom improved business for everyone, even those not dealing in electronics. As head of Hazrat Trading, Ranchhod was turning a profit every year, making money for the parent company again and again. Manjula bore two more children: a second son in 1962, a second daughter in 1969. Ranchhod, traveling for three or four months at a time and working long hours when he was in town, missed much of his four children's growing up; later he would say with regret, —I never even knew when my sons started school.

His business was to sell everything: ready-made shirts, quick-release ice cube trays from Japan, saris he designed himself by cutting and pasting patterns he found appealing. In the bazaar he spotted colorful traditional Fijian bark designs on paper, and arranged them in a block for shirt fabric that became a bestseller. He followed his own taste, ordering black velvet scrolls that featured the map of Fiji in colored thread and glitter; for a time, nearly every Fiji Gujarati home had one prominently displayed.

But nothing was as sweet as that first deal: the surprised, shocked faces of his elders who could hardly believe that this boy, this headstrong, illiterate boy, could turn such a profit. He had disobeyed orders, he had used his own wits, found his own sources, and won. And that spirit stayed with him.

Business was a constant challenge, not only against the market but against what was expected of him. It was a realm in which he was able to earn a grudging recognition and respect, certainly from outsiders and to some extent from his own family. And through it, Fiji became home.

To be a Narsey in Suva in the 1960s and '70s was to live a rarefied life: to be a big fish, albeit in a tiny pond. Every housewife in the city knew your surname, had bought a yard of cloth or a plastic hanger or a handkerchief from one of your uncles, cousins, or employees. At the town's major retail intersection, your family name stood in tall yellow letters, facing off smartly with the white-run department stores whose corporate headquarters were in Australia or New Zealand. The latest goods came through your shop, and you could satisfy any passion from audiocassettes to zoom lenses.

By day you were a boss; by evening you drank—Ranchhod was old enough now—at the Merchants Club. There, your account was always open, your father's photograph was on the wall, and someone you knew was always ready to share a round of whiskey, poker, and gossip. Ratanji, one of the club's five founding members in 1952, was president in 1967; his main feat was arranging for a giant refrigerator from America to hold sufficient quantities of beer, juice, and soda. The club was exclusively for Gujarati men, merchants, who were excluded from the white bars and did not want to drink in the native Fijian ones. On Christmas Day they opened it to wives and children for an annual party. Ratanji and his dear friends Narotam and Kalyaan cooked the goat stew.

With the duty-free boom and the income from Hazrat Trading, for the first time it was both possible and profitable for Narseys to consider a capital investment. Ratanji's ambition for the company could now take more concrete form—literally. Fiji's first concrete factory had opened, and with it the potential to build a real, modern department store.

Narseys occupied two prime pieces of real estate, dominating the intersection of Renwick and Ellery streets in downtown Suva. On one corner were Ranchhod's offices and the duty-free store, along with a few tenant-shopkeepers. That building had been erected of Oregon timber in the early 1900s to house the original presses of the *Fiji Times*, back when Suva first became the capital of Fiji. It was sturdy enough for decades to come.

But across the corner, the clothing and housewares departments of Narseys filled up four narrow wooden structures on the plot where Motiram had originally set up his tailoring shop. The decades had taken their toll. In 1966, Ratanji commissioned architects to design a modern two-story building for the site.

Blueprints completed in July 1967 showed how construction would unfold in three phases, to allow business to continue unimpeded. Mango and other fruit trees would be cut down. On a vacant section of the land that had once served as a vegetable garden, a temporary wood-and-tin shed would be erected to house the retail operations during construction.

The new building was finished in October 1969. On the ground floor, glass doors opened into a broad, vinyl-tiled retail area with interior fittings imported from New Zealand, flexible enough for the changing needs of a modern department store. Out back, rolling aluminum shutters and a modern loading dock allowed for smooth daily deliveries. An elevator glided upstairs to spacious offices, storage areas lit by skylights, and a tearoom for the staff.

It was the perfect symbol of Ratanji's grand designs for an empire: a gleaming two-story edifice in a one-story town constructed of wood, iron, and tin. Where other buildings displayed their posts and pillars, the new Narseys was Fiji's first curtain-wall building, supported by concrete beams and columns hidden behind a "curtain" of glass and aluminum. Its piling went down seventy feet into the earth—a foundation that could accommodate growth up to seven floors.

After its completion Ratanji went on an extended vacation. For the first time, he took his wife with him, perhaps hoping to satisfy a lifetime of complaints. The plan was to tour the Far East, where he had business contacts, visit their daughters in Toronto and London, and catch their son's doctoral graduation ceremony in Iowa City.

In Japan, they posed for photographs with geishas, ate bowls of noodles and strangely sticky rice, visited the zoo. At the Tokyo airport, they checked their baggage, weighed down with gifts for their children and grandchildren, for the flight to Toronto.

In the waiting area, Ratanji clutched his chest, gasped, and collapsed. Perhaps stress had taken a toll on his health, or perhaps it was simply his time. At age sixty-two, he was dead of a sudden, massive heart attack.

. . .

Only once in their lives did all eight of Ratanji's children gather in one place: at his funeral. As the body was flown in from the east, his far-flung children, whom he had planned to visit, flew in from the west: Kamu from London, Lila from Toronto, my father from Iowa. The others were already in Fiji.

Ratanji left two wills, one in Fiji, one in India. The latter, typewritten in Gujarati, was registered earlier that year in India "because I have reached an advanced age and whether I live or die is in God's hands." The rest was matter-of-fact, describing each beneficiary in legal terms. Ranchhod, for instance, was "my son Ranchhod, occupation shopkeeper, from Navsari, living in Suva . . . Khatri by caste." Cash and company shares were divided among the children. The two youngest sons, my father and his brother, inherited two houses in India. The youngest son was to live in the family house in Fiji, on the condition that he care for his mother there for the rest of her life.

But Ratanji left no written instructions for stewardship of the company. Uncle Magan had died a few years earlier, during the construction of the building; his shares had been divided among his own children, with no one gaining a decisive majority. After the thirteen-day period of mourning for Ratanji, the board of directors met to decide the company's fate.

The Narseys board was not accustomed to meeting. It had expanded from its original size, five members with five hundred shares each, to thirteen cousins and uncles holding more than one hundred thousand shares among them. Minutes were filed regularly, in accordance with the law; they listed members present, members who sent apologies for their absence, decisions made, topics discussed. And they were pure fiction.

The truth was that Ratanji had made the decisions; Chiman, as company secretary and his father's protégé, had recorded them; and everyone else went along. Ranchhod was not the only shareholder who had been instructed, for many years, to keep silent.

So the official minutes of the meeting of May 16, 1970, provide little clue as to the discussion that took place. Three members lived in India; presumably the other ten were present. Ranchhod's version is that his brother Chiman simply proclaimed himself head of the company.

Ranchhod was galled. By now he had learned to keep his temper largely under wraps, at least around his elders, so he waited for someone else to speak up. Thakor ("Tom") was the living person with the most shares, and had been co-director with Ratanji; surely he would say something.

But Tom was nodding in agreement.

At last Ranchhod, summoning all the calm he could muster, said, —Brother, not like that. The board should decide. This seat is empty, who should it be? And if there is more than one person, we should have an election, do it properly.

But no one in the family had any experience with debate, disagreement, or voting. There was a shocked silence.

—No, no, said Tom at last. —Everything is fine; there is no need to do all that.

The minutes, as filed in the Narseys Ltd. folder at the Registrar of Companies in downtown Suva, state simply, "It was resolved and agreed that Mr. Chimanlal R. Narsey be appointed as a Director to fill the vacancy created by the death of Mr. R. M. Narsey."

Ranchhod might have hoped, but he would have been naïve to think, that a different decision could have been reached. Chiman had started in the company at age nineteen, risen through all of the departments, and learned the inner workings of management. He was in the number-two job before his father died. Everyone knew that Ratanji was grooming Chiman as his replacement, and no records indicate that Chiman's performance was anything but exemplary.

But Ranchhod would always believe that things should have been different. Word had come to him, he maintained years later, that his father was about to depose Chiman. A business associate in Hong Kong had told Ranchhod that his father was planning the move as soon as he returned to Fiji. Ratanji, the man said, intended to put Ranchhod in Chiman's seat instead.

What interests me about this rumor is less its veracity—a tale older than I am, regarding a company now dismembered—than the light in my uncle's eyes as he told me of it. Sixty-six years old, suffering from a rare and terminal lung disease that left him weak and coughing like a much older man, suddenly he seemed to me a mere boy. Still wanting, and working desperately to convince himself of, his father's love.

And as I write these lines I am aware of a great anxiety in me. Do I really want to revive the story of these disputes—reigniting, perhaps, a second-generation rivalry among several sets of cousins over whose father deserved to run the company? It can hardly make a difference now. But the hard feelings persist; in interview after interview, my father's relatives dig out old grudges like favorite scabs. A storyteller among storytellers, I listen; then I write, despite my doubts as to whether or not I have the right. For I, too, have inherited the family traits: stubbornness, quick temper, the bearing of grudges, and perhaps a deep desire to understand. We tell one another these stories over and over, as if the telling has some value, is itself part of the mesh that holds our family together, even if the content is of being torn apart. And from time to time we vow to stop telling certain tales, or to cut ties and step back into more distant relationships, or to put an end to the gossip and the quarreling altogether.

But these vows are like the pale petals of a Japanese maple outside my writing window this late March: beautiful, fragile, impossible to keep.

With the passing of his father and his uncle Magan—his protector and comforter and mentor, the only man who really understood him—Ranchhod was truly an adult. Thirty-five years old, he would now have to navigate the swamp of family politics alone. Because of his act of outspokenness, Ranchhod believed that his brother saw him as a threat and held a grudge against him ever after. Over small details and a larger vision for the company, they butted heads until Ranchhod chose retreat, of a sort. He would be king of his own corner of Narseys, and increasingly confined to it.

At home, there were other stresses.

His youngest daughter was constantly sick, and no one knew what was wrong; later she would be diagnosed with scoliosis so severe it required corrective surgeries. Then Manjula became pregnant again. Their fifth child, a girl, lived only a few hours. They dressed her satin and lace, and placed her in the coffin with a milk bottle in her arms.

It had been a hard birth, and Manjula was confined to bed for months afterward. It became clear how much work she had done, in her steady and unassuming manner. The burden of caring for the younger children shifted to the eldest daughter, with help from Ranchhod's sister and sisters-in-law, who naturally resented the extra work. Ranchhod had no idea how to handle domestic quarrels; Manjula's calm temperament had shielded him from them. From his children, he demanded obedience of a kind unrealistic for even those of the quietest nature.

When they failed, he took out his belt. And used it, beating the flesh of his flesh until, one time, the buckle hit so hard it drew blood. The child was crying, shaking, trembling; twelve years old, on the verge of adulthood, but clearly no adult. And not the real target of his rage, not the real cause of his frustration.

Ranchhod put the belt away, and never used it again. The scar, which would last for decades, was inflicted around the same time that the company's reins were passing to Chiman. There was so little that Ranchhod could control.

Years later, my cousin would recall this last and worst beating by saying, *At this stage if someone said it they would call it abusing.* At the time, though, it was a father's prerogative — and an echo, perhaps, of many generations, many childhoods. For everyone in our family has an opinion or an anecdote of the family temperament, variously described as hot-tempered, quick to judge, stubborn, *jabri* (shrewish) for women, *garam* (hot) for men. Whether they speak of it or not, everyone also knows the underside of this temper falling on the children, for which the modern English word "abuse" is an uncomfortable fit. No one has yet found a framework that can hold the whole telling.

Alone among my relatives, my uncle Ranchhod — after listening to my carefully rehearsed, pre-interview spiel about how this book would be public, how he should tell me if he wanted to keep anything off the record — shook his head impatiently. *That's your job,* he told me; *I trust you, dikraa.* Dear; daughter. Perhaps he knew he would not survive to read or vet these words; perhaps he knew that each storyteller makes his or her own version, and that the stories themselves belong to no one. And if any further justification or absolution is needed for telling this story, perhaps it is the weight and light of that trust.

I do not believe that merely airing a story heals it; but perhaps it can be a kind of honoring, of all the pain.

. . .

Over the next decade and a half, Narseys continued to grow under Chiman's leadership. Suva's duty-free business faded as other ports learned how to compete, but other enterprises sprang up. Narseys diversified into manufacturing, led by an energetic young cousin of Ranchhod's who had seen his first glimpse of the world while the two traveled together on a buying trip in 1977. Within a few years the cousin, eager to bring Narseys into the age of industrial progress, persuaded Chiman to let him start a plastics factory. At its peak in the 1980s, Narseys consisted of the plastics factory, the glass-front department store, Hazrat Trading, the Ratan shoe factory (named for Motiram's mother), a retail shoe store, an audiovisual outfit run by Chiman's eldest son, a wholesale liquor division, some rental real estate, a store that sold sewing machines, and major stakes in a flour mill and a sanitary-napkin factory.

Though Ranchhod had never managed to separate himself from his father's firm, he wanted a different fate for his children. He borrowed money to send his eldest son to study accounting in India, and incurred another loan to pay for his older daughter's wedding. In 1983, when both sons were old enough, they decided to buy a small tailoring firm. Each time, Ranchhod turned to the "bank of Gujarat," the informal network of Gujarati shopkeepers and businessmen who financed one another's ventures as a way of helping loyal friends, as well as investing their own profits for a percentage return.

This debt came on top of the regular loans from Narseys that virtually all of the partners were taking, and which ultimately were part of the company's downfall. By the 1980s, Narseys wages were too low to sustain the lifestyle that family members felt they deserved. The company financed cars, mortgages, "world tour" vacations, even extraordinary household expenses for almost all of its dozen shareholders. Some were under the impression that they were merely taking advances on their salaries; accounts were kept in the office, but no scheme of repayment was introduced, and most had no idea how much they or anyone else owed. As "loans to company directors" made up a greater and greater portion of the bottom line, regular minutes and annual reports were filed in the official books for meetings that never took place and spreadsheets never seen or discussed by the shareholders.

This hidden story was deeply out of sync with the official one and, as always in such cases, taboo to discuss. When someone tried to raise an issue, as Ranchhod occasionally did, he was immediately admonished; decrying his cousins and uncles as "a bunch of yes-men" hardly helped his cause. One cousin would later describe the company as a "gravy train" whose seemingly limitless supply no one wanted to interrupt with dissent. The chief executive, Chiman, was hardly in a position to rein in the spending or introduce fiscal austerity; his own debt was among the highest.

To outsiders, and as far as most of the families knew, Narseys was riding high. Stylish mannequins and the latest electronics sparkled from glass storefronts downtown, and virtually every year a new venture was announced, each financed by a bank loan. Ratanji's legacy, the stately building of glass and concrete, turned out to be a dual one. In retrospect, the mortgage undertaken to build it seems to have set off a corporate habit of borrowing on a large scale.

As business conditions in Fiji changed, it was hard for the tradition-minded company to shift gears completely. The retail side became less and less profitable, but creative bookkeeping rearranged the manufacturing and indenting/wholesaling profits to show a positive bottom line in all departments. Then Chiman decided to close Hazrat Trading, combining its activities with the Narseys wholesale department. Ranchhod found himself without a unit to run.

After years of relative autonomy, it was a bitter pill. Ranchhod found himself assigned trivial duties: chaperoning his divorcée sister on a pilgrimage to India, working as backup for Jayanti in the retail department.

Yet Narseys continued to expand, the story of its prosperity embellished even as each new venture added to the scaffolding of debt and creative bookkeeping. The company took out loans not only for capital investment but also for operating expenses. At the end it would be dismantled bit by bit, revealing that much of what had held it up was air.

Two events triggered the collapse: a coup and a death.

In May 1987, native Fijians staged a military coup whose stated aim was to end Indian domination of the island's economy. Looting, violence, and another coup four months later set off a panic. By now the pattern was familiar to Gujaratis, who typically had relatives or networks that extended to other countries where they had become victims of just such an economic backlash. Most Fiji Gujaratis who could afford it—especially those whose businesses and wealth were prime targets for looters—began looking for a way out.

The men of Narseys leveraged their business and political contacts to emigrate. Ranchhod's brother Jayanti fled to America, where he had a married daughter. Through a tailoring client, Ranchhod's sons managed to obtain hastily procured visas to New Zealand. Ranchhod and Manjula followed. Eventually they would all resettle near the Gold Coast of Australia, where his elder daughter sponsored them, and where the weather was warm and familiar.

The New Zealand and Australia that accepted Ranchhod's family in the late 1980s were far friendlier than they had been only a short time before. Almost since its inception as a British colony, Oceania's largest continent had determined to be a "white Australia." Its early settlers squeezed the Aboriginal population into ever-smaller areas, then imported "coloured" labor from nearby islands as well as China and India. At one point Chinese made up twenty percent of the male population of the mining province of Victoria. But the backlash came swiftly, and typically. A race riot by white vigilantes in 1857 was followed by anti-Chinese restrictions, which paved the way for xenophobic legislation that sought to restrict all Asian and other nonwhite immigration. As in South Africa, the British refused to sanction overtly racist laws, and this became an impetus for Australians to seek independence. One of the first legislative acts of the autonomous federation of Australian states was the Immigration Restriction Act of 1901. It introduced the infamous dictation test, widely copied around the world, whose primary goal was to keep out nonwhites. The "white Australia" policy was articulated as one of survival, a cornerstone of the national identity. The country's powerful agreed that they needed a growing settler population, but only of a certain stripe. Not until 1958 was the dictation test dropped, and Australia began accepting part-Asians and light-skinned Asians (such as the Dutch of Indonesia and the "burghers" of Sri Lanka), as long as they did not look "to be less than 75 percent European in appearance." White citizens' "coloured" spouses were still being deported, and white Europeans were actively recruited and given economic stipends and bonuses if they migrated to Australia.

Still, a momentum for change was building. During the 1960s, thanks to the civil rights and anticolonial movements, ideals of racial nondiscrimination took hold among First World policymakers and their constituents. In 1965, the United States repealed its ban on Asian immigration, using instead a system of quotas for each nation. In 1966, Australia began allowing nonwhites with technical or professional skills to enter, and several thousand Asians filtered in. At last, in 1973, the 1901 act was fully repealed.

Then Australia opted for an even more progressive system than the United States had, one that would not discriminate on the basis of race, color, or national origin. Instead, each potential immigrant would be evaluated on a "points" system, earning a score based on such factors as education, technical or professional training, and relatives already in Australia. "White Australia" was dead. Under this system, a handful of Fiji Khatris had made their way there well before the coup, including Ranchhod's older daughter, whose husband qualified by virtue of his accounting credentials.

In New Zealand, change had come more slowly—only a year before the coup, just in time for the Fiji Indians. New Zealand was an inward-looking, isolationist sort of place, with more sheep than people and glad to keep it so. But it was also polite, civil, and liberal: New Zealanders did not like to think of themselves as racists. They were certainly not like the barbarous whites of South Africa, for example. Besides, in the early 1980s New Zealand was suffering a population decline so drastic that newspaper cartoons joked, "Last one out, turn the lights off." Self-deprecating humor masked a national anxiety and an economic crisis in the making. The country was experiencing its own miniature "brain drain" as educated and skilled young New Zealanders left for better work opportunities abroad, in Europe and America. Something had to be done to boost the country's educated elite. In 1986 New Zealand allowed its doors to swing both ways. For Ranchhod's family, emigrating after the 1987 coup, it was the luckiest of timing.

And then, in May 1988, Chiman died.

Back in Fiji for the funeral, Ranchhod attended another emergency board meeting. The irony did not escape him: his chance to run the company had come too late. Retired, committed to staying with his family in Australia, he tried to give advice to whoever would listen. When he left Fiji again, cousins took control and worked to keep the firm running.

But there were new challenges, never faced in Narseys' eight decades in business. Fiji's economy was in crisis as its major trading partners, Australia and New Zealand, instituted economic sanctions, hoping to pressure the coup leaders into restoring a legitimate government. Indian emigration was draining the country of its skilled professionals, business owners, and workers; nearly forty thousand people left Fiji in the three years after the coup, more than in the entire decade up to that point. Tourism was nonexistent. Manufacturing slowed as skilled workers and managers emigrated. Exports and imports were cut off. In every possible sense, business was bad.

And Narseys was vulnerable. With three strong partners gone and no system in place for nurturing leadership, the company felt at times rudderless. Infighting erupted; everyone had his own theory about what was going wrong.

—*It was Chiman who ran the company into the ground.* —*No! Chiman was a saint, a good man who helped everyone.* —*Too nice, he never said no.* —*He liked to play the big man, giving out cash that wasn't his own.* —*Everyone was used to the company being a gravy train. They killed the golden egg goose.* —*It wasn't his fault; there were too many dead dummies who didn't work hard, who never thought of the good of the company, only themselves.* —*Who are you calling a dead dummy!?* —*And by the way, you owed money to my father, and I intend to collect!* —*You cheated us in that deal.* —*I don't know why he never liked me, us.* —*How they treated us when we were young . . . when we were old . . . when we were poor . . . when we worked so hard . . .*

The elders blamed the younger generation for abandoning traditional ways; the younger men blamed those who failed to adapt with the times. Cousins overseas blamed mismanagement by those who remained; those who stayed blamed the emigrants, who sought to cash out their company shares to start new lives. Did migration accelerate the decline of the business, or did the dismal economic climate precipitate migration? Whatever the case, years of bickering and turmoil culminated in a board meeting on the evening of May 7, 1992, shortly after the workday ended. According to the official minutes, ten shareholders were present. Ranchhod was not among them. The meeting began at 5:40 P.M.; the men talked for an hour and twenty minutes. The minutes recorded simply, "It was finally resolved to liquidate the assets of Narseys Limited."

Liquidate: it was a fluid, poetic word for a process that many family members experienced as brutal. Over the three years it took to dissolve the company, the Narsey temper flared up again and again. Minutes were written and rewritten as participants objected to how their remarks had been characterized. Some who expected payouts for their shares were shocked to learn that they were deeply in debt to the firm, and said they had no way of paying. Some objected to the official audits and had their own audits conducted. Face to face and in transcontinental memos and faxes, they argued over prices, valuations, processes—until eventually every last building and business was bought by a family member, sold off to the highest bidder, or simply shut down.

The day in 1994 that the Narseys store closed its doors for the last time, Ranchhod was in Brisbane, Australia. It was October: spring at the south of the world, the days beginning to grow long, hot, and bright.

For once Ranchhod was glad not to be in Suva: not to have to walk past the empty glass display windows and darkened entryway, the permanent CLOSED sign indicating, in a way, the family's shared and humiliating failure. It would have broken his heart, it would have filled him with rage; in the Gujarati idiom, it caused his liver to ache. No one had sweated more than he had for the company, he felt; he had wandered night and day in the jungle, it had made him who he was.

He was not a refugee but a kind of exile. Brisbane, on Australia's sunny Gold Coast, was pleasant enough; his four children and their families lived nearby, and with only a little imagination he could still feel and smell the warm breezes of the South Pacific. In the white man's land one could be comfortable; one might seize opportunities and make one's way. But one would never feel quite at home. Only for the sake of his sons had he migrated.

But on closing day, he was grateful for each of the one thousand eight hundred miles of sea that separated him from the epicenter of his grief.

Ranchhod would travel back to Fiji once more, for his younger daughter's wedding. While there, he would begin coughing uncontrollably—a condition that, upon his return to Australia, was diagnosed as a rare lung disease. Slowly, over a period of years, his lungs would turn rigid as bone. It was becoming more and more difficult to breathe.

In 2003 his last two grandchildren were born: twin boys, to Ranchhod's younger daughter, who considered them a medical and divine miracle. Two sons, two daughters, with two children each. — Now my family is complete, Ranchhod told Manjula. He was now the oldest brother left, Jayanti having died in 1999 in California. Already Ranchhod was on oxygen twenty-four hours a day, in constant pain, unable to speak for more than a few minutes without coughing. A few months afterward, shortly after the New Year and his sixty-ninth birthday, he went into the hospital for the last time.

A year before, he had asked his doctor how long he had to live. The doctor had looked at him with sympathy: — Every day that you wake up, Ranchhod, thank God for it.

Now, with his family around him — including Chiman's widow and youngest son, who had also moved to Australia — he made his peace.

— If you have hurt me, I forgive you, he told each of his loved ones.
— And if I have injured you in any way, please, I beg your forgiveness.

In a ritual act, he had each one place a teaspoonful of water in his mouth.

Then he slipped off into a deep morphine sleep, a prayer to his favorite goddess on his lips.

At the funeral, members of the local lawn-bowling club, of which Ranchhod had been an avid member and the first "black" president, came and sat among the gathered clan. Two granddaughters spoke, eloquent and openhearted and beautiful as only teenage girls can be, one barely able to make it through her sentences. My father and my uncle Manhar, the two surviving sons of Ratanji and Kaashi Narsey, were there to pay their respects. Arrayed around the coffin were wreaths and bouquets sent by Ranchhod's sisters and other kin all over the world: Toronto, London, California, New Zealand. And Fiji, where the youngest cousin was still running Narseys Plastics and where the Narseys name still stood on a wooden building at a downtown corner, recently designated as a historic site. Someone else now looked out the second-story office window where Ranchhod had spent the good part of thirty years, those he had come to think of as his best. The boy who had once regarded the wild island as intolerable had grown, in exile, into an elder who came to see Fiji as a true paradise. If there was heaven on earth, surely it involved beaches and sunshine and one's own people all around; drinking buddies, feasts, people recognizing and respecting you when you walked down the street, listening to and laughing over your stories.

pArt thRee: CItIZeNS

1984

Estimated size of the Indian diaspora: 4,599,063
Countries with more than 10,000 people of Indian origin: 33

1. South Africa
2. England and Wales
3. Guyana
4. Trinidad and Tobago
5. USA
6. Fiji
7. United Arab Emirates
8. Canada
9. Singapore
10. Surinam
11. Saudi Arabia
12. Oman
13. Netherlands
14. Yemen (PDR)
15. Kenya
16. Kuwait
17. Tanganyika
18. Qatar
19. Bahrain
20. Muskat/Muscat
21. Iraq
22. Zambia
23. Mozambique
24. Iran
25. Indonesia
26. Thailand
27. Australia
28. Nigeria
29. Germany (FRG)
30. Hong Kong
31. Jordan
32. New Zealand
33. Libya

6. BRAINS

We have built universities, technological institutions, and national
science laboratories but they are emptier than before because they
are constantly being drained . . . Indeed, our entire educational
system has become a big liaison and passport office.
 — "India," paper presented at an international conference
on the "brain drain," August 1967

Ratanji and Kaashi (*Fiji*)   Narotam and Benkor (*Fiji*)

↓ |
↓
Kamu (*England*)
Chiman (*Fiji*)   Sarasvati (*India*)
Kanchan (*Canada*)   Pushpa (*Fiji*)
Jayanti (*USA*)   Tara (*Fiji*)
Ranchhod (*Australia*)   Champak (*USA*)
BHUPENDRA (*USA*)   *m.*   BHANU (*USA*)
Manhar (*Fiji*)
Lila (*Canada*)

*I*N THE SUMMER of 1963, my mother and father stood a few feet apart on the same dock, gazing up at the same ship. The *Oriana* was a gleaming white ocean liner about to embark for the western coast of North America, thousands of miles across the pure blue thrash of the Pacific.

They did not know each other, yet.

My father, Bhupendra, twenty-one years old, was traveling from Fiji to the New World to study. My mother, Bhanu, age sixteen, was at the dock to see her brother off. The two young men were the first of their community to go to the United States for education. Their fathers were friends and drinking buddies; over casual conversation, each had made the decision—despite some reservations—to buy his son one-way passage. And both mothers were on the verge of weeping.

As the families said their farewells, only a tiny hint of the future could be heard, a stage whisper from my mother's elder sister to their brother:
—Keep an eye on that young man; I think he will be good for Bhanu.

And so my mother glanced at my father for the first time.

She noticed his loose-fitting pants, how he kept calling to his mother, pointing out to her various features of the ship: —Ma, look at this, he said, —and this, Ma, and this.

—Isn't he nice-looking, my mother's sister said, nudging her.

—Maa! Maa! my mother mocked, bleating like a sheep. She was still in high school, a popular girl, star student, and basketball center; her mind was not on marriage. As she watched her brother and her father's friend's son disappear up the gangplank, she had no idea that this stranger would become the most important man in her life.

I imagine the very beginning of each of my parents' lives, long before they converge: egg and sperm meeting, dividing, differentiating, a bundle of human tissue hurtling toward human being. In the third week after conception, before either of my grandmothers even knows she is pregnant, a certain layer of cells known as the ectoderm begins to thicken. This is the beginning of neural development: what will become the brain.

My father's brain, my mother's brain. By the time of birth, eight and a half months later, it is doing everything it will ever do—controlling bodily functions, taking in sensations, learning. According to the Enlightenment philosophers of Europe, it is a tabula rasa: a blank slate awaiting mathematics, morality, language; a repository of free will. In the Hindu understanding, it is the reincarnation of an ancient karmic stream already destined to grow, migrate, and make me.

As Bhanu and Bhupendra grew up, their brains became more than their individual organs. Among the most educated young people ever produced by their community, they migrated in their twenties from the Third World to the First. The leap was momentous, not only for them and their future children, but also because it was part of a worldwide pattern so remarkable that it developed its own experts and statistics, its own terminology: the brain drain.

Coined in 1962 to describe the large-scale migration of skilled technocrats from Britain to the United States, the term was quickly co-opted to describe a related, even more dramatic phenomenon: the movement of educated professionals from developing countries, particularly India and China, to developed nations, particularly the United States. Critics saw the brain drain as a large-scale theft by the world's wealthiest nations of the intangible assets of countries that could ill afford to lose their brightest young people. Apologists defended what they saw as merely the free market at work. "Brains go where money is," argued one, while, in the version preferred by *Science* magazine in 1965, "Brains go where brains are . . . where there is a challenge . . . where brains are valued." Thousands of articles and books, hundreds of thousands of academic and conference hours, and even several rounds of hearings before the U.S. Congress and the United Nations were devoted to various aspects of the brain

drain: solutions to the problem, if it was a problem; analysis of the statistics, laced with regret that better statistics were not available; and pur-
ported calculations of the lost value to its native country of each
"drained" brain (estimates ranged from $20,000 to $75,000). My parents'
brains, and those of millions of others who migrated during the 1960s
and '70s, were no longer their individual properties alone; they were commodities for the West.

At root, the experts wanted to know what I, child of such migrants,
also wonder: How did these men and women, crème de la crème, come
to travel from one world to the next? And why—despite their deeply
rooted histories, despite the difficulties of exile, and even sometimes despite themselves—did they stay?

When my mother speaks of her childhood, it is a rush of sensory details,
tastes, smells, sounds, flowers and plants and weather patterns of her
beloved Fiji, where she was born and, except for a few childhood years
in India, raised. I grew up in Michigan knowing that Fiji tasted of
tamarind plucked fresh from the tree, climbed by her, a fearless girl in a
school skirt, throwing the stiff brown pods with their dark, sweet-sour
meat down to her friends, who were all afraid to climb. I felt the wet heat
of daily five-minute rain showers, drying off in just minutes in the tropical sea air. I dream-ate mangoes every way they came: green, sour, tart,
sliced with salt; or pickled in chili oil, sugar, salt, fenugreek; or sliced ripe
and orange; or smoothed into soup. I knew the pleasure of her childhood mischief, running easily away from an arthritic-kneed mother; or
of mixing yogurt, salt, mustard seed, chili, and cucumber into *raita* and
eating the whole bowlful atop the tin roof alone as she read her schoolbooks. Of playing basketball: organizing the first girls' intramural team
at the Indian school, designing uniforms (short, sleeveless dresses with
pleated skirts and green trim), running and dribbling and leaping across
the courts at the botanical gardens, losing almost every game to teams
of Fijian girls who seemed twice as tall. Shopping for luxurious dress fabrics at the Narseys store, where she once saw the governor's wife shop,
and where her father in flush times would tell the "uncle" behind the
counter,—Give Bhanu whatever she wants. Begging her parents, futilely,
to let her learn swimming after school, to take Saturday music lessons,
to go to New Zealand to study. Watching her father drink all weekend

with his friends; fleeing to the movies whenever she could. Hearing her uncle Kalyaan drink, fight, and curse in the next bedroom through the thin walls, raging at her aunt till he passed out, night after night after tropical night.

In many of these ways, my mother's childhood was typical for a girl of her community in those times. The youngest of five children, she was devoted to both of her parents. She learned household chores but was not above wriggling out of them, and spent her free time going to the movies, gossiping, and philosophizing with friends. They made their own adventures and discoveries: finding golf balls near the city course, cutting them open to make rubber bands for their hair; wading through rice paddies at recess, coming back to school with muddy knees. What set Bhanu apart from her giggling girlfriends, then and into adulthood, was education.

From the beginning, Bhanu did well in school. She skipped grade two and then grade four, and ranked in the top ten students of her class most years. Some of this remarkable academic success was due to her love of her teachers, and some to her brother, Champak, who served as tutor, tormentor, and the competition to beat.

Only a year apart—he was born in July 1945, she in September 1946 —the two siblings were close. When Bhanu had to go to the dentist to get the last four of her baby teeth pulled, at age seven, it was Champak who took her by bus to the hospital's dental school, and who comforted her as best he could when blood dripped on her favorite pink satin dress. He was always challenging her to do better in school, nagging her to stay awake and study, asking her why she couldn't place number one in her class, as he did. All through primary school, she raced to keep up with his record.

School was the Baal Mandir, literally the Children's Temple, set up by Indians in Suva to educate their own, although a few native Fijians also attended. Bhanu was smart and worked hard but was no bookworm. She was a ringleader among her friends, and always kept up with the latest fashions. She played the female lead, Sita, in a holiday play based on the epic Ramayana; she often fell asleep over her schoolbooks, and had little passion for reading or mathematics.

Pictures and places, though, fired her imagination. In geography class, she pored over the atlas, spun the globe, and drew intricate, color-coded maps adorned with facts and figures: geological riches and natural resources, climate and annual rainfall, major imports and exports. Her geography notebook traveled the school, shown off by teachers in other classrooms as a specimen of exemplary work. Her imagination traveled, too: Europe, Australia, Antarctica. The climate and minerals of the islands. The history of the British Empire. The Seven Wonders of the World: she hoped she might one day see them all, though it was a remote wish—just as, when photos of the moon missions came out in *Life* magazine, she thought how wonderful it would be to go there.

Meanwhile she went to school devotedly, doggedly, even on her sisters' wedding days when everyone said, —Just skip a day, what does it matter? They did not bother to state the obvious: that for a girl, education was nothing, and what Bhanu would learn at a wedding mattered more for her future than anything taught at school. In eighth grade she was chosen to be head of the class on Mondays, and led her team to earn points by cleaning the school, scouring the bathrooms, picking up trash. Such skills were reinforced by other classes, for which the students were bused to a local home economics school. The girls learned to make scones, set a table, knit, crochet, and bake a cake, while the boys studied carpentry.

For the first seven grades, classes were in the Hindustani language, with one English lesson a day. In eighth grade, the school became serious about English. Bhanu and the other Indian students were able to pass written tests in English, despite having little conversational experience, but now, suddenly, they were required to speak English at all times. Those caught speaking another language anywhere on school grounds were fined a penny—which they had to wear on a chain around their neck for the whole day. The Fijian penny, with a hole in its center, lent itself well to such punishment.

Eighth grade was also the year when school itself became serious. Bhanu had to focus on the year-end examination, a national set of qualifying tests for high school entrance. If she did well in all subjects, she could go to Dudley High, a Methodist institution that was considered the best girls' school on the island. Champak was already at the best boys' school, a Jesuit-run high school, and she wanted nothing less than her brother. She studied harder than she ever had in her life.

At the time, not a single girl from the Khatri community in Fiji was in high school. Most did not even bother to take the qualifying exam, opting instead to drop out after the eighth grade, either to marry or to wait for marriage.

But Bhanu was determined, and her parents were indulgent. She felt especially close to her father, Narotam. As the youngest child, she had perhaps the most undivided time with him. They ate oatmeal together in the mornings, and Narotam allowed her to play sports and go to the movies with girlfriends—freedoms that her uncle and aunt, who lived in the same house and had no children of their own, thought unwise. When Bhanu did well in the eighth-grade examinations, earning a place at Dudley and her brother's grudging admiration at last, her mother was ill and could not attend the graduation ceremony. It was Narotam who beamed proudly from the audience as Bhanu accepted a prize for having the highest marks of any student in her class.

Still, Narotam was a traditional man whose main priority for his daughters was marriage. Bhanu started ninth grade with Narotam saying, —All right, but this is the last year. When she begged to keep going, Narotam relented and allowed her one more year.

At the end of tenth grade, another set of national tests came up. Narotam told her that she could continue only if she scored an A on the exam. She leaned into her studies as hard as she could, staying up late to cram as many facts and figures into her head as she could, driven by an ambition for which she had no female role models. How much of what we do at age fourteen or sixteen is a decision? And how much is a simpler drive for survival: an unspoken, interior understanding of what will help us to become ourselves, and the instinct to reach toward it—a tropism, like a plant that bends toward the sun?

Sun on a concrete step, a mother's finger: these are among my father's earliest memories of his childhood in the village of Navsari, India. Growing up, my father had no American dream. America was Elvis Presley on the phonograph and the Voice of America on the radio, while India was *Bhaarat Maataa,* the nation as mother and goddess. Bhupendra was her son as surely as he was the sixth child of Ratanji and Kaashi Narsey.

On cool winter mornings before school, Kaashi would bundle the children in sweaters and take them to a neighbor's sunny stoop to warm up.

Then they walked to school together, Bhupendra holding his mother's finger all the way. They were good times, my father says now, an old sweetness in his eyes; the good old days.

By his own telling, Bhupendra's childhood was idyllic. His very birth, in Navsari on April 8, 1942, was deemed auspicious: that week, his father, Ratanji, closed a deal on buying a property next door. Ratanji vowed that upon his death the house would go to the baby who had brought such good luck.

As a child Bhupendra was his mother's unabashed favorite; she fed him from his own special plate, which none of his siblings were allowed to touch. His nickname at home was Bhagwaan, the common word for god. His two older sisters, Kamu and Kanchan, helped raise him; along with Chiman, Ranchhod, and Jayanti, they made up the first set of siblings. Bhupendra was the oldest of the second set, which included Manhar, a year younger, and Lila, whose birth is his first memory.

Just shy of four years old, he sat on the stairs overlooking the commotion downstairs, where his mother lay in labor as people came in and out of the house. Then the midwife left, and there was a baby to play with, and Bhupendra saw himself as her protector. Years later, when Lila enraged their mother by rolling rotli for dinner too slowly, it was Bhupendra who ran to the kitchen. As their mother hit Lila, screaming, —I'm going to kill you, he intervened with a knife.

—Here, he told his mother calmly, —if you want to do it right. This brought their mother to her senses, and she stopped.

But Kaashi never raised a hand against Bhupendra. In school he was favored as well: he spent only a week in kindergarten before the teacher sent him off to first grade, since he already knew his numbers and alphabet—taught by his older siblings and his mother, in spare moments. If intelligence is a product of early love and attention, surely Bhupendra began with a head start.

The first lessons that the brain must process arrive through the body, and the heart. From birth or even before, pleasure is a need met, deeply satisfied; pain is deprivation. As infants, we know everything (taste of sustenance, comfort, love-hate) through the mother; then through the other bodies moving through our rooms, creating shifts of light, smell, and sound. Next we step outside. Strangers, streets, school; these too teach us. And when we begin to go farther, to learn things our families cannot teach us, we begin to grow up.

For my father (as for me), the primary source of this extrafamilial knowledge, this deep initiation into the world beyond the family, was books. Once he learned to read, books took him into the realms of the gods of science and history, of other languages and the alien concepts embedded within them: Hindi, Sanskrit, English. And later, or along with all of these, the inner realm of himself.

His quickness made him a teacher's pet. Year after year, all the children sat on the floor or low benches except Bhupendra, who sat on a chair at a proper desk, next to the teacher. In return he came to love education. In third grade, he ran a fever during final exams but insisted on going to school; his mother came and sat with him through the examinations. Every morning the children chanted a traditional Hindu mantra:

> Lead us from darkness into light,
> from the unreal to the real,
> from the cycles of life and death to the everlasting.

Bhupendra took the teachings to heart. Studying scripture, he memorized Sanskrit *slokas* well enough to correct visiting priests tartly when their tongues slipped. He and his school friends followed the religion's unwritten rules without discussing them; he did not eat in the homes of his "lower"-caste friends, and the "higher"-caste boys did not so much as accept a glass of water in his. In Fiji his father and older brothers had all but dropped such caste taboos, but at home in Navsari, caste purity was very much alive—so much so that no one needed to explain or speak of it. It was part of the subtle education he absorbed, woven into the fabric of a village whose traditions seemed eternal.

The only gap in Bhupendra's life was his father, whom he saw only every three or four years. Ratanji inhabited the distant and fuzzy world beyond Navsari, a world known to Bhupendra only through his geography textbooks and scattered family anecdotes, although almost all of his older male relatives lived out there.

In 1946, when Bhupendra was four years old, Ratanji had just taken the helm as director of Narseys. When Bhupendra turned ten, Ratanji was opening a shoe-distribution business and a drinking club for Gujarati merchants in Fiji. As Bhupendra entered his teenage years, Ratanji was expanding the tailoring and clothing shop into a department store, with new divisions selling liquor and electronics. Business took Ratanji not only to Fiji but also to Hong Kong, Japan, Australia, England; and once to New York, where his connections landed him a radio interview on the Voice of America, to be broadcast in Asia. He telegrammed home, and at the appointed hour the clan in Navsari gathered in Kaashi's front room. The year was 1956 or '57; Bhupendra, precocious, had skipped a few grades and was in high school.

The main room of the family home, with its dark wooden walls and raw floor, became an informal amphitheater focused on a chest-high cabinet radio—the latest model, brought home by Ratanji himself on an earlier trip. Aside from the plank swing that hung from the ceiling, on which eight adults could easily crowd together, the radio was the largest piece of furniture in the room. Someone turned the dial, past the national radio stations with their patriotic news and classical tunes, and found the Voice of America. The program was in English, which only a few of the dozens of family members packed into the room could understand. Even Bhupendra, who was taking English in school, could hardly count himself fluent. Still, as his cousins and aunts jostled and hushed one another, Bhupendra leaned in close and listened, over thousands of miles of radio hiss, to his father's voice.

Weeks later, a vinyl recording of the program arrived by post. Bhupendra and his brother placed it on the turntable of their gramophone, cranked the handle, and watched with dismay as the heavy needle irreparably scratched the surface. The record was designed for a more modern turntable, and was now ruined. They would have to wait a few months or years to hear their father's voice again. And they would never know what, exactly, Ratanji had been saying, though they were sure it was profound and important.

If his father's absence had been unique, perhaps it might have caused Bhupendra more grief. But in fact, few fathers were present in the neighborhood, and it had been that way for a long time. Bhupendra knew that paternal migration had begun at least two generations earlier, with his grandfather Motiram. Now, almost all of his uncles and older cousins were overseas, in Fiji, South and East Africa, London, and elsewhere. The men sent back money and visited when they could; where passports have been lost, the journeys of the fathers can be tracked by the births of the children. This, too, had come to seem a normal part of the rhythm of village life.

Besides, at the crucial moments in Bhupendra's life, his father always seemed to arrive, like a hero in the movies: Bhupendra's bout with typhoid, his primary school graduation, moments when decisions needed to be made about his future. Bhupendra learned to accept his father's gruff, periodic love and also, when the visits inevitably ended, to survive without it.

Instead, his childhood was filled with family, faith, and school. Grade school was math, science, geography, Indian history, and Gujarati. High school brought a new subject, world history, in which they memorized the English kings (why did so many have the same name?) and surveyed the spread of the British Empire. They also added languages: Hindi, English, and a choice of a fourth—Persian for the Muslim boys, Avesta for the Parsis, and Sanskrit for the Hindus. In English class, for the first time, Bhupendra was told to spell his first and last names. The first he managed; the second request confused him.

—What is my last name? he asked the teacher.

Like his brothers and uncles before him, he was an Indian with only one name confronting the English system of two names. And as with them, the outcome was somewhat arbitrary.

His teacher happened to know that one of Bhupendra's uncles owned a building, on which a second name was engraved in Gujarati. It was not Narsey, which was his father's last name and the name of the store in Fiji. Instead, it was a longer version of the name his brother Ranchhod had chosen, Hazrat: destiny. In block letters the teacher wrote it down: H-A-J-R-A-T-W-A-L-A. The *J* was the teacher's interpretation of a Gujarati letter that is pronounced more like *jh* or *zh*; the *wala* was a common suffix that is transliterated equally often as *walla* or *wallah*. Bhupendra copied out the English letters, and *Hajratwala* became the spelling that he, alone in his entire family and indeed in the world, would adopt as his own—a memento of his own unique moment of encounter.

. . .

As Bhupendra started his second year of high school, his younger brother, Manhar, entered high school as well. The boys took classes from 10 A.M. to 5 P.M. each day and did their homework each evening under the direction of a private tutor—a rare luxury that was one of the fruits of Ratanji's success overseas. Because the high school was across town, their mother arranged for them to take lunch each day at the home of the family priest, who lived behind the school.

Before they went, she gave them a lecture.

A man who has always used knife, fork, and spoon may look at one who eats with his hands as more casual, lacking in etiquette, perhaps even primitive. But eating with one's hands carries its own complex rules, which any Indian village child comes to know. A Hindu eats, for example, only with the right hand, never the left—which is reserved for bathroom functions—and never both; eating with two hands is something only very small children or people who are somehow incapacitated may do.

Bhupendra and Manhar, of course, knew this much. Now their mother schooled them in the finer points.

—Now you are about to eat at a Brahmin's house, so eat neatly! Don't mush everything together like you do at home! Tear off one little piece of bread and put a little vegetable in it, like this.

She demonstrated, and continued. —Mix a little rice with a little daal, and eat that before mixing more. Don't make a big soup on your plate.

At the first meal, Bhupendra hesitated, watching closely how the priest and his family ate. It was the first meal he had ever taken outside his family, and he wanted to make no mistakes, to bring no shame upon himself or his kin. He saw that they were doing as Kaashi had described: They broke off pieces of rotli, with which they scooped up vegetables. They built a bunker of rice in which to pour the soupy daal, instead of letting it slosh all over the plate, then blended it neatly, bite by bite. Bhupendra copied them, feeling his discomfort and fear of embarrassment subside as he mastered the new skill. Eating with them daily, he developed a habit he would keep the rest of his life.

In the most subtle of ways, my father's manner of eating sets him apart from, and some would say above, the rest of our people. Whatever he eats now, whether tacos or Szechuan chicken or home food, his plate is always neat; he takes one bite at a time and chews it calmly, in a disciplined way. And I wonder how it was that he thoroughly internalized the rules set before him for two years as a teenager. Did he begin eating in the high-caste way at home immediately, perhaps showing off a little in front of his own family, exhibiting his own social mobility? Or was the shift gradual, as over time it simply became too much to maintain the gap between the home way and the outside way? Or was practicing encouraged by his mother at home, in the effort to save him — and herself — from embarrassment at the priest's home? Whatever the case, it was a first step out of the narrow confines of his family's home and caste. And even today, when my mother serves rice, she knows to pause a moment, to let my father first shape it into a barrier on his plate, before pouring the daal within it, neat and contained.

The priest told Bhupendra and Manhar religious fables over lunch and sat with them in meditation afterward. Later it was said that the reason both brothers did so well in school was that they had eaten the Brahmin's food, which in the Ayurvedic system of traditional medicine would be called *sattvic:* balanced, pure, healthy for the body-mind. Over vegetables and flatbread, rice and daal, they imbibed not only the ideal foods conducive to learning but also a greater share of the priest's blessings. This informal aspect of their education, the family believed, made both boys unusually brainy.

Along with his religious tutelage, in high school Bhupendra broadened his interests. He and his friends walked along the railway tracks of Navsari, conversing about philosophy, school, the world beyond. To practice his new languages, he wrote to the *Rotarian,* the magazine of the international Rotary Club, to find Hindi and English pen pals elsewhere in India and throughout the world.

One day he came home with a request: Could he take an afterschool elective? The school was offering music classes, taught by a sitar maestro and classical singer who was so famous that he sometimes performed on the national radio station. Bhupendra thought it was a magnificent opportunity.

To his surprise, his mother was anything but pleased.

The performing arts were for low-caste people, Kaashi remonstrated, and no child of hers would be involved in singing and dancing and carrying on. Performers were vagrants, all but begging on the streets—traveling minstrels, showmen—or mingling with courtesans, dancers, and other entertainers of dubious provenance. Becoming a musician was like joining the circus; you might like the clowns, but you wouldn't want your son to become one.

Surprised, Bhupendra rallied enough to make a counteroffer. There was an art class, too; could he take that?

Drawing, painting: still a questionable enterprise, in Kaashi's view. In the village, artists sat on the street with their boards and paints, or climbed scaffolding to paint the buildings and temples of the rich. The Western model of museums and concert halls, of a high art performed by, not only for, the elite, had not yet penetrated the village of Navsari. People of the royal caste, however remote from royalty themselves, did not become artists; they hired them.

But, reluctantly—perhaps unable to dash her favorite son's hopes altogether, or perhaps eager to keep him out of the corrupt world of music—Kaashi gave her consent to the art class. So Bhupendra learned about pencils, charcoals, paints; perspective, composition, color; the human eye, the artist's eye. He started with flowers and still lifes, progressed to bodies. And he took yet another step beyond the world of rules that had circumscribed his ancestors, following instead a path toward a liberal, worldly education.

Along the way, he studied hard.

The unofficial policy of the community was that boys went to join the family businesses abroad; usually this came to pass naturally, when they flunked out. But Bhupendra did not fail. He passed grade after grade, his brother Manhar one year behind him. Bhupendra became the first, among all of his siblings and first cousins, to graduate from high school.

What came next? Kaashi wrote to Ratanji, who wrote back: —The boy is studying, no point in wasting his education here in Fiji. Ratanji decided to visit India to seek a solution.

Meanwhile, Kaashi sought counsel of her own. She summoned to the house a beggar-prophet, one of the wandering wise men who meandered from village to village exchanging fortunes for alms. She asked about the fate of her brightest son: What would become of him?

The prophet listened. Perhaps he looked at the boy's star chart, or simply closed his eyes and deliberated; perhaps he was pondering the meal or money my grandmother was about to give him. Then he delivered stunning news:

— If this boy does not leave the house before he turns sixteen, he will become a monk and never give you grandchildren.

There is so much we do not know about our own lives, so many ifs and perhapses that guide us toward becoming ourselves. These days we might consult horoscopes or tarot readers, herbalists or therapists, but their advice is simply that: advice, a new perspective to be weighed and considered, one potentially useful reflection upon our situation. My grandmother's generation was, in a way, the last in my family to take destiny seriously. To take the word of a wandering prophet, and make of it a life decision, requires a kind of faith I do not possess. Somewhere between my grandmother's time and mine, in the westward migrations of diaspora, there came a moment when such pure belief—called, now, superstition—was left behind.

Had Kaashi been worldlier, perhaps she would have dismissed the prophet as a quack and kept my father at home to attend the local college, which offered a course in accounting. Perhaps she would even have resisted any decision that would take him away from the fold, and my father would have remained immersed a while longer in the circumscribed sphere of her influence: family, tradition, food, caste, village, home. Perhaps, from this protracted cocooning, swaddled some years longer in her nest, he would have emerged a different man.

But as it was, she took the fortuneteller's word as we might take a product of hard science, as if the man viewed Destiny through a telescope whose gaze was simply more powerful than the naked eye. For a woman of her time, it was a devastating vision.

A fable from the life of a Hindu saint and commentator, Shankaracharya, brings home the nature of my grandmother's dilemma. I came across a translation of this tale in a text written decades later by my father. He asked me to edit the manuscript, which in draft form included this passage:

As a boy, Shankar was swimming in the river when he was attacked by a crocodile. As his mother stood on the bank watching, the river goddess came and offered a choice: save the boy's life and have him become a monk, or let him die. Of course it was a difficult choice . . .

My comment in the margin was, "Why was it a difficult choice? Not obvious to a Western reader." What mother would not first save her son's life and only later consider his career choice?

But my father explained the difficulty: "Either way, she would lose her son." A religious man not only renounces worldly possessions; he must also shed attachments of any sort, including family ties. For Kaashi, who longed to see her sons settled with wives and families of their own, Bhupendra's childhood piety now seemed an ominous portent. The idea that her baby could be swept into the harsh life of a renunciate was unbearable.

—No matter what, she told her husband, —I want this boy out of the house.

My father's memories of 1957 are, naturally, distant, made more so by the fact of his multiple migrations ever since. Each time we move, we must leave something of ourselves behind; perhaps then the map of a diaspora consists, like a constellation, mainly of gaps. And these distances gape in our memories, as in our personalities; we lack the physical objects, buildings, people whose presence might remind us of what we once were, might lend us some continuity. Now in his sixties, my father can barely believe he was once that boy, it was so long ago and far away. So when I ask him to amplify this moment—what was it like when he and his father decided his future?—he cannot remember whether the conversation took place in person, by sea mail, or through the intermediary of his mother.

But he remembers its content: the questions he was asked, and the answers—inadequate—that he gave.

—What, Ratanji asked Bhupendra, —do you want to do?

From a father to a son, the question was rare enough that Bhupendra had no ready answer. He was fifteen years old, and loved to draw. —I want to be an artist, he said.

His father shook his head; how could one support a family as an artist? Bhupendra thought again; a doctor, perhaps?

But Bombay was teeming with doctors, both quacks and legitimate practitioners, his father objected. These were the years before medicine became a prestigious and profitable occupation; most Indians received their primary care from healers, pharmacists ("chemists"), and midwives. Doctors were called to the house only in emergencies, often in the middle of the night; and besides, medicine required years and years of schooling. Again, it would be a hindrance to family life.

Architecture, then, Bhupendra suggested, thinking it a fine compromise between art and science. His father again considered, and again rejected the notion. How many houses could be built, after all? Each family needed only one, and most already had a home; surely one could not make a living designing houses.

Bhupendra was out of ideas. He asked his father to choose.

For Ratanji, the fact that he weighed his son's opinion at all was a sign that the question was confounding. In all of his experience and that of his forefathers, occupation was a primary function and a natural outcome of hereditary caste. The son did as the father had done, and that was all. Occupations had shifted slightly over a century, from weaver to tailor to trader, but that was a matter of economic need, not personal desire.

But times were changing. Ratanji, given his own minimal schooling, had no basis on which to choose a profession for an educated boy. So he asked around.

A cousin had just opened a chemist's shop, and said that was a very good line of work. People will always need painkillers and balms, Ratanji reasoned. And since the family concern in Fiji was now a department store, in a few years Bhupendra could come and open a dispensary.

By good fortune, Gujarat University in Ahmedabad, the state's commercial capital, had just launched a five-year pharmacy program. It was part of India's new push to invest in science and technology education. When the school year started in June 1957, Bhupendra and his parents were on an overnight train to the city. They toured the campus, paid his tuition and room and board, arranged for daily milk delivery at his dorm room so he could make morning tea, and stayed one night at the Hotel

Chetana. The next morning, after a tearful embrace, his parents took the next train home.

Bhupendra did not know, quite, how it had happened that he was suddenly cast out—for an education, yes, for an opportunity no one else in his family had been given, but cast out nonetheless. Aside from a few clothes and books, his possessions consisted of a bedroll, a small Primus stove and pot, and a stash of tea and tea spices. Neither these supplies nor any situation he had encountered in his fifteen years had equipped him for life outside the family and the village. He had never gone to sleep without his family nearby, never woken up without mother or aunt or sisters to ask if he was hungry, to urge him to eat. He had never taken a meal in a restaurant, let alone a huge cafeteria like the one where students ate.

Alone in the big city, he cried for three straight days.

On the third morning he pulled himself together enough to try making a cup of tea. Twice he burned the milk; the third time he succeeded. Slowly he began to adjust to his new life. The barely conscious question *Why me?* receded until years later, when he learned of the prophecy that was the real reason he was sent away from home.

At home, his parents also wept and worried over whether their teenager could fend for himself. A month after dropping Bhupendra off, Ratanji came for a surprise visit, just before his return to Fiji. Unable to gauge his son's academic progress, he was nonetheless glad to see that Bhupendra's room was clean, his bed made, his books neatly lined up on a shelf. Ratanji worried that the food might be institutional slop, and bought Bhupendra a bottle of ketchup to pour on rice if nothing else was edible. But the bottle of bright red sauce—foreign to Gujarati cuisine—was destined to stay on Bhupendra's shelf untouched; even if he had developed a taste for it, he would have been embarrassed to bring his own condiment to the cafeteria.

Bhupendra did make use of his father's other gift: a bank account with an allowance of ten pounds a month. With hundreds of rupees at his disposal each semester, Bhupendra was easily the richest boy in the dorm. Three times a week he treated his new school friends to dinner and a movie in town, keeping a diary of the films they saw. They studied together, took snack breaks and practiced English at the nearby canteen, and applied their budding scientific skills to such experiments as wiring their metal bed frames to electrocute the bedbugs that, from time to time, infested their mattresses. And so my father's wandering days began—not as an ascetic, but as a student of the world.

In the 1950s, Bhupendra and his classmates enjoyed some of the earliest fruits of India's independence. Their prime minister, the nation's first, was Jawaharlal Nehru, who as a boy had loved to tinker in a small laboratory set up for him in the family mansion. Although his breeding and political activism had directed him to the study of law and history, in his youth Nehru had also made time for geology, zoology, and botany at Trinity College in England; among his classmates was a grandson of Charles Darwin. "There are three fundamental requirements for India," Nehru wrote in 1940, looking ahead to the independence he hoped and trusted would come: "a heavy engineering and machine building industry, scientific research institutions and electric power."

In this belief in progress, Nehru was diametrically opposed to his compatriot in the movement, Mahatma Gandhi. Gandhi, who had observed how industrialization destroyed rural livelihoods, favored reverting to a village-based, nontechnological economy based on handicrafts such as spinning and hand-weaving. But after independence and Gandhi's assassination, it was Nehru who had the task of grappling with practical means of addressing the suffering of India. "It is science alone," Nehru wrote, "that could solve these problems of hunger and poverty." As prime minister he set about putting that solution to work, cultivating the scientific brainpower that he saw as essential to India's future.

In 1947, as one of his first acts, Nehru laid the foundation stone of the first national laboratory in Delhi. Within a few years he broke ground on the first of the research universities later known as the Indian Institutes of Technology, on the site of a large detention camp where the British had held protesters during the historic 1930 salt march. Over the coming decades, this investment would pay dividends as the institutes gradually developed an international reputation for producing some of the world's most skilled engineers, computer scientists, and entrepreneurs.

Nehru also named scientists among his top advisers and incorporated scientific investment into each of the "five-year plans" that governed the new country's spending. Government funding for scientific research grew from 24 million rupees in 1947, when Nehru took office, to 550 million rupees by the time he died in 1964—an increase of 2,200 percent. And he began funding education at a phenomenal rate, raising no less than thirty new universities between 1947 and 1961—as well as encouraging new programs, especially in the sciences, at existing institutions.

Under British rule, Bhupendra and most of his classmates would have had neither the wealth nor the connections to gain a higher education. "University" had been virtually synonymous with "England," where Nehru, Gandhi, and other elites had studied in the pre-independence era. Now, thanks to the efforts of these largely foreign-educated leaders, the knowledge of the world could be taught to young Indians in their own country, by their own countrymen—in shiny new laboratories complemented by a garden, behind the school, of pharmaceutical herbs.

The realm of science that Bhupendra entered as a fifteen-year-old must have seemed a kind of rigorous and thorough explanation of the world, a relief from the chaos of the Hindu calendar with its constant fluctuation between auspicious and inauspicious times, of the Hindu gods with their impenetrable whims that, in boyhood, he had done his best to track. Science spoke to his already logical, mathematical mind. In one more barely perceptible step away from his family, he soon began, privately, to eschew some of the beliefs of his mother and sisters as superstition, replacing them with Western medical knowledge. The clear equations and cause-and-effect rationality of a scientific education were, for him, natural and easy to embrace.

First, however, he had to understand its vocabulary—in a foreign tongue. His college was a "mixed" one, meaning that the students came not only from Gujarat but from all over India. English was ostensibly the common denominator and therefore the language of instruction.

But what the students shared most was that they had no idea what their professors were saying. Their high school English proved radically insufficient for practical use. The first time someone said "Hello" to Bhupendra, he froze. He knew the textbook meaning of the word, of course, but not the proper response.

In the classroom, although his professors spoke slowly, Bhupendra struggled to follow the technical vocabulary, which was far beyond his previous exposure. Each night he sat with a pharmacy textbook in English and his old science books in Gujarati, looking for diagrams that matched. "Triangle" meant, apparently, *trikone*. "Distillation process" was *nisyandan nikreeyaa*. Every word was different, and at the end of six months came the midyear exams.

When the results arrived, he had to write to his father in Fiji: —I have good news and bad news. The bad news is, I have failed every single subject in the program. The good news is, I am still number one in the class!

His classmates, twenty-five students who also came from regional high schools where they had studied only in Bengali or Tamil or Marathi, had had the same problem. Bhupendra's scores, though failing, were the highest.

Luckily, Ratanji saw the humor in the situation. For years afterward he bragged about his son who was "number one failing," and he let Bhupendra stay in school. Bhupendra managed to pass the year-end exams, and all of the exams thereafter.

As the boys—there were only two girls in the program—struggled through the material, they also bonded, like any group of adolescents thrown together far from home. Bhupendra's world grew. He studied Urdu, for the beautiful script and poetry, and made Muslim friends for the first time. He took German, and added German pen pals to his list of correspondents. And he entered doorways forbidden to him in the village.

With a friend, he took lessons downtown in art and, for the first time, his beloved music. He learned the scales and principles underlying Indian classical compositions, and dabbled in Hawaiian guitar lessons. He found he had a knack for rendering images in watercolor, in pen and ink, and in a near-invisible form of embossing created with only a sharp thumbnail. He painted birds: white lines on black paper, an exquisite and delicate trio with sweeping arcs for tails, intricate feathers. Turning to the human figure, he chose the natural aesthetic object for a heterosexual male teenager. In drawing after drawing he explored the curves and lines of the female form, rendered in realistic detail, draped sometimes with fabric—and sometimes not.

Despite these extracurricular activities, he never lost track of the reason for his freedom. He kept his grades high and stayed in school even as his class steadily shrank, his peers succumbing to language and other barriers.

Then, in his fourth year, urgent missives began arriving from home.

By now only his youngest sister, Lila, lived in Navsari with their mother. The two older sisters were married; all of the older brothers had gone to Fiji; Bhupendra and his younger brother, Manhar, were in university (the latter in Bombay). Kaashi felt abandoned. She started drinking heavily, and wreaked her alcoholic rages on her only remaining daughter. Every few weeks Lila would sneak off to the post office to telegram Bhupendra: —Situation bad, come home quick. And Bhupendra would board the Friday night train, arrive home on Saturday morning, and do what he could before taking the Sunday night red-eye back to school. Sometimes he fetched antacids for his mother's stomach pain and administered seltzer water; mostly, he listened.

That my father remembers his childhood up to this point as joyful is no mean feat, considering that he saw his father only every few years, that his mother beat the other children, that he was discouraged from pursuing his artistic and musical interests, and that he barely knew his older siblings. Migration had split the family apart, yet family life stumbled on as if uninterrupted. Now, driven by spirits, Kaashi ranted of its difficulties. Her husband traveled the world, she seethed, but never took her anywhere. She was alone; none of her children cared; she would die alone, any moment now.

For Bhupendra, it must have been as if the sweet flesh of his childhood had suddenly split apart to reveal an ugly, rotten pit. He developed a lifelong distaste for alcohol, but kept trying to help his mother. His final summer in university, he took an unpaid internship at a chemical factory in Navsari, to be close to home. It was then that, for the first time, he found himself a target of his mother's rage.

The notion of privacy within the family was nonexistent. Bhupendra realized that his mother would not approve of the frankly secular images he had created in college, but he could not bear to part with them. He stored them in the only place in the house that was remotely his: his bedroll.

One day Kaashi discovered them, and she was outraged. In a screaming fit she made her displeasure clear. Perhaps it was as if all her fears about the corrupting influence of the arts had come true; he was misusing a gift that should be used, if at all, only for religious images, not for such filth.

Somehow that summer passed, and in December 1962, Bhupendra—frivolous or not, lusty or pious—made both of his parents proud. He became one of only five from his original class of twenty-five to graduate.

Once again Ratanji was in India, this time to escort his most educated son to Fiji. There, Bhupendra was at last to be taken into the fold of the family business. Kaashi thought it was high time her son married; at twenty, he was more than ready by the standards of the community. His "art," along with his habit of acquiring female pen pals, must have been in the back of her mind; on a rare family vacation in the hill station of Pune, he had shocked everyone by hopping on the back of a motorcycle driven by a strange girl, who turned out to be one of his correspondents. A big biscuit-manufacturing family had a daughter the right age and would have welcomed an educated son-in-law in their extensive commercial concerns, but Bhupendra said no. He never saw the girl; he simply was not ready to marry, he said.

His father did not force the matter, instead taking him on the scenic route to Fiji. First, Ratanji shepherded him through the rounds. At the Civil Hospital in Surat, Bhupendra was vaccinated against smallpox and cholera, to meet Fiji's requirements for anyone coming from India. In Bombay, he obtained his first passport, containing handwritten permission from the government of India to visit Ceylon, Singapore, Australia, and Fiji.

In Singapore his passport was stamped with a landing pass, good only for the few days that the ship was in port. There Bhupendra was introduced to, and declined, another prospect fancied by his parents. In Sydney, he met a pen pal who showed him around the city. As they entered a department store, he bragged to her, —My father has a store just like this in Fiji. Of course, Bhupendra had not yet been to Suva, and had no way of knowing that the towering glass and steel department stores of Australia were skyscrapers compared with the row of street-level wooden shopfronts that were the Narseys empire. He entered Fiji on September 6, 1962 —by coincidence, the day Bhanu was celebrating her sixteenth birthday.

· · ·

Bhanu had passed the tenth-grade exam, but with a B.

As her classmates began eleventh grade, Bhanu resigned herself to not going to school. By the terms of her deal with her father, she would stay home, learn to cook and clean, and become educated in the ways of being a good adult woman. A cousin was to be married in Tavua, on the other side of the island, and Bhanu was dispatched with her aunt to help out a week before the wedding.

But while she was gone, the high school principal paid a visit to Narotam at the shop. She wanted to know why Bhanu had not started the school year with her class. The next day a teacher who had taught Bhanu history and Hindi stopped by. —Send her back to school, the teacher begged; —she is a smart girl, she should study. And by the end of the week Narotam telephoned the relatives in Tavua. —Her teachers are driving me crazy, he said (in Gujarati, *maaru maathu khaai jataa chhe*, they are eating my head). —Send her back.

With this reprieve, Bhanu started working her way through eleventh grade as her brother was finishing twelfth. Champak, who had earned top marks in his Catholic high school, had somehow gotten it in his head that he wanted to go to America to study. He had already applied to a Catholic university recommended by his principal, located somewhere named Iowa; had shown his father the admissions letter; and had asked, and asked, and asked. Narotam's standard reply was, —We'll see.

So Champak waited. But he was not waiting idly.

Unknown to his parents, Champak had started dating an Indo-Fijian girl from the nearby town of Vatuvanga who was a class ahead of Bhanu. In his senior year, Champak had taken to meeting Sita nearly every afternoon.

One day sometime in the spring of 1963, shortly after graduation, the amorous young couple were ambushed. Acting on a tip, his uncle Kalyaan had followed Champak to the meeting place, caught him with the girl, and dragged him home. There, he faced his parents' wrath and tears.

Champak was Narotam and Benkor's only son, and the only male descendant of his paternal grandfather; all the others of his generation were girls. Only he could carry on the family lineage, and its honor. He had to, just had to, marry a Khatri girl, his parents told him. Or else.

Narotam shared his woes with his friend Ratanji Narsey—who, remarkably, offered a solution. Ratanji was sending his son Bhupendra to America in a few days' time. Perhaps a ticket could still be purchased.

Narotam did not have much money to spare, but given the emergency, he scraped some together. Did Narotam recall his own youthful love affair, in his case with the movement, and his own father's formula of migration as discipline, migration as correction? Just as he had been sent to Fiji to keep from becoming "lost" to Gandhi's political movement, he would now send his only son to America. He told Champak to pack his things.

Less than a week later, Bhanu found herself at the Suva dock, waving goodbye to her closest sibling and only brother as he disappeared up the gangplank.

Bhupendra had not expected to find himself bound for America, either.

Upon arrival in Fiji, Bhupendra was treated as an honored guest. Under his father's orders, his brothers refused to let him help in the store, since he was educated. There was no firm plan; Bhupendra had thought his father wanted him to open a pharmacy, as part of the department store, but the weeks and then months wore on with no talk of work. Whenever he asked, he was put off: — Yes, yes, soon.

By then his mother and younger siblings had moved to Fiji as well, leaving a distant cousin to occupy the homestead in Navsari. The family's migration was complete. But Bhupendra was growing bored. Amusements and outings with his nieces, nephews, and sisters-in-law wore thin; hanging around with the menfolk in the store, with no work to do himself, seemed absurd.

So he took up his favorite hobby. At the downtown bookstore, he bought a sketchpad, drawing pencils, and a set of watercolors. And he used his right thumbnail, grown a few millimeters long on purpose, for an invisible art.

As I look at his delicate etchings of 1963, it seems to me my father was dreaming my mother long before they met. The technique requires holding an image in one's mind, without benefit of sketch or tracing; the line of the thumbnail is the only tool. One image takes at least a week to make, painstakingly, touch by touch.

To see the images, one must be equally inventive. They have no color, only texture, so you must hold them up to the light at a favorable angle. Then a woman is revealed, leaning forward, her nipples erect. Or a face turns in profile, the curve of her cheekbone, eyelash, and jaw implying longing and desire. Or a girl walks into a canopy of leaves, nude except for her high heels. In the great tradition of Indian erotic art, the aesthetic and the moral are said to be merely different manifestations of the divine —yet it is easy to see why Kaashi objected to my father's portraits of girls, the frankly sensual arcs of their bodies, their gazes hinting at a romantic imagination that, surely, a Hindu mother does not want to know her favorite unmarried son possesses.

I do not think, though, that my father experienced a dualism in his mind between art and faith. I think he was simply an enthusiastic—the word in Gujarati, *hunsyaar*, can also mean intelligent, engaged, passionate—young man. He was absorbed in the process of drawing and painting, as in childhood he had been absorbed in the Sanskrit chants. In giving himself over to each with his full attention, he was performing what some might call the purest form of meditative practice. Perhaps he even experienced moments of grace, of touching the universal through the ordinary: newspaper photographs, pretty girls from his imagination, and wild hibiscus flowers that he tore from the trees in Suva and laid on the kitchen table, to render in delicate, meticulous still lifes.

My mother picked hibiscus to wear behind her ear, strung marigolds and carnations into garlands for doorways and deities, wove strands of jasmine into her braids. In Suva in 1963, as Bhupendra idled away months waiting for his life to begin, sixteen-year-old Bhanu was choreographing folk dances for local festivals and finishing high school, her future blank and uncertain before her. With girlfriends she mused over the ideal characteristics of a husband.

—He doesn't drink, said one.

—Or smoke, said another.

—He doesn't live with his mother, said Bhanu, and they laughed. To be a bride without a live-in mother-in-law would be a rare treat indeed; they all knew of the trials that could await one, the *dukh*—suffering— that a mother-in-law could impose.

For an example, they had to look no further than the matriarch of the prominent Narsey family, recently emigrated to Fiji from India. Why,

Kaashi was known to be a witch—with the dual connotation that word held in both English and Gujarati. With her older sons' wives she quarreled relentlessly; one daughter-in-law was often seen running away from home, declaiming loudly of the suffering the old woman had levied upon her. Better to marry a man whose mother was dead or at least lived far away, Bhanu thought.

But it was musing in the abstract. In reality, Bhanu did not intend to marry anytime soon. Although many of her classmates were already betrothed, and her sisters had been married at her age, Bhanu had her sights set on a possibility that was, for her time and gender, a radical thought: higher education.

The grand journey of Bhanu's life to this point had come when she was a child. Born in Fiji, she had been moved back to India as a baby with her mother and sisters. Then an uncle came back from Fiji bearing the news that her father had bought a grand bungalow there, with a new-fangled electric icebox that could keep food cool for weeks at a time. The uncle bought her a pair of shoes, saying she would need them on the ship. And then she was traveling across the sea.

Six years old, Bhanu learned to work the ship's systems to her advantage. She kicked off her pinchy new shoes whenever she could, roaming barefoot, outwitting and outrunning the elderly cabin "boys" whose job it was to chase her down and enforce the rule against bare feet. Ship life was full of fearsome adventures. Bhanu had never used a sit-down toilet, so on her first try she climbed up and squatted with her feet on the rim, and nearly fell in. There were separate mealtimes for children and adults, as well as separate Indian lunches and dinners; she organized her days to attend as many meals as possible. In a Christmastime bobbing-for-apples contest, she won the top prize: a box of white chocolate.

Now, ten years later, emboldened by her brother's example and her own academic success, Bhanu was dreaming of a bigger prize. —I want to study to be a doctor, she told her father. —Send me to New Zealand.

Narotam gave his typical response: —We'll see.

Bhanu knew what that meant. A young Khatri girl in Fiji might sooner imagine herself in a space suit headed for the moon than to dream, even secretly, of study abroad. Her people did not send their daughters un-chaperoned to the movies, let alone across the sea.

And then Bhanu became the first girl of her community in Fiji to finish high school.

It is difficult to describe how rare my parents' academic success was at the time. In the merchant families of our clan, the notion of going to school was not even a generation old. My grandfathers had attended only a few grades, my grandmothers none. When Bhupendra was five or six, an older boy whose family lived on the other side of the village well was about to become one of the first Khatris to finish high school. It was a phenomenon so unusual that the neighborhood children came around just to see. Keeping a respectable distance, understanding that they must stay quiet, Bhupendra and the others would form a loose circle around the two-foot-wide desk set up in the courtyard. Then they would simply watch the boy study.

In both India and Fiji in those years, the British system of education was in place. Each student had to pass end-of-year exams in every subject in order to advance to the next grade. Sooner or later, most sons of the community reached an exam they could not pass, at which point they went to join their fathers in the shop—whether that shop was in India, Fiji, South Africa, or one of a handful of other destinations where our diaspora had spread itself.

As for girls, those who failed were prepared to wed. Just as often, they were pulled out of school in order to be married. Most of Bhanu's sisters and girl cousins had dropped out somewhere in the elementary grades. Only one Khatri girl in memory, Bhanu's friend Padma, had made it to high school; but finding the Methodist rules too strict—she was not allowed to wear the traditional dot on her forehead, or bangles on her arms—she dropped out. Years later Padma would tell Bhanu this was the greatest mistake of her life.

But at the time, Bhanu's friend was simply following the norm of the community. Failing or dropping out was no shame, for either boys or girls; anyone who kept going in school was deemed a rare intellect. You could count on one hand the number of graduates in the community. They were automatically set apart.

And it was this setting apart that would become a marker of both my parents' lives. For my grandparents, the stakes were high. Suddenly the world was bigger and wider; it could swallow up their children as easily as it might embrace them with open arms. Migration was no longer a desperate measure, as it had been for them and their forebears, a solution to an economic problem; it was a choice their children were clamoring to make. And it was impossible to know the right decision in advance. As the doors to many countries swung open, one had to watch one's children walk through them, and trust in destiny to ensure that the lessons one had imparted would hold.

One afternoon Ratanji came home to discover his son engrossed in painting a hibiscus in full, glorious bloom. He was furious.

— Did we educate you, did we bring you to Fiji, to waste your time like this?

— But what am I supposed to do? asked Bhupendra, who had no work or study to occupy his time.

So his father set him a task: the family tree.

One photocopy of the tree remains in my father's, and now my, files. In his finest Gujarati, Bhupendra inked the generations of male names dictated by his father. He then adorned the branches with curvaceous twigs and heart-shaped leaves, inscribing the history of his family.

From Kaashi he learned that he had had another brother, a boy who lived only long enough to be named: Giridhar. His mother wanted the boy on the family tree; his father did not. Ratanji had his way, but my father kept the knowledge. Decades later, when he typed a new version into his first computer, he would list Giridhar as the fourth son, and himself as fifth.

On the branching tree he drew in 1963, he set the names of the next generation — his young nephews — into flowers, coddled by soft, rounded petals. His own twig ended in a bud not yet opened. Inside its optimistic folds waited my brother, nameless and formless as any future.

I am with the other girls, the wives and sisters and daughters, in the shadow tree that cannot be perceived at high noon.

Without work or income, Bhupendra continued to say no to eligible bachelorettes suggested by his parents. After the family tree was completed, and as no wedding bells were imminent, Ratanji declared that Bhupendra's term of idleness had lasted long enough. He dispatched

Bhupendra with his uncle Magan to find the appropriate government office and obtain a license to practice pharmacy in Fiji.

At the licensing office, the official was apologetic.

—Mr. Narsey, he told Uncle Magan, —I want to tell you that this man is more educated than I am. Your nephew is the most educated pharmacist we have on the island. But I am so sorry, I cannot give him a license.

Bhupendra's degree was from India, the man explained, and Fiji recognized bachelor's degrees only from Britain, Australia, New Zealand, and Canada.

Bhupendra was outraged, his patriotic spirit offended by the suggestion that India's degrees were inferior to those of the white Western nations. Ratanji wanted to send him to complete the required two-year certification course in New Zealand. But Bhupendra suggested that instead of two years of repetitive course work, he could spend two years earning a higher degree: a master's in manufacturing pharmaceuticals. The move would prepare him not only to open a pharmacy but to set up a manufacturing facility in Fiji. Ratanji agreed, so Bhupendra began looking into graduate programs.

He recalled that a few of his peers back in India had talked about going to America to study. And so he approached the door of the U.S. consulate in Suva, entered a small office where the Stars and Stripes hung, and walked for the first time onto what was, technically, American soil.

If Bhupendra's dream, in 1963, had been to live in America, being a student was one of the few ways that he could have accomplished it. Born in India, applying for a visa via Fiji, he fell into what the U.S. Congress back in 1917 had established as the "Asiatic barred zone," a region from which immigrants were deemed wholly undesirable. The bar was effective; the most recent census of 1960 had found fewer than nine thousand people from India living in the United States. Some were old enough to have entered in an earlier time when migration was free, and most of the rest were visiting students and scholars.

Christopher Columbus's error notwithstanding, no one knows when the first Indian arrived in North America. A slave from India may have been among the possessions imported by an early settler of Salem, Massachusetts, in the 1600s; a handful of sailors, merchants, and swamis from

India were said to have landed at East Coast ports in the late 1700s and 1800s. The earliest documented arrivals were students, in 1901. Enrolled at first in East Coast institutions such as Cornell University, they came with scholarships from various Indian educational societies or funding from their own families, and soon made their way to California's large universities as well.

The student presence was quickly overshadowed by a larger group: hundreds of Indian laborers on the West Coast. These men, mostly Sikhs from the Punjab region of northwestern India who had become world travelers by virtue of serving in the British Indian army, were drawn first to western Canada by rumors of high wages and a voraciously expanding economy. As Canada reacted with immigration restrictions to squeeze them out, some traveled south.

To their new bosses in the American West's lumber mills, railroads, farms, mines, and quarries, they were a godsend: strong and hardworking, cheaper than the whites, less particular about their working conditions than the Japanese, and younger than the Chinese—to whom America's borders had been closed for more than twenty years. That change had come about after white vigilantes burned down Chinatowns throughout the West Coast in the 1870s. The arsons had proven such a success—culminating in congressional passage of the Chinese Exclusion Act of 1882—that, rather than being pacified, white vigilantes learned that mob action was an effective form of political expression.

In comparison with other groups, the number of Asian Indians arriving in the United States was small, never exceeding one thousand annually. Still, within a few years of arrival, they were subject to a tide of anti-Asian xenophobia.

In 1906, an anti-Chinese riot enveloped Vancouver, with three hundred whites mobbing the Chinese quarter, tearing down and then setting fire to their shacks. The same year in San Francisco, Japanese scientists studying the aftermath of the city's massive earthquake were stoned and told to go home.

In 1907, the violence reached Asian Indians.

CROWD NUMBERING 500 DRAGS DUSKY ORIENTALS FROM THEIR HOMES, triumphed a headline in one of the towns where violent mobs attacked "Hindoos," as all Indians, regardless of religion, were known. In settlements as large as Seattle and as small as Live Oak, California, white men fearful that their jobs were being undercut by cheap immigrant labor rioted to drive out hundreds of Indian, Filipino, and Chinese workers. Political leaders raced to follow up on their constituents' violently expressed views.

In 1913, California's Alien Land Law stripped Asian immigrants of the right to own property, forcing quick sales and economic devastation on those few Indian laborers who had managed to save money to buy their own farms. In a reflection of how dramatically the xenophobic focus was shifting, by 1920 the commissioner of the state's Bureau of Labor Statistics would report "the Hindu" to be "the most undesirable immigrant in the state" and "unfit for association with American people."

The rioters' victory was enduring. California and other western states shaped the national debate on Asian immigration for decades to come. In 1917, the U.S. Congress barred Indians from migrating to the United States and prevented those already in the country from bringing over wives. In 1923, the Supreme Court ruled that Indians could not be granted citizenship, which was limited to "whites." The Court admitted that both science and history classified the races of India as Aryan and "Caucasian," following a taxonomic system under which the other categories were "Mongoloid" and "Negroid." But, the unanimous decision said, "the common man" would identify Indians as nonwhite and would "instinctively recognize and reject the thought of assimilation" with them. The following year, Congress extended the immigration and citizenship ban to all of the so-called Asia Pacific Triangle, closing the leaks and putting an effective end to what newspapers of the day had termed "the Asian invasion."

Students, however, enjoyed some exemptions to the ban. Without the option to become American citizens after graduation, Asian students were generally temporary visitors, not immigrant threats. During the 1920s, when the borders were otherwise tightly sealed, more than a thousand students from India arrived to study in U.S. universities. In 1935, an Indo-American surveying his countrymen estimated that five hundred Indian students were scattered throughout the United States, making up one-ninth of the Indo-American population.

A few of these scholars managed to remain, and even rise through the ranks. In 1944, the Senate Committee on Immigration heard expert testimony that at least fourteen Indian scholars and scientists were holding key positions in American industry and universities.

The Senate hearings were part of a quixotic effort to reverse the draconian immigration bans. Indo-American activists, with a few allies in Congress, sought to prove that they were indeed desirable citizens, willing and able to contribute to America's urgent needs. By this time, World War II had brought slight relief to the long-maligned Chinese Americans; Congress, throwing a bone to an important ally and attempting to stave off charges of Nazi-style racism, had just consented to let in 105 Chinese immigrants each year. Chinese in America were also, after a hiatus of six decades, being allowed to apply for citizenship.

Prominent Indo-Americans, including a doctor, a former senator, and community activists, lobbied for the same treatment. It took two more years to overcome congressional and labor opposition. At last, in 1946, President Truman signed legislation extending similar provisions to Filipinos and Indians. Japanese, Koreans, and other Asians were still banned; yet America's freeze on Asian immigration was beginning, ever so slowly, to thaw.

In this climate, educational exchanges became a pet cause of a few senators who wanted to create international goodwill cheaply, without spurring a backlash. Quietly, Congress authorized a series of small programs that allowed more foreign brains to come and study in, and contribute to the knowledge of, the United States: the Fulbright Act of 1946, the U.S. Information and Education Exchange Act of 1948, the Mutual Educational and Cultural Exchange Act of 1961. Many of these "exchanges" were really a convenience for employers hamstrung by restrictive immigration policies. U.S. psychiatric hospitals in the 1950s, for example, frequently hired foreigners under the pretext of educational exchange to fill difficult and low-paying positions that failed to attract American doctors. In 1952, as part of a broader package of changes to immigration law, certain restrictions on foreign students were relaxed, and they were reclassified as nonimmigrants.

This series of technical changes had the effect of allowing more Asian students to enter the United States on temporary visas—without opening the floodgates to either a large, permanent Asian population or the resulting political backlash. It increased foreign students at a fortuitous time for university coffers, filling empty slots left by the boom generation of G.I. Bill scholars. It was a win-win situation. A Columbia University sociologist, studying student migration to the United States, describes how "it became American policy to encourage and facilitate educational exchange" in the postwar period:

> Educational programs were certified for foreign students; consular procedures were devised to inform foreign students about their rights and obligations as nonimmigrant aliens; tests were developed to insure some minimum competence in English in those who hoped to study in the United States; scholarship and fellowship programs for particularly gifted foreign students were enacted.

Taken together, the measures were a huge success. America's class of foreign students arriving in 1963, the one that Bhupendra was considering joining, would be nearly forty thousand strong: four times as many as in 1950. And each year, it would continue to grow.

Bhupendra's timing was thus impeccable, if innocent. Years earlier, he might have found little official encouragement to study in America; later, the great rush for American visas and passports might have crowded him out. But on the day he walked into the American consulate in Suva in early 1963, there were no long lines, no waiting period, no jostling for attention. The place looked empty except for a man behind the information desk, who came around with a friendly smile and an easy manner that Bhupendra would come to associate with America itself.

He showed Bhupendra a current directory of U.S. universities and colleges. *Consular procedures were devised to inform foreign students . . .* Sitting at a small round table in the air-conditioned office, with its large picture window overlooking Cumming Street, Bhupendra browsed through the directory at his leisure. He found five schools that offered a master's degree in pharmacy with a specialty in manufacturing, and went back to the desk. The consulate official showed him where the schools were on a map, told him how to apply, and said he should take the language exam required of all foreign applicants. *Tests were developed to insure some minimum competence* . . . Just a few months earlier, the U.S. Immigration and Naturalization Service had announced that it would help schools by allowing them to have prospective students take the TOEFL, the Test of English as a Foreign Language, abroad rather than coming to the United States for it. So Bhupendra sat again at the table to take the test, and the man scored it right away. Bhupendra had passed and could go now, the man said.

—Don't I need a letter, some kind of proof? Bhupendra asked.

—No, we will send it directly to the universities, the official said. This was another recent change, designed to help U.S. schools recruit foreign students.

—But what if someone asks for proof?

—Son, let me tell you, in America people believe everything you say until you give them a reason to think otherwise. They will believe you.

To my father's people, America was uncharted territory—a country where few of their kind had ventured, where one might easily become, in the Gujarati idiom, lost. *Poiro khowai jahe,* the boy will become lost, busybodies warned his mother. "Lost" meant to become rootless, tailless; to forget the ways of the clan. It was equivalent to another phrase my grandmother had to endure: *Poiro bagri jahe,* the boy will become ruined, spoiled—the same adjective used to describe rotten fruit.

Privately, Ratanji and Kaashi shared the same fears. Kaashi wanted her son married before he went anywhere. They would have preferred England or New Zealand or Australia, where they had more relations and where the culture was not, perhaps, so wild and free. A handful of traditional Khatri families had settled in California, a handful elsewhere, yet most of America might as well have been the Wild West for all that the Fiji Indians knew of it. And it was true that at least a few of the community's young men were known to have found their American dream in the arms of a white girlfriend, mistress, or wife.

Ratanji trusted his son's opinion about the best educational course to pursue, but America made him queasy. It was a place that could ruin, or at least confuse, a boy.

In the spring of 1963, a few months after his visit to the consulate, Bhupendra received one and only one graduate admissions letter. It was from the University of Colorado at Boulder, which he vaguely remembered as being somewhere in the middle of the map. He had not yet benefited from one aspect of American policy—*scholarship and fellowship programs for particularly gifted foreign students were enacted*—but he was not worried: his father was paying his tuition. He would study two years, add another degree to his list of accomplishments, and come home to rejoin his family.

To Kaashi, the risk of losing her son still loomed large. Though the family was migratory, till now everyone had followed the path set by Motiram back in 1909: from India to Fiji, with occasional voyages back, surrounded always by a close network of kin and clan. Bhupendra was the only son about to be set adrift, far from his people, in a vague kind of danger. So she tried to extract a guarantee.

—Promise me, she said to him one day shortly before his departure, —promise me before you go that you will come back and marry a Khatri girl.

—No, Bhupendra said, —I cannot make that promise.

To his mind, trained as it was by the Hindu scriptures, such a promise could not be made lightly; once spoken, it was a sacred vow that could not be breached.

—I have no idea what I'm going to do in the future, he told his mother.

—Then at least promise you will marry an Indian girl, she begged.

—No, he said, —I make no promise at all.

And thus when he boarded the ship to America, he did so unfettered: free to make his way as he chose, to see all that America had to offer. Trying to be gracious to the dozens of relatives who pressed gifts into his hands, and trying to distract his mother or perhaps himself from the grief of parting by pointing out various features of the ship, he did not notice the fair, slim girl with dark eyes at the dock.

Bhanu wanted to keep studying, but she did not know what her father would allow her to do. So she pursued several avenues at once.

She took the Cambridge Overseas exam, which would have qualified her to seek admission to British or Commonwealth universities. While awaiting the results, she applied to stenography school in Suva. And she worked on her father, asking him to send her abroad. Champak was studying in America, she argued; why couldn't she go to New Zealand, just a short hop away?

When the exam results came, she was thrilled: Grade I, the highest category possible, in biology, mathematics, English, religion, history, geography, and English literature. She could easily gain admission to a university in New Zealand.

But Narotam hedged. —Just wait, he said each time she asked; —just wait. And he nixed the stenography course: —No daughter of mine is going to be a secretary.

One day at last he came home with a clipping from the *Fiji Times:* a few lines of a classified ad. Applications were being accepted, it said, for physiotherapy students at the Fiji School of Medicine. A man who worked at Narotam's shop had pointed it out, had said it was a good line of work for a girl. Narotam, still a Gandhian by temperament, had always hoped that one of his children would enter a profession in which they might help others. And unlike the university's M.D. program, this one did not require students to live in the dorms; they could commute from home.

Bhanu dared not ask her father what exactly physiotherapy was. It was her ticket to school, and she could not endanger it with any hesitation. She agreed immediately.

When she tried to research the field at the public library, she found nothing helpful. She went to meet with her high school principal, and asked her. Something to do with massage, the woman said; something to do with polio. Armed with this paltry information, Bhanu went to the interview, riding shotgun in her father's flatbed truck from the store.

Physical therapy or physiotherapy had a relatively short history in the Fiji Islands. The program at the medical school had started only the year before, with three students; this was to be the second class. In the 1950s Fiji had had a polio outbreak, and physiotherapists had been imported to massage the limbs of the afflicted. That was what everyone knew.

The interviewer asked Bhanu if she knew what physiotherapy was. Bhanu gave a vague answer that included, somewhere in it, the words "massage" and "polio." The woman smiled; another student who had no idea. Well, she would find out soon enough.

—Classes start in May, Bhanu was told. —You will receive a stipend of nine pounds per month, tuition is free, and we will send you your class schedule in the mail.

The luxury cruise liner carrying Bhupendra and Champak floated smoothly across the surface of the Pacific: one week to Hawaii, another week to Vancouver, two more days to San Francisco. The *Oriana,* part of the P&O line, was organized in the English manner, with "upperclass" and "lowerclass" facilities; Bhupendra and Champak were not allowed on the upper decks.

While Bhanu's brother learned to play Ping-Pong and, with his Jesuit-school English, mingled easily with the other passengers, Bhupendra passed the time reading and hanging out with the few other young men from India. At night there was dancing, and Bhupendra enjoyed being around the pretty English girls, though conversational English remained a challenge.

Food was another. One evening the meal was spaghetti. The Indians watched in confusion as the other diners swirled their forks gracefully round and round, then into their mouths. When Bhupendra tried it, the noodles slipped and slithered every which way. By the time his fork reached his lips, the rebellious spaghetti had splashed — if he was lucky — back onto the plate.

An American priest who often sat at their table offered salvation. — You can eat it like the Americans, he suggested, showing the Indian students how to chop the strands of spaghetti into bite-size segments that could more easily be shoveled into the mouth. It was another lesson in eating, and one of many hints that my father would pick up about what makes an American an American.

At the port of San Francisco, Bhupendra's father had arranged for the two young men to be met by a distant uncle, Ratilal, who was one of the first in the community to migrate from India to America. Uncle Ratilal told them the story of his success. He had arrived in San Francisco with nothing, and met up with some other Gujaratis from the Patel community. Like him, they had no education, no English, no capital, and few skills that seemed marketable in America. They worked as housecleaners. Ratilal had begun cleaning offices; a commercial janitor's pay was somewhat higher, and he could work without supervision — almost like being his own boss. Cleaning two or three offices each night in downtown Oakland, he came to know the night-shift workers, including the owner of a low-end hotel. As they swapped stories about their lives, Ratilal told the man how he was saving almost all of his earnings: he lived in a hostel with a shared kitchen and bath, ate rice and daal for no more than a dollar a day, and kept the rest squirreled away. The owner took a liking to him, and one day said, — Look, you're saving all this money, why don't you buy this hotel from me?

Ratilal looked up at the tall building, several stories high. — I never imagined I could own such a big hotel; my parents don't even own a house in India, he said.

But they worked it out, and Ratilal bought the building: the Will Rogers, an SRO—single room occupancy—hotel in downtown Oakland.

By the time Bhupendra and Champak arrived in 1963, Uncle Ratilal had three such hotels and a house of his own. America, Ratilal told his two young visitors, was a place where such miracles could happen. He invited Bhupendra and Champak home for meals, showed them the sights, and put them up at the Will Rogers among the old men who paid rent weekly and drank in the shadows of the city's neon signs. When it was time, Uncle Ratilal also arranged Greyhound bus tickets for them: for Champak, to Iowa; for Bhupendra, to Colorado.

Riding the bus two nights and three days, Bhupendra gazed out the window at the ever-changing landscape, the scenery so unlike either India or Fiji: dramatic peaks of the Sierras, snow-tipped even in late summer, followed by the broad flatlands of Nevada and Utah, punctuated every several hours by city lights, the diesel and grease smell of busy stations. The bus wound up and through the Rockies, crested a peak, and coasted down to Boulder, a city set like a jewel in a valley of forested mountains. — Wow, thought Bhupendra, — what a place I have chosen!

He had written in advance notifying the university that he would arrive several days before classes started. The bus rolled into the university stop, the door opened, and there stood, he thought, his welcoming committee: an Indian man his own age, whose name turned out to be Bhupendra, too. The other Bhupendra was also Gujarati, also studying pharmacy, and had the same faculty adviser. But he was not on official assignment; he had just been walking by the bus stop, he said, and paused to see who would get out.

It felt like a good omen. Bhupendra took Bhupendra to the foreign students' office, which assigned him a host family until classes started, and a dormitory thereafter. The adviser shared by the Bhupendras was a German, whose strong military personality was intimidating; even his children addressed him as Sir. A handful of other Indian students were in the program, and Bhupendra fell in easily with them. They warned him that the German would make him take two years' worth of calculus.

— I haven't come here to study mathematics, Bhupendra said. In their first meeting, to decide upon a course schedule, he told the adviser, — I know enough calculus.

— No Indian kid knows enough calculus, came the reply. Still, the man allowed as how, if Bhupendra could get the head of the math department to sign off, he could skip the prerequisites.

Bhupendra had no calculus textbooks with him, so he bought a paperback study guide at the university bookstore for $3.95 and spent three days working through it. When he felt ready, he set up an appointment with the math chairman, hoping the man had a more favorable view of Indian students.

In 1963, if there was anywhere in America that people were used to seeing Asians outside of urban Chinatowns, it was in the math, science, and engineering departments of universities. Bhupendra and his classmates, new arrivals from India, China, and elsewhere in Asia, were at the vanguard of a new wave of immigration to the United States that was about to reshape many aspects of the nation, perhaps none more than its academic and scientific landscape. Studying for their degrees in the great plains and valleys of the new land, trudging through snow to classes and laboratories, they were making history.

Less than a year before Bhupendra arrived, in October 1962, a minor adjustment had been made to U.S. immigration law, designed to "facilitate the entry of alien skilled specialists." Since 1946, one hundred Indians annually had been granted permanent resident status—but far more applied each year, which had created a backlog of hundreds. The 1962 law cleared a good portion of this backlog, allowing some of those who had already applied for a change of status—specifically, those who could prove their credentials in science and engineering—to become immigrants. The number of Asian scientists and engineers obtaining the small, government-issue green cards that indicated permanent resident status immediately tripled, causing the *Boston Herald* to publish a few lines of pithy commentary:

> Send me your trained, your skilled,
> Your eager students straining for degrees,
> The cultured cream of all your learned scores.
> Send these, the brainy masters, Ph.D's
> We're courting class along these golden shores.

By the time Bhupendra graduated, the trend of Asian "brains" defecting to America would become a steep upward curve. He and his peers would face the prospect of going home after graduation not as a predetermined fate, but as a heart-wrenching exercise in free will.

The math chairman wrote an equation, then showed it to Bhupendra:
—What is this?
—Triple integration.
—And how do you solve it?
—You start from the inside and work your way to the outside.
The questions were basic, and Bhupendra was not actually asked to solve a problem. The math chairman wrote a note. Bhupendra, jubilant, met with the German, who commented, —You are the first Indian to walk into my office with this letter.
To enroll in a class in manufacturing, the subject Bhupendra had come to study, there was one more hurdle. The adviser pointed to a machine in his laboratory: —Do you know what this is?
—A tablet rotary press.
—Do you know how to operate it?
Bhupendra paused. He had seen such machines, capable of pumping out hundreds of tablets per minute, only in textbooks; in India they had worked on a simpler press that made one pill at a time. He considered bluffing but feared he would be asked to demonstrate.
—Not right now, but I'm sure I can, he replied instead.
That honest but confident reply won him a place in the course, while his compatriots were stuck doing two years of prerequisites.

. . .

Bhupendra's English was still rudimentary, his manner that of a boy from the upper stratum of a village. One day he forgot to bring his pen to class, and wanted to borrow one for a moment to write down an important point. He turned to the student next to him. In Gujarati one would say, *Bhai, mane taari* pen *aap ni:* Brother, give me your pen. "Give" and "lend" are the same verb; the polite and temporary nature of the request would be understood. The language has no equivalent for "please."

—Give me your pen, Bhupendra demanded urgently of his neighbor.

—No, said the other student, pulling away and giving him an odd look. Bhupendra was furious, filled with an impotent rage.

People problems seemed to plague him. One roommate was too loud, another too messy. One roommate insulted him; the next insulted him even more. After his eighth housing rearrangement in less than two years, Bhupendra realized that the problem might lie with himself.

But this realization came toward the very end of his time in Colorado. By then, his volatility—his portion, perhaps, of the notorious Narsey temper—had had a grave consequence.

His studies had gone well, with A's and B's in his classes and only a slight delay in writing his thesis as he waited for the results of his laboratory experiments to bear fruit. He had traveled to California, Las Vegas, and the Grand Canyon; he had taken a summer job selling encyclopedias. Now, with one semester left in Colorado, he was focused on planning for his future. In one of his weekly letters home, he asked his father whether Narseys was ready to open a pharmacy or a pill-manufacturing factory.

—No, came the reply; his father's brother Magan, the managing director of the firm, was very ill, and no new projects could be considered.

—Come home anyway, Ratanji wrote.

The truth, though, was that Bhupendra was changing. His image of himself in a white coat, dispensing painkillers and balms to the old ladies of Fiji at the back of the Narseys department store, had shifted and blurred and slowly faded. In his laboratory in Colorado, he had learned to operate not only the tablet rotary press but also the other modern machinery, to mix and document the results of his experiments with test tubes and beakers, Bunsen burners, solutions, distillations. He was studying how quickly the colors in pill coatings faded, according to various conditions; it was an important topic, since people tended to discard pills that had lost their color, even if the medicine inside them was still stable. Fascinated now by pharmacy's theoretical and mathematical aspects, Bhupendra wanted to continue in research. A patriot, he was interested in returning to India someday, to share his knowledge with his motherland; but Fiji, lacking a community of intellectual peers or scientific research facilities, was far less appealing.

He wrote home and told his father he would like to pursue a PhD.

— What is a PhD? came the reply. — And how much will it cost?

— It is the highest degree possible to attain, Bhupendra wrote. — It will take three more years.

Ratanji said he could not afford such expense. — Come home now, he wrote.

Instead, Bhupendra set about developing Plan B.

His F-1 student visa allowed him to work up to eighteen months after graduation; the U.S. government considered this practical training to be, in theory, an extension of a student's education. Bhupendra calculated that if he found work for eighteen months, he could save enough money to start a doctoral degree. In his typical methodical way, he applied to a hundred pharmaceutical companies for a position. He also applied to several doctoral programs.

Every one turned him down.

He went to meet with his adviser. — What might the problem be?

The advice he received was invaluable, if a bit late: — Don't use anyone's name as a reference without asking them first.

— Oh! Well then, will you be a reference for me?

The adviser paused. — You should ask someone else, I think. Ask a professor whose course you got an A in.

Bhupendra nodded and left, confused by the odd American etiquette. One day in the mail he received an anonymous envelope: a copy of a letter of "recommendation" about himself, written by the adviser. Apparently someone had taken pity on him and forwarded the letter so that he could see what it said. Bhupendra read it, reeling. The letter spoke candidly of Bhupendra's umpteen changes of address, his short temper, and apparent difficulty getting along with people. With such an evaluation from his primary adviser, it was no wonder his mailbox was filled with nothing but rejections.

This unpleasant lesson in American candor was a profound shock to Bhupendra, raised in an Indian value system of loyalty, family-feeling, and helping one another along. He no longer knew if he could trust any of his three references, and he had no idea what to do.

But the cruel moment also contained a gift: a glimpse of truth, and the potential for transformation. Away from his family and the milieu in which arrogance had served him well, Bhupendra realized that the Narsey temper was a problem he would have to learn to control.

For now, though, the damage was done. Bhupendra set about completing the last hurdles in Colorado. On the way to his oral examinations and thesis defense, he was turned back by the department's sole Indian professor, a Dr. Himmat Mehta, who chastised him for his rumpled appearance. Bhupendra went back to the apartment, ironed the cuffs and front panels of his shirt—the only bits that would show under his suit jacket—and aced the interviews. At commencement, his black gown and cap sported a dignified gold tassel, indicating his master's degree in science. It was August 1965, and his graduating class of ninety included one Iraqi, one Afghani, and four Indians, including Bhupendra. He sent a photograph home, himself in graduation robes against an American flag; Ratanji made dozens of copies for all the family members.

Meanwhile Bhupendra set about trying to repair his career prospects. Once again he came up with a plan.

The great industrial heartland of America lay east of the Rockies, so Bhupendra decided to go east. He had bought a huge old Ford, cheap, from a fellow student, who had also taught him how to drive it. Now he would take Interstate 80 toward New York, pausing in each major city to seek work. His father had stopped sending money, so Bhupendra's only assets were the car, $100 remaining from the $1,500 his father had given him two years before, and his expensive textbooks. If he reached New York without finding a job, he figured, he could sell everything and buy a plane ticket to Fiji.

In Lincoln, Nebraska, he stayed a night at the YMCA; the university's doctoral program had already rejected him, so he kept on moving. In

Iowa City he stayed at another Y, for three dollars. The next morning he stopped by the University of Iowa. At the pharmacy building he filled out an application, skipping the most difficult section by writing simply, "References provided upon request." Then he drove on.

In Chicago, he counted his money: he had fifty dollars in his pocket. He was not going to make it to New York. In his rented room at the downtown Y, he sat down to calculate.

A night at the Y with private room and shared bath: six dollars. A day's worth of food: three dollars. Gas and miscellaneous: one dollar. At ten dollars a day, he could last for five days. It was a Monday.

If by Friday he had no job, he guessed he would go back to Fiji.

In Washington, D.C., the nation's highest politicians were working to get him to stay—not Bhupendra as an individual, of course, but skilled young scientists from the Third World. As early immigration policies were shaped around the need for labor, so was the legislation being drafted and debated in the summer of 1965. Instead of bodies, what America needed now was brains.

By the 1960s the Cold War had become a national obsession. American superiority over the Soviet Union was measured by every conceivable scorecard: votes in the United Nations, comparisons of gross national product, medals won in the Olympics, shifting maps of small Third World countries. Now President Lyndon B. Johnson was aiming to import the talent America needed to emerge victorious in at least two arenas: the space race and the nuclear arms buildup. Aerospace engineers and nuclear physicists were worth their weight in plutonium, but all scientists, whether or not they worked for the military, were counted as valuable recruits for Team America.

The legislation that had eased restrictions on foreign students back in 1952 had also paved the way for further change. That act had been a comprehensive rewrite of U.S. immigration law, technically abolishing the ban on Asia and setting up a new formula that looked like equality, although it was actually a clever piece of strategy. The quota of immigrants from each country was set at one-sixth of one percent of the population of that country's natives already in the United States—as measured by the census of 1920. By basing future growth on the 1920 population, the act guaranteed that historically tiny groups, like the Indo-Americans, would remain tiny, while larger ones, like most European Americans, could grow. Just to be sure, a special provision capped migration from the old "Asia Pacific Triangle" at 2,000 total. And to be extra-sure, immigrants with fifty percent or more Asian ancestry were charged to Asia, whatever their current citizenship, so that third-generation Japanese from Brazil or Pakistanis from England could not sneak in under non-Asian countries' quotas.

Precisely because the 1952 act preserved America's racial profile, it had passed political muster. For Indo-Americans, whose quota of 100 immigrants per year remained the same, it had no numerical impact at the time. What it did change was the type of people who could come, and this would turn out to have a more lasting effect.

Previous legislation had given first preference to relatives of Americans, with small occupation-based quotas. But the 1952 law had turned that practice on its head. First preference was now going to those with skills "urgently needed in the United States." Fifty percent of each nation's quota was set aside for these professionals.

Doctors, scientists, engineers, and health workers found that their brainpower could launch them to the front of the immigration queues. They lined up quickly. While the quotas for such nations as Great Britain and France went unfilled, those from Asian nations with substantial educated populations and tiny quotas, including India, were soon booked up for years in advance.

At the same time, American companies and universities were clamoring for talent. From 1952 to 1965, U.S. research and development funds nearly tripled, paying for a 242 percent increase in scientists working in R&D. America's universities were producing too few U.S.-born students to keep up with this voracious pace, yet U.S. law was keeping out the brains who could satisfy the demand. Tinkering with immigration law and creating new access for students and exchange scholars was no longer enough. As a series of U.S. presidents fighting the Cold War recognized, large-scale recruitment of foreign scientific talent could not occur without changing the basis of immigration policy: the national-origin quotas themselves. Presidents Truman, Eisenhower, and Kennedy had all placed large-scale immigration reform on their agendas, without success in Congress. Now the issue had landed in Johnson's lap—and this time it seemed to have a chance.

The civil rights movement had created a climate in which, for a brief moment, politicians scrambled to exhibit racial tolerance. Corporations favored changes that would bring cheap labor, trained up to U.S. standards (often overqualified, even) but willing to work for less, for jobs that were going empty. Public xenophobia against Asians, which had blocked immigration reform since the turn of the century, was at an all-time low, with Americans' enemy radar refocused against the Soviet communist threat.

The time seemed right for far-reaching change, and many minds and mouths and pens were hard at work on Capitol Hill, hammering out the precise compromises and phrases that could make it happen. Politically and perhaps astrologically, the stars were lining up.

At the Y, Bhupendra lingered in the lobby each morning until someone left a newspaper behind. After combing the *Tribune* classifieds (free), he budgeted another dollar a day for nickel phone calls; the calls saved on gas, which was 31 cents a gallon. He drove around filling out applications, and soon learned to skip the offices and restaurants with signs reading NO DOGS NO JEWS NO BLACKS.

In the university towns where he had lived until now, people were used to seeing foreign students; the Americans he had encountered were comfortable with, and even intrigued by, his ethnicity. Chicago in 1965 was another story entirely. Within a year, it would explode in race riots that would rock the nation. For Bhupendra, it was the site of his first encounters with the color line that W. E. B. Du Bois had called the problem of the twentieth century, the racially polarized America divided starkly into white and black—with no category but "black" for anyone who was, like Bhupendra, darker than a paper bag. In Chicago people either went out of their way to avoid him, mistaking him for a black man, or approached him speaking in Spanish, thinking he was Puerto Rican.

The week went by, and Bhupendra's billfold grew slimmer. On Friday morning, a two-line ad in the *Tribune* said simply, "Analytical Chemist. Gas Chromatography. Apply in person." Bhupendra had taken a special elective in the new technique and had written a paper on how it could be used to test for steroids in athletes' urine. The emerging technology, which measures the rate at which a molecule breaks down, would later be developed into such applications as the Breathalyzer test for drunk drivers.

Bhupendra drove out to Morton Grove, a northwestern suburb near the airport. His interviewer was the head of quality control and R&D at a firm called G. Barr Company. Bhupendra filled out an application and wrote down his grades—including an A in the gas chromatography course. The man interviewed him on the spot, without asking him for references.

—Do you know what a propellant is?

Bhupendra paused. It was Friday; without this job, it was quite possibly his last Friday in the country. But he decided it was risky to fib on a technical point.

—No, I don't, he replied, —but I have learned this much and I have come this far and I'm sure I can learn it.

—When can you start? was the next question.

—Now, he said.

He was hired to start on Monday, at a salary of seven hundred dollars a month, far beyond his expectations. But there was still one problem: how to meet his expenses on Friday and Saturday. He told his story to his new boss, who was so impressed—or pitied Bhupendra so much—that he took twenty dollars from his own pocket. —We'll take it out of your first paycheck, he said.

With that, Bhupendra set out to find an apartment.

He spent a few evenings after work looking for a place to stay, but Morton Grove was a white suburb. Apartment complexes bore the same offensive signs; many building managers refused to even open the door when he knocked. At last he found a motel with a low weekly rate. Within a few weeks, though, the manager told him he had to leave.

—But I'm paying you on time, aren't I?

The manager shook his head. Someone had complained about a dark man living permanently at the motel. He would have to go.

Drawing upon his limited experience in America for a solution, Bhupendra drove out to Evanston, the home of Northwestern University. There, on campus, he hoped to find a friendly refuge among people who were used to foreign students and visitors. At the student housing union, he found a listing for a shared apartment, four rooms. Three were occupied by white students, but the landlady was willing to rent the fourth to him. He sighed with relief, and settled in for a twenty-minute commute each way.

· · ·

Over just such issues, America was exploding around him. In the summer of 1966, Dr. Martin Luther King Jr. made Chicago a focal point of his civil rights campaign, and the city was awash in protest marches, fiery rhetoric, and violent backlash. Bhupendra paid enough attention to heed his coworkers when they warned him which white neighborhoods to avoid driving through, even innocently, and especially at night. Otherwise, he felt little personal involvement. Despite his experiences with racism in Chicago, it was not a problem that had much to do with him. He was a visitor in this country, not a part of its internal squabbles, and he intended to do his best to avoid getting caught up in them.

Bhupendra had jotted a quick note home to let the family know where he was working, but moving, and moving again, had led him to neglect his weekly letter home. Nearly a month went by, until one day a supervisor called him in and asked, —Have you written home lately?

It turned out that his uncle Magan, a Rotarian, had written from Fiji to the Rotary Club in Chicago saying, —I have lost my nephew. They looked up the company's name and called. Immediately Bhupendra rushed to send a cable home, letting them know that all was well.

Settling in, he found among his possessions a book given to him by a cousin long before, which he had never read: *How to Win Friends and Influence People,* by someone named Dale Carnegie. He opened it, skimmed the pages, and was captivated.

Carnegie's mass-market paperback, a popular bestseller that had sold millions of copies since its publication in 1936, was like a light bulb popping over Bhupendra's head, as he would say later. Bhupendra saw his own behavior illuminated—under the anecdotes of how *not* to behave. Still carrying the shock of America's perspective on his behavior, via his professor's "recommendation" letter, he was receptive to Carnegie's lessons about tact, negotiation, and seeing the other person's point of view. And he was young enough to change, to leap out of his old skin and into a new, perhaps more American, self.

When I interview relatives now about my father, it is as if this later self has eclipsed the impetuous young man he says he once was. —He was always *bhagvaan ni gaadi,* one brother says; the image is of a vehicle moving smoothly, frictionless, undisturbed by bumps and ruts on the ground; God's own train. —Your father sits in meditation, doesn't he?

one cousin remembers: *dhyaan maa pare,* to fall into concentration, as if it were a deep well down which one might calmly, coolly, endlessly float.

Decades after his epiphany, my father would write in the front page of the copy he gave me as I finished college: "As I look back, I can see that I was self-righteous, arrogant and argumentative. Oh, yes, I 'won' all the arguments with my family & friends. I could catch them at every little point they misspoke. I was sharp. I knew it all. I could tell what they were doing wrong & how flawed their thinking was . . ."

And he added a wish: "May this book bring you life time of happiness as it has brought me."

My father spent the winter of 1965 and the spring, summer, fall, and early winter of 1966 practicing his new outlook on life in Chicago. Through the changing seasons he drove to work each morning, arriving at 8 A.M. at his new company, which turned out to be an underarm deodorant factory owned by the Pittsburgh Railways Company. A train carrying pressurized gas pulled up behind the plant. Someone brought Bhupendra a sample from the tank. He tested it, using his new gas chromatography skills. Then he signed the piece of paper that allowed the assembly line to start. Gas pumped into hundreds of small aerosol cans that would become deodorants with different brand names, with slight variations in scent or formula. At 5 P.M. he signed off to close the line, and drove home.

In his bachelor quarters he would open a can and heat something up on a hot plate, eat, read a bit, and go to bed. Occasionally he experimented with cooking, though he lacked most of the essential ingredients of Indian cuisine. Devon Avenue, tucked into the northwestern corner of Chicago just a few miles from Bhupendra's apartment, was not yet the Little India of shops and restaurants that it would become in the next decades, as tens of thousands of Indian immigrants streamed into the city. The latest census, in 1960, had found only sixty-eight natives of India in Chicago, and Devon was just another anonymous boulevard. Bhupendra made do with short-grain rice instead of basmati, and vegetable curries improvised with powdered garlic, ginger, and chili; the fresh ingredients were too exotic to be found in American grocery stores. Lacking also the essential spices of cumin, coriander, mustard seed, and turmeric, his concoctions did not taste much like home food; but they were the closest thing he had. He knew no one other than his coworkers and co-tenants, spent weekends driving around Chicago neighborhoods and trolling the stacks of the university libraries, and sometimes visited the city to tour the great museum.

One day he set out for the Art Institute with a more precise mission in mind. He pressed and put on his suit, packed his art portfolio, and traveled downtown to the venerable and dignified building on the lake-front whose broad steps, flanked by two marble lions, majestic columns, and arches, announced its importance. He had made an appointment to show his work to a professor there.

In the office, the professor marveled at his portfolio, particularly the "invisible" images etched by hand: — This is amazing; I've never seen anything like it. Bhupendra had secured a small exhibition at the student union back in Boulder, and now he hoped the professor could help him find his way in the Chicago art scene. But when Bhupendra asked how to go about showing his work, or studying further, the white professor's face hardened into an expression now familiar from landlords, employers, strangers: — All that is very difficult, he said.

Bhupendra stood, thanked him for his time, and went back to his room in Evanston.

In Chicago for a conference, I stand a few hundred yards from the Art Institute, on the shores of Lake Michigan, and think of my father's time here. Nearly forty years later, he tells his Chicago stories in more or less good humor, only hinting at the difficulties by saying, "I learned a lot about America the hard way." I can barely believe the doggedness of his quest for that first job, and the miracle of success. The lake is so vast it might be an ocean, the curve of its watery horizon stretching toward strange, unseen lands: Indiana, Wisconsin, Michigan. Its waves, which appear blue from a distance, up close are green and murky, lapping fiercely against a concrete shore. Opposite, past the grand museums, is a downtown filled with old, imposing brick buildings; gleaming new sky-scrapers that seem to be held up by glass alone; and the fierce chill wind that blows between them.

While in Boulder, Bhupendra had written long, chatty letters to his eldest sister in London. Perhaps he had rambled on a bit too long about a pretty girl named Penny, her sweet blue eyes. He realized this news must have traveled when his father wrote with a new offer: — There is a girl, if you are interested. She has studied . . .

American girls were good for movie-and-dinner dates, Bhupendra thought, but the cultural gap was so large that he had never seriously considered settling down with any of them. He knew he was not in danger of becoming "lost." But neither was he ready to marry.

He wrote back, equally neutral and practical in tone: — That's good, but I have no money to come to Fiji. I am saving for my PhD.

What holds a diaspora together across oceans, national boundaries, generations? Watching my cousins enter arranged marriages, I have wondered why a young person born and raised in Fiji or Hong Kong should feel any affinity to one raised in New Jersey or Toronto, even if they are from the same caste. But for my grandparents, the suitability of such a match was a given — and more than that, an urgent requirement.

My father had grown up in India, my mother in Fiji; the currents of their lives and families had, up to this point, carried them many thousands of miles apart. In a sense their marriage was arranged by education, within a world of possible prospects that was delineated by caste. Aside from their degrees, indeed, all that they shared was caste: a supposed purity of blood enforced by culture and economics, supported by a continuity of belief and a politics that these days we might call "identity."

Among Khatris the elements of this identity included religion, history, geography, food, and certain habits of drink, dress, and speech. In the 1980s in Michigan, my parents met a Khatri family in a grocery store when the wife overheard my parents discussing the selection of fish; she recognized the pronunciation of the word (*maachhli*) as distinct to our caste. Astonished and delighted to find each other, they developed a friendship that remains strong to this day.

In India, arranged marriage plays certain societal roles: solidifying alliances between families, ensuring continuity for the sake of the ancestors, maintaining entrenched power within the most powerful castes. In diaspora, arranged marriage is crucial for different reasons. Where geographical return is impossible or uncertain, marriage is itself a type of return. To join one's blood to the blood of one's caste is always a homecoming; one is no longer at risk of being "lost."

This simulated homecoming functions not only in the lives of individuals but also in the life of the community as a whole. As the Khatris became a diasporic people, arranged marriage was what ensured the survival and transmission of old ways of life. With each young person's wedding, everything worthwhile — identity, honor, community coherence — was either preserved or lost.

With so much at stake, no marriage could be left to the vagaries of youth, or to a thing as unruly as love.

In October 1965, Bhupendra's sister Lila, recently married in the time-honored manner, moved to Toronto with her new husband. On the telephone with her, perhaps Bhupendra heard loneliness; and he himself had not had any face-to-face contact with family for more than two years. He wanted to go and visit her.

But under the terms of his student visa, if he left the United States he would have to reapply from abroad. Bhupendra wrote an appeal explaining his dilemma, and addressed it to President Lyndon B. Johnson, White House, Washington, D.C.

One day at work he received a phone call. The voice on the other end identified himself as an immigration officer from the Chicago office. — Did you write a letter to LBJ?

— Yes, Bhupendra said.

— Well, you could have just come in to our office. Come in and pick up your visa.

"The Immigration Service official is often the only representative of the Government encountered by the foreign student during his stay in this country," noted a commentary in the Immigration and Naturalization Service newsletter during this period. The INS saw itself as the first line in recruiting and welcoming skilled talent, a national priority. The commentary went on to stress the importance of providing "the student and his family with a lasting, favorable impression of our Government."

As for President Johnson, he can perhaps be forgiven for not answering Bhupendra's query personally. On October 3, 1965, the president was at a ceremony at the Statue of Liberty, signing the Immigration Act of 1965. Technically an amendment to the 1952 act, it was underplayed by nearly everyone, including its supporters. "This bill that we will sign today is not a revolutionary bill," Johnson announced. "It does not affect the lives of millions. It will not reshape the structure of our daily lives or, really, add importantly to either our wealth or our power."

In fact, the act would reshape not only the daily lives of millions but also American immigration policy itself. It was a complete reversal of decades of exclusion. It abolished the racial "national origins" basis of immigration policy, substituting current nation of citizenship. And for the first time since 1882, it admitted Asians on the same terms as all other peoples of the world.

For the long-excluded Asians, the act was revolutionary. The barred zone was finally and unequivocally retired. Citizens of all nations could now compete on an equal basis in each category, although no nation could exceed twenty thousand per year. For those with skills and education, the act was a godsend. Of the seven new categories of "preference" that would guide decisions on who was allowed in, two were designed for them: "Needed workers" could apply with employer sponsorship, as skilled white workers had been able to do since 1952. And those with certain "urgently needed skills" could apply on their own behalf, without a job offer in hand; proof of training was enough.

At the same time, certain provisions of the law were crafted to preserve America's white majority. Even as the act opened up immigration from Asia, for example, it tightened Latino immigration, which had been fairly free of restrictions. And with four of seven preference categories reserved for immediate relatives of American citizens, policymakers had reason to believe that the ethnic makeup of the incoming population would still skew white.

The first provisions went into effect on December 1, 1965, and INS employees worked overtime through the holidays to handle the "initial flood of applications" from those eager to take advantage of the new openness. Within a year, the number of skilled immigrants admitted would double. By July 1968, the INS newsletter would note "several unintended and unexpected side effects." Chief among these was the fact that the two occupational categories—"needed workers" and those with "urgently needed skills"—were dominated by immigrants of color, particularly Asians. The act had "spurred demand in these categories to new highs," causing a years-long waiting list for some nationalities.

The eleven-and-a-half-page act of 1965 would alter the demographic makeup of America, redouble the worldwide ripples of anxiety about brain drain, and transform the fate of millions of people around the world, including my parents—whether or not they had yet realized that they wanted to become Americans.

In Toronto for two weeks that December, Bhupendra had a taste of family life for the first time in two years, playing with his sister's young children, buying them clothes and a red plastic car they could sit in and "drive." Lila and her husband, recently arrived, had little money. She would need a coat for winter, Bhupendra told her, and offered to buy her one. She demurred; she would make do with her sweater, she said. —Come on, you'll die, he said. She would wear her first winter coat, bought for an extravagant $150 and with fur on the collar, for more than ten years.

As for the matter at hand, the question of my father's future, it would have been my aunt's first natural line of inquiry: —So, brother, when are you getting married? And Bhupendra asked whether she knew the girl mentioned by his father.

I have heard two versions of what happened next.

According to my aunt, she praised Bhanu as the perfect girl for Bhupendra, and his response was, —In that case, sister, I'll marry her.

But my father, telling me the story, describes it differently: "She told me your mother was a snob, stuck-up, walked around with her nose in the air." He took his sister's opinion with a grain of salt, he says, and flew back to Chicago.

When Bhupendra received his letter of admission to the doctoral program at the University of Iowa, he wrote home with the good news. He would defer enrollment for one semester, in order to make the most of the eighteen months of work allowed on his student visa, then start his PhD program in January 1967. He planned to have saved $2,500 by that time: a full third of his income from the factory, and just enough to cover tuition, room, and board for one year.

Ratanji's next letter said, —We will pay the airfare; just come and see the girl.

Bhupendra wrote back that he would come for a visit but was making no promises about marriage. Each month, on green graph paper, he plotted his earnings, expenses, and savings: one millimeter equaled five dollars. By his calculations, he could not yet afford a wife, however lovely and talented the girl might be.

My mother did not know she was the subject of this transpacific correspondence.

In the three and a half years since her brother had left for America, Bhanu had grown up a great deal. She was twenty now, about to graduate from the physiotherapy program in which her father had enrolled her. But Narotam was not there to see it.

Bhanu had witnessed his final heart attack, tried to resuscitate him with her fledgling medical skills, mourned even as she tried to comfort and support her mother. They waited to tell Champak the news until his exams were over, several weeks later, but perhaps from his Iowa dormitory he sensed a disturbance: he failed the term. Bhanu's life was changed.

No more was she the daughter of a well-to-do businessman, able to buy whichever dress fabric suited her fancy. Her uncle Kalyaan tried to run the store alone for a while, but eventually it became insolvent. Kalyaan was taken in by Narseys, where Ratanji, an old friend of the family, set him behind the ladies' wear counter. Everyone knew that Kalyaan gave away more than he sold, trading handkerchiefs and pantyhose for "favors" from female customers, whom he took into a curtained fitting room for "payment." He kept a bottle of whiskey behind the counter and went to the club after work; arriving home late, drunk, and often violent, he vented his frustrations on his wife. From their side of the thin wall, Bhanu and her mother listened to the arguments, crashes, and weeping. They waited for the dull calm that came when at last he passed out.

By day, in the neat classrooms and smooth corridors of the hospital, Bhanu studied anatomy, physiology, all the things that could go wrong with the body, and the modalities a physiotherapist used to heal them: heat, exercise, massage. To work with patients who needed aquatherapy in the medical school's heated pool, she learned—alone among the Khatri girls she knew, and years after her parents had barred her from after-school swimming lessons—how to swim.

In her second year of physiotherapy school, Bhanu had to let go of her overseas dream. She had been chosen for a World Health Organization scholarship to continue studying physiotherapy in New Zealand, where medical facilities were more advanced. But her mother drew the line, knowing that her late husband would not have allowed it. The scholarship went to another girl in the program.

At home, finances grew tight; Bhanu had to go to a neighbor to borrow money for Champak's tuition. Relatives pressured the widow to get this last daughter — pretty, sociable, modest, and eminently eligible — married off. Bhanu was the right age, already overqualified for most of the island boys, and the brief wave of gossip over Champak's affair had blown over. Plenty of marriage offers were coming in; it was foolish not to take advantage of them.

And there was another issue, one that usually went unspoken, but that loomed large nonetheless. For girls there was no question of becoming "lost"; they were rarely allowed to wander far. But a girl could still be ruined, in fact or in reputation; she could be ensnared in *lafraa*.

Lafraa is translated, in my Gujarati–English dictionary, as "botheration," and further amplified as "improper worldly trouble or connection." For a respectable girl, even a hint of lafraa means trouble, a tangle of a particular romantic sort.

One afternoon a Narsey cousin stopped Bhanu as she walked home from the medical school, and asked whether she had Champak's address in America. She had it at home, she replied, and he said he would walk there with her. They were seen by several people sitting on porches as they passed, and by the time they reached home, Bhanu's aunt had been notified and was frantic with rage and shame. She barely waited for the boy to get the address and leave before shouting at Bhanu. And the next day the neighbor girls asked, — What were you doing with him?

— Doing? Bhanu said. — I wasn't *doing* anything.

In such a climate, a girl had to be careful. She understood her mother's worry, yet she did not want to marry a mere *dukaan-wala*, a shop boy; she was holding out for an educated man. And she wanted to finish school herself. She was enjoying her classes and practical training, and she knew marriage would end her professional aspirations.

To console her mother, Bhanu vowed that there would be no problems. When the time came, she promised, she would marry a boy chosen by her family. And in the meantime, she would finish school and steer clear of any lafraa. So when a boy slipped her a love note on the bus, or when she noticed one or two young men who just happened to be standing around every day as she walked from the bus to home, their eyes following her, she was not tempted. She remembered the drastic reaction to Champak's transgression; for her, any sign of "botheration" would mean immediate marriage and an end to her education and profession. No boy was worth that.

In December 1966, Bhanu bought her mother the first pair of shoes she had owned since traveling by ship from India: open-toed chappals, to wear to the physiotherapy graduation ceremony.

Around this time Bhanu also heard the second of what would later prove to be tiny hints of the future. She was choreographing a folk dance for a winter festival, and several of the young Narsey girls were in the troupe. The brother from America was in town, and sometimes chauffeured them to and from practice. On the last rehearsal before the performance, the older girls stayed back to make flower garlands. One of them, the daughter of Chiman Narsey, trying to get Bhanu's attention, shouted, "Bhanu kaaki, Bhanu kaaki!"

Bhanu looked at her, puzzled; *kaaki* was the word for a particular type of aunt, the wife of one's father's brother, and she was no kin to Chiman Narsey's daughter. Guiltily, the girl clapped a hand over her mouth. They must have been teasing one of the brothers at home, Bhanu thought, smiling. And she forgot all about it, almost.

Unknown to her, the young Narsey man who dropped his nieces off at dance practice was in Fiji with an agenda. It was not entirely his agenda, but his father's: Ratanji had been keeping an eye on his late friend's daughter, the young woman with the medical training. She was some kind of nurse, he had heard, well mannered and educated, an ideal match for his overeducated, wandering son.

He had even taken steps to ensure that there would be no complications.

Ratanji was a shrewd businessman who did not hesitate to play hardball. His drinking buddies were Fiji's powerful, the businessmen, bankers, and government officials whose favors could often be earned with a round of drinks or a bottle of Johnnie Walker Gold Label. Other Gujaratis came to him for help in navigating the bureaucracy, and he did an informal trade in obtaining licenses, passports, and visas for people. Information is power, and in this way he managed to know everyone's business while, like an experienced poker player, playing his own cards close to his chest.

Among Bhanu's potential suitors was a young college graduate from India whose father was working in Fiji. The father had asked Ratanji for help in obtaining a visa so that his son could visit Fiji to seek a bride. Bhanu, the only educated girl on the island, was of course of great interest.

Wanting his own son to be the prime candidate, Ratanji sat on the application for several months. — It's coming along, he assured the anxious father each time they met.

Now that Ratanji had succeeded, at last, in summoning Bhupendra to Fiji, he was trying to obtain his son's agreement to the match. But the boy, made headstrong perhaps by his years of independence, was causing a problem. He wanted first of all to see the girl.

It was an act that proved more difficult than it might seem. Arranging a meeting was out of the question; it would start the gossip rolling, and would reflect badly on both families if the match did not work out. Then a wedding came up, and Bhupendra's brother Ranchhod and their cousin Ratilal took charge of the matter.

At the wedding banquet, when Bhanu sat down to eat, they pointed her out to Bhupendra: a slender girl in a pink sari.

— Pretty, very nice, Bhupendra said.

As my father considered my mother for the first time, did he imagine what it would be like to have her as his wife, raise a family with her? Having visited the warmth and good foods of home, was he realizing that he had already spent three and a half years alone in America, fending for himself in the snowy plains of a foreign land? Or — more likely, more logically — were his thoughts already turning back to the challenges of survival and the semester ahead, to the precarious financial situation reflected on his graphs, and to his need to be, at least for the moment, free of spousal obligation?

Cousin Ratilal worried that the girl might be taller than Bhupendra. When Ranchhod noticed that all the guests were rising from their seats and walking through a certain doorway to wash their hands after eating, he positioned Bhupendra near the post and put himself and Ratilal in a spot across the way where they would have a good view. As she passed, they noted with satisfaction that she was an inch or two shorter.

They told Bhupendra she was a nurse; she wore white clothes to the hospital. One day Chiman came running with a newspaper with her name in it, the college results published. It said she had earned a diploma in physiotherapy. —What is that? they asked Bhupendra, who explained it as a sort of specialized nurse, who would massage your back or feet when they hurt. Truthfully, he did not know much more about the field than they.

But his mother, riveted by visions of a daughter-in-law to rub her tired legs at the end of the day, was thrilled. The pressure increased. A kind of impromptu family meeting was held: Everyone sat down at the kitchen table and asked Bhupendra, —When will you get married?

Again he objected. —I have three years of study left and only enough money for a year; if I take a wife, how will I support both of us?

—Leave her here, said Ratanji.

—No, that's not right.

Ratanji was furious. But Bhupendra, who was as stubborn as his father, held firm, and boarded a plane back to America alone.

As my mother in Fiji memorized the muscles and sinews of the body, my father in America was studying the molecular composition of pheromones. As my mother—slim, fair, lovely—was catching the eyes of local boys as she walked uphill toward the Fiji School of Medicine, my father—intense, dark, handsome—was going on dates in America, writing to one of his sisters about a girl with beautiful blue eyes. And as my mother was entering the virtually unknown world of the working professional Khatri woman, my father began to understand a little more about both America and himself.

Bhupendra flew back into the Chicago airport just as it reopened after a record twenty-three-inch snowfall. The city was virtually shut down, looters had raged through certain neighborhoods, and so much snow had fallen—an estimated seventy-five million tons in a ten-day period —that the city sent some south in railcars, as a post-Christmas present for the children of Florida.

To save a month's rent, Bhupendra had placed his car, with all of his belongings in it, in storage. Now he retrieved it—pleased to find that, despite the cold, it started—and drove toward Iowa City, 220 miles away, where the next phase of his academic career was to begin.

About an hour from his destination, he stopped at a roadside restaurant for a cup of tea. When he got back in the car, he pulled his seat belt on, a good habit he had developed even in those days when the law did not require it. A few minutes later, he hit a patch of black ice. The car spun, flipped over a few times, and landed in a ditch.

When he opened his eyes, all he saw was snow.

Unhurt but shaken, he climbed out of the car and saw that it was a complete wreck. He flagged down a snowplow, and then another motorist stopped. The driver offered him a ride and a deal: he would get the car towed and deliver Bhupendra's belongings to him if Bhupendra would sell him the car for fifty dollars. A week later, they met and Bhupendra gave him the title. On campus he would not need a car anyway.

He deposited his Chicago savings in the Iowa State Bank & Trust, wrote a rent check for a new apartment at ninety dollars a month, and went for an entry interview with his adviser, Seymour Blaug—a man as different from his previous adviser as India was from Iowa, a man he would come to think of as his angel.

—Do you have a scholarship? the professor asked.

—No.

—How are you paying for this?

Bhupendra told his story and said he had just over $2,500 saved up—enough for a year.

—Then how will you pay for next year?

—I have no idea, but something will come up.

—Do you have a job?

—I can't; my visa doesn't allow me to work.

—A teaching assistantship, then?

—No; I applied, but they do not give them to first-year foreign students.

—All right. Wait here.

After a few minutes Blaug returned and said he'd talked with the dean.

—You have a TA-ship that pays a stipend of $250 a month, and reduced tuition of $1,000, so now your money should last two years. But pay just a semester at a time. I'm giving you these classes, and if you get all A's, you will be eligible for a four-year international student scholarship.

Scholarship and fellowship programs for particularly gifted foreign students were enacted . . .

—No problem! said Bhupendra.

—It's very tough; your competition is all Indian and Chinese students.

—No problem, Bhupendra repeated. Heaven had been good to him throughout his academic life; surely getting A's now would not be a problem.

Bhupendra might not have been worried, but in 1967, the fact that his competition was all Chinese and Indian was a matter of great concern in the world beyond Iowa City. What had once been a trickle of Third World students into U.S. schools was becoming a tidal wave. That academic year, China and India accounted for about 11 percent, each, of the total number of foreign students in the United States. Canada, previously the largest supplier of foreign students, had slipped to third place. And large numbers of Third World students were responding to the 1965 law tailored for the world's intelligentsia: they were not going home.

The persistent tendency of educated people to migrate from areas of lesser to greater opportunity has, now, a certain inevitability; it has become an established, obvious phenomenon. In the late 1960s, however, it was both new and troubling. The loudest protests came not from U.S. xenophobes but from Third World patriots. The great mass of America's imported brain trust—70 percent of it, according to the most reliable figure—originated in what the United Nations termed LDCs: Less Developed Countries. Debate on the floor of the world body in 1967 and 1968 was fierce.

The LDCs, many of which had just barely achieved independence, saw the brain drain as a throwback to, and extension of, the bad old days of colonialism. Instead of being stripped of their minerals and natural resources, now they were being relieved—without compensation—of their most valuable resource, their brainpower. The representative from Dahomey called it an "odious bleeding" of Africa, a continuation of the slave trade; of Nigeria, it was noted that the nonreturn of a single medical graduate was a serious loss to that impoverished, doctor-sparse nation.

In response, the United States and other First World nations expounded a new philosophy they called "internationalist." Scholarship and ideas ought to be free, they argued. Developing nations, rather than maintaining a petty focus on national boundaries, should look at the big picture. Didn't all of mankind benefit from such achievements as reaching the moon?

The General Assembly passed a resolution expressing grave concern, and several U.N. bodies conducted studies. Scholars convened special sessions all over the world to consider the matter: 1967 in Lausanne, Switzerland; 1968 in Ditchley Park, England; 1972 in New Delhi. A 1967 bibliography on brain drain listed three thousand books and articles published by academic, governmental, and popular presses, with hundreds more expected to be included in future editions.

The Swiss conference, one of the first, opened with a dramatic and often-repeated, if ill-substantiated, statistic: over 90 percent of Asian students who came to the United States for training never returned home, according to the president of Cornell University, James A. Perkins. In *Foreign Affairs,* Perkins had written an influential article laying out the "cruel" dilemma for American policymakers: It was a contest not between greater and lesser powers in the world, but between U.S. foreign policy and U.S. domestic needs. "While with one hand we give laboratory equipment, train teachers, send our own teachers, build buildings," he wrote, "—all on the very simple propositions that the modernization of the underdeveloped world is in our immediate and demonstrated self-interest and that the critical component of a modernizing society is its modernizing men—with the other hand we take away not only the raw materials but the very people who have been so carefully trained to develop them." As one UNESCO writer wryly commented, "There is the gravest ground for suspecting that the existing pursuit of knowledge in the world is not directed to what is desirable or necessary in the interests of the world as a whole but may well be oriented almost exclusively to the needs and desires of the most advanced societies in the world."

A few American liberals were sympathetic not only to the Third World's dilemma but also to their own constituents, domestic trade unions; they made efforts to fight the tide. Senator Walter Mondale called the problem "particularly urgent" and, in 1966, introduced two ill-fated bills. One died in committee; the other, authorizing a $50,000 study by the Department of Health, Education, and Welfare, passed, but the study was never conducted. Instead, another was published that "seemed more concerned about accommodating [foreign medical graduates] in this country than with encouraging their return home," a later study noted.

Some nations made attempts to retain their talented young; India, for some years, refused to allow the TOEFL, the language test my father took in Fiji, to be administered within its borders. But this limited migration only slightly, to those who could afford a quick plane trip to Dubai or Sri Lanka to take the exam. The more draconian proposals of some Third World nationalists and First World liberals — seal the borders, deny permission to emigrate — were never seriously considered, and the waiting lines at U.S. embassies throughout Asia and Africa continued to grow over subsequent decades.

As globalization has rolled on, Americans' fears have morphed: now we fret about factory jobs going to Mexico and China, the outsourcing of call centers to India and Bangladesh, and illegal immigrants' impact on low-wage, low-skill American workers. Concern about highly educated newcomers seems quaint and has for the most part dissipated, though its echo remains in the occasional rhetorical barb aimed at H-1B workers in Silicon Valley. It is difficult to remember how in the 1960s and '70s the brain drain roused passions as heated as those surrounding our current immigration crises. If America could have acquired only my parents' brains, transplanted them like kidneys into jobless or skill-less Iowans and Michiganders, surely it would have: a white physical therapist, a white scientist, without problems of assimilation or language or race. But our brains are hardwired to our bodies and minds, and when my parents — and others of their generation, educated professionals with much-needed skills — came to the United States, they brought with them their whole history, the history of their skin.

At the peak of the debate, the question of return — which foreign students were going back home, in what numbers, and why — was both paramount and impossible to track. Logistically, students shifted apartments frequently and traveled back and forth internationally; often there was a gap of some months before the change of official status that could turn them from visiting aliens into permanent ones. And then, their intentions also shifted. A survey of Indian students in the United States, published in 1970, found that about half had planned at the beginning of their studies to return home. By the end (5.8 years later, on average), three out of four were planning to "drain."

But Bhupendra knew — didn't he? — that he planned to go home, either to Fiji or to India, just as soon as he had his PhD. And maybe a bit of work experience in America; that couldn't hurt, either.

. . .

At home in Fiji, Bhupendra's mother was making her own long-range plans. While Ratanji was fuming, Kaashi was scheming. Legs aching, she still wanted Bhanu as a daughter-in-law.

She decided to pay a visit to Bhanu's mother. After all, she had not one but two unmarried sons.

I try to envision my grandmothers meeting in the house on Foster Street in Suva, halfway up the hill between the town and the hospital, with a view of the hot blue sea.

By the time I first saw this house, where my mother had grown up, it was a dilapidated version of its former self. It was covered in a coat of bright turquoise paint that was peeling into the humid air. On a long veranda—the one where my grandfather had collapsed of heart failure—two women were rolling out papadums and setting them to dry in the sun.

Now the house has been torn down, the large plot a scrabble of dirt and weeds. An antique tamarind tree is the only familiar sight—the one my mother climbed as a girl, nearly a lifetime ago.

Did my grandmothers have a view of the tamarind tree through a window as they talked? Did they sit on a sofa, or at the kitchen table? Did one serve the other biscuits, tea? What niceties were exchanged before they got down to business; who held the power, the trump card; what were their expectations of success or failure? My mother's mother would have worn the white cotton sari befitting a widow; my father's mother, wealthier and still married, might have worn something finer but, respecting her peer's status, not flashy.

Benkor listened to Kaashi's proposal.

Like everyone else in town, Benkor knew Kaashi Narsey and her quarrelsome reputation; knew also that Kaashi's youngest son and his bride would, by community custom, be the ones charged with taking care of her, living under her roof as long as she lived. Could she sentence her last daughter, educated and vivacious, to such a fate?

When Kaashi had finished speaking, perhaps Benkor tilted her head, put a finger to her chin. After a moment she spoke, in her slow, succinct manner:

—*Nallo to nai sakko,* she said. —*Parn moto, sakko.*
With the younger son it's not possible. But with the older, possible.

Possible, impossible, plausible, implausible: perhaps any child telling her parents' story must be a secret narcissist, entranced by the chance drama of her parents' meeting, the improbable string of twinkling lights that lead somehow to the explosion that is her own body. Though my parents' arranged marriage had more in common with a business deal than a love story, for me the tale carries all the intrigue of a passionate romance, and one with a most desirable outcome. When my grandmothers parted that afternoon, did either of them perceive with certainty the pattern of the future? When they gestured and negotiated toward a match, did they envision the grandchildren who would ensue from such a union? Did they predict, or even love, a decade in advance, me; the possibility of me?

Bhupendra, unaware of his mother's strategizing, finished his semester with all A's. He had beaten the competition: as long as he maintained a B average, his tuition would be paid for the next four years.

And his graph-paper chart, revised, looked healthy. He still had most of his Chicago money. He wrote home: —If the girl is not yet married, I can afford to marry now. I can come for the summer.

My mother knew of proposals in the wind, but she was intent on enjoying her new career. She was earning the stunning sum of thirty pounds a month, and with that, along with savings from her student stipend, she planned to buy a used Volkswagen Bug from her favorite physiotherapy teacher. Miss How, who would be returning home to the United Kingdom soon, agreed to supply driving lessons as well.

Bhanu also was preparing her trousseau. She bought one or two new saris a month, hemmed them, and had the matching blouses tailored. Then she folded them neatly in a trunk for the day, sometime in the uncertain future, when she would be married.

Ratanji, receiving Bhupendra's letter in Fiji, was furious. His obstinate son, who had wasted money coming and going as if it were nothing, now wanted to visit again? Bhupendra should have married and left the wife behind for a few months, as he'd been told. For that matter, he should have moved back to Fiji after his master's degree; what was this nonsense about more study, when by now he was surely more than qualified to open a pharmacy in the back of the department store? Why should Ratanji pay for another round-trip airfare? How could he be sure the investment would pay off this time?

It fell to Bhupendra's brothers to speak reason to their father. Ranchhod and Chiman, both married and with children of their own, waited for a calm moment before approaching him.

—Father, one or the other said, —you know how stubborn our brother is. Now that he's decided to get married, he *will* get married—and what if he marries one of those American girls?

Ratanji wrote back: —Fine. Come in the summer.

Bhupendra placed his belongings in storage for the summer and decided he would move himself and his bride into married student housing in the fall. The university-owned apartments, at forty-eight dollars a month, were subsidized; rent would be forty-two dollars less than he paid for his current off-campus housing.

When the housing clerk asked his wife's name, Bhupendra explained that he did not know yet—but that he would certainly be married by next term, and to please write down Mrs. Hajratwala.

And Kaashi paid another visit to Benkor, who replied, —Possible. Yes.

To my mother, everything after this point is a blur, weeks and months from which she emerged with her entire life altered. There were days of nerves and decisions and instructions, things to do and undo. She gave notice at the hospital, finished the driving lessons with Miss How, explained why she could no longer buy the car.

Bhanu knew a few things about her new family and husband, but it was difficult to separate fact from rumor. Her older sister Pushpa—the one who had whispered so presciently in Bhanu's ear on the dock four years earlier—said that the Narseys lived in such luxury that the women changed outfits twice or thrice a day. Meanwhile Bhupendra's father, perhaps confused by his son's explanations of his studies, was bragging that

Bhupendra had invented penicillin—a claim that Bhanu, having taken several science classes, knew to be patently false, though she was mature enough to hold her tongue.

The way Bhanu saw things, it was enough that Bhupendra was more educated than any boy on the island, more educated than any other among the slew of proposals she had received. Her mother and Pushpa approved of the match. And there were positive signs about her new family: Ratanji had shown generosity by hiring her uncle to work at Narseys when the family's fortunes waned, and the Narsey sons were known as gregarious, respectable young men. Beyond all of that, two of Bhanu's wishes were about to be fulfilled: she would live far away from her mother-in-law, and she would at last have a chance to travel overseas. She wondered if she could bring her collection of *Life* magazines with her.

Bhupendra flew into Fiji's main airport, on the western side of the big island, late on the night of Monday, June 12, 1967. His brother Ranchhod picked him up, and they drove four hours to Suva in the east. Bhupendra had just enough time to shower and dress before his 8 A.M. Tuesday appointment at the registrar's office. No one was taking any chances that he might change his mind again.

In the waiting area, future husband and wife sat next to each other, not speaking. Bhupendra noticed again how pretty she was. In his worldly travels he had learned a little about how to converse with a stranger. Begin with a compliment, Dale Carnegie had advised, and perhaps those words of wisdom rose somewhere out of his subconscious as he looked down at the inches of bench between them, upon which was the trailing end of her pink chiffon sari. He complimented its dainty floral pattern; and when she said she had embroidered it herself, he lifted the cloth to praise the work. —Pretty, very nice, he might have said. Later his family would be scandalized: Not yet married, and already fondling her sari! He could not touch her yet, but he could touch the vein of her threads, what her hand had touched and made.

The wedding itself was meant to follow some days afterward. But Bhupendra's uncle Magan was deathly ill, suffering from cancer of the fundus of the stomach. It was Bhupendra who had interpreted the doctors' report, drawn a diagram of the organ, and explained it to his family.

Every few days Ratanji would call Bhanu's uncle and say, —Make the preparations, Magan is feeling better, we'll have the wedding tomorrow afternoon.

Then, hours later, he would call back and say, —Forget it, he's not well now. Let's postpone.

At home, Bhanu was making her own financial calculations. By now her family was in precarious circumstances. She and her uncle were the breadwinners, but Kalyaan's income was minimal. They were not only maintaining their household but also paying Champak's tuition in America. And the wedding expenses had to be borne by the girl's family.

Bhanu had saved four hundred pounds from her physiotherapy stipend and salary. Now that she would not be buying Miss How's car, she could use that money for the wedding. If they kept it simple, she thought, it would be enough.

As they waited for their wedding date to be set, my parents did not court, date, or even talk much. Spending time as a couple alone was considered both unnecessary and unseemly. One exception was the day Bhupendra took Bhanu to the U.S. consulate, where they showed their passports, their marriage certificate, and Bhupendra's student visa. The consul official stamped her passport with an F-2 visa, the category for student wives: no waiting period, no delay. They went home, their union recognized now by two governments. On paper, and by day, Bhanu was a daughter-in-law; she visited her in-laws' home daily to sit with Uncle Magan in his sickroom. At night, she went home to her mother's house.

One morning, Ratanji called with a different message. Magan had passed away in his sleep.

As the home of her in-laws filled with mourners, Bhanu's own home bustled with wedding preparations. A priest was consulted to calculate an appropriate date, taking into account the thirteen-day mourning period for Magan, auspicious and inauspicious astrological hours, and Bhanu's menstrual cycle. Finally the wedding was set: 2 P.M. on July 10, a Monday.

The celebration would be understated, out of respect for the newly dead. In financial terms, this reduced scale was a fortunate stroke for Bhanu.

Only immediate family members were invited, and the crowd was less than fifty. Her sisters, cousins, and cousins' wives came to help, cook, and fuss. Bhanu's only personal guest was Miss How, her favorite teacher; even her dearest childhood friends and neighbors had to stay away. Instead of a dinner banquet, Bhanu's family would serve afternoon tea and homemade snacks: the white milky fudge called *burfee* and the trail mix–like *gaathiyaa.*

After weeks of waiting, the ceremony itself was perhaps anticlimactic. In a haze of anxiety and fatigue, early mornings of ritual and duty, neither of my parents remembers their thoughts during the central moment of their wedding: the four circles they made around the sacred fire, with the priest murmuring Sanskrit verses and their families looking on. Their necks were garlanded with flowers, their foreheads cluttered with red powder and raw rice, their wrists tied together symbolically by a red silk scarf. There was no ritual kiss, no clinking of champagne glasses. They sat again before the priest, their places reversed now as a sign of their changed status. And their hands, in the wedding photos, are clasped together.

The wedding photographer was Bhupendra's younger brother, Manhar, who gave the two rolls of color film to Bhupendra, who waited to have them processed back in Iowa. From Woolworth's, Bhupendra bought a small journal and decorative contact paper, and improvised a three-by-five photo album. He mailed it to Fiji so that the families could see it; it traveled with relatives to London and South Africa, then to Toronto, and from there his sister mailed it back to him in Iowa. It was the only copy.

The young couple were themselves making a series of similarly complex transitions.

Three days after the wedding, after the wrap-up rituals, my mother moved into the Narsey home. She had closed her savings account and given the balance to her mother—one hundred pounds, left over after the wedding expenses. To her in-laws' home she took only a small tin suitcase, which had been her sister's when they came as children from India. The saris that Bhanu had been buying herself each month easily fit inside. In the wedding altar, the place reserved for two new trunks stuffed with clothes and household goods as the bride's trousseau had been empty; Ratanji, sensitive to the family's financial circumstances, had told her relatives not to prepare them, saying diplomatically, —We are providing enough for her.

It is hard for me to imagine my parents' state of mind upon marrying a stranger. They have tried to explain: *That was just the way it was, every-one we knew did the same, it was no big deal.* But I think it must still have been a big deal, as any marriage is, any first sexual encounter. In a society where everyone has the same experience, certain experiences may go unarticulated for many lifetimes. Among the events that pass in silence, at least in the public record, are whatever wishes or fears or regrets a woman takes to her wedding night.

For a woman of my mother's generation, this moment—an almost ritual deflowering, with no prior preparation, not so much as a first kiss or date—was routine. For a woman of mine, it is nearly impossible to fathom. The question itself—*How did it feel?*—comes from a different world, is unanswerable; across the gap between my parents' young selves and me, perhaps there are no words to convey the actual experience, the *feeling.* In my family I have some hint of it through whispers and rumors, the network of news that is called, because it is women who convey it, gossip.

One of my cousins had to explain to her new sister-in-law the facts of life, several days after the honeymoon. The girl had not known anything, and her husband had not been tender. They were driving, and pulled into a gas station as my cousin explained to her what was happening, what part of the man entered what part of the woman, how it could feel, and what would happen next. The girl opened the car door and threw up.

Another cousin's wife, my own age, married when I entered college. Her mother-in-law asked my mother to explain the facts of life to her. By the time I graduated, she had three children. Yet it took her several more years to understand that the loud sounds her husband made at night, the way he stopped breathing from time to time, were not simply the normal way a man sleeps; he had a sleep disorder that required treatment.

I like to think that my parents' education protected them from the worst of such silences. I like to think that my father was a thoughtful man, and that my mother, having studied anatomy and sneaked peeks at *Cosmo* centerfolds, had some idea of what was about to happen. I like to think that there was, in the weeks and months and years after their wedding, a kind of courtship that had elements of the sweetness, romance, and love that I myself have known. And that one of those nights, if not the first one, they found a mutual pleasure that would, eventually, make me.

But not yet: they had already discussed a practical matter. I can imagine my father broaching the subject of birth control gently but directly, feeling awkward perhaps but knowing that it was his role to take the lead in such discussions. I can imagine my mother, perhaps shy at first, giving voice to her own bold, opinionated nature. They agreed; she would go on the new birth control pill. They would wait until Bhupendra finished school to have a child.

On the night of July 13, 1967, approximately four years after that first chance non-meeting on the dock, my parents slept at last in the same bed, in the Narsey home. Weeks of waiting and days of exhausting ritual had taken their toll. The newlyweds' slumber was so deep that neither stirred when a thief reached in through the open ground-floor window, surveyed the goods on the nightstand, and stole all of their 24-karat wedding gold. Gone was Bhupendra's slim new ring from his in-laws, inscribed with his initial *B;* gone were Bhanu's new black-beaded necklace and red bangles signifying her married status.

Gain and loss, give and take: these are the fundamental tropes of migration, the ebbs and flows that are as certain as travel itself. What Bhanu gained was a good husband, a chance to travel, a lifetime of intellectual companionship, and the opportunity to develop her mind rather than stagnate. What Bhupendra gained was a helpmeet, a lifetime of domestic companionship, someone who could understand both where he had come from and where he wanted to go; an ongoing connection to and taste of home. What they lost was what Bhupendra had already begun to leave behind, and what Bhanu had not known she was so much a product of: a culture and family that had formed an inextricable web — from which they were already extricating themselves — and the intimacy of living among the intangible textures of their childhoods. When I think of my young father in the nook of the porch in India, immersed in his textbooks and in the flow of village and community and family around him, with no contradiction among them; when I think of my young mother climbing tamarind trees and tossing down the sweet-sour pods of fruit whose taste I know only from dried plastic packages or tubes of paste, I feel that only I know what has been lost. They at least had the pleasure of living through their childhoods, of knowing precisely who and from whom they were, once. Perhaps only we of the next generation — raised among strangers, eating the fruits of our parents' risks — can taste the true proportions of bitter to sweet.

They reported the theft, replaced the necessary jewelry, and did without the rest. A modern couple, they were the first in their families to go on a "honeymoon" — two, in fact.

The first was a bus trip around Fiji's main island. Its formal purpose was to introduce Bhanu to the extended Narsey clan. In truth, she, raised in Fiji, knew them better than Bhupendra did. Thus they began a life-long pattern of Bhupendra greeting people as if they were familiar to him, coached by Bhanu as to their identities and precise relationships.

The second "honeymoon" was suggested by a distant uncle who lived in Tonga, where, he told Ratanji, there was a lovely hotel in town, perfect for sending the boys over with their brides. But to Bhupendra's parents, a young couple traveling alone did not seem proper. After some consideration, the family agreed to a compromise: the newlyweds would stay at the uncle's home, and Bhupendra's mother would go along too, as chaperone. It was the first public honeymoon in the family.

For the next four weeks, Bhanu and Bhupendra lived with the Narsey clan. Bhanu helped with household chores and took a crash course in homemaking from her mother-in-law, majoring in Bhupendra's favorite foods. She wrote down Kaashi's recipes for *garam masala* and the other spice blends that were each family's signature, which Kaashi had in turn inherited from her own mother-in-law, Maaji; she learned that her husband's family liked sugar in their daal. Her new sisters-in-law, they of the troublesome Narsey temperament, had been sternly admonished by Ratanji not to cause her any trouble: — This is an educated girl, she doesn't know anything about housework, it's your job to teach her. And so Bhanu found them civil enough; moreover, they did not, as it turned out, change outfits several times a day.

When it came to gender roles, Ratanji Narsey was as conservative as they came. His own daughters were struggling in Toronto and London, encumbered by being raised without English, education, or independence. Even a decade later he was enforcing the rule against the women of his family working outside the home; one of my cousins recalls with frustration that she was not allowed to do anything with her high school and secretarial degrees while in Fiji.

But for my mother he made an exception. Perhaps he sensed that in America a different type of woman would be needed. He had never liked America, not for a boy alone, subject to temptations of every kind. But since his son seemed bound to live there at least a few more years, he had chosen a suitable bride.

On September 6, 1967, they celebrated Bhanu's twenty-first birthday. Four days later, she and Bhupendra flew to America in time for the start of the new school year.

That semester, nearly five thousand wives and children of foreign students were admitted to the United States. Like the others, Bhanu had tried to steel her nerves for a new life. Her stomach, though, was another matter.

It was two nights and three days by train to the interior. Besides saving money over airfare, my father thought that riding the rails would be a romantic way to introduce his bride to America's scenery. Amtrak in 1967 had limited culinary options. Bhanu was not vegetarian; she had grown up eating chicken and lamb. But every Amtrak meal featured beef, which she had never tasted. Even the soup was beef broth; it looked to her like blood and smelled worse.

For a whole day Bhanu ate nothing but the *chevdo* snack mix they had brought from Fiji. During a brief stop in Cheyenne, Wyoming, they ran to buy potato chips and rushed back to the train; the thin air at more than a mile high caused Bhanu to feel out of breath, which made her panic. Fiji was at sea level, and she had never experienced the effects of high altitude before. She felt nauseated till they got off the train in Cedar Rapids, Iowa.

A forty-dollar taxi ride brought them to Iowa City. It was a Saturday, and the campus was quiet. After picking up the apartment key from the university office, they sat in the Quadrangle for afternoon tea and apple pie, one of Bhupendra's American favorites.

To Bhanu, everything in America would stink for weeks. The restaurants had an odor altogether different from anyplace she had had to eat before. Fiji had continental-cuisine restaurants, but no one she knew had ever eaten at one. The closest thing was the home economics class at the missionary school. She had learned to make scones and trifles, but the instructors had been careful not to offend their students' mostly vegetarian sensibilities.

Their apartment, Unit 1013, Finkbine Park, was an aluminum barrack that smelled of gas. Located in a cluster of military-style trailers that had been erected as "temporary" housing for veterans coming back to study on the G.I. Bill, it was showing the wear of twenty years. Not only that, but it apparently had lain empty all summer: cobwebs hung from the corners, and a layer of dust coated every surface. Bhanu insisted that they clean before doing anything else.

Bhupendra found a friend with a car to take them to Kresge's for detergent, a bucket, a sponge mop, a broom, and a few other essentials. They scrubbed until six or seven that first evening, then outfitted the apartment with their few belongings, along with two pillows, two knives, and two forks that a previous roommate had bequeathed to Bhupendra. Then they slept, in what would be their home for two more years.

Neither Bhanu's degree nor her visa status allowed her to work in the United States; the diploma from the Fiji School of Medicine was not generally recognized outside that region. So Bhupendra had suggested that Bhanu take classes, too. She thought she might study home economics, which she loved, or continue in physical therapy. On Monday morning she and Bhupendra went to the physical therapy department to find out how to gain admission to the program.

Bhupendra introduced himself and his wife to the head of the physical therapy clinic, who ushered them into his office. The man addressed Bhanu: —Are you a PT already?

Bhanu could barely understand his thick American accent. —Yes, I am, she told him.

—OK, on Wednesday there is a board exam in Des Moines. Can you go?

It turned out that the clinic was desperately understaffed; he wanted her to work, not study. Bhanu said yes, and the man made a call. He arranged to register her for the exam, though every deadline had passed. The application also required a photo; luckily, Bhanu had an extra passport photo in her purse.

Des Moines was two hours away, and Bhupendra asked if there was a bus, as they had no car. Bhanu said she had no books to study with; they were all coming by ship from Fiji, which would take three months.

—Dear, he said, —here's my office; whatever books you want, you take. Then he called in a student named Nancy. —Give this lady a ride tomorrow night to Des Moines, and help her study, too.

So Bhanu spent Monday evening and all day Tuesday with Nancy; whatever Nancy studied, Bhanu also reviewed. In the evening they went to Des Moines, where they stayed in the nurses' quarters of a hospital. Bhanu, finding herself away from family overnight for the first time in her life, copied everything Nancy did. She was shocked at the showers without doors, but went ahead; she had no idea how to navigate the self-serve breakfast line in the cafeteria, but took one of everything that Nancy took, including an egg-salad sandwich whose taste she would remember, decades later, as simply *gross*. Then they went to take the exam.

Iowa's state capitol was the most impressive building Bhanu had ever seen. She walked up its grand stone steps, through statuesque marble pillars, under a tremendous and ornate golden dome. In a huge, high-ceilinged hall, wooden desks were spaced four feet apart. The papers were distributed, and Bhanu gazed with confusion at the rows of circles. No one had explained to her the notion of a multiple-choice exam or the system of mechanical scoring that had recently come into vogue.

Part one was basic sciences, and much of the material was new to her; but she circled answers in the exam booklet. After a while the exam monitor, walking through the rows, told her not to write in the booklet.

—Then how will I answer? she asked, and the monitor tried to explain to her how to fill in the circles, but she did not understand. She looked around and saw that Nancy was busy doing something with the paper that had only circles on it. When the monitor was safely away on the other side of the room, she hissed for Nancy's attention and gestured her confusion. Nancy held up her paper and showed her first answer, and Bhanu finally understood.

By this time, an hour and a half of the three-hour exam had passed. Parts two and three were more practical and more directly related to physical therapy, so Bhanu found them easier. When the results came back a month later, she had passed those two, but had failed the first part by two points. Without the license that the exam conferred, she could not work. She arranged to audit fall classes in anatomy, physiology, and physics, and registered to take the exam again.

The snow began to fall.

Iowa in winter was a frozen sea. Bhupendra taught Bhanu to cross the glacier step by step, from their graduate student barracks to town or to the Quad, pressing her new rubber boots, fortified with two or three pairs of socks, against the slippery ice. They both fell, again and again. They had no money for a whole winter wardrobe of Western clothes; she pulled a thin sari around her, and a jacket over that. Her lab partners in anatomy class laughed at her over the cadaver they were slowly dissecting that semester: — How can you wear such a beautiful dress with such ugly shoes?

At night, since the barrack's tin wall had no insulation, Bhanu and Bhupendra slept with scarves wrapped around their necks and over their heads. They placed their slippers near the bed so they could step right into them without touching the cold slab. The sole source of warmth was an ugly metal furnace protruding into the living room, fueled by heating oil and vented through a pipe out the roof.

One day when Bhanu was home alone, she turned to see the whole furnace glowing red, from the barrel all the way up the chimney. She shut it off, then went outside. Flames were shooting from the roof. Bhupendra, on his way home from work, passed a neighbor walking the other way. — Your house is on fire, the other student calmly informed him, and Bhupendra started running for home. By the time he arrived, firefighters were already on the scene, putting it out. It was natural for such heaters to build up soot and catch fire, they explained.

Between classes and crises, Bhanu set about making the metal trailer into a home. She and Bhupendra covered the rotting wooden countertop with contact paper, and purchased a straw mat to shield the furnace from sight. A graduating student sold them a sewing machine for twenty-five dollars, which Bhanu used to convert some of her trousseau into curtains. A pink sari became the front curtains; a blue one covered the bedroom window. They bought a large and tremendously ugly rocking chair; Bhupendra drew a pattern for a slipcover, and Bhanu sewed it.

They did the same with a used sofa. She scrubbed the aluminum pots they had bought for ninety-nine cents apiece till they gleamed, and covered a metal Crisco can (before the days of cardboard "cans") with contact paper to use as a utensil holder. The habit of making a home wherever she was became a skill that Bhanu would use again and again.

Another was the skill of building community. When a fellow Gujarati student was to be married, Bhanu agreed to help with the wedding; they made eight cabbages' worth of curry. For the university's annual International Festival—an event commended by the local INS officer as an example of how universities might foster international "friendship and cooperation"—Bhanu helped cook traditional dishes and choreograph folk dances. At Divali time, Bhanu joined in preparing a feast with the members of the Indian Student Association, which had just enough critical mass to hold holiday dinners, while Bhupendra helped with the organizing. The festivities included a talent show, where one of the speakers was a serious young graduate student who would later fashion—in part from the isolation of being a foreigner in the white land of academia—an influential set of postcolonial theories. Gayatri Chakravorty Spivak, whose essay "Can the Subaltern Speak?" is considered a seminal text of the field to this day, is known, among other things, for wearing boots with her saris.

My parents were fashioning their own theories of America. To them it seemed above all a land of opportunity, friendliness, and welcome. Certainly there were moments of difficulty, of nausea and homesickness—but where else in the world could you walk into a stranger's office in your first week in the country and be met with such generosity: job, books, scholarship, smile?

It was on the night of their first shared Divali in America, among a community of foreigners reenacting a ritual of home, that Bhupendra took one of his favorite photographs of Bhanu. She was dressed in a sky-blue sari, one of a pair that Ratanji had bought in India for his two youngest daughters-in-law. Her hair was swept back into a scarf-bound ponytail, and her eyes were dark and limpid in a fine, pale face. For decades Bhupendra would carry the photo in his wallet, a reminder of a sweet time.

One weekend the barrack apartment was filled with a special kind of warmth: family. Bhanu's brother, Champak, had driven the 140 miles from Ames, halfway across Iowa, to visit. Bhanu cooked what she could to summon the scents of home: rice, chicken curry, rotli. The rice was not basmati, the chicken lacked certain spices, the rotli were made from all-purpose flour rather than the special finely ground whole wheat they were used to, but it would do.

Champak could see how his baby sister had grown. Married now, and cooking a whole meal! How odd that they were all assembled here, in Iowa, perhaps the whitest place in the country or even the world, having somehow traversed oceans and skies, passed through cornfields and prairies to eat this meal together. Bhanu spoke in Gujarati, and Champak answered in English, his mother tongue stiff and awkward from disuse. Four years in America, he had had adventures he could not share with her, at least not yet.

As he took the first bites of spicy chicken, his mouth filled with tastes he had not known for years. And his eyes filled with tears. Not nostalgia, not homesickness—his palate had become American, the food simply too spicy for his taste buds. He ate it all and asked for more, nose running. And they laughed as only family can laugh.

In January, Bhanu retook the portion of the exam she had failed. Waiting for the results that spring, she learned about the thaw. One morning they stepped out of bed—into water. The barrack was set into the earth, below ground level, so snowmelt had seeped under the crack of the doorway. They spent the day cleaning and sponging, then hung the thin carpet they had recently bought for fifty dollars—to keep their feet a little warmer on the icy slab—on a clothesline, where it took two weeks to dry.

Bhupendra was working from 7 A.M. to midnight in the lab, and sometimes Bhanu went with him after dinner, helping to wash his test tubes. Meals in those months were simple vegetable curries, or sometimes Campbell's tomato soup, nine cents a can, with crackers. For a dollar or two they might treat themselves to a meal out, venturing out on weekends to split a slice of apple pie with ice cream in the Quadrangle, share a burger at McDonald's—she was getting used to beef—or splurge on a midnight movie, ninety-nine cents, with popcorn they popped on the stovetop at home and sneaked into the theater.

In April, Bhanu learned she had passed the exam. That very day, the clinic director telephoned the Omaha office of the Immigration and Naturalization Service. Over the phone, Bhanu was issued a visa number and given a verbal OK to work.

My parents were aware of their personal good fortune, but not of the supremely good luck of their timing. That spring, 1968, the last provisions of the new Immigration Act were being phased in, still being publicized and understood; the quotas were not yet full. Within the year, so many would-be immigrants would discover and apply for the new categories that INS officials warned of a backlog of at least two or three years. By the end of the decade, the process of getting a work visa and permanent resident status—an immigrant's first official step toward the dream of American citizenship—would require formal paperwork and years of waiting.

But for Bhanu, arriving almost accidentally at the height of the brain drain, the coveted green card appeared in a few weeks and without fanfare, in the mail. Printed in blue ink on white paper, the green card took its name from the wavy green lines printed over half of the laminated surface, over the photograph. Bhanu was smiling, dark hair smoothed back from her face with a fragrant oil, her sari's flowered border visible over her left shoulder. As her spouse, Bhupendra could have applied for permanent residency as well, but then he would have been required to register for the draft; with the conflict in Vietnam raging, he decided to stick with his student visa. Bhanu's card, dated June 5, 1968, advised her in tiny print of the necessity of keeping the government informed of her address, and noted, "If 18 years or older, you are required by law to have this card with you at all times." She was one of seventeen thousand aliens with "urgently needed skills" admissible under the third preference category in 1968.

"We are in the international market of brains," U.S. Secretary of State Dean Rusk was quoted that year as saying. India had just, for the first time, made the list of top ten countries providing immigrants to the United States. My parents were impressed with American efficiency, grateful for the kindness of authorities eager to help them, and warmed by the welcome that was, in part, a quirk of history.

Nine hundred dollars a month.

Bhanu's new salary was a virtual fortune, especially considering that Bhupendra was already covering their monthly rent and expenses from his graduate student fellowship. They remained frugal, but soon Bhanu's earnings bought their first car. It was a new Fiat 850, the smallest car available, light blue, stick shift, for $1,800. They went to visit Champak, and he often made the two-and-a-half-hour drive to visit them.

Champak had worked hard in his first years in America, taking odd jobs as babysitter, dishwasher, and construction worker to pay for textbooks and rent. He had loved Ames, Iowa, from the first day he arrived there; he told his sons many years later, "I just felt safe here." Thousands of miles from home, endowed with a new freedom, he also played hard. His American friends called him Champ. Handsome, athletic, and outgoing, he had had a series of white girlfriends. Slowly, he broke his news to Bhanu: he was seriously dating a farmer's daughter named Nina. He did not tell her that the girl's father had promised him a house, a car, and a stake in the family farm if they married.

At Champak's graduation, Bhanu and Bhupendra spent the whole day with Nina. Bhanu came home and cried. Indeed, it seemed her brother was lost. What would the family back home say? How could Champak be happy with someone from a strange culture, who did not even know how to cook his favorite foods? And what would become of their widowed mother, without a proper daughter-in-law whose home she could go to in her old age?

Although Bhanu was younger, and bound to respect her older brother, she resolved to try to speak reason to him.

By the time she did, perhaps something had soured in the relationship; or perhaps the taste of home that Champak had experienced in the Iowa City barrack every once in a while was enough to remind him of who he was. Bhanu never asked what happened to the farmer's daughter. All she knew was that when she did speak to Champak about marriage, he seemed ready to settle down.

—Name a girl, he said.

Bhanu, surprised, thought she would have only one shot. She named their lifelong friend Tara, whose family lived across the street. She showed him Tara's letters to her, written in fine English. It was Tara who, the day before Champak had been sent off to America, had teased him about his then girlfriend—through a locked screen door, so that he couldn't retaliate—with the words *Sita Sita, velaa velaa* ("Sita, shame!").

Champak nodded. They wrote a letter home, Bhanu telling her uncle that it was either Tara or the Iowa farm girl, and that he had better arrange the match. Champak wrote on the back, "What Bhanu has written is right."

Within weeks, he had borrowed money from his little sister to buy a plane ticket back to Fiji for the wedding.

Bhanu felt that a tragedy had been averted.

Though his father had been an Indian patriot, Champak seemed never to have considered resettling in India. Fiji and now the United States were comfortable places to live; India was distant, dirty, poor, even foreign.

But for Bhupendra, who had grown up in India, the dream of going home remained alive. Within their circle of friends, when the talk turned to India, Bhupendra could often be heard expressing clear ideas of what his homeland needed, of what he would do there just as soon as he reached home. "If I were prime minister . . . ," he would begin, launching into his ideas about education, politics, development.

So as 1969 began, in anticipation of graduation, Bhupendra had to decide where to apply for jobs. Each foreign graduate faced the same difficult decision: go home, or try to stay in America?

In Calcutta I met a man of my parents' generation who had studied in the United States, then gone home to take his place among India's elite. "I didn't want to spend the rest of my life as a second-class citizen," he explained.

In San Francisco, a writer friend who had immigrated from India in the early 1960s explained her choice to become an American. In the years of Kennedy and civil rights and the expansion of freedom, "this was such a welcoming country," she said. "You could be free here."

For Bhupendra, the question was logistical. His father, struggling to handle the large Narseys enterprise after Uncle Magan's death, was not prepared to capitalize a new pharmaceuticals division. Bhupendra thought he would work, gain expertise and prestige, and then strike out on a business enterprise of his own, either in Fiji or back in India.

He also wanted to teach; after nine years in universities, academia was more his home than anywhere else, and the campus environment appealed to him. He sent his curriculum vitae to universities and companies all over America, as well as a few other places in the Western world.

But the U.S. academic job market was tight, plagued by a sudden glut of PhDs. Bhupendra's initial efforts bore little fruit. This time, though, he had a strong advocate in his adviser-angel.

Professor Blaug told Bhupendra that the way to get a job was to present his research at the annual pharmacy convention, where industry recruiters and academics gathered to talk shop. The 1970 convention was to be held in Washington, D.C. Professor Blaug tutored Bhupendra through writing an abstract proposal and then, when it was accepted, rehearsed the talk with him: correcting his English pronunciation, advising him to stand up straight, alerting him when his eye contact faltered. He also schooled Bhupendra in the fine art of networking: — Tell everyone you meet, whether they ask or not, that you are looking for a job. And carry a stack of résumés to give out.

So Bhupendra and Bhanu flew to the nation's capital. She toured the city alone during the day, and they met for the convention's social events every evening. His talk went well. Afterward, in the hallway, Bhupendra ran into Dr. Mehta, the professor from Boulder who had told him to iron his shirt. As instructed, Bhupendra told Dr. Mehta that he was looking for a job and offered him a résumé.

—I just met someone, Dr. Mehta said. —Wait right here, don't move!

For more than half an hour Bhupendra stood in the hallway, the conventioneers flowing around him. He dared not move. At last Dr. Mehta came back, and said he had arranged an interview for Bhupendra.

—Tell him you'll do anything, Dr. Mehta instructed. —I told him you'd sweep the floors, clean the bathrooms, whatever!

The position, as it turned out, was far from janitorial: it was for a director of research at a San Francisco pharmaceutical company. But when the recruiter, who was the company president, looked at Bhupendra's résumé, he grimaced.

—Your name is very long, he said. —Can we call you Bob?

Bhupendra thought about the fact that, with only weeks before graduation, he had not a single job offer in hand. Yet he found himself shaking his head.

—When I learned English, he said, —"refrigerator" was a very hard word. But I learned it. You have only one word to learn, not a whole language. I think you can learn to say "Bhupendra."

Astonished, the man laughed. And he invited Bhupendra to bring his wife to a company-sponsored cocktail party in his suite later that evening.

Bhupendra was still dreaming of being a professor. But he agreed to fly —first class—to an interview for the position in San Francisco as director of research. A few universities also expressed interest, so he planned a round of interview trips to Omaha, Houston, and Madison.

His parents, too, were airborne. Ratanji and Kaashi were on their ill-fated round-the-world vacation, timed so that they would arrive in Iowa for Bhupendra's graduation ceremony. But while Bhupendra was interviewing in San Francisco, Bhanu received a telephone call at work informing her of Ratanji's massive heart attack in the Tokyo airport. His body was being flown to Fiji.

Rain pounded the asphalt as Bhanu made her first long solo drive, thirty miles north on State Highway 27, to the Cedar Rapids airport; Bhupendra had caught the first flight home. Since they had been saving most of Bhanu's earnings, they had enough for two round-trip tickets to Fiji. But as noncitizens, before they could leave the country, they had to obtain a "sailing permit" from the Internal Revenue Service, certifying that they owed no taxes. They also had to obtain reentry permits from the Immigration and Naturalization Service. Bhupendra canceled his remaining job interviews, and they set about visiting the bureaucrats.

There were hassles. The IRS agent overcharged them and insisted he was correct, so they had to pay a few hundred dollars, for which Bhupendra would later successfully file an appeal. Then the IRS would accept only cash; they went to the campus bank, showed their Chicago bank statements, and somehow persuaded the manager to allow them to transfer and withdraw hundreds of dollars for the tax and the plane tickets to Fiji.

As they packed their bags at last, Bhupendra received a call from the San Francisco firm. They wanted to hire him, at the impressive salary of twelve thousand dollars a year.

"Well . . . ," Bhupendra said. He was searching for the proper English phrase for accepting the offer without sounding desperate. Having pulled out of his university interviews, he very much needed the job. Industry had not been his first choice, but this was a case of—what was the American saying?—a bird in the hand being worth three in the bush.

"All right then, fifteen thousand," said the boss. The man had mistaken his hesitation for a negotiating tactic.

"OK, yes, thank you," Bhupendra stammered. Here was another lesson in American etiquette and strategy, one that he and Bhanu would later laugh at. Amid the grief and stress of the moment, though, the job offer was merely a relief.

After landing in Fiji, they went straight to the Narsey home. Ratanji's body was laid out in the front room. Kaashi, in white widow's garb, sat at the head. All of the siblings, including Bhupendra's sisters from London and Toronto, were arrayed around the coffin.

Kaashi addressed Chiman, her eldest son, who was now the head of the household.

—Take money from our account for the girls' airfare, she said, motioning toward her daughters, then added, —But Bhupendra is here at his own expense.

Bhupendra was shocked. He had just spent three thousand dollars in taxes and airfare, and given up the chance to teach at a university, in order to reach Fiji in time for his father's funeral. Was his mother angry that he had brought his wife? He had not expected to be reimbursed, but neither had he expected to have the fact emphasized so publicly.

He bit back his grief and rage. Bhupendra and Bhanu joined the circle, and sat. For the next thirteen days, they mourned.

The hordes of experts who studied the brain drain in the 1960s and '70s wanted to know most of all how, when, and why the brilliant young minds of the Third World decided not to go home. Many reports and surveys attempted, futilely, to zero in on the precise moment of decision-making. I believe a migrant encounters this crossroads not once but again and again, as if in a recurring dream.

Had my parents been welcomed home warmly, assured of a place in the Narsey empire, perhaps they could have chosen this moment of grief and openness to take the path back to Fiji, close to both of their widowed mothers. As it was, though, they returned to Iowa sobered.

They did not yet know where they would live the rest of their lives, but for now, San Francisco seemed as good a choice as any. In Bhanu's farewell card from the International Wives Club of the University of Iowa, signed by forty-three women whose names show their origins all over the world, one friend wrote, "Best of luck—drop me a line when your husband makes Prime Minister!"

When Bhupendra officially changed his status from student to permanent resident, he fit the typical profile of a skilled immigrant at the time. He was among the 2,900 Indian scientists and engineers who obtained green cards in 1970, the largest cohort of skilled technical "brains" from any country in a single year since 1950. He was twenty-eight years old, like nearly half of the scientists and engineers entering the United States in the late 1960s. Like him, most skilled immigrants were Asian, male, and students. Seven out of ten had physically entered the United States before the landmark Immigration Act of 1965; they had no way of knowing what changes were in the works on Capitol Hill. They just happened to be in the right place at the right time.

In places like Boulder and Iowa City, international students on campus still formed tiny cosmopolitan enclaves set into mostly white, provincial surroundings. But my parents' new destination was different, and so were the times. In the first half of the decade, before the landmark 1965 act, just as Bhupendra was arriving as a student, a mere 3,355 Indians had immigrated to the United States. In the second half, as Bhanu was achieving green-card status, nearly 28,000 Indians had done the same. This eightfold increase in immigration was greater than that of any other national group. And by 1970, one in four "aliens" registered in the United States was living in California. There, Bhupendra and Bhanu hoped to find Asian grocery stores, festivals, and real community.

In San Francisco, Uncle Ratilal took them apartment hunting. He was very light-skinned, an asset in approaching the doors with FOR RENT signs. On his advice, Bhanu, who owned pants and dresses by now, wore a sari every day of the search; that way, as Uncle Ratilal did not have to explain, people could tell that she was Indian rather than some less desirable race. Still, when the landlord or manager spotted the dark young couple hovering hopefully in the background, the apartment would have just been rented; they had simply forgotten to take the sign down, they explained.

After several days of this discouraging pattern, they at last found a one-bedroom apartment in the city's western district, the Sunset, just a few blocks from the beach. They settled in, and Bhanu found work; luckily, California was not one of the eight states that said physical therapists had to be (or intend to become) U.S. citizens. Pharmacists did, but Bhupendra's research position did not fall under the state licensing rules for those who dispensed pills to the public. Bhanu learned the downtown bus routes to the physical therapy clinic, while Bhupendra drove to his laboratory farther south on the Peninsula. They traded in the tiny Fiat for a luxurious, light blue Ford LTD. On weekends they might bundle up to visit the fog-stroked Ocean Beach, wander the gardens of Golden Gate Park, or check out random, free entertainment such as the annual dog show, where they marveled at the luxurious lives of the primped and pampered American pets. Bhupendra took lessons in oil painting. Bhanu went grocery shopping in Chinatown, overjoyed to find real vegetables and fresh spices. They were ready, they decided, to start a family. Within a few months, she was pregnant.

The day I was born, my father sent three telegrams: one to the Narseys store in Fiji, one to his sister in Toronto, and one to his sister in London. By luck or fate, he also received a telegram: a job offer from a university in the far south of the earth.

It was fortuitous timing in more ways than one. Bhupendra had just been told that his position was likely to be eliminated, since his company was being swallowed by a larger firm. With the Vietnam War in its sixth year, the United States was a frightening place for draft-age men. And the new academic position was in New Zealand, just a hop away from Fiji, where both of my grandmothers still lived. Having experienced the trauma of trying to travel to his father's funeral from a great distance, Bhupendra and Bhanu felt it would be better if they lived closer to their aging mothers. Besides, Bhupendra had always wanted to teach.

So they arranged for their car to go ahead by ship, sold or gave away most of their furnishings, and embarked on another round of official visits: To the tax office once again to pay what they owed to the United States and obtain the permit that would allow them to leave. To the Indian consulate, for permission for Bhupendra to use his passport to travel to yet another set of ports. To the New Zealand consulate, for a six-month renewable visa, with "wife and daughter" included on Bhupendra's passport.

Finally, they drove all over San Francisco, capturing images of a picturesque city they did not expect to see again. My father took most of them, through a lens of unabashed romance. In the albums of the early years of their marriage, these last vistas join endless photographs of my mother in a sari, her hair pulled back tight and black, cheekbones high and pale: with hibiscus blossoms in the city's botanical garden, or leaning into the wind at the Golden Gate Bridge, or, earlier, against a giant California redwood with me in her womb.

Once more, they crossed the Pacific.

Dunedin, at the southern tip of New Zealand facing the Antarctic Circle, was a university town of 82,300 with neat houses built on gentle green hills, remnants of an ancient volcanic crater. Bhanu and Bhupendra shopped for, and purchased, their first home together: a one-story house with two bedrooms at the end of a cul-de-sac, backing onto a golf course, for eleven thousand dollars. Their new nation had more sheep than people, and the vast majority of both were white.

New Zealand and its influential neighbor, Australia, were not yet interested in reaping the rewards of the brain drain. By long policy and practice, New Zealand had virtually no minorities and thus (as Bhupendra liked to say) no minority problem. The indigenous Maori were, like Aboriginal populations all over the Western world, so reduced and impoverished as to be nearly invisible in the towns. Since World War II, newcomers from Britain and elsewhere in Europe had been welcome without restrictions (many were even given free or "assisted" passage); for everyone else, permanent entry was at the discretion of a cabinet minister. The university applied for an exemption on Bhupendra's behalf, and he thought it quite an honor when he received a personally signed letter from the Department of Labor, Immigration Division: "Dear Sir, I am pleased to tell you that your application . . . has been favourably considered . . ." He would be migrating this time not as an unannounced student riding a public bus over the mountains, but as practically a local dignitary.

The promise held. In that lambswool landscape, our family's ethnicity was an exoticism too rare to be a threat; there was none of, say, Chicago's racial hostility. New Zealanders expressed a friendly curiosity that was returned by the young migrants as they learned the subtleties of yet another land. When their next-door neighbors invited them for "tea," they were surprised to find themselves enjoying not a hot drink but the evening meal. When Bhanu became pregnant again and asked to wear her saris to work—they were expandable, so she wouldn't need to buy maternity clothes—her supervisor agreed, on the condition that she wear a different one every day so that everyone could enjoy a variety of the beautiful fabrics. Bhanu would tell the story for years, of the offer and her reply and the way she sneaked in a repeat or two, without her supervisor noticing.

Within six months, though, they knew the transcontinental move had been a mistake—in financial terms, at least. Bhupendra's salary was a third of what it had been in San Francisco, but he had assumed expenses in New Zealand would be commensurate. It was a shock to find that rent, utilities, food, clothing, and everything else that made up daily life was as expensive as it had been in the United States. Even with Bhanu's physiotherapy salary, they were barely making ends meet, and unable to save any money at all. So once again, Bhupendra sent out résumés, trying to find a way back to the United States.

But after a year he had had no luck. Their status as permanent residents expired, requiring a visit back to the United States to preserve it, which they could not afford.

Luckily Bhupendra had always been good at coming up with a Plan B. Every seven years, professors at the university were due a sabbatical, all expenses paid. He and Bhanu agreed that they would make the best of life in New Zealand, and if after six more years they still wanted to leave, they could use the sabbatical year to try to make a go of life in America again.

Meanwhile Dunedin was peaceful and calm and, if nothing else, a decent place to raise children.

Six days after my second birthday, my brother, Nayan, was born, a healthy eight pounds, six ounces. One girl and one boy: Bhupendra and Bhanu felt their family was complete. Bhupendra's position as an international scholar, a senior lecturer at the university, gave him the kind of small-town prestige that was familiar and comfortable for a Narsey son. The *Evening Star* published his photograph with an above-the-fold headline about a conference in the pharmacy department, and when he walked downtown with one or both of his children, waitresses and shopgirls recognized him as that nice Indian professor with the cute brown babies. His interest in the arts became a grace note to his life, receding into guitar lessons and membership in the Otago Art Society, where he had a couple of small exhibitions.

Bhanu worked full-time as a physiotherapist and kept a busy domestic life, learning to replicate the tastes of home without a single Indian grocery store or restaurant. Instead of making green mango pickles, she marinated the native gooseberries, tart and sour, in an approximation of home's pickling spices. For the leafy greens of the tropics, she substituted plain spinach. In place of cilantro, she grew a patch of parsley in the backyard. The local newspaper found her, too: SPICE IS THE VARIETY OF INDIAN LIFE, read the headline. The article began:

> Step into the Wakari home of Mrs Bhanu Hajratwala and you can tell immediately by the delicate scent of spices wafting from the kitchen that this is no ordinary New Zealand home.
>
> In fact, all it would take to make you feel you have entered a different world altogether would be for Mrs Hajratwala to greet you in her sari.
>
> "But with all this snow lying around, I'm afraid you'll just have to forgive me for not wearing one today," the attractive mother of two, clad in Kiwi-style jumper and slacks, joked . . .

In the article my mother claimed to like the cold, but in fact the constant fog and drizzle wearied my parents. Having grown up in the tropics, they found the climate depressing: only one or two sweater-free days a year.

In New Zealand, even more than in Iowa, Bhanu and Bhupendra were conscious of themselves as representatives of a people, a race; and they sought to educate, to put the best face forward, as well as to build their own community. With friends, they started a local organization called the Dunedin India Society, made up of "people from all walks of life who are interested in the Indian way of life." The society celebrated festivals, held dinners, and published a spiral-bound cookbook as a fundraiser. When the town's cognoscenti sought advice on things Indian, it was the society's president, Bhupendra, who took the calls at his university office or at home.

One night well past midnight, Bhanu and Bhupendra were woken from a sound sleep by a call from the police station. A young Indian man had been found drunk out of his mind, with Bhupendra's business card in his pocket. Could Bhupendra come down and pick him up?

The young man was a refugee from Uganda whom my parents had befriended. His entire family had been massacred before his eyes by the henchmen of dictator Idi Amin, who shortly afterward had expelled all Indians from the country. In Uganda, as elsewhere, Indians—including Gujaratis—had formed a shopkeeper class. They became a prime target of the extreme and violent form of nationalism that the dictator espoused, their plight the most vivid and traumatic example of "pariah capitalism" that our diaspora had encountered. After the 1972 expulsion, thousands of refugees lived in camps for months and were eventually shuttled out of Africa to any country that would take them. Many ended up in England, while others were sponsored by charities and churches in the United States, Canada, Australia, West Germany, and New Zealand.

In Dunedin, a Protestant church had sponsored the young man and two other Ugandan families. One airport arrival was captured by an article in the local newspaper headlined ASIANS ARRIVE. The photograph showed three white men from the church and a Ugandan Indian family of five, all looking expectantly at my father, who, as translator, must have been the only person in town whose words they could mutually understand.

On a personal level, Bhanu and Bhupendra met with acceptance and respect. As ambassadors of their people, they performed remarkably.

But sometimes they longed for the easier comfort of home: to go offstage, to speak without translation, to be understood without anyone making a special effort. Despite outward signs of settling into New Zealand, Bhupendra's dream of returning to India remained alive. Dunedin India Society aside, the cultural isolation of their life in New Zealand was profound. The whole South Island of the nation had no Indian restaurants or grocery stores. Any cultural event had to be organized by my parents and a handful of others. The few dozen other Indians in Dunedin were mostly students or visiting scholars, who came over for meals but, unable to secure permanent permits, orbited home after a couple of years.

And Bhupendra felt a loyalty to his motherland. Even after a dozen years away, he still wanted to make a contribution. Bhanu, who had not lived in India since childhood, was game.

So Bhupendra wrote to his brothers in Fiji, asking if they would consider providing Narseys capital for a pharmaceuticals factory in India. He wrote to Indian universities seeking a position, and was asked to interview for a full professorship at the University of Bombay. He arranged to present a paper at an all-India pharmacy conference, so that the New Zealand university would subsidize his airfare and hotel expenses. In December 1975 all four of us went on a trip to India.

Those were the years when a visitor's first glimpse of scenic India, emerging from the Bombay airport and driving into the city, was the view of whole families crouching in giant sewer pipes at the edge of the world's largest slum. I was four years old, and wide awake.

—What are they doing? I asked my father.

But he was nearly as bewildered as I at the answer he gave me. —They don't have homes, they are living there.

For Bhupendra, it was the first trip back to Mother India in thirteen years. He was shocked. Everywhere we went, we were surrounded by desperately thin children who begged for the humblest of items: coins, chewing gum, even ballpoint pens—a commodity that, like blue jeans and cosmetics, was cheap and ubiquitous in the West but dear in India in those years. In Patna, the capital of India's poorest state, where Bhupendra presented his pharmacy paper, my parents remember being served dinner in a fine hotel by a waiter in a shabby uniform. He was so thin that he looked as if he rarely ate a full meal, and said he had eight school-going children to support. Bhupendra gave him eight ballpoint pens, a treat for the children, and tipped the man the entire price of the meal, saying, —Buy some good food for your children tonight.

I don't remember this incident; perhaps I was sleepy, or in bed already, or simply immune to the implications of the moment. Years later, hearing him talk about making this tiny gesture—"It was all I could do," he says—I realize the helplessness he must have felt. He was encountering a motherland in the grip of a social transformation so chaotic and massive that it seemed incomprehensible.

As an economy, India was screeching and grinding through a belated industrial revolution, experiencing the birth pains of shifting from a semifeudal British colony to a semisocialist democracy, trapped in a new cycle of dependence on massive foreign aid to stay afloat. As a nation-state less than twenty-five years old, the land had suffered partition and its accompanying near–civil war, a six-week war with China, and a war for Bangladeshi independence that had sent millions of refugees into India. As a people, Indians were midway through a population explosion that would leave them a billion strong by the millennium, with millions pouring from the villages into the cities to compete for scarce, low-paying jobs. Taken together, these national traumas shaped a grim day-to-day reality that left Bhupendra disoriented and disconnected from the country he had always considered home.

For Bhanu, the connection to India was even more remote: she had lived in India a few years as a child, in her ancestral village of Gandevi, but had returned to Fiji at age seven and never come back. In Bombay she was part tourist, part investigator, calling real-estate agents and viewing neighborhoods and apartments while Bhupendra went to interview at the campus. Entering its gates, he passed rows of beggars, and could not imagine hardening himself to the sight every day; was this the new India, or was it an India he had never noticed as a child?

He was offered the position, and asked for a higher salary. The man hiring him would not negotiate, but added, —Of course, you will be able to supplement it.

How?

By taking bribes from rich students, under the guise of "tutoring," in exchange for passing marks.

A sensation of betrayal runs through the brain-drain literature, and is mutual. Beginning in the 1960s, a war of words had been raging. Those who did not return home were called "gypsies" or "traitors." One Indian academic mocked the expatriates with their unreasonably spoiled wives, who wanted Brylcreem in tubes rather than in glass jars, and who complained during their occasional visits about even their posh lifestyles full of luxuries: "In India, cars are not promptly serviced, refrigerators become noisy, and telephones do not function." Another Indian science writer argued by analogy, comparing those who deserted their homeland to ungrateful children: "If the neighbours of a family are richer and have better living standard, then the children of the family cannot be expected to start living with the neighbour forgetting their own parents."

On the other side, an Oxford scholar observed that young scientists in India suffered "lack of appreciation of their work, insufficient means for research, difficulties in obtaining equipment and last but not the least, pettiness and jealousy" from older colleagues. A Yale University dean told the *New York Times* that he could not in good conscience advise a young Indian engineering graduate, offered a $10,000 job in the United States or Canada, to return home "where there is a high risk that he will be a clerk-typist for the next 10 years." The *Washington Post* reported that neither India's government nor its industry could absorb even half of the 600,000 graduates who moved into the job market each year, and the Indian government itself conceded that it was educating far more scientists than it could employ. A special Indian census of 245,000 scientific and technical personnel found that one in ten were jobless, while nearly two in ten were employed in fields outside their training "either on their own accord or due to the lack of opportunities in technical employment." If a man with a master's or doctoral degree in science was lucky enough to work in his field, he could expect to earn a median pay of about 300 rupees per month—approximately $50.

The census did not comment on or explore the possibilities for supplementary income.

My mother, recalling the trip of 1975, remembers sitting in their Bombay hotel room after the job interview, watching my father weep.

"He said, 'What have they done to my country?'" she tells me.

My father, listening quietly as she describes this, nods. "I felt that I had left my country, like a wife, to someone else for safekeeping, and—"

I am thinking about how I have seen my father cry only three times in my life. I watch his face for a trace of the anger or disappointment he must have felt then, although the evenness of his voice does not betray it. He sits in the stuffed beige recliner that is his customary spot in their comfortable family room, surrounded by a luxurious blend of Western and Indian décor, and suddenly, as he fails to finish his sentence, I see his eyes fill with an old grief. He drops his gaze and turns away.

Turning away from India, in 1975, was the end of a dream.

. . .

After India, we finished our jaunt through Asia, seeing the sights in Singapore and Thailand, getting stuck a few days in Manila. In some airports we had to stand in several lines, since legally I was an American, my father an Indian, my mother a Fijian, and my brother a Kiwi. Our passports filled up with purple, green, blue, and black circles and triangles and squares, the stamped authorizations of various nations.

Back in Dunedin, my father wrote a letter to his mother: —Now I don't think I can live in India. My heart is heavy with the poverty I've seen there. India has changed . . .

One of his brothers wrote back, rebuking him sharply: —India is as it has always been. You have become spoiled; it's you who have changed.

But my parents had made their decision, and were beyond the age of bowing to familial pressure. Independent of the wishes of the extended clan, they wanted to secure their own future now. The dream of home —of finding a place to settle down, raise their children, and get ahead— persisted.

Slowly all the reasons for staying in the South Pacific dissipated. Bhupendra's mother, Kaashi, passed away, and it was as if the possibility of making Fiji home expired with her. Bhanu's mother moved to Iowa to live with Champak and his bride, now the parents of two sons. Though my mother told the New Zealand newspaper reporter that we went to India every three years and to Fiji frequently, in truth we did not have money to travel much. It was difficult to save. Wages were low, expenses and taxes high, supporting a range of social services: daily milk delivery, free health care, nurses who made weekly home visits when children were born. My father's charts of savings showed no progress. My mother grew vegetables in the backyard, cut our hair at home, and sewed most of our clothes, including my father's ties; but while we were never poor, my parents felt they would never get ahead, as they could have in America.

At the university, my father was one of three Indians to hold the rank of senior lecturer. But none had ever been promoted. Assistant professor, the tenure-track position, was permanently out of reach, the dean told him apologetically. It was a white university in a white nation. My father had published papers, served on committees, earned the respect of students and colleagues. The dean would write the best recommendation letter he could.

So when I was seven years old the world changed again. My father was due for a sabbatical. We would use the year to try to move back to America, to leave behind the land of sheep. It was time to pursue, in earnest, the American dream.

The popular conception of inertia these days is of paralysis: someone stuck in a dead-end job or unable to make necessary life changes. But this is only one meaning of a scientific concept that consists of two corollaries: bodies at rest tend to remain at rest, but bodies in motion tend to continue to move. In the 1960s one Cornell University professor applied this idea to the brain drain. Creating a mathematical model of migration patterns, he coined the term "cumulative inertia" to describe the probability of moving in terms of the previous moves an individual has made. A federal study summarized the theory thus: "Briefly put, the more one moves, the more likely he is to move; the longer he stays in one place, the more likely he is to keep on staying. This tendency is quite evident in the data on mobility of PhD's." My father was one of these mobile PhDs, and the federal study, published in 1971, was as good an explanation as any for why my parents moved that winter to New Zealand—and why, seven years later, they were bringing us back to America.

Bhupendra lined up a yearlong research fellowship with a respected professor at the University of Florida. Champak sponsored Bhanu through the sibling provision of the 1965 immigration law. Green cards for everyone but me, the U.S. citizen, came in the mail within months.

In Gainesville, though, it turned out that the professor had built his reputation by running a postdoctoral sweatshop for Indian and Chinese students. On top of a full week's work, seminars were held on weekends at the professor's home; once the door closed, no one was allowed to leave. At the lab, every trip to the bathroom was timed, every page of notebook paper counted.

After two weeks of working twelve-hour days, Saturdays and Sundays included, my father called his old professor, his angel, in Iowa City: —Please, get me out of here.

The University of Iowa offered him lab space, projects, administrative support: everything but a salary. We gave up the apartment and the rented furniture and made the two-day drive to Iowa City, where our brown Ford LTD promptly broke down. My father applied to other universities for work, and in the spring came a choice: Buffalo or Detroit. Some god flipped a coin, and in June 1979 we became Michiganders.

Bhanu stayed home, for the first and only extended period in her life, as a full-time housewife. That first year in Michigan, she wanted to get us children settled after the series of sudden moves and new schools. I started third grade, my brother started first, and because our mother was home, we walked home every day for a hot lunch.

Meanwhile she was battling with the state of Michigan to be recognized and certified as a physical therapist. After a lengthy exchange of letters and a series of hearings, the state's physical therapy board ruled that the three-year degree Bhanu had earned in Fiji, her twelve years of work experience, and her testimonial letters from several bosses were not equivalent to a four-year degree.

Bhanu was caught in a trap that snared, and continues to snare, many foreign-educated professionals in the United States. It is an imperfect mechanism of the brain drain that allows immigrants to be admitted on the basis of their skills but does not guarantee them the local licenses necessary to practice those skills. The professor who becomes a taxi driver, the doctor who opens a motel—these are stock characters in any South Asian community in the United States. Within a few years Indian doctors in Michigan would organize to combat the problem of licensing of foreign physicians and other medical professionals. But in 1980 there was no advocacy group lobbying for either individual cases or widespread change. Like Bhupendra, denied a license to practice pharmacy in Fiji more than a decade earlier, Bhanu found that she was required to go back to school.

And so my mother became a student again. A heavy steel-gray desk, a university leftover from my father's department, was transported downstairs; a faux-wood-paneled room off the basement with blue shag carpet was transformed into her study. She was given some credits for her previous course work, but she had to take or retake freshman composition, physics, biochemistry, and other subjects: a total of four semesters. She pulled out the rusty old study skills she had learned at her brother's side in Fiji and set to work. Champak, in Iowa, could not help her now, but my father did sometimes. And I remember quizzing her from handmade flashcards as she memorized such things as the small bones of the hands and feet: carpals, metacarpals, tarsals, metatarsals. For psychology, she navigated a wheelchair for part of a day and wrote about the experience of disability. I was eight, then nine years old. When I was nearly ten, she went to work at the Henry Ford Hospital in Dearborn, a thirty-minute commute away.

In New Zealand, Bhanu might have become small and huddled; our lives there were always slightly shabby, as if the gray of the skies had settled over our skins, clothes, hopes. In Fiji she would have been one of several daughters-in-law, bickering for position in a chaotic and quarrelsome extended family. In India she could have lived a life of middle- or upper-class privilege, with a household of maids to supervise.

In America my mother bloomed like a tropical flower, colorful with a thick, strong stem, petals as sturdy as bark. She became a career woman who, with my father's careful financial planning, built a physical therapy practice so successful that within a few years it was netting six-figure profits, and would eventually put both of her children through Ivy League–caliber universities. She never slacked off on what she saw as her main duties as wife and mother, waking at dawn to make breakfast and pack lunches for all of us, making sure we had a homemade dinner most nights of the week, even if we had to warm it up and eat before she herself came home from work. She served as a social hub for a community of Indian (mostly Gujarati) families whom my parents befriended in Michigan, who lavishly praised her cooking and entertaining skills. She kept up with family obligations, sent cards and gifts at the right occasions, remembered birthdays and important holidays, and took us as often as possible to visit our nearest relatives in Iowa and Toronto. She seemed tireless, though of course she was often tired, developing insomnia and suffering chronic shoulder pain from leaning into her clients' deep-tissue massages several hours a day. Later she would recall the Michigan years as a blur: *I can't believe we did so much, it was crazy!*

Slowly we became—all four of us—American. For Bhupendra and Bhanu this would become clearer with each visit to India or Fiji. Although they tried to blend in, to do as the locals did, the mask was less and less perfect. The changes were physiological: they could not drink the water, had to be careful about what they ate, were bothered by pollution. Toughened instead to midwestern winters and life without housekeepers, they had become, in some barely perceptible way, softer. Toward the end of each trip they longed for the climate-controlled neatness of America's suburbs, the quiet order of their own lives.

The changes were also, of course, psychological. They found they simply could not understand *why* certain things were as they were, *how* people could stand to live that way. As their mothers and sisters described folk cures and beliefs, as their uncles and cousins quaffed whiskey and claimed it was good for their health, my parents listened politely, and afterward sympathized with each other over their people's ignorance. Over the years they fine-tuned a sensibility for when to intervene with real medical advice and when to let things be. They became accustomed to queries from relatives near and far: what should be done about an ache in the hip, what were the side effects of a medication, did a knee or shoulder warrant surgery, what did this paper from the doctors or the hospital mean? Such translation was a part of what they came to understand as their unofficial "social work," a service to the community whence they came. It was a connection but also a separation, a kind of setting apart — and setting above — that they negotiated, over a lifetime, together.

In time they found they were not the only ones. Their new Indian community in Michigan was composed of engineers and doctors, physical therapists and pharmacists — educated men and a few women like themselves, also far from home. The 1980 U.S. census, taken just as we moved to Michigan, found Indo-Americans to be the immigrant group with the highest proportion of university graduates and professionals. They also had the highest incomes of any major immigrant group, a fact that one pair of census analysts found remarkable, given that "almost 80 percent of these immigrants had been in the United States ten years or less." That U.S. immigration policy had been virtually designed to ensure this outcome was not mentioned, and rarely noted even by Indian immigrants themselves. What mattered was that they were no longer "Hindoos" who were "unfit for association with American people." Indo-Americans had become a "model minority."

In 1984, after waiting the requisite five years of continuous United States residence, my parents filed applications for U.S. citizenship. Bhanu's form listed a traffic ticket of $40 (paid), along with memberships in two physical therapy associations, the Gujarati Samaj (which my parents described on the form as "Indian Culture Society"), and the Canton Business and Professional Women's Association. Bhupendra's application listed five pharmacy associations, the Gujarati Samaj, and the science honor society Sigma Xi. Both provided their most recent addresses and occupations, ten fingerprints, and a bit of Gujarati script in the box labeled, "If your native language is in other than roman letters, write your name in your native alphabet in this space." They answered no to three questions about Communist involvement, two questions about Nazi affiliation, and various queries about whether they had ever been members of the nobility, mental patients, prostitutes, habitual drunkards, polygamists, drug traffickers, or deportees. They answered yes, they believed in the Constitution of the United States, and yes, they were willing to pledge allegiance to the United States and bear arms for it if required by law. On November 19, 1984, they were sworn in at Detroit's Cobo Hall as citizens of the United States. They were given naturalization certificates that confirmed their new citizenship status, listing them for identification purposes as being of "medium" complexion, with black hair and eyes, and noting their height and weight.

On each certificate, in a section for "distinctive marks," someone had typed, in capital letters, the word "NONE."

Where does one generation's story end, and the next begin? I am not a parent, but I have a sense that a parent's story must find some of its resolution in the next life — in the story of the child. This, at least, is the traditional belief, of which I caught a glimmer of understanding at my brother's wedding in 1998.

Our mother planned the wedding like a war. For months, a year ahead, she was making lists, dreaming of centerpieces and massive menus. Her own wedding had been such a simple affair, with only close family members, only tea and snacks. My brother's wedding, by contrast, featured five hundred guests, many of whom were treated to not one but several grand meals over the course of two August weekends. The previous winter, all four of us as well as my future sister-in-law had made an advance shopping mission to India, to buy the necessities: Dozens of outfits, so that all of the main players could change at least twice a day, with coordinating shoes and bangles and bindis. Stacks of saris to give away as gifts. Centerpieces for the tables; garlands and decorations for the doorways and altars. Multipage invitations, purchased after a day's selection in the stationery alley of Bombay, printed in Gujarati and English. Upon our return stateside, our mother set about requisitioning and organizing the food, dishes, holy items, and whatnot into large labeled boxes in the basement, arranged in chronological order for each day of the festivities.

No one could say she would have done more for an Indian daughter-in-law.

Behind the public festivities was a rough, raw story. My brother's bride was a Michigander of half-Finnish, quarter-Irish, quarter-Norwegian descent: a white girl. They had begun dating, secretly, in high school, my brother sneaking out the side door of the garage at night. When in college he revealed his love interest to our parents, they wept, raged, and tried to persuade him to change his ways. He broke up with Heidi, saying, —I can't do this to my parents. But within weeks they were seeing each other again.

By the time Nayan and Heidi moved from dating to engagement to marriage, my parents had bravely shifted with them. They paid for most of the wedding and a lavish scuba-diving honeymoon—unchaperoned —to Fiji. Besides the multiday Hindu wedding, they gamely participated in a Catholic wedding and separate country-club reception. Indian daughter-in-law or not, my mother would not be robbed of the pleasures of a grand wedding.

Because I was my mother's lieutenant, on call for anything that needed to be done, running hither and thither to retrieve items or make arrangements, the two weeks before and during the wedding are a blur. So I do not remember which day it was that I saw, between errands, one of my aunts sitting on the swing in my parents' family room, weeping.

Another aunt asked her what was wrong. Aunt #1 said she was remembering my grandmother, Kaashi, on her deathbed nearly thirty years earlier. Though Kaashi had eight children and more than twenty grandchildren, her last words—so this aunt said—were of my father: —Where will his day end?

By the time his mother died, Bhupendra had traveled from India to Fiji to America to New Zealand, but he did not yet seem settled. My aunt was weeping three decades later because my father's wandering had ended, in her eyes, in tragedy, with my brother's marriage to an "American" woman: the first white flower to blossom on the brown limbs of the family tree.

Failure, success; gain, loss. I do not think my parents see their lives or ours as tragedies, by any measure. Rather, they have adopted an admirable attitude of constant possibility. They travel frequently, and seem not to have lost the desire for novelty. Perhaps a lifetime of migrating creates such an openness, a continuation of the inertia toward motion.

"When we left San Francisco," my mother tells me, "we thought we would never come back."

We are crossing the Bay Bridge after an inordinately fancy dinner at an eighty-year-old castle built into the San Francisco cliffs. We are celebrating my birthday and my parents' anniversary, which fall on the same weekend. I live now in the city where I was born. They live in the suburbs one hour east, where they have moved for a sunny retirement after twenty harsh Michigan winters, and I am driving them home. Gazing at the bridge lights strung across the black waters, my mother says to my father in the back seat, "Who would have thought we would cross this bridge so many times?"

Sometimes my mother's voice fills with the wonder of a child from a small, small place, who feeds her imagination with *Life* magazine, never thinking she might see with her own eyes the fantastic, almost unbelievable lands depicted there. She and my father have embarked on a project to put all of their photographs into albums, a project that is reminding her, she says, of a lifetime's worth of travels. The only place she has not been that she read about in *Life* in the 1960s is the moon.

"Perhaps one day," she muses, "when they take passengers there." She is barely sixty. After all that my parents have seen, it seems possible.

7. SHELTER

Narotam and Benkor
↓

Sarasvati
Pushpa
Tara and Dhiraj
Champak |
Bhanu |
↓

Harish
MALA
Shobha
Meena
Pratibha

"*f*OR TEN YEARS *I cried.*"

In the dark of my apartment, my cousin Mala's words come through the tape recorder, strong and clear over a white noise that reminds me of rivers, though I know it to be highway traffic; it murmurs, this second voice, like the sound of time passing. I interviewed her on the road, driving up Interstate 5 from her home in Los Angeles toward mine in San Francisco. Our mothers are sisters, but Mala and I grew up on separate landmasses: she in Fiji, I in the United States. With a twelve-year age gap between us, I hardly knew her, though I had heard whispers and rumors that made me curious. Other relatives spoke of her past with a mixture of pity and admiration, and I hoped to learn why as we talked. We had six uninterrupted hours as we traveled toward a ceremony that would celebrate the first pregnancy of my brother's wife.

Every married woman bearing a child in our community undergoes this ritual, a day of prayers and special foods: the *srimant,* the rite by which the father's family seeks the blessings of the household goddess for the birth. During the ritual, our family would ask the goddess to accept the unborn child, and future children from this stranger's womb, into the clan.

It seems a beautiful sentiment, to arrange divine reception of the child before its birth, linking the reincarnating soul to its worldly home. But if the child is a girl, this acceptance is only temporary. When she marries, the family and its goddess will release her; the ritual will be repeated, and this time her groom's family goddess will be propitiated. For a married woman no longer belongs to her own father's lineage; she is not written into the family tree or counted with the ancestors in that line, nor is she to return to her childhood home as a family member, but only as a guest. And in every generation, some women more than others bear the burden of this shift in status, this alienation from parents and siblings, this journey to become a stranger-daughter in another's home.

As Mala's sons played with their Game Boys in the back seat and the golden fields of California's heartland rolled past, I turned on my tape recorder, and she began to tell, for the record, the story of her life.

Mala was the oldest girl. Both of her parents were born and mostly raised in Fiji; both had spent a few childhood years in India. Her mother, Tara, was seventeen when her marriage was arranged to Dhiraj, a tailor who was almost seven years older than she and who turned out to have little luck in business. They lived in a small shack behind his tailoring stall, and they got by because Tara's parents sometimes sent rice or other staples to help them make ends meet. Poor but prolific, Tara and Dhiraj were married in 1957 and had a son in 1958, Mala in 1959, another girl the next year, and another boy the next. This second son had a hole in his heart, however, and did not survive long after the miracle of birth. Mala's first memory is thus of female suffering: her mother weeping at the funeral, a deep and terrifying sadness. And then, the necessity of life going on: within a year, another girl was born.

Dhiraj decided to shift his growing brood from Suva, where numerous Indian tailors competed for customers and living expenses were high, to a backwater town on Fiji's northern coast. They would live in Tara's childhood home, where her father—Narotam, Mala's and my grandfather—had settled when he first arrived in Fiji three decades earlier. There, Dhiraj hoped, he could raise his family in peace and prosperity.

The town of Tavua lies somewhat inland, near a hill under which surveyors discovered gold back in the 1920s. The most beautiful local feature is a river that flows wide and dark blue through banks dense with taro plants, whose broad leaves bear a fecundity of green that perhaps only a woman who has given birth many times can truly understand. Our grandmother, who washed clothes and pots in the Tavua River and carried water to and from its banks, was such a woman; so was her middle daughter, Mala's mother; and so would be Mala herself. The taro grows, its roots and leaves are dug up for food, and somehow it grows again and is never lessened.

Despite the river's beauty, Tavua lacks ocean vistas, so its tourist trade has always been nonexistent. Business in Mala's childhood was most brisk on payday, when the gold miners came to town to cash and spend their paychecks. One spending place was a small shop on the dusty main road where Dhiraj and Tara stocked such goods as cotton dresses, imported blue jeans, thin polyester shirts, leather sandals made in India, canvas sneakers from Hong Kong, and rolls of printed fabrics in cotton and polyester. The mine workers sometimes paid in nuggets of pure gold, slipped from the island's depths into their pocket depths, and these Mala's father or mother would inspect and weigh on a jeweler's scale kept for that purpose behind a glass counter filled with necklace-and-earring sets and neatly folded packets of underwear. With such earnings, D. Haris & Co. —for that was the shop's name—eked out a living for a family of seven.

But the clapboard house was showing its age. What with the constant maintenance it required, childbirthing, and householding, Mala's mother had enough work for two or three of herself. When Mala was ten years old, her mother suffered a nasty kitchen burn that left her temporarily disabled on one side, shortly after bearing another girl. It fell to Mala to care for the baby, Pratibha. Mala also became responsible for much of the daily maintenance of home and family: cleaning, cooking, bathing, feeding, fetching, changing diapers, and walking her siblings to the three hours of school they had each day.

Tavua's one-room schoolhouse filled up in the mornings with farm children from the surrounding rural areas; afternoons were reserved for townies like Mala and her siblings. Many of the town children learned just enough to write out a receipt and calculate a bill, then dropped out of school. Mala loved her classes; she went as often as she could through her junior year of high school, when she failed the year-end exams. She would have liked to repeat the year and try again, but her father decided she was old enough to start helping out in the store.

By now Narotam's half-century-old house had been condemned, and the land was sold. Dhiraj moved his family to a newer home; the store was doing well enough. Behind the sales counter, Mala learned how to run the register while keeping one eye out for shoplifters; how to restock the inventory; how to measure and cut cloth. She had a way with the customers, deftly unrolling the long bolts of fabric they wanted, or could be persuaded to want, for shirts, dresses, salwar kameez, and curtains. She was sixteen, then seventeen years old, and the community had an eye on her future. Marriage proposals arrived as regularly as new shipments of goods.

But Dhiraj and Tara were in no hurry to marry off their loquacious eldest daughter. They were a close family, and she was both a good daughter and a good worker: solid and capable, the one to whom her siblings turned when they needed to borrow strength—or a laugh, for Mala's eyes often sparkled with secret humor, and when she chose to loose her tongue, her wit was sharp and quick. Her parents wanted to wait for a good home for her, preferably one that was nearby, prosperous, and suffused with kindness.

In Los Angeles one evening during my interviews with Mala, her husband came home and surprised me with a sheaf of four pages that he had composed during empty hours at his parking-lot job, headlined, *I MadhuKant born on 01-01-1956 and my History how I grew in Lautoka Town in Fiji Islands.*

Madhukant's story is written in blue and black ballpoint, in neat cursive, the pen having pressed down so hard that the words of each page are written over impressions of the words from the page before, in capitalization as idiosyncratic as Emily Dickinson's. It covers his education, the growth of his family's business ("Wholesale Bussiness by Buy Variety Goods such as Canned & Plastic Packet food items, Cotton and straw Hats & Caps, Ready Made Garments, Insenses and Kerosene Light Stoves, from Big Chinese Direct importers. We 40 to 50% percent profit and Travel in Station Wagon Car . . .")—and the most romantic story anyone in my family had told me.

"Once I went to Tavua Town to Sell goods to shop Name D. Haris & Co," he wrote. "There my eyes fall on his daughter name Mala."

Mala had her mother's sturdy build, large curves on a large frame. At 5'7", she was close to Madhukant's height, and if one were setting out to breed packhorses or steer, one would dream of making such a match. Her hair hung down to her waist and was thick as a mane; her face was a smooth, tan oval, and within it her light brown eyes sloped slightly downward, creating a softness that might lead a man to imagine great gentleness, as of a mare or a she-elephant.

"The owner told his daughter to get a cup of Tea for me. When she brought the Tea accidentally My Hands her hands. She looked at me and I looked at her and she smile than I fall in Love with her."

Madhukant told his parents, who agreed to send a go-between with a proposal. At first Mala's parents said no, as they had to all other offers; she was still only seventeen, there was plenty of time, and better suitors might yet come.

But as it turned out, this bid was different. The old lady who was playing matchmaker came again, singing the family's praises: their store was thriving, Lautoka was only an hour's drive away, and, most important, the boy was driving his parents mad with his stubbornness.

—He will not marry any other girl, the messenger said almost beseechingly. —You must say yes!

If you are a good daughter from a Khatri family, there is a moment in your life when compliance and softness are called for: the moment of the marketplace, when your marriage is to be arranged. This is what all of girlhood leads up to, and it is a time when lowering your eyes, bowing your head, wrapping yourself daintily but not vainly, maintaining a quiet interior smile and neutered expression that is neither bodacious nor sullen, keeping legs and lips pressed together—all of these qualities serve you well.

Later, toughness is the primary characteristic of female survival. The capacity to survive any and all of a husband's ways, a mother-in-law's whims; to do the cooking and cleaning of a whole household, without rest or complaint; to adapt to a new family, town, sometimes country; to bear, suckle, and keep twenty-four-hour watch over children, ensuring not only their physical safety and needs but also their moral character; to have tea and sweetmeats ready for whatever visitors may happen by; to pitch in at festivals and weddings for marathon cooking sessions that may begin as early as 4 A.M., or last all night, feeding hundreds— these are only some of the tasks of a woman. To say here "married woman" would be a tautology, since all women are married—it is part of the definition—unless they are not yet married, in which case they are girls, or unless they belong to some curious other gender which never marries, tragic and suspect. But why dwell on the exception, unspeakably rare? Mala did not know anyone who hadn't married, she herself was healthy and normal and good, so of course she would do as her parents wished; they knew best, and had only her happiness at heart.

She was a joyful girl who smiled merrily at all of the customers, just being friendly, favoring none; none had made any special overtures that she could recall. Which boy was it, then, who wanted her above all others?

—The one from Gosons who comes, said her parents.

Gosons was the name of the Lautoka store, a play on the father's name: Govind's sons.

—Which one? There are two who come.

—The younger.

—If you think it's right.

—Yes, but what do you think of this boy?

—Whatever you think . . .

And so they were engaged, in January 1977. The bride and groom, with their parents and two designated witnesses, went to the registration office. A magistrate asked each of them whether they consented. In the evening, Mala's family hosted a cocktail party for Madhukant's relatives.

The government of Fiji considered them legally wed, but for the families it was more like an engagement; only the Hindu ceremony would consecrate the union. Madhukant's sister was also engaged, to a man who was working in Australia, and the family wanted to hold a joint wedding. So they waited.

"Before Married very time I go to their Shop in I brink at her and She Brink at me," Madhukant writes. This courtship lasted five months, until "On 12th May 1977 We got Married." The groom was twenty-one years old, and his bride seventeen and a half. In Madhukant's telling, the wedding is the perfect ending to a fairy-tale romance.

But every fairy tale must have a villain.

The first migrants in our community were women: they traveled from their homes to their husbands' villages upon marriage. Mala's mother and her mother-in-law had both made the journey, as had all their female forebears, and now it was Mala's turn. An ancient tune still sung at weddings acknowledges the path: "Stranger, do not weep as you go to your new home . . ." The word for stranger is *pardesi,* literally "from another country"—a term applied now, in the age of globalization, to Indians who live abroad. But the first foreigners, the first to have to make their way in strange environments, were women.

And so, although her new home was only an hour's drive away, Mala knew she was entering a different world. Naturally she was cautious, and somewhat shy. Normally outspoken, she worried about saying the wrong thing. In front of her *saasu,* her mother-in-law, she tried to stay modest and quiet.

For this, to her dismay, her saasu scolded her: —What's wrong with you, can't you talk? So Mala tried to summon up her confident, talkative self. But when she chatted with a neighbor, her mother-in-law complained, —Why talk outside, you have no one to talk with in the house? And despite the family's affluence, Mala's saasu retained a frugal-to-a-fault sensibility. She would send Mala to the market with a few dollars for vegetables, and Mala had to return with change and to-the-penny accounting—then endure a grilling as to why she had bought such expensive onions and potatoes.

Mala found no sisterly bonding with the other two daughters-in-law, as each strove in her own way to shelter herself from the barbs. Within weeks, Mala realized that navigating her mother-in-law's criticisms was to be the major preoccupation of her new life.

Mala's saasu was, to all appearances, living the Indian dream. For a woman of her generation, she had the coveted triple blessing: her husband was still alive, her children had all married within the caste, and all of her sons' families lived with her under the same roof. It was an ideal scenario, not only by tradition but also in practical terms. With three daughters-in-law at home to carry out the daily homemaking tasks, she could enter a state of virtual retirement. Knowing that they were duty-bound to respect and obey her, she could exercise virtually unlimited authority.

The part played in a Western fairy tale by the wicked stepmother is, in much of India, played by the powerful and evil mother-in-law. From traditional folk song to Bollywood film, she is an archetypal character: the bitch-power, the devil woman, the old hag whose tests must be overcome for our heroine to advance into her own power. Whole soap-opera series revolve around the drama of mother-in-law versus daughter-in-law, and it is rare that a family saga unfolds on big or small screen in which the malicious older woman does not make an appearance, an instantly recognizable caricature or cameo. Certain actresses have made a career of playing this walk-on part.

Offscreen, almost every daughter-in-law has horror stories, especially if she has lived with her in-laws for any length of time. Some of these complaints are no doubt exaggerated or manufactured, but in my own family, I have witnessed one aunt complaining to guests at the dinner table, *My daughter-in-law doesn't know how to cook at all,* as the younger woman serves a multicourse meal she has spent all day preparing. Another says to her daughter-in-law, who has just walked in the door from a full day's work and is preparing to make dinner for the family, *Your kids are so spoiled, it's your fault, can't you keep them quiet?* And another rants to anyone who will listen, *That girl has put a spell on my son, he does everything she says, he can't even fart without her permission, they go out to the movies and leave me alone here, what will become of me, they are just waiting till I'm dead!* Certain mothers-in-law have made a career of acting the martyr part.

Married in May, Mala was pregnant by August. One day she felt queasy at the sight of the blackish eggplant curry that her saasu had told the daughters-in-law to prepare for lunch. Mala craved instead a simple fried-potato curry, made the way her mother would have prepared it. Not wanting to bother anyone, Mala stirred it up herself, cooking enough for the other women to share.

—Who said you could make that? her saasu demanded as they sat to eat. —Aren't you ashamed, eating all by yourself?

—Oh, but there's enough for everyone, please have some, Mala said.

But her mother-in-law, fuming, left the table and walked all the way to the store, to complain. Madhukant came home in the middle of the workday to berate Mala: Why was she making trouble? Talking back to her husband was out of the question; his temper was fierce.

When Mala recalls those early years, her voice grows quiet: "I couldn't say anything, I'd shut up and sit and cry and cry. If anything happened I'd just sit and cry. I said nothing."

As Mala's pregnancy wore on, it was a tumultuous time within the family, filled with daily explosions. All three brothers and their father worked together in the clothing store that Madhukant's father, Govind, had opened as a young man. Each of the three sons joined as he came of age, helping Govind to expand to wholesaling and importing goods from Asia. When Madhukant, the youngest, joined, they formed Gosons Enterprises as a partnership with four equal shares and the father as chairman. Madhukant and the middle brother traveled within Fiji to take orders from other shopkeepers; it was during this time that he had met Mala.

But now, Madhukant often found himself separating his brothers when their arguments turned physical at the shop. They accused each other of mismanagement, secrecy, and even theft; when their tempers reached a fever pitch, they would attack each other with fabric scissors, kitchen knives, anything that came to hand. Sometimes neighbors called the police to break up the fights.

The brothers' disputes were mirrored at home, amplified by their mother's character. When dinner was to be shrimp, for example, Mala's saasu counted out two shrimp per person before cooking them in spicy tomato broth. At the table, the children of the eldest son, being children, fished for as many shrimp as they could land in their bowls, three or four apiece. The younger sons' children were left with only broth; then the wives argued, and their husbands fought. Once the eldest brother stood and knocked over the whole pot, splashing tomato-red soup everywhere.

Another day the middle brother threatened to move his family out of the house. Mala watched, stunned, as her saasu clutched the heavy kerosene jug they kept in the kitchen.

—I'll drench my body, then light the match! How can you do this to me! the old lady shrieked as the whole family looked on. Her voice punched through the walls, so loud that Mala was sure all of Fiji could hear them. By morning the rumor would have traveled throughout the family networks on the islands.

Mala stood back, out of the action, as the others begged the old woman not to commit suicide by self-immolation. Someone wrestled the kerosene away; someone else snatched up the matches. Another held her until, at last, her flailing turned into sobs and she collapsed into a chair.

Eventually, that night, the house was quiet again, if tense. Like everyone else in the family, Mala was upset and shocked. But there was also a more immediate sensation: relief. For once, she had not been the target of the old lady's rage.

In the end, despite the old woman's tantrum, the middle son did move out. Within a year, so did the eldest brother. They managed to keep the business together, but with their residences separated by a few blocks, Mala was left alone all day with her saasu and her infant daughter.

Mala had never been afraid of hard work; she had shouldered her share of a large family's workload all her life with good cheer and competence. What did frighten her was her saasu's random outbursts and constant, malicious oversight, and the sense that nothing she did could or ever would please this woman. Mala never knew whether she would be chided for starting to cook something without supervision (arrogance) or for failing to start the cooking (laziness); for speaking up (impudence) or keeping quiet (aloofness). Whatever she said or did, wore or ate, all seemed fair targets and subjects for criticism.

One day, for example, the mother-in-law gave her own marriage necklace to Mala, saying, —Here, daughter; wear this and be happy. The *mangal sutra* of black and gold beads is traditional in our community, and is the mark of a married woman, with sentimental value equivalent to that of a wedding ring. The words *sukhi rehje* were a traditional blessing from elders to the young, and Mala accepted the gift. Perhaps it was a peace offering, a sign of a calmer life to come.

But a few days later, as Mala was wearing it, she noticed her saasu glaring at her. —That's mine, give it back! the older woman growled.

The battle raged on, daily.

In the Mahabharata, thought by scholars to be four thousand years old, a virtuous woman is described as follows:

> She was always attentive to her husband and whatever he did
> she did the same . . . She did not stand outside the house or

hold long conversations with anyone. She got up early, did the household work with her own hands . . . and looked after her parents-in-law.

Other wifely virtues included washing her husband's feet, never showing anger, attending to the needs of all family members, and being "the first person to get up in the morning and the last one to go to bed."

This consensus on a woman's role has the deepest of roots, and is woven throughout the sacred literature as well as popular culture. While a Hindu man's life is traditionally divided into four stages, each representing a stage of his spiritual growth, a Hindu woman's is divided into only three. Daughter, wife, widow: each is a relative status, a reference to her role vis-à-vis male kin. And of the three, by far the most important, the one that all of history seems devoted to praising or regulating, is wife.

Within a year Mala bore her second child. The birth of a son, as fulfillment of a prime obligation of a daughter-in-law, should have eased some of the pressure on Mala, but it did not. Instead, her in-laws isolated Mala from her own family even more than custom demanded. If her parents came to visit, it was unpleasant and difficult to talk intimately, since Mala's in-laws would not leave them any privacy and, on the contrary, would pass the time making disparaging remarks about Mala. Tavua was only an hour's taxi ride away, but her saasu placed conditions on each visit that made it difficult to find the time. If Mala wanted to make the trip, she had to rise well before dawn to prepare a full lunch: curry, rice, daal, and the daily portion of two types of flatbread—white flour for Madhukant, whole-wheat flour for her parents-in-law. Then she would have to boil the morning tea, separating a cup without sugar for her diabetic father-in-law; lay out breakfast; do the dishes; and clean the kitchen. Only then could she hurriedly dress and catch a 6:30 A.M. taxi. After reaching Tavua at 7:30, she might spend a few precious hours with her parents and siblings, but by 11:30 A.M. she had to be home to serve lunch and start dinner. And her saasu would complain that she had come back so late, and why did she have to go anyway?

Eventually the verbal abuse Mala had to endure before and after each trip dulled the joy, to the point where the few hours' respite hardly seemed worthwhile. Her parents counseled her to visit less and, instead, to focus on getting along with her in-laws.

Mala's children were one and two years old when Gosons bought a piece of land for $100,000 and took out an additional loan of $500,000 to build a nine-unit shopping complex along Lautoka's main strip. Business was booming.

But within the family, the feuding continued. One day the fistfighting between the brothers was so fierce that their father, trying to break them up, got pushed to the floor. Black-and-blue bruises blossomed on his fragile old skin.

At last their older sister, now married and living in Australia, came to intervene. She called a family meeting. If the three brothers could not get along, she said, they should go their separate ways. The store and its assets should be divided, with each brother running his own portion.

After plenty of heated discussion, the men agreed. The sister told Mala and the other two wives, —You will have to help your husbands in their businesses now. Will you support them?

—Of course, said Mala, —why not?

The great cyclone of 1985 was a calamity for the entire town of Lautoka. At Gosons Enterprises, most of the inventory—from clothing to tricycles—was waterlogged and ruined.

But for the dueling family, the storm proved a blessing. Cash from the insurance company was easier to divide up than the goods would have been. The physical space already had three clear divisions, but the brothers quarreled over which storefront was more desirable; in the end their sister had to step in again.

Designating the spaces on three pieces of paper, she made them pledge to abide by Destiny's decision. Then they drew lots.

The space that Destiny gave to Madhukant had no storefront on the main street. He decided to open a wholesale business and named it, optimistically, Madhusons (thus far, he and Mala had only one son). With this, he began his own transformation, from dutiful youngest son to head of household.

Years before, as a young man visiting India, Madhukant had made a

My parents shortly after their wedding in 1967. They carried these photos of each other in their wallets.

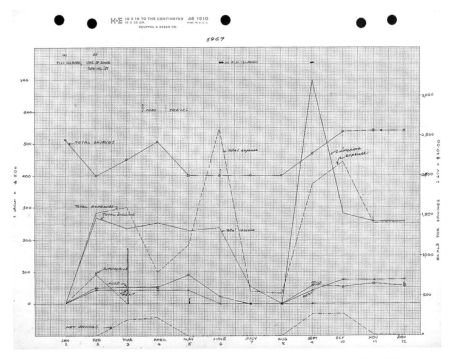

My father's graph of expenses in 1967, the year my parents married. The spike in June represents his wedding trip to Fiji, and the one in September shows their trip back to the United States.

Champak and Tara in 1969, just after their wedding.

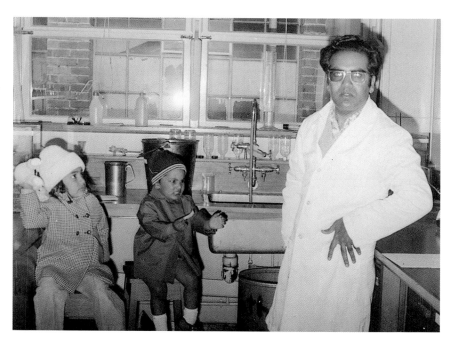

The young professor and his children, New Zealand.

LEFT: *Our first stop in the United States: Disneyland, 1978.*

BELOW: *In our new home in Canton, Michigan, ca. 1979. Note the tropical wallpaper mural.*

*Growing up
in Michigan in
the 1980s.*

My brother, Nayan, at his wedding in 1998, with our uncle Champak.

Mala with her family on their first trip to the United States, when I first met her at my brother's wedding and learned part of her story.

My mother (left), Mala, and Mala's mother-in-law with Mala's daughter, Kirthi, 1978.

Jaydeep (far left) and his family in Kalyaan, outside Mumbai, India, 2001.

Minal Khatri (third from right) with her siblings and cousins at her sixteenth birthday party in London, 2002.

Raju (Roger), the entrepreneur, at his wedding in Toronto, showing a gift, ca. 1987.

Dhiren, the table tennis player, with his trophies, early '80s.

Praveena with her students in the new, post-apartheid South Africa, 2002.

Hemesh, the Hong Kong import-export businessman, in 2001.

The next generation: my nieces with their cousins, 2007. Left to right: Ava Naasko Hajratwala, cousin Ella, Zoë Naasko Hajratwala, cousin Sonia, Téa Naasko Hajratwala, cousin Trina. They all live in suburban Michigan.

pilgrimage to a temple devoted to Hanuman, the monkey god of Hindu epic literature. There Madhukant had witnessed miracles—including an exorcism, a priest flogging a malevolent spirit out of a possessed woman —that gave him a powerful faith. Now his parents were making a trip to India, a sort of retirement journey for his father. When they came back, they brought Madhukant a vial of holy water from the temple grounds.

Drinking it, Madhukant felt a profound peace come over him. He was transformed. Where once he had been a poor student with little knack for the details of running a business, now he felt he could make the most of what he had been given. He became confident, and business started to feel natural to him; he could see, suddenly, how to make profits. Once each week he recited a lengthy praise-hymn to Hanuman, performing a full ceremony of worship to the god whose temple had given him such aid.

For Mala, the change was also dramatic. She rushed through her morning chores, cooked breakfast and lunch early in the day, sent her children off to school, and then joined Madhukant in the store. There she brushed up the skills she had learned in her parents' shop: tracking inventory, packing and unpacking wares, sorting merchandise, keeping accounts. She enjoyed a few hours' shelter from her saasu's gaze before returning home to cook the evening meal, put her children to bed, clean the house, and collapse into a heavy sleep.

That was her life six days a week. On Sundays, when the store was closed, Mala did not rest. Her in-laws demanded that she prepare a special labor-intensive feast, lamb-lentil stew and barbecued meatballs with all the trimmings. In addition to her daily chores, she also had to scrub all the floors and the dozens of old-fashioned louvers that covered the windows.

Mala's twenties were passing in a blur of activity and exhaustion. Still, working double duty in the shop was preferable to spending every waking hour with her mother-in-law.

On their son's seventh birthday, Madhukant and Mala decided to hold a celebration. Both of their families were invited. Mala's parents had another family event to attend, and came to the party a couple of hours late. As they walked up the path toward the house, Mala's father-in-law began shouting at them.

The curse words he used were so terrible that no one in my family will repeat them to me, although everyone seems to have heard the story. He excoriated them for their tardiness, then turned his harsh language to vilifying the lazy, worthless daughter they had given in marriage.

Mala's father told Mala to pack her clothes. — You don't need to stay in this house, he said.

Of the three stages of the Hindu female life cycle, the middle one, wife, is the one she must achieve and then hold on to at all costs—so much so that one classical heroine, upon the death of her husband, is said to have followed the God of Death all the way to the gates of the underworld in order to restore her husband to life and save herself from being a widow. One of the worst slurs one can call a woman in Gujarati, a curse word akin to "cunt," is *raan:* widow. For a divorcee there is no word, the phenomenon being so uncommon that we must insert, on the rare occasions when a reference is necessary, and always in that special undertone of projected whisper that is reserved for shame, the English word.

Mala had tried nearly every strategy available to her. Fighting back was never an option: it would mean thrashing upstream against not only her husband and his entire family, not only the community and its gossips, but also millennia of expectations of what a woman should be. So she had attempted to anticipate her saasu's wishes (but they were everchanging); to enlist allies (but who in the household or neighborhood would take her side?); and to explain her point of view to her husband (but he had made it clear that it was her job to get along). When those failed, she bit her tongue and worked as hard as she could. But even silence and accommodation were not working; the escape route her father had offered meant divorce.

Growing up, I had heard of only one case of divorce in the entire history of my family on both sides. It was a miserable story.

My father's sister, Kanchan, left her husband in the 1950s and obtained a divorce from the *panch,* the five-man council that held jurisdiction over caste affairs in their village in India. The ruling was a rare triumph but also a great shame. Until her dying day Kanchan spoke of it only if pressed and then only obliquely. Whatever relief she might once have felt in freedom from her drinking and gambling husband had long since washed away in years of bitterness. Her father, then her brothers, and then her son took care of her materially, yet she was miserable, always living under the burden of her social-outcaste status. A woman without a husband is rootless in the world, shamed, and dependent forever on her male kin, who will always resent the burden. Such a social death was considered by many a fate worse than actual death—literally, in the case of the high proportion of Indian wives who attempt or accomplish suicide each year. Outside of marriage, for a woman, there was nothing.

Mala, sobbing, refused her father's order. She would soldier on, and remain *wife.*

In retaliation for her parents' ill manners in threatening to take her back, Mala's in-laws cut off all contact with her family. They stopped delivering wholesale goods to Dhiraj's store and demanded immediate, early payment of outstanding invoices. If Mala's parents called the house, her father-in-law would curse them on the phone before hanging up. They were not allowed to visit; she could not visit them, or go to any family events where she would be likely to encounter them.

"In-law" among our people is *vevaai,* a particular type of kinship between two families. It is not, as the English term might imply, a matter of legality or technicality. Each marriage links not only individuals but clans; indeed, entire structures of community and caste persist only through such ties. One's vevaai, the parents of one's son- or daughter-in-law, are kin toward whom certain obligations exist. The severing of that relationship is thus an extreme and violent measure.

In 1987 Mala bore another son, Mithun. She was not allowed to go to her mother's home for the traditional convalescence period, nor were her parents allowed to come and see their newest grandchild.

Mithun's birth came at a dramatic time for the country. An Indo-Fijian was elected prime minister for the first time in the islands' history. But within weeks the military, composed mostly of native Fijian soldiers, revolted. As the army took over the government at gunpoint, looters took advantage of the momentary chaos to rampage through stores, most of which were owned by Gujaratis. It was Fiji's first military coup.

Fiji's shopkeeping Indians were fearful and exhausted, and so was Mala. She had wanted to have her tubes tied after the birth, but her mother-in-law had staged one of her infamous tantrums, ranting about how it was a sin. Mala had come home without the procedure.

Through the grapevine, she heard that her parents had weathered the coup. Through the grapevine, she sent word of her son's healthy birth.

Every day I was crying, Mala says of this period of exile from her family. But if the extremity of the punishment was intended to increase her submission, it backfired. Cut off from her parents, feeling that she had little more to lose, Mala stopped trying to please. When her mother-in-law launched into one of her interminable complaints, Mala just shrugged and said, — Go ahead, talk, just keep talking about it!

Once unloosed, her tongue began to shriek, as if the years of self-repression had gathered an unholy force behind her words. Even if the words themselves were relatively mild, Mala found that she was often yelling them loud enough for neighbors three or four houses away to hear. — Say what you want, go ahead, talk talk talk!

One day the next-door neighbor, a kind Indian doctor, encouraged Mala to keep on shouting. — Yes, child, tell them. They've kept you so oppressed and fearful. Don't be afraid, speak your mind!

This advice, from a respected elder, emboldened her. She continued to shoulder her workload as a dutiful daughter-in-law, but spoke up when pushed to do more than that. She redefined her own sense of dharma, or moral duty, and decided to live it in her own way. Duty did not require suffering everything silently, as she had once believed. Respect meant speaking politely, but one had the right to verbal self-defense, to expression; so she spoke up, muttering at some times, shouting at others. Responsibility, hard work: these she continued to accept, but not beyond the point of fairness.

Still, she wept. When her grandmother was on her deathbed, Mala was not allowed to go to her for a last visit. When the old woman died and custom dictated that Mala's in-laws show their respect, they sent Madhukant as a representative; even he was instructed not to go home for the wake but only to attend the impersonal ceremony at the funeral home. It was an intentional slight.

In 1991, Mala's youngest sister, Pratibha, whom she had all but raised, was to be married. Mala was not allowed to go to the engagement ceremony.

But Pratibha was a force to be reckoned with. It was Pratibha who had urged Mala years ago, —If they yell, why don't you yell back? It was her advice that Mala was finally heeding. And it was at Pratibha's urging that a delegation, consisting of their parents and two community elders, arranged to visit Mala's home to meet with her in-laws. They would open up a dialogue after five years of stony silence.

Anticipation as well as tensions ran high in Mala's household as the meeting date neared. Mala could not wait to see her parents again, but she was terrified at the prospect of the quarrel that was sure to break out. But Madhukant was also fed up with the drawn-out drama. Older now, a father of three, and more confident—perhaps as the one who held the household's financial purse strings—he told his parents, —My parents-in-law are coming to talk. You be quiet and listen.

At the meeting, Mala's parents wept and begged: —How long can we live like this, not seeing our daughter's face?

Mala's in-laws, pressured thus by their son and by the community, relented. They agreed to let Mala, accompanied by her husband, attend Pratibha's wedding.

But they were under no obligation to make it easy. A wedding lasts at least three days, but Mala's in-laws told them to go only for the most important day, leaving early in the morning and coming back home before dark. Nevertheless, it was a thaw. The family reunion was tearful, tinged with joy as well as pain for the lost years.

Afterward, Mala told me wryly, "I became *jabri* myself."

Jabri is a complicated word, one of the rare Gujarati terms whose meaning is unambiguously negative. Its possible meanings include shrewish, naughty, wicked, difficult. Once in a while it can be pronounced with a kind of grudging admiration, or admitted to be necessary, as in "Sometimes you've got to be *jabri* with these people." The *Modern Combined Gujarati–English Dictionary* lists only the masculine: *jabar,* powerful, strong. *Jabri* is the feminine version. And as in English, a woman claiming strength or power can be translated, more or less, as "bitch."

In Mala's case, becoming jabri entailed no wild or cruel behavior— only that from time to time she might, for example, cook something on her own initiative. One holiday she made a large batch of sweets and left them out for everyone to enjoy. Her mother-in-law complained, —The children come home from school and eat all this junk! You're letting them have bad habits!

An earlier Mala might have been cowed, might have gone to her room and wept. But the new Mala answered back, —I made it for them to eat, so they eat. I'm at the shop all day, I can't police them. But if it bothers you, why don't you get a safe, lock up all the food, and dole it out one morsel at a time?

A few days later, she told the children to start coming to the shop directly after school. There, she made tea on an electric kettle in the back storeroom and gave them store-bought snacks so they could eat their fill before heading home.

Then her mother-in-law complained, —You're wasting money buying them outside food. What, home food isn't good enough?

But Mala and Madhukant could afford a few snacks. In the post-coup years, real-estate values throughout Fiji had plummeted as shopkeeping Indians fled what they viewed as a newly hostile business and political climate. Pre-coup, Indians had made up a majority of Fiji's population; by 1996, with thousands emigrating to Australia, New Zealand, and beyond, they were only 44 percent.

Madhukant was his parents' youngest son, though, and it was his place to stay with them. Besides, for those who stayed, there were profits to be made. Within a few years Madhukant picked up a three-bedroom house for the bargain price of thirty thousand dollars. He also bought a commercial property: two large shops, four offices, two flats, and three warehouses. The same year, their youngest child, Pranil, was born. It was 1993, and by now Mala had the *himmat*—inner strength, courage, will—to ensure that her childbearing years were over. She told the doctor she wanted her tubes tied right after the birth, took the extra day's rest, and came home. When her saasu yelled, Mala said mildly, —Go ahead and yell.

The house still belonged to Mala's father-in-law, but Madhukant and Mala were paying all of the household expenses, which encompassed the old man's whiskey needs and a $20,000 remodel, including a new ceiling and floor tiles. When their daughter, Kirthi, turned sixteen, they paid for a decent wedding and saw her settled with a suitable boy from a respectable shopkeeping family in the capital, Suva.

Fiji, nine decades after the first Gujaratis migrated there, was comfortably home. Mala and her family spoke not only Gujarati and English, but also Fiji's Hindustani creole and even a few words in the native Fijian tongue. Madhukant had become, by a process of attrition and acquisition, one of Lautoka's most prominent businessmen. At home in the islands' balmy climate and cultural mélange, they had no desire to emigrate.

But in 1996, suddenly, Fiji's lawlessness started to feel personal.

The first time that Madhusons was looted — windows smashed, goods stolen, premises ransacked — Madhukant was furious. He cleared the mess, paid for repairs with the insurance money, and reopened. Within two months, though, the store had suffered three more break-ins. In one instance, a witness told him that seven police officers, arriving on the scene in response to the blaring burglar alarm, let the robbers escape and instead took goods home for their own families.

Accurate or not, the tale is one of a genre of such stories, and indicates how native Fijian authorities were widely perceived to be indifferent to crimes against Indians — especially Gujarati shopkeepers. Adding to Madhukant's troubles, he could no longer afford to keep his shop insured; the shop had five large glass display windows, which were such a high risk that the insurer demanded higher premiums. Livid, he vowed to leave Fiji.

Like his peers before him, Madhukant researched his options. Australia, New Zealand, Canada: all three countries accepted migrants via a point system, but it was weighted toward those with close family relationships and professional qualifications. And then, in 1997, he saw an item in the newspaper about the U.S. immigration lottery.

On a whim, he decided to apply. Maybe Destiny would favor him this time.

Most Americans are shocked to learn that each year our government's computers randomly select 55,000 lucky winners from all over the world to immigrate to the United States. These newcomers have no close family ties, no urgently needed professional skills, no large sums of money to invest—indeed, no grounds to become Americans except desire. We are accustomed to thinking of our immigration policy as somewhat rational, despite plentiful evidence to the contrary. The lottery is perhaps the most obvious Exhibit A.

The lottery's first incarnation, passed in 1986, was a gesture at balance for those who had begun to feel that America was letting in far more brown and black immigrants than was entirely desirable. In its early years the lottery favored those "adversely affected" by the Immigration Act of 1965. That act, prioritizing professional skills and family connections, had been carefully designed to maintain European American population dominance—but not quite carefully enough. Chain migration meant that people who had originally "drained" as professionals from Third World countries had been able to sponsor large numbers of their family members, who might or might not be educated; these in turn sponsored others, leading to a skew in the family categories of immigration—the very ones that, it had been thought, would ensure that America stayed populated with European stock. The fact was that most white Americans had no close relatives in Europe anymore; Europe was one of the areas "adversely affected." The lottery, with only 10,000 winners in its early years, could hardly stem the tide, but perhaps it could add some balance.

Partly it did so by reserving a quota of forty percent for Irish nationals, many of whom were already illegally living here. Its second function, then, was as a sort of unofficial amnesty program, which, not coincidentally, guaranteed its congressional sponsors the strong backing of the Irish American vote. Each individual could mail in up to 1,000 applications per year. It was truly win-win legislation.

Over the years the program was tinkered with and regularly threatened with elimination, but preserved in its essence until the great immigration battles of the mid-1990s. Faced with the accusation that the program encouraged illegal immigration, its sponsors chose to preserve it by eliminating the Irish privilege and making winners subject to penalties if they were already here illegally. Rather than amnesty, then, the lottery became what it is now, a long shot at the world's grand prize: becoming an American.

To qualify to enter, all you need is a high school education or a specified equivalent; citizenship in a country that sends fewer than 50,000 immigrants a year to the United States by other means; and the ability to write down certain pieces of information correctly on a sheet of paper. Among the approximately 6 million people who entered in the same lottery season as Mala and Madhukant, 1.3 million were disqualified for not meeting one or more of these requirements.

Madhukant filled out the paperwork, which was surprising in its simplicity: plain white paper with name, address, telephone number "if possible," country of citizenship, date and place of birth, and the same for each of their three sons. (Their daughter, married, was too old to qualify as a dependent.) He made out one form in his own name, one in Mala's, and taped—not stapled—a recent photograph (1½" by 1½") to the page. Then they signed their names.

Madhukant mailed the two envelopes together to his friend in Los Angeles, who had agreed to go to the post office and mail them so that they would arrive "between noon on February 3, 1997, and noon on March 5, 1997" at the specified address: DV-98 Program, National Visa Center, Portsmouth, N.H. Wherever that was.

By 1997, the lottery was so massive that the post office in Portsmouth sorted each continent's applicants according to its own designated zip code. For Oceania—consisting of Australia, New Zealand, Papua New Guinea, and "the countries and islands in the South Pacific"—the zip code was 00214, and the odds were long. Mala and Madhukant were competing for one of 844 visas to be distributed in their sixth of the world. By the strange logic of the law's formula, Europe had more than 23,000 visas up for grabs and Africa more than 21,000, while Asia had just over 7,000 and Latin America fewer than 2,500.

In West Africa that spring, hundreds of people rioted and hurled stones at the central post office of Sierra Leone, where thousands of lottery entry forms were found to have been dumped into the sea. In Washington, D.C., the lottery survived yet another congressional attempt to eliminate it as an irrational policy; Ireland's ambassador was reportedly "instrumental" in keeping it alive. In New Jersey, immigrants from India officially became the state's largest group of new arrivals, according to new figures released by the Immigration and Naturalization Service; it was also the first year that Indians made it into the top three immigrant groups nationwide (after Mexico and the Philippines). They were therefore ineligible for the lottery, although Bangladeshis and Sri Lankans could apply.

In Fiji, Madhukant opened an envelope, and shouted aloud.

And Mala began packing for her first plane trip.

Los Angeles from the air is a patchwork of grays: concrete, slate, pitch, smog. For someone who has grown up on an island verdant with palm trees and cane fields, where the longest road is a 315-mile loop around the entire landmass, the greater Los Angeles metropolitan area is an awesome sight. On the approach, the endless gray dissolves into S-shaped blocks of townhouses and tract homes; just before touchdown comes the green shock of racetrack, then runway lights shimmering against the dark glass skin of hotels.

Mala took in the scenery and the excitement of her three sons, but her own thoughts were focused, as they had been for most of the eighteen-hour flight, on survival. What would they do in America, how would they live? Would they, who had done only one kind of work their whole lives, be able to learn a new trade at their age? Would she be able to keep track of new details, and would she need to learn to use a computer? How much was rent, food, schoolbooks for the boys?

These and other questions were the purpose of this, their first scouting expedition. Mala was hesitant about leaving the only homeland she had known, but her parents, siblings, and even sister-in-law were encouraging the move. They had to leave for the children's future, everyone said; Fiji's economy was shrinking, crime was rising, and the islands were no longer a paradise, at least for Gujaratis. And relatives already in the United States had invited them to visit and see how they liked it.

Besides, it was August 1998, almost a year after Madhukant's name had been drawn in the lottery. If they wanted to keep their options open, they had to activate their green cards by getting them stamped within United States borders.

I met Mala and her family during this trip at my brother's wedding in Michigan. My first impression of the family was of a series of Russian dolls, identical in form but scaled in size, the kind you could put one inside another: Madhukant was the tallest and roundest, followed by

Mala and, in turn, their three sons, aged nineteen, eleven, and five. All of the boys were friendly, boisterous but not seething with resentment like most American adolescents; Vinay, the eldest, had a permanent twist of one ear that reminded me, rather sweetly, of a baby elephant. During the endless days and nights of wedding-related cooking, Mala taught me to make a special kind of sweet bread cooked only at weddings, and we stood side by side for what seemed like hours, as they had to be pan-fried individually. As we talked, she struck me as friendly, enjoyable, and even a bit independent—spirited, not just another subservient daughter-in-law. I don't remember exactly what was said between us, but it occurred to me that she was a woman willing to speak her mind. At the time, I knew nothing of the path she had taken to become so.

Of the cities they visited on that trip, Mala and Madhukant found Los Angeles the most appealing. Its vastness—it is ten thousand times the size of Lautoka—was daunting; but a large city would offer more opportunities for work, community, and Indian groceries. The climate suited them. And apparently it had an abundance of motels, which was a good line of work to pursue, according to friends and relations all over America. Among Gujaratis, especially those with an entrepreneurial bent and no higher education, the motel business was said to be a no-brainer.

They decided to go back to Fiji, close up shop, and take the plunge. They would claim their lottery prize.

In the late 1990s, the national media were abuzz with stories of South Asian immigrants to California: the H-1B visa holders, the brilliant computer scientists and engineers from the subcontinent who were flocking to Silicon Valley to be part of the Internet revolution. Their story merged with, and seemed a natural sequel to, the saga of the brain-drain generation, those polite professionals who had assimilated so smoothly into America's suburbs, universities, hospital staffs, and engineering firms.

Pushing up underneath this visible, model-minority diaspora was, however, another South Asian community, composed of relatives and refugees and illegals who threatened not only America's borders but the South Asian American community's vision of itself. They were working-class, either minimally educated or unable to apply their overseas educations to white-collar work in the United States. They were most visible as taxi drivers and newsstand operators, at 7-Elevens dispensing change and cigarettes, or behind bulletproof glass at gas stations and late-night liquor stores.

It was this quieter diaspora, one that was ultimately deeper-rooted and longer-lasting than the Silicon Valley megatrend but that never appeared on the cover of *Forbes* or *Time*, that Mala and Madhukant were about to join. With their rudimentary Fiji public-school education decades behind them, neither would be able to read English well enough to browse the help-wanted ads in the *Los Angeles Times* classifieds; their oldest son, Vinay, by then twenty, would have to become their first translator in America. He would explain to his parents, as best he could, the terms of the lease on the one-bedroom Hollywood apartment where all five of them would live. He would go with Mala to a parent-teacher conference when little Pranil, in a seven-year-old's tantrum, decided to fib to a teacher that his parents were beating him. Vinay would also take computer classes, decide which computer they should buy, and attempt with little success but good humor to teach his father to use e-mail. And when he started working the graveyard shift at a motel, where he would do his homework in the quiet of the night, and a man walked in and held a gun to his head and demanded the cash from the register, Vinay would speak to the police afterward in his most polite English before coming home in the middle of his shift and crawling into the bed that was his, in the living room next to the television, next to his younger brothers already deep in dreams.

But all of that was far ahead of them, in the unforeseeable future. Landing at LAX on August 5, 1999, they waited to be picked up by a Fiji friend's relative. One of their suitcases had somehow been lost in transit, so after waiting for it to no avail, they finally emerged from baggage claim and customs only to realize they had no idea how to recognize their contact person. They were behind schedule, the terminal was crowded, and they worried they had missed him. Mala suggested calling, but when they tried to use the pay phones, they could not understand how the American dialing system worked, nor did they have the proper coins or phone cards.

Hours went by. Madhukant said, —We have no business in this country; let's go back. Over the next years, each time life in America threw up another hurdle, this would become a mantra of sorts for him. He kept thinking of the inventory he had put in storage in Fiji, the property he had not sold but leased out, holding on to it as a kind of insurance policy in case they needed to return. And then he would remember, or be reminded of, the break-ins. Even as they were finalizing their immigration paperwork by fax, the shop had been broken into once more; the fax machine, along with everything else of value, had been stolen.

It was Vinay who convinced his anxious parents to stay calm amid the chaos of LAX. — Just wait, he repeated; — just wait. And they did. Finally, as in the happy ending of a Bollywood movie, the man walked up to them, they all exclaimed and embraced in relief, and they picked up their bags and went home with him. That was their first day in America.

Within a week, they heard through the Gujarati grapevine that someone knew someone who was looking for a responsible couple to manage a motel on Alvarado Street. Good, Mala thought, we can start to work. Though their hosts were generous, she felt uncomfortable being someone's guest indefinitely; the whole point was to start their new, American lives. So they took their luggage — the lost bag had arrived — and moved into the motel. The manager's quarters were cramped for a family of five, but if it all worked out, Mala thought, this job would be a convenient way station. They would learn how to manage things, save some money, and then perhaps buy their own motel, as so many had done before them.

By the turn of the millennium, the Asian American Hotel Owners Association, which despite its inclusive name has always consisted mostly of Gujaratis, could boast that its members owned a full forty percent of the hotel and motel rooms in the United States. They had twenty thousand hotels with more than a million rooms, ranging from skid-row to high-end boutique, and were a fifty-billion-dollar economic force. If you have spent a night in the past decade in what the industry calls "economy lodging" (a Days Inn, Motel 6, or Holiday Inn Express, for example), it is more likely than not that you were staying in an Indian-owned room.

How that happened, over a period of twenty-five years or so, is a story that in its outlines is rather simple; anyone who has played the Monopoly board game can grasp it. First you cobble together enough dollars (property, cash, loans, whatnot) to buy a hotel on a well-traveled route. Soon the customers come through. You use the revenues you earn to buy more property. The key is to imagine that you are playing not strictly as an individual but as a real human being with family members whom you care about, or at least who you wish would move out of your living room. You don't want them to go bankrupt from paying rent to you, as in the board game; you'd rather have them running their own motels, or one of yours, and have casual passersby pay the rent.

The first Gujaratis to penetrate the motel game started out in San Francisco in the 1950s. As a port city, it had a constant flow of travelers as well as a steady supply of long-term hotel residents, men with drinking or other problems who never quite got it together to manage a place of their own. In the long tradition of immigrants finding an economic niche, a handful of Indians realized the benefits of managing, leasing, and eventually owning such motels. First and foremost, you did not have to pay rent yourself, cutting out one of the biggest line items in any household budget; second, the work did not require special credentials or education, or even fluent English. By 1963, a social scientist studying the phenomenon found twenty-two families owning dozens of the city's skid-row motels in the area between Third and Sixth streets just south of Market. All of them were from a particular Gujarati caste, the Patels, who would eventually come to dominate the industry to such an extent that today you can buy T-shirts celebrating the Patel-motel connection.

For the first Patels, the motels were not only a way of making a living; they were also community hubs, a place for new immigrants to stay while they got their footing. A few Gujaratis of other castes also entered the business, and some individuals struck out beyond San Francisco. What really made the trend take off nationwide was an unlikely combination of government investment in interstate highways, the oil crisis of the 1970s, and Walt Disney World.

I first heard this history from a Patel named Ramesh Gokal, one of the pioneers of the Indian motel business, who happened to be friends with some of my relatives in New Jersey. They had all emigrated at some point from South Africa, which gave them a solid basis for camaraderie. Gokal, a friendly and frankly intelligent man of whom it might be said that every subject is his favorite subject, was glad to outline for me the early history, which I later confirmed through other sources, that had shaped the economic landscape in which Mala and Madhukant found themselves in the late 1990s.

Mid-century, America was at the height of its love affair with the automobile. When Disneyland opened in Southern California in 1955, one of its star rides was Autopia, where Americans who had presumably driven miles to get there could enjoy driving bumper cars around a track. The following year President Eisenhower signed the Federal-Aid Highway Act, spreading $25 billion among the states to create what would become known as the interstate highway system. A decade later, a series of new connectors had been built, including the country's longest north–south routes: Interstates 75, 85, and 95, which connected the high-population regions of the Midwest and the Northeast all the way south to the tip of the Sunshine State. Flying over Florida in a helicopter in search of a location for his next great theme park, Walt Disney found the spot where the highways connected, a swamp near a sleepy town called Orlando. He began dredging it, and on October 1, 1971, Walt Disney World opened.

It was the beginning of a boom. Dozens of motor hotels, or motels, sprang up along the interstates leading into Florida. Families in cars, recreation vehicles, and caravans traveled up and down the highways, stopping overnight to refresh themselves and perhaps dip in the tiny cement pools. The motels' new owner-investors were mostly white, empty-nesters, former corporate executives looking for a relaxed retirement business. Having a motor inn along the interstate was, says Gokal, reaching back to his roots for an African analogy, like diamond mining.

Then, in the mid-1970s, the fuel crisis hit. Gas shortages and skyrocketing prices put an abrupt end to the era of autopia. It was time for the diamond miners to get out; their grown children did not want to inherit empty motels, and these were the years when, as Gokal put it, "you could lie on the interstate for an hour and a car wouldn't hit you."

Meanwhile, the number of Indians in the United States was creeping upward, thanks to the 1965 Immigration Act. Some of these professionals had hit the glass ceiling, or found themselves itching to be their own bosses; some, because of state-by-state licensing rules, were unable to practice in the field they had been educated in; some found themselves with extra capital they wanted to invest. A few were new immigrants arriving on business visas, which they obtained by agreeing to invest a certain amount of money in the American economy. Like Gokal, most had heard from their San Francisco relatives or connections about the easy money to be made in motels. California was already too pricey for most of them, but in the Midwest and South, they could find plenty of properties for sale, cheap. Gokal himself bought a twenty-six-room motel in North Carolina in 1976. By 1978, when he sold it, he owned five more. Eventually he became partners with the broker who was selling him the properties, and together they sold dozens of motels to other Indians. The Monopoly game was in full swing.

From Gokal's perspective, and the community's, the Indian buyers were bailing out the American sellers, offering them cash during a period when no one else would buy. Others, though, saw it as opportunism; you can imagine the conflict if some people are playing the game as lone rangers, while others are applying the ethics of teamwork and dealmaking. Half a dozen motel property brokers told the *Washington Post* in 1979 that they hated doing business with Indians, who were "a headache" and tended to do "things not customary in this country." Gokal's ancestors in South Africa would have found the arguments familiar: Indians lived so cheaply that they could undercut the white competition; they were dirty, the rooms smelled of curry, and so on. White owners put up "American-owned" signs, although it was a bit too late—like appealing to the public to stay at your Park Place when your opponent has built hotels all across the board. More significant forms of discrimination came from banks and insurers, who denied loans and policies to anyone named Patel, and from large hospitality chains that shut Indians out of buying their franchises. When the community tried to make up for these lapses, by self-insuring and loaning funds to one another, the Justice Department launched an investigation of a mafia family-type "scheme"—based on suspected immigration fraud, allegations of travelers' checks crossing state lines, and suspicious similarities in names.

Eventually, the Indian motel owners realized they needed to organize. With the help of a few key white allies in the industry and in state politics, they began using their collective economic clout to negotiate with bankers, insurers, and franchise chains. The president of Days Inn conducted an internal study rating his firm's Indian-owned properties versus others by a series of measures including quality of service, timeliness of franchise payments, and so on. Surprising themselves, his staff found that the franchise's Indian-owned inns were, on average, more profitable and of equal or higher quality. By 1985, the Associated Press was reporting that "nearly every exit of Interstate 75 in Georgia has an Indian motel owner." By 1994, a single company had six hundred Indian franchisees.

By 1999, when Mala and Madhukant entered the field, many Indians owned multiple motels or hotels. Property values were high, boosted by continuing demand from other Indo-American buyers. For newcomers with limited resources, the best place to get a foot in the door had become not the owner's desk but the manager's apartment.

Mala did not know the complex array of social and economic factors that led to the position she was taking, yet she and Madhukant were drawn to motel work for the same reasons as hundreds of other Gujaratis before them: housing included, little English needed, no experience necessary. The only job qualification seemed to be a willingness to be available twenty-four hours a day. Mala was used to hard work, and she understood the basics of how to handle customers and their moods. The hours and chores could be distributed among all family members; Vinay and even Mithun were old enough to take turns at the front desk.

Perhaps most importantly, they knew others had done it. At my brother's wedding Mala had met our second cousin from Orlando, whose husband's family owned four hotels around Disney World. In the Hollywood hills, just a few miles away from Mala's home, I interviewed an aunt who had come to America in the 1960s and raised her children behind the motel desk, pretending not to notice customers holding their noses at the curry smell; we talked at her dining room table, overlooking a sapphire lap pool that in turn overlooked a plunging valley, as a real-estate agent ushered a rap star through her custom-built home, which she was considering selling.

Such success stories were everywhere in the air. The motel business had been providing them to Indo-Americans for a quarter-century now, so Mala and Madhukant felt it was a good bet.

But for those starting out, the business was not glamorous. It meant cleaning rooms and dealing with people who ruined the sheets, stole towels and even lamps, called the manager's line with drunken giggles in the middle of the night. It meant shifts spread over twenty-four hours, which made family outings all but impossible. Still, Mala thought she was ready.

The problem, though, was that the owner had either left unclear instructions, or left instructions that were clearly at odds with what Mala and Madhukant had understood. The hired desk clerks refused to teach them anything about the office work, instead relegating them to maids' chores. Mala and Madhukant cleaned the rooms, did the laundry, swept the hallways; they were managers in name only, and as Mala would later say, "We didn't come to America to learn to be maids." That line of work she knew well enough.

After six weeks of clashing with the surly motel staff, they moved out. In an apartment on Vermont Avenue, with no furniture, they plotted their next move.

Across the street was a massive hospital, at least a dozen stories high. Mala looked at it every day and thought, There must be jobs there, sweeping or cleaning up at least. So she crossed the intersection and went in, and walked around the corridors — each one exactly the same.

After a couple of turns, she realized she was confused and lost. She didn't see any place to fill out an application, and she couldn't work up the courage to ask one of the passing nurses or doctors what to do. Finally she saw a green exit sign and hurried out, walking all the way around the building to get back home. She gave up the idea — how could she work there if she could not even find her way around?

Through the grapevine, they heard about another motel opportunity. They decided to try it again; perhaps Alvarado Street had just been an unlucky experience. This time it was a bigger hotel, with much more responsibility — an overwhelming amount. They started learning the job, managing the staff, and trying to understand the systems of reservations, check-ins and check-outs, and payments. They had been at the motel just a few weeks when a phone call came from Fiji: Madhukant's mother was dead.

Mala and her mother-in-law had never become friends. But when the older woman grew ill with old age, it was Mala who had washed her soiled clothes and bedding, helped her to use the toilet, and cleaned her body afterward — all part of the dharmic duty of a respectable daughter-in-law, wife, woman. In Lautoka for the funeral, Mala thought, *Well, perhaps now she's found happiness.* In any case it was good to be back in Fiji for a visit, and to see her family again.

They flew back to Los Angeles, but by now they had lost their motel position. Instead, they moved into an aging but affordable apartment complex in the area of Hollywood known as Little Armenia, near the apartment they had rented previously while in between motels. Again they looked for work.

Mala had soured on motels, but she didn't know what other kind of job to seek. A neighbor told her to go to the unemployment office, that the people there would help her find a job. Vinay, who by now had enrolled in computer classes and taken a job as night desk clerk at a Comfort Inn, looked in the telephone directory, called a number, and asked for the address of the nearest unemployment office. Then he mapped the bus route for Mala, explaining what to look for and where to change lines.

Mala took the two buses, asking the drivers each time to be sure. When she reached the office, the staff pointed her toward the computers, where she could research the current job listings.

But Mala had never used a computer. After a few moments she got up and left.

The apartment-lined block of La Mirada opens onto one of the main north–south arteries of Hollywood and of greater Los Angeles, Vermont Avenue. It is quintessential L.A., an endless stretch of strip malls and utilitarian office buildings, with residential areas tucked into the side streets. Some blocks to the north is the hipper enclave of Los Feliz "Village," where the retail turns to chic cafés, boutiques, and an independent bookstore. To the south lies nothing but more of Vermont Avenue, for miles, all the way through Compton.

Eventually Mala strung together two part-time restaurant jobs, and Madhukant found work as a valet, parking cars. After a year or two they moved to the manager's quarters of the apartment complex on La Mirada. That meant two bedrooms instead of one, a break on the rent, and, on weekends, a more or less steady stream of tenants knocking at the screen door to turn in rent payments, to complain about something needing to be fixed, or to ask to be let into their apartments after locking their keys inside. One afternoon during a visit, I sat on the courtyard steps with Mala's youngest son, Pranil, who was giving me the rundown on the residents: one vacancy, one other Indian family, two Filipino families, eleven Armenian families. In return I was trying to answer his questions: how does God make the clouds move, why is the sky sometimes purple?

From behind a screen door, two identical fat boys with dark curls stared at us. They were obviously twins, maybe three or four years old. I smiled and gave a small wave. They started shouting. Pranil cocked an ear.

"They said shut up," he reported dispassionately. "They said you can't sit here. They said you have to go now." I thought the three of them were communicating in the special child language, the mumble that only other children understand.

"Where are they from?" I asked him in Gujarati.

"Armenian," Pranil said.

"Oh—you understand Armenian?" I asked in English. Behind the screen door, the twins' father came and shouted at them, pulled them into the apartment.

Pranil nodded. "I could speak some too."

The twins appeared again, scratching at the door.

"*Nyada*," Pranil told them.

"What does that mean?"

He had to think, to translate. "It means, like, Don't touch."

At school, Pranil was in English as a Second Language classes. When the forms had come, Mala filled them out honestly, which is to say that under "other languages spoken at home," she wrote "Gujarati and Hindustani"; how smart her children were, to have three languages! The result was that both Mithun and Pranil were placed in ESL classes. Mithun soon placed out, but Pranil would stay in ESL for the next eight years. In the neighborhood he picked up not only Armenian but also Spanish, and noticed how the Armenian children he knew had somehow managed to be tracked into mainstream English classes, though he himself spoke better English and was not in fact fluent in either Gujarati or Hindustani. In seventh grade, he would test at fourth-grade reading and math levels.

His parents were navigating their own bureaucracies with somewhat greater success. Inside the apartment, Mala directed my attention to two plaques newly hung on the living room wall. One said:

MGM Plaza
Employee of the Quarter
Madhu Kant
Parking Department
1st Quarter 2002

Madhukant's job, valet parking at the movie studio, was now full-time and included benefits and frequent overtime. The other plaque said:

McDonald's #5806 presents
Mala Kumari
Employee of the Month
November 2001

Mala was working the early shift at a McDonald's just around the corner, a job that took her away from her family at dawn but allowed her to be home for most of the boys' afterschool and evening time. One afternoon shortly after they had settled into the apartment, Pranil and Mithun were playing outside when Pranil pointed to a woman and said, —Here comes Mummy!

—No, it's not! said Mithun, the older.

—Yes, it is! insisted Pranil. He was right; Mithun simply hadn't recognized their mother out of a sari, in her polyester McDonald's uniform.

It wasn't long before Mala found it tiresome to wear saris at all. Pants felt too constricting, but outside of work she wore tops with long, loose skirts that allowed her to enjoy the freedom of fabric moving about her legs. Her silk, nylon, and cotton saris in an array of bright colors were folded away into suitcases under the bed, reserved for formal community functions.

Mala's second job, which she had taken to try to save money for a visit home to Fiji, was at a sweets shop twenty-three miles south of Hollywood, in the Little India area of Artesia, California. By the time of the census of 2000, 1.9 million people of South Asian origin—Indian, Pakistani, Bangladeshi, and Sri Lankan—were living in the United States. Of these, one in five lived in California, and their profile was now more diverse than that of the 1960s brain-drain generation. Unlike their suburban professional predecessors, the working-class immigrants tended to cluster geographically. Artesia's newest neighborhood was one place where they gathered, conspicuous and unassimilated, filling two or three blocks with sari shops, restaurants, groceries selling spice mixes and family-size sacks of basmati rice, and vendors of Bollywood videos and compact discs.

For Mala, the commute to Artesia took an hour and a half via two trains and a bus. But the job paid in cash, and being in Little India meant she could pick up the Indian groceries they needed. Vinay had also taken a second job, as a ticketing clerk at Singapore Airlines. "Life is hard," Mala told me. "I can't say it isn't. My mind spins trying to think what to do, how to do it." Her clock was set ten minutes early, to give her a head start on her already long days. She was almost never late. From her coworkers at McDonald's, she was picking up more Spanish than English.

Several years later, they are still in the apartment on La Mirada, but life has become somewhat easier. With the help of their saved money and employee-rate tickets from Singapore Airlines, the family has been able to make a couple of trips back to Fiji—including once for Vinay's arranged marriage to an accountant raised partly in Fiji, partly in New Zealand.

Mala now keeps her clock set at regular time. When it buzzes at 5:20 A.M., or sometimes in the silence a minute or two before, she leaves her sleeping husband and climbs out of bed. She is nearly fifty years old, her limbs are heavy, and sometimes her lower back or legs ache; but her will is strong. If it is summer, the Los Angeles sky is already light and hazy; if winter, it is dark, and sometimes stars peek through the smog.

After her ablutions, she sets the chaa on the stove: milk, water, black tea, sugar, and her own family's blend of spices, an authentic ancestor of the "chai" sold in trendy cafés throughout the City of Angels. Keeping one eye on the tea, which is prone to boiling over the sides of its pot the second she steps away, she stirs together a quick breakfast, perhaps some eggs and/or toast and/or *sheero*, a hot semolina cereal with ghee and sugar. A big morning meal will be necessary to fortify her still-sleeping family: Madhukant, who will soon rise to drive to his job at MGM, where

he now works in the parking office rather than parking the cars himself;
Mithun, who will take two trains to his engineering classes at California
State University's Los Angeles branch; and Pranil, who will ride with his
father to eighth grade at one of the city's failing public schools, with a
student–teacher ratio of 40:1 and where he has already had several rounds
of gang-prevention education.

Across town, Vinay is also rising to take the first shift at the motel he
manages with his new bride. After her visa papers came through, they
stayed in the apartment on La Mirada for a few months, then decided to
move out on their own. Unlike some in the community who want their
families to stay together under one roof, Mala encouraged the move; she
knew better than anyone the costs of too much day-to-day closeness between mother- and daughter-in-law. The Days Inn in Lawndale where
Vinay and his wife live and work is, needless to say, Indian-owned. It
stays relatively busy, being convenient to both the beach and the airport;
a sign in the lobby advises guests that breakfast is available from 6 A.M.
to 9 A.M. and includes a complimentary copy of *USA Today.* "Today's
Weather" is reported in black marker on the whiteboard as being 80 degrees, a sign that rarely needs changing. On a typical morning Vinay is
checking out guests, loading mixes into the Minute Maid juice machine
at the free breakfast bar, fielding a backpacker's series of questions about
bus lines and whether the motel's wireless Internet service is working (it
isn't), and conveying instructions to the cleaning crew and the motel's
airport shuttle driver. The driver, originally from Guatemala, has worked
for so many Indian motelkeepers over his past nine years in the country
that he has mastered several Gujarati phrases, including a rhyming prayer
("Sing god's praises as you eat your lentils and rice") and some less-than-
pious words (*Saalo gaando chhe!* or, roughly, "He's a crazy bastard").
Vinay is debating whether to keep the airline job; his wife has a day job
as an accountant. One thing they are clear on: they are managers, not
maids. If a customer throws trash in the elevator, or a room needs to be
straightened up, they call on the staff to take care of it. "Once you start
cleaning up, you have to do it all the time," Vinay's wife explains to me.
They have learned the American concept of boundaries.

Mala spares them a thought as she puts away last night's clean dishes
and packs her husband's lunch. If nothing is left over from last night, she
cooks a quick vegetable curry for him and gets a head start on tonight's

dinner. The tea boils; she strains it into a pot, gulps down her own cup, and hurries into the shower, ignoring the stubborn black mildew spots on the ceiling above the stall. There was a time when she would have climbed a stepladder every other day to scrub away the spatter of stains, but now the mildew has won the battle, enduring her curses but little physical challenge. Scrubbed clean, she sprays herself with a floral deodorant from the dollar store and pulls on her daily uniform: a grayish polyester shirt, long black skirt, multicolored tie, and matching polyester vest. This last item she calls, in Fijian-Hindi-English patois, a "coatee," and she hates it for being scratchy, unflattering, and most of all hot. By the time she is dressed, the household is awake. She will leave the breakfast dishes to her sons, who, after long years of coaxing and haranguing, have been trained to do certain chores. At 6:20 A.M. Mala grabs her heavy black imitation-leather purse and strides out the door, down one long block, through double glass doors, to clock in at 6:27 or so.

She has graduated from the two restaurant jobs and works now in the hospital she was once afraid to enter, having mustered her courage to go in, find the human resources department, and ask for a job. At $9.30 an hour, with health benefits, it is a definite step up. She assembles and delivers food, mostly to patients in the obstetrics ward who are about to have babies. She tries to pause once a day to walk casually over to a patient's window and, chatting all the while, look out toward her own home; from certain rooms on certain floors, she can see the back corner of the La Mirada Apartments. In the middle of the day it feels good to get a glimpse of the shelter she has worked so hard to provide for her family, and for herself.

Each time I talk to or visit Mala, some minute variation in her schedule has taken place. Always, I am fascinated by the minute-by-minute way she maximizes her time, the quantity and weight of her responsibilities, and how lightly she bears them. She is amused by my interest, but indulgent as she recites yet another iteration of her schedule: she has taken or dropped another part-time position; she is working weekends or not, sometimes an earlier shift, rarely later.

Despite the hard work, though, her life is her own, in a way that years ago seemed impossible. So when she complains of fatigue, as she does sometimes, it is in the most good-natured of ways. At the end of the day she may be exhausted, but she can sit in front of her own television on her own sofa and watch satellite television from India for half an hour, with no one to tell her to do otherwise. Frequently, when she reflects on her life as a whole, she says something like, "This is freedom."

In December 2006, Mala won another employee award. This time it was for Best Customer Service of the Year, hospital-wide, for a "hostess," based on surveys filled out by her patients. She received a certificate suitable for framing, some gifts, and tickets to the nurses' holiday party. In the raffle drawing at the party, she won a rice cooker.

It wasn't quite like winning the U.S. lottery, but it was nice.

8. BODY

To assimilate means to give up not only your history but your
body, to try to adopt an alien appearance because your own is not
good enough, to fear naming yourself lest name be twisted into
label . . .

— Adrienne Rich

Bhupendra and Bhanu

MINAL
Nayan

*D*EEP IN THE MARROW of every story is a silence. Having struggled, all these pages, to be transparent, not to overwhelm the stories of others with my own, now it is my turn to emerge, solid. And I hardly know where to begin. I have practiced the art of submergence — invisibility, assimilation — all my life. To metamorphose, now, from neutral narrator to embodied character, self, seems a great act of exposure. Vulnerability, guilt, freedom, sympathy: Which thread shall I pull first? How shall I unravel or construct, from all of my memories and aches, one true pattern, one set of possibilities — one spine?

I might have been named Gita, Saroj, or Sudha. I might have had trouble in school, been raised under the shadow of Mars, and brought good luck to my house. The telegram my father sent from San Francisco to Fiji at my birth was un-mystical:

> BABY GIRL BORN 742 PM MONDAY JULY 12TH STOP
> BHANU AND MINAL IN GOOD HEALTH LETTER
> FOLLOWS BHUPENDRA

It was 1971. My grandmother in Fiji forwarded the vital information — date, time, time zone — to her astrologer in India. He wrote my horoscope, which predicted all of the above. Based on an ancient calculus, the stars said my name should start with *G* or *S*. My grandmother sent a gift for "Gita."

But I had already been named, as my parents reminded her: *meen* meaning "fish," *al* meaning "like." *Minal,* she who is like a fish. They were college-educated, beyond superstition; they had named me for a friend of my mother's, just because they liked the sound of the name. They declined to read the trajectory of my life ahead of time: lucky and unlucky years, characteristics of a compatible mate, probable paths of education, marriage, and health. Nor did they perform the sixth-night ceremony, when a pencil and paper are placed under the baby's crib, for the goddess of destiny to write.

And so I was raised free of predestination.

But not entirely.

My parents believed in destiny, even as they doubted the importance of ritual in shaping it; and the telegram my father received that day—the job offer from the south of the planet—was a kind of proof. With or without a written horoscope, I entered the world with a lucky footprint.

Within six months I was an emigrant, collecting the first international stamp on my passport. I slept all the way from San Francisco to New Zealand in an airline bassinet, aided by a lick of whiskey.

In the normal manner, I progressed from howling to cooing to, eventually, words. In New Zealand I believed we had our own special language, a delightful singsong made up by my parents. It was a code we could use in the public park, where we fed our stale bread-ends from the week to the ducks, or in the grocery store to discuss the funny-looking woman nearby, say, or complain about prices that were too high. No one could decipher our secrets. We used it just for fun, too: My mother said it was time to *inter-pinter* the laundry, to move it from washer to dryer. A bumpy road was so *gaaber-goober,* she complained. She could double any word or name to humorous effect, or for emphasis: Minal Binal, TV BV, bowling phowling.

It was only when we visited India, when I was four years old, that I understood there was a world of other people who spoke the same funny way. Gujarati was a lilting, rhyming language, and with a child's knack I absorbed it completely in the six weeks of our visit. By the time we left India, I had forgotten all of my English.

. . .

I never thought of myself as an immigrant until I began writing this book. Because I was born in San Francisco and now live in San Francisco, my mind skipped over the years of disruption in between; I believed I was only the child of immigrants, the so-called second generation. But the truth is, I have lived through multiple migrations, shifts from one world to another; and these geographic shifts were mirrored and amplified into emotional, mental, and even sexual ones. Each time I cross a border, I feel the push and pull in my body, a cacophony of competing desires. And always there are choices to make: what to assimilate, what to reject. Is it true that we are always, as migrants, and the children of migrants, attempting to choose what my parents call "the best of both worlds"? Or is it possible to transcend—no, not transcend, but enter into—the dualism, the splitting, the uncertain interstices between the worlds? Is it possible to integrate, even heal, the trauma of crossing; of many crossings?

Back home in New Zealand, my Kiwi babysitter was forced to learn a few basic words in Gujarati for a few weeks, until my tongue acclimated again. *Water, hungry, yes, no.* Eventually I would become adept, like all children raised with more than one language, at code-switching, knowing instinctively when to use Gujarati and when to use English. Meanwhile Mrs. Maclean acquired *pani, bhukh, haa, naa.* She fed me Jell-O and a soft-boiled egg for lunch every weekday while my parents were at work. She was our next-door neighbor, and my mother also traded recipes with her—rotli for trifles, curries for brandy snaps. Her daughters, Philippa and Vicki, became my best friends. We were partners in spitting watermelon seeds, hunting for golf balls on the nearby course, and taking swim lessons at the Y. We watched television, and I developed a secret crush on Adam West as Batman. I called their grandmother Gram, and had no memory of my own.

Five years old, I walked unchaperoned—the streets were that safe—every day to and from Maori Hill Elementary School, which, despite being named for the indigenous people of New Zealand, was populated by a couple of hundred white children, one Maori boy, and me. My teachers had innocent, storybook names: Mrs. Lion, Mrs. Stringer, Miss Babe. Once I lost a 24-karat gold earring on the way to school; a neighbor's son found and returned it. And when one of my kindergarten classmates asked his mother, *Why don't Minal's hands ever get clean?* and she reported this to my mother, they simply laughed: Kids say the darnedest things.

I remember our years in New Zealand as happy ones. Traveling back, I have felt a nostalgia for its green hills and cool southern fog, an unaccountable joy, even a sense of home—the original landscape that my body remembers. But when I was six years old, I began peeling the skin from my lips, obsessively, till they bled. My parents tried everything: scolding, spanking, a trip to the pediatrician. I remember the bitter taste of iodine on my fingers, the night mittens; but none of it worked.

I believe that as children we know things, in an almost prescient way, as animals understand earthquakes; that we absorb mysterious signals, the unspoken anxieties of adults, and the plans that are being hatched around us. Did I sense that my parents were planning to shift continents again, and that they were (although they did not say so, perhaps not even to themselves) afraid? Did I take this fear, worry, and uncertainty into my own small body? When I was seven years old, the world changed.

My parents had decided to move back to the United States. When they broke the news, they tried to sweeten the deal: in America they would buy me one new doll every month, for a whole year. Like legions before me, I was seduced by the New World's promise of wealth beyond imagination.

After touching down in Los Angeles, we toured Disneyland and I picked up a Mickey Mouse cap with ears and my name embroidered in yellow script. This rite of passage was followed by a series of moves whose reasons I understood, vaguely, as being connected to my father's work. Of Gainesville, Florida, I remember the terror of roaches, which I had never seen before. In Iowa City, where we lived for a year, our lives seemed brushed by a glamour that only America could offer. One of my classmates was the son of a minor television star. My best friends were redheaded twins whose father had spent time in India and given them Indian names; when I went to their house for a sleepover, I saw with amazement that they each read a book at the dinner table. The twins borrowed my Indian outfits, and my mother choreographed a Gujarati folk dance at our school's winter show. Christmas was, for the first time, storybook white, and important. My parents bought a plastic tree and gifts, to help us fit in. I sang Christmas carols in my second-grade classroom, where we stood for the Pledge of Allegiance every morning and had *The Hobbit* read aloud to us every afternoon. I learned to ice-skate, to sled, to transform deep drifts of snow into roly-poly men and hollow angels.

By the time my father found a permanent position in Michigan, we all had migration fatigue. With each move, I had had to start over: friends, neighborhoods, teachers, schoolyard lingo.

Looking through old class photos, I can't play the *Which one am I?* game with current friends or lovers. Every picture has only one brown girl. Here she is with babyish pigtails, here with a sixth grader's version of a sophisticated braid; here with eyeglasses, now braces; embarrassing shadow of mustache; eyeliner and lipstick; straight teeth, feathered hair, contact lenses. Which one am I? The answer is clear, yet I hardly recognize myself. I was a foreigner to everyone around me, and therefore to myself as well.

And was this queer feeling a part of my destiny, a quirk of history, or some mixture of both? Was it the rich soil in which a certain sense of being different would later take root? Was it a predictor of how I would choose to live my life? Whatever its nodes and branches, in Michigan my sense of being an alien would come into sharp focus.

Our new home was next to an elementary school in the Township of Canton. It was a three-bedroom, white brick house, and when you walked in the front door, to your left was a wallpaper mural of the tropics. Installed by the previous owners, bequeathed to us along with the red shag carpeting and the Ping-Pong table in the basement, the mural covered the entire wall with a beach panorama: palm tree, waves, sand, sky. The opposite wall was tiled in mirror, so that entering the house you could have the illusion of stepping directly from suburban Michigan into, say, Hawaii, the Philippines (where the previous owners were from), or Fiji. This surreal environment was our formal living room, a new concept to me: a whole room that hardly anyone used.

Instead we spent our time in the decidedly more prosaic family room, whose only artifice was fake wood paneling. It opened onto a dining nook, kitchen, and stairs leading down to the basement. I had my own room, with cream-and-gold princess furniture, shelves for my books, and a growing collection of dolls. Property values here, thirty-five miles from Detroit proper, were stable, the real-estate agent had told my parents; most importantly, the schools were "good."

"Good," in the most segregated metropolitan area of the nation, turned out to have a very specific meaning.

In campus towns in New Zealand and Iowa, our brown skin had been exotic, too rare to be a threat. But if our previous neighbors had had no sense of a Race Problem, suburban Detroiters were all too aware of it. Eight years old, I touched down in an electrified pond, all ions already polarized.

At first, or on the surface, it was all right. No one threw bottle rockets at our house. We were the good darkies: brown, not black; immigrant professionals, not blue-collar workers competing for scarce union jobs. But the sense of unbelonging was palpable, and tinged with tensions I could not have begun to name.

"Where are you from?" asked one of our Canton neighbors. New Zealand, we said. "Oh—did you drive?" came the next question, revealing the distance we had traveled. Another's son said, peering into our garage, "But it's illegal to have only one car!"

In elementary school I tried the new games, though the coordination of my arms and legs with the seemingly endless variety of round objects and their desired destinations eluded me: dodge ball, kickball, T-ball. Boys played Smear the Queer and King of the Hill; girls played foursquare or stood in knots talking about boys. My hearing became unreliable.

"Does *anyone* like mangoes?" someone asked.

I did not catch the tone, so delighted was I to hear mention of my favorite fruit. "I do!"

She turned on me: "*David* Mengel? You *like* him?"

"Oh," I said, "no, sorry," and stepped back, confused and embarrassed.

I began to be quiet. My childhood receded as I tried not to mess up in the new world. This was the year my mother took off work to help us settle in, so every day my brother and I came home for lunch: SpaghettiOs or Campbell's soup, Ortega tacos, grilled cheese sandwiches. At night I slept on *Peanuts* sheets where Charlie Brown, Lucy, Linus, and Snoopy frolicked around a motto that nicely summed up the playground ethic: "Happiness is being one of the gang." But more and more often, at recess

I flew solo on the swings, or played alone in the naked winter woods behind the school, carving words and pictures with my mittens in the snow.

My new world, the school and subdivision I was learning to navigate on my purple Schwinn bicycle, had once been cornfields. Canton had become a rural farm community just after the two great transportation breakthroughs of 1825. A canal had opened a route through the Great Lakes so that New Englanders could spread themselves onto the new homesteads of Michigan, and the Detroit–Chicago road was laid down, blossoming with tiny, convenient stops for stagecoaches. In 1834 this particular stop was named, in a fit of nineteenth-century orientalism, for a city in China. Neighboring Nankin and Pekin eventually changed their names (Westland, Dearborn), but Canton stuck. As the "Sweet Corn Capital" of Michigan, Canton produced six thousand bags of corn a day as late as the 1967 harvest.

That year, by a conjunction of racial progress and racial antagonism, Canton started to change. By the time I arrived, the corn town had been reshaped by two decades of white flight from Detroit. But it would take years—a decade more of growing up, and a decade of living away from Michigan—for me to learn this silent history, and years more to understand how it shaped me.

My elementary school teachers encouraged me to write poems and wild stories, and filled my journals with praise: "Minal, you are such a talented writer. I love reading your work." And I wrote back: "Dear Mrs. Kurnick, I love you." My New Zealand education had put me ahead of my American peers, and I was sometimes so bored that I asked for more math problems. On report cards my teachers gave me high marks but worried, "Sometimes, Minal seems to be a loner and I'd like to see more interaction between her and other classmates." Instead, I took refuge in my schoolwork and in books; my parents took me to the public library nearly every weekend, even as they tried to encourage me to develop other, more social interests. From the library I checked out armloads of Nancy Drew, the Hardy Boys, and other mysteries starring fearless young people who always ended up with a complete understanding of all of the clues clustering around them. I read the "Little House on the Prairie" series and felt a nostalgia for a history that wasn't mine, for a time when girls licked maple-sugar candy made of syrup poured on snow, and the prairies were tamed by homesteaders clearing their flat acreages of forests, of Indians.

February is Michigan's cruelest month, when the wind chills the air to minus twenty degrees, the snow turns dingy, and spring is still months away. In the February of my third-grade year, just a few months after our move, unemployment in southeastern Michigan stood at twelve percent, not counting those who had given up looking. The region had lost 87,500 jobs in a year, more than half from the auto industry.

The economic cruelty trickled down: boys made fun of other boys wearing cheap flannel shirts from the sale bin at Kmart.

"I used to have a shirt like that," someone would say.

"Yeah?"

"Yeah, then my dad got a job!"

In the fall I started fourth grade and our elementary school held a mock election; Ronald Reagan won by a landslide, foreshadowing the national consensus a few weeks later. I was one of three who voted for the Independent candidate, having overheard my father say, "He's very good; too bad he won't win." My parents could not yet vote, but they were rooting for Reagan's sunny "Morning in America" platform; later they gave money to the English-only movement that was gaining speed in California. When the school sent a questionnaire asking "Languages spoken at home, other than English," my father wrote "NONE," to avoid the possibility of my being placed in a bilingual class.

But America's political waters were tricky, filled with contradictory positions we each had to negotiate for ourselves. My parents decided to teach me to read and write Gujarati, having first obtained permission from my classroom teacher, who thought I might benefit from the intellectual stimulation. Mum had started working at the hospital; Pappa's schedule as a tenured associate professor was more flexible, so for an hour a day he and I sat at the kitchen table with the curling Gujarati alphabet as I sounded out stories about squirrels (*siskoli*) and lions (*sher*).

At school I started to get headaches. At home my parents began inviting over other Indian families they met at the PTA, at the grocery store, at the mall. The night before Halloween, our house was hit with eggs and tomatoes, marking an annual bacchanal known as Devil's Night; the crab apple tree in our front yard was dressed in loops of toilet paper. Our Muslim friends who lived in Canton were used to such treatment; the woman wore the headscarf, and their home was a target all year round. My teachers said I was beyond my class level, and suggested I skip fifth grade. My doctor said I was nearsighted and needed eyeglasses to stop the headaches.

So at age eleven, perched uneasily on a forest-green Naugahyde seat, peering out the windows through my new Wonder Woman spectacles, I started riding the bus to Pioneer Middle School. I did not feel like Wonder Woman. Overnight, it seemed, the children around me had changed, become harder. I learned new rules. You were not supposed to look anyone in the eyes; as between dogs, eye contact was a challenge met with immediate, fierce barking. "Ya got a staring problem," a girl would snarl, gums bared, or "Take a picture, it'll last longer." I began to grow breasts, which they could see; I began to bleed, which they could perhaps smell. I began to understand the world as composed of me and Them.

To board the yellow bus each morning was to run a gantlet. The back was the territory of the bad kids, who brandished illicit cigarettes and curse words. But sitting too far forward meant that They could throw bits of sandwich or paper at you. If you got on last with your violin case, you had to depend on the mercy of a stranger to let you sit, and mercy was in short supply.

"Tits!" hooted Billy, the biggest because he'd flunked eighth grade twice. "Why do they call you Tits?" The bus driver turned up the radio; it was always the same Top 40 station playing the week's Top 40 songs in reverse order, counting down to number one. Someone started a chant, and everyone joined in: "Meener Wiener Meener Wiener Meener Wiener . . ."

I started to hate Them; to hate my body, which was growing foreign even to me; and to hate my parents for choosing a stupid name that made me a target. Those bus rides could not have been more than twenty minutes, but in my memory they stretch an eternity, occupy most of three years. They were far more terrifying than the voyages back and forth across the Pacific, when I had not known what lay ahead.

Some classes were a refuge, like orchestra, where we were all nerds together, huddled behind our full-grown instruments. My father was pleased that I was receiving the music lessons he had been denied, to develop an appreciation for the arts. In social studies, we were assigned to imagine our school as a self-contained system. My final project resembled nothing so much as a prison blueprint, complete with forced labor and armed guards.

But math was worst of all: poor Mr. Barnes, a thin, balding man who loved numbers, not children, his desk littered with spit wads whose origins he could never discern—how could he have protected me? The class was self-directed; Mr. Barnes sat at his desk and did his work as we did ours, and my hair filled with spit wads. It must have been satisfying to create, in a black mass, constellations of white.

I can sympathize, now, in Buddhist fashion, with the boys in the back of the class or the teacher up front, see how they were all suffering. But if I try to get inside my own head at that age, I can barely catch a glimmer. I remember completing math units furiously, comforted by the neatness of equations and rules, with a momentum that put me nearly a grade ahead by the end of the year. Speeding through the numbers brought a kind of numbness that made it possible for me to bear the weight of relentless, minute decisions: how to act, what to wear, whether to move.

Should I run my hand over my hair to get the spit wads out?

Should I ignore it, not to give Them the satisfaction of a response?

Would it be better if I gave Them the finger?

Would it be worse?

Would it be better if I had designer jeans?

I pretended invisibility as much as I could, and They pushed and pushed for a reaction. It was like a game but it was a war. I had to have a wall.

One day a fat, pasty boy named Rob started screaming, pounding the desk, shouting, "Stop it! Stop it!" as if he were having a seizure. I don't know what they'd been doing to him just before, but it was he who cracked, and everyone shrugged and muttered, "Crazy." Someone took him away. He was back the next day, and it was worse than ever for him. I had no doubt it was traumatic stress: emotional misfit syndrome. I saw that his wall was not strong enough.

I erected mine tall and circular, a region of the imagination that was inviolate, where no one could touch me. Its bricks were fear, shame, silence.

Even my parents had to be outside. My mother had been a Popular Girl, the ringleader who led her classmates on the basketball court and illicit field trips through the tamarind groves of Fiji. My father had been the smartest boy in his class in a place where being so brought not ostracism but admiration. They were social success stories; I was a failure. I did not think they could possibly understand me.

Besides, I was ashamed of anything that made me different—and my parents were most certainly the core of my difference. I was ashamed of what they wore, what we ate at home, what I called them: Mummy and Pappa. Normal kids had Mom and Dad, I learned when a classmate read one of my school journal entries and laughed; from then on, I referred to my parents as Mom and Dad. Such parents would have given me a name, skin, clothes that would be totems of protection, would have let me do the things that made a girl normal: date and stay out late to chat about boys. True, my mother never sent me to school with chicken curry instead of a sandwich, but that level of culinary assimilation was not enough. I wanted an *American* family, dinners of roast beef or meatloaf—fantasy meals I read about in the pages of my young-adult novels. In these exotic flavors, I imagined, I would taste what it was to be American. Somewhere in there, between tuna casserole and a first date, between MTV and *Sixteen Candles,* somewhere in the interstices of rock concerts and miniskirts, was the secret to happiness, the way to be one of the gang.

So when my mother visited school one day and a note fell out of my locker saying, "You have B.O.," I mumbled, "Must have been meant for someone else." One more brick for the wall. When I came home with my face smeared with violent pink, I looked at my mother's shocked face and lied, "We had a lipstick fight on the bus," as if it were mutual. One more brick.

Because I told my parents nothing, they read my diary. I stopped writing.

At school, people who had seemed friendly laughed with the bullies; I stopped trying to make friends. In the cafeteria a tough girl put toenail clippings in another girl's sandwich; I stopped eating, and threw away the lunches my mother packed each morning. On the balance beam a group of boys surrounded me with taunts; I stopped going outside. I found a study hall where I could sit through my lunch hour, facing the wall.

If my retreat was thorough, it was hardly calm. A few years later in high school we read *Lord of the Flies,* William Golding's parable of children enacting adult wars. We had to answer the question, Which character could I fit? I wrote about Roger, the sadist, who was the first to kill: "In middle school there were many many times when I wanted to kill somebody: To maim them, to hurt them physically as much as they had hurt me emotionally." I switched to the present tense. "I imagine them cowering before me begging for mercy while I subject them to ultimate degradations." More than a decade before the Columbine school shootings, neither bullying nor revenge fantasies were taken seriously. My teacher wrote "Wow," and gave me an A+.

Home was a different world, a swirl of schedules and expectations that seemed increasingly foreign. My mother cooked Indian food most nights; my parents' friends were all Indian. When we went to dinner at someone's house, my father sat with the men in the living room, my brother went off to play with the boys, and my mother and I went to the kitchen. Girls my age already knew how to roll out perfectly round rotli, and our mothers warned, only half jokingly, that it was a skill we'd have to master if we ever wanted to get married. Mum despaired, since mine came out "like the map of India"; I was, perversely, determined to keep it that way.

Still, my rotli rebellion did not excuse me from all responsibility. I was coached to ask "How can I help?" and "Does anyone need anything?" and to clear the adults' plates, wash dishes, serve tea. Mostly I fulfilled the role of dutiful daughter as well as I could, bringing home A's, practicing the violin and Indian classical dance before my weekly lessons. Within my wall I contemplated suicide, and felt even more self-loathing that I could not go through with it. It was just a fantasy. I read Anne Frank and thought *she* had the courage to die; the Holocaust did not seem too great a metaphor for my pain. I read Camus. I read *Animal Farm* and knew Orwell was right about the people who ran the farm: they were pigs. I read Stephen King's *Carrie* with glee and decided my revenge would be to become famous, and show them all.

Underneath, I still longed to be named Ann, as I had written in an elementary school journal; to have friends, or at least a place to sit at lunchtime. I feathered my long hair with a curling iron each morning, wore blue eye shadow, cajoled my parents into getting me one precious pair of Jordache jeans. I kept my mouth closed to hide my braces, and took my glasses off whenever I didn't need to see the chalkboard. On Saturday mornings, while my brother watched cartoons, I lay in bed, listening to Casey Kasem's *American Top 40* on my clock radio and writing down song lyrics so that I could mouth the words on the bus and pretend not to be different, pretend to be a part of things. To be normal, American, normal.

It did not occur to me that my difference was immutable.

In 1980, the year I started fourth grade, the Census Bureau counted 387,233 "Asian Indians" in the United States. The main feature of our presence, one study noted, was that we were "inconspicuous" and "rapidly assimilated." Economically, academically, on paper we fit smoothly into the middle class.

But another piece of our demographic condition in that moment, uncounted and unaccounted for, was loneliness. Among immigrant groups, Indo-Americans were the most geographically dispersed. Rarely did the researchers find Indians concentrated in specific, urban neighborhoods, and these too were relatively small. For the most part, while Cubans congregated in Miami, and Vietnamese created Little Saigons across California and the South, the post-1965 Indians with their professional educations ended up all over the country, often in the white suburbs. Isolation was built into our patterns of immigration and assimilation, as surely as hair follicles in our brown skin.

I knew the handful of other Indians in my school because the community was small. Their fathers were engineers or doctors; one family ran a motel; the mothers stayed home or took modest part-time jobs. We were a microcosm of the most educated, most professional, and thus wealthiest immigrant group in the nation. And at fewer than four hundred thousand spread across a nation of 227 million, we made up a scant one-fifth of one percent of the U.S. population. If you rounded out the math, we would make up zero percent.

These days, when Hollywood debutantes sport Bollywood fashions and "chai tea" is available at every Starbucks, it is hard to remember the America where I grew up: an America where people did not recognize our ethnicity, where we were constantly mistaken for black or Hispanic or anything but ourselves, where when we said "Indian," they asked us, "What tribe?" Living in San Francisco, where a new yoga studio seems to open up every month, I am tempted to forget that other America which regarded anything foreign with suspicion, where half an hour of yoga and meditation in our public-school classroom had our town's delegation of the Christian right raging. My parents' survival tactics worked in the world of adult professionals, where their own fully formed selves and their colleagues' veneer of civility protected them. But children have no such social screens; my environment was unfiltered, toxic as tar. And as in my junior high school, Indians as an American group had no critical mass, no power, and no political identity.

Elsewhere in the diaspora—Fiji, London, even Toronto—my cousins were raised in Indian-only communities, which held tight to their cultural values by virtue of neighborhood, close networks of kin, and sheer numbers. Our parents also wanted to "preserve our culture," as if culture were a mango to be pickled in chili and brine, not a thing that evolves with its environment. But in the American suburbs of the 1970s and '80s, even gathering places were scarce. In and around Detroit, our nexuses of culture were limited to two grocery stores, two "sari palaces" for clothing, one or two Indian restaurants, and a Hindu temple in a distant part of the suburbs, an hour's drive away. In place of outings with cousins and constant oversight by neighborhood aunties, we were driven to the occasional Indian dance classes, talent shows, and dinner parties that our parents dedicated a good share of their free time to organizing.

One generation's grounding may be the next's limitation. The daughters reject the mothers' comfort food, their ways of feeling beautiful, the yards of silk and slashes of kohl. The sons do not want women who will serve them tastes of home, but women who will lead them into new worlds. Not every daughter, not every son; but sooner or later, a generation diverges, and makes its own way further into the new world than the parents' first dream envisioned. Perhaps each migrant should be warned at the border: Your children will become foreigners to you; are you prepared? It would cut the rate of chosen migration by half.

Somehow we were meant to absorb "culture" on the weekends, stay true to our parents' values, yet accomplish full-fledged assimilation at school. To our parents this meant we must have, above all, good grades. To each other, my peers and I were friendly in our homes or at "community functions." But if we passed in the halls at school, we looked away. Some

Indian girls managed to slide into the popular cliques, wearing foundation a shade lighter, boycotting their mothers' cooking for fear the curry smell would seep out their pores, mastering the fine arts of the giggle and the tight pink sweater and the precise sassy angle at which books should rest on hips. The rest of us would have settled for inconspicuous. I stayed away from the popular Indian girls, not wanting to compromise their status; they did not come near me at school, however close our families might be. As for my fellow misfits, I despised them almost as much as myself. We, too, made sure never to be seen with one another.

It was not until I went to college and compared notes with other Asian Americans, raised in the white suburbs, that I realized my alienation had a racial component. I had thought I was an outcast because I had the wrong clothes, or the wrong karma (I spent many of those study-hall hours in junior high school trying to remember if I'd ever been mean to other children at a younger age). Because almost everyone I saw was white, I never thought of myself as not-white. I felt different, but I did not know why; I tried to be "normal" and could not understand why I failed to be so. I was a brown body, and did not know what that meant: that blending in completely would be impossible, that I could never disappear into the "melting pot" described in our history lessons on the ideal American immigrant. Racism was, perhaps like sexuality, one of the unspoken mysteries of the adult world. It was a word we did not have then, though I felt its outline daily, a white loop in my chest, a constriction around the live wet thing.

Michigan's racial structure was densely layered, built not only around our hearts but into our landscape. I have come to understand that the uniformity I witnessed around me was not imagined but constructed: a landscape shaped by successive waves of racism.

Its bones were laid down two centuries ago, during the westward expansion of America, accomplished by genocide and racial exclusion. In India and Africa, the "white man's burden" was the rationale for conquest; its corollary in the New World was "manifest destiny." Before 1808, Native Americans from a dozen tribes inhabited most of Michigan's 57,000 square miles. Less than sixty years later, tribal lands amounted to only 32 square miles.

The change was made possible by a land ordinance carving up the vast area, opening it to white homesteaders, the German and British and Scandinavian immigrants whose descendants would become my class-mates. The law was carefully crafted to deter settlement by free black Americans. It divided the Territory of Michigan "into several numbered townships, each six miles square in area. The townships themselves were divided into 36 sections, each one square mile in size. Each section, as necessary, was further subdivided into quarter sections."

Here was the grid on which the next wave of conquest would take shape. "Subdivisions," once units of land available for purchase by set-tler families, would become the units of suburban community.

Long before we arrived, the subdivisions had divided further; one could no longer buy an 80-acre farm for $100. Our house, on a lot 65 feet by 135 feet, was in section 10, the most densely populated fraction of the six-square-mile Township of Canton, in a subdivision named Carriage Hills II. Neither carriages nor hills were in evidence, but no one seemed trou-bled by the fiction.

Our subdivision's development was linked to a massive demographic shift that had begun before World War II. As African Americans migrated up from the South for jobs in northern cities, whites abandoned those cities. They paved over more and more of the plains, inventing subur-ban sprawl to satisfy a need—not simply for land, but for white land.

In Detroit, four days of rioting in July 1967 accelerated the centrifu-gal motion. That was the year that Canton began to grow houses faster than corn. A few years later, the National Association for the Advance-ment of Colored People sued for educational integration in Detroit—a move that would forever influence the suburban definition of a "good" school. The public schools I attended were among the best.

The fight dated back to the 1954 *Brown v. Board of Education* decision, in which the Supreme Court had said that separate white and black schools could never be equal. But the ruling alone did not integrate Amer-ica's schools. With the law on their side, civil rights activists had to wage a city-by-city legal battle against fierce, sometimes violent, opposition. In Pontiac, Michigan, for example, the Ku Klux Klan blew up ten school buses the week before a busing order was to be implemented. Against this backdrop, NAACP lawyers pressed their case in a Detroit courtroom.

Two decades of urban disintegration had already left Detroit itself mostly poor and mostly black. The city was ringed by suburbs that became increasingly white in direct proportion to their distance from the city, like a photo-negative image of a spiral galaxy. As everyone involved in the court case soon realized, meaningful integration would have to involve the outer, whiter areas. A map published in the *Detroit News* showed the proposed remedy: busing 780,000 students between the city and fifty-two suburban school districts. A thick line made the affected suburbs look as if they were all an extension of Detroit.

Beyond that line lay suburbs not threatened by integration, and these became a haven for white families. In Canton, just outside the desegregation border, the effect was immediate and dramatic.

In 1970, the year that the NAACP sued Detroit's school board, a township land-use plan would later report, "Residential construction activity in Canton began in earnest." Land across the desegregation border was suddenly valuable, and farmers started to sell to developers.

During the four years that the desegregation case rose through the courts, 6,500 new homes were built in Canton. At the same time, Detroit was losing an average of 31,000 people a year. The Census Bureau ordered a rare midterm count in Canton in 1975; it showed that the township had more than doubled, from 11,000 to 26,000 residents in just five years. Most newcomers were from the other side of the line.

By the time my family arrived in 1979, Canton's population had almost doubled again. Our white brick house next to Miller Elementary School went up during this boom. So did the school itself, the grocery store where we shopped, the interstate entrance ramp that my father took on his drive to work, and the office complex where my mother would open her physical therapy clinic. Our elementary schools ran year-round, with students on staggered schedules; young white families were moving in faster than schools could be built.

Eventually the Supreme Court overturned the busing plan—in the process, "making a mockery of" *Brown*, according to the dissenting opinion by Thurgood Marshall. Not a single Detroit-area student was ever bused. But the controversy had terraformed Detroit's suburbs. White flight was the most effective grass-roots response to the civil rights movement and its demand for integration.

. . .

Our new neighbors were not people with a history of greenness. They had scratched their way to the suburbs; they traveled in and out of the dangerous city; they were bent on defending their turf.

Literally, sometimes: the dad next door was obsessed in his pursuit of golf-course green. Twice a week he mowed his lawn, alert to any shoot of dandelion or crabgrass. Upon finding one he would root it out, poison its vicinity, complain pointedly to my father over the fence. And always the weeds would come back.

We joked about the neighbor and his lawn obsession, but we never spoke of race. Detroit was a world away, and although my father went there every day to teach, its people and problems might as well have been taking place on another planet, for all that we in the suburbs knew or, mostly, cared. The other Indian families we knew never went to the city.

Race itself was a deep silence, even when it slapped us in the face—as when, in Montgomery Ward one day, a white salesclerk slapped my mother. What I remember of this incident is not the initial violence, but my mother, hysterical, and my father, arms around her, hustling us all out of the store. I had never seen my mother scream and swear. For years afterward, my parents would say only that Montgomery Ward had "terrible customer service."

Only last year, as I was completing this manuscript, did my mother tell me the whole story. "I don't know if it was racist or what," she said to me in the first telling, but later, "It was definitely racist because the person behind us was a white lady, and the clerk took her first." As my mother angrily protested that day that she had been waiting longer, her hand came down on a parcel that, as it happened, contained the clerk's sister's hat. —How dare you crush my sister's hat? said the clerk, and struck my mother across the face.

In the same conversation, my mother told me of an incident that I do not remember, but which occurred shortly after we moved to Michigan. I would have been about eight or nine, my brother two years younger. We were playing in the yard of the school next door when a boy our age came by and started calling us names. *Niggers*, he said, and pulled a knife.

My brother and I climbed onto our bicycles and rode home, with the boy following. My mother was in the front yard, gardening, and I told her what had happened. My mother took the knife, got the boy to tell her his phone number, and called his mother to come and pick him up.

As far as I know, my parents never talked to us about the *n*-word, at this time or later; nor did we have any other conversations about racism. Without language, my adolescence has seemed a string of disassociated images, seen from above or by a camera: two blond girls, tall, advance on a seated brown girl; two brown children ride away fast on their bicycles. These flashes bear a certain kinship to the memories of survivors of trauma, and share the basic confusion. Distress, fear, violence without a known cause turns inward, and grows. Without language, a child believes it is all her own fault.

As my mother tells me the story of the boy with the knife, a faint body-memory resonates: myself as a child standing behind my bicycle with its blue-and-white wicker basket, the slight, familiar shadow of my brother beside me, my mother talking in a low voice to another child. Almost. The memory, if it is there at all, is mostly a physiological fear, reinforced so many times over the next few years that even today, few things tense my muscles more than a pack of white adolescent boys, if I must pass by them.

But I do remember our yard, the wire diamonds of the fence separating it from the schoolyard, the magnolia seedlings my parents planted along that fence, and the crab apple tree in the center of the yard, with its bright, hard, bitter fruit. And when I think of us in Michigan, when I think of Asian Americans dispersed one nuclear unit at a time all over the suburbs of the 1970s, I think of us perhaps like crabgrass: almost lawn, but not quite. An irritation, a tinge of blue: ocean, distance. We could not grow in smooth, parallel stalks—blades of one size easily tamed by the mower—but in small family clumps, irregular, rough-edged. We put down roots quickly. Once introduced, we were nearly impossible to get rid of.

Getting rid of Asians was a particular Detroit obsession. In the Motor City, what was bad for the auto industry was bad for everyone; and in the 1980s, Japan was the auto industry's Public Enemy No. 1.

In southeastern Michigan, every other person (literally, 48 percent in 1980) worked in an automobile-related job. Kids could call out models and years of cars speeding by on the highway, the way I imagine farm children know their goats. When the auto industry crashed, everything crashed.

The immediate culprit was the oil crisis of the 1970s. Suddenly Americans were abandoning their beloved gas-guzzling Thunderbirds and Cadillacs in favor of fuel-efficient Japanese cars. The resulting economic shudders were early throes of what these days is called globalization. At the time, it was simply called "It's because of motherfuckers like you that we're out of work."

Those were among the last words one Asian American heard before he was beaten to death by two laid-off white autoworkers. The distinction between a Japanese manufacturing mogul and a second-generation Chinese American draftsman/waiter was lost on Vincent Chin's attackers. They called him "chink" and "nip," as well as "fucker," before pounding him on the head with an all-American baseball bat.

That was 1982; when the killers were sentenced to probation and a fine of $3,780, Asian American activists rallied for justice and created a movement. But I was in sixth grade, and the suburbs were far from the demonstrations. In southeastern Michigan, Asian Americans were less than one percent of the population. I did not know about Vincent Chin.

What I knew were vague hints of danger. Ghosts rang the doorbell, then ran away. My parents fielded crank calls in the night, kids who scoured the phone book for funny-sounding names. Nothing on the outside of our house was allowed to give away our ethnicity. We did not drive a Japanese car because it might be keyed in a parking lot or have a rock thrown through its window. For the two decades that my parents lived in Michigan, they owned only Fords. Assimilation was our sole strategy, the totem we believed would protect us.

When I learned to drive, at sixteen, my first car was another Ford: a dark blue, gently used Mercury Capri hatchback, turbo. My mother's physical therapy practice was thriving. We moved to a new house with a swimming pool in a wealthier subdivision named Beacon Hill; still no hills. I parked in the driveway, as the other two Fords were in the garage.

It was fall of my senior year, and things were better. I had found a niche at the high school newspaper, a well-funded and award-winning perk of our wealthy suburban public education system. I was applying to universities out of state. I studied French and joined the school's French Club, where we called each other by newly minted French names. While other girls chose exotic appellations like "Angelique," I reveled in the simple "Marie"—at least once a day, I had a name that everyone could pronounce. Then, one crisp winter morning, I came out of the house and saw the antenna of my car twisted in a crazy Z shape.

As I went closer, I saw that the antenna had been used to scratch something into the hood. I squinted, trying to make out the first word. It seemed to say SAND, which made no sense to me; maybe SCRAM?

The second word was unmistakable: NIGGER.

"We're not even . . . ," I thought with surprise. I got into the car and drove to school. I did not feel anger or grief or fear. Shame pushed up my rib cage, and I pressed it down; like everything else that was odd about me, starting with the color of my skin, I hoped no one would notice the car. I focused my confusion on the choice of epithets. The suburbs of Detroit were too segregated for me to know that ten miles away, the nation's largest Arab American community was taking shape; "sand nigger" was a slur coined for them.

As for me, I was getting out.

In truth, when I fled Michigan I was not escaping racism, of which I had no conscious understanding; I was, like any American adolescent, escaping my parents. And I was escaping India, that part of it which lived in our skins, in our home.

"Indian only" might have been the sign hanging over our family's social life, although I do remember a couple of weekends with my mother's white boss and colleagues. These times stand out in memory for being the exceptions that proved the rule. My parents entered and exited the white world daily, but I did not live this part of their experience. Instead I perceived their lives, their essence, as Indian, and saw mine —the life I led apart from them, the six hours of school daily—as American. My parallel world was increasingly important; it expanded to eight hours, ten, twelve, as I studied more, participated in more extracurriculars, and lived more at school than at home. Between home and the world, between the India whose values my parents wanted to impart and the America in which I lived and learned to breathe, there seemed to be no overlap. Or rather, I was the overlap, and always there was the sensation of straddling, of being stretched.

The older I grew, the wider the gap I had to ford. It was a generation gap, not particular to my family alone, and at its core was a deep silence:

sex. As my white friends dated, talked about their crushes, spent hours on the phone with boys, and more, I did not. My brother and I had known all our lives that our parents expected us to have arranged marriages. Someday I was supposed to have a say in who and when and how —but not really whether—I would marry.

I was fourteen years old when I first said the No. It was in the basement of my parents' best friends' house. We kids were running around the blue-tinged concrete covered in rugs, the Ping-Pong table, the pillars that held up the house; in suburban Michigan, the basement is the size of the whole abode. Our parents used these subterranean rooms for storage, laundry, rec rooms, and large dinner potlucks, when the Ping-Pong or pool tables overflowed with trays of fried bread, spicy chutneys, and oily vegetable curries that warmed us on cold winter nights. It might have been Christmas; I might have been wearing jeans and a trendy sweater with glittering threads, like the other teenage girls, though our fathers always wanted us to wear Indian clothes, just once in a while, because we looked so pretty in them. The men wore acrylic sweaters and polyester-blend pants and talked about the auto industry, the presidential race, the economy, the auto industry again. The women talked cooking and family; they wore saris a few seasons old, from the last trip to India or the last family wedding, under thick cardigans they clutched together at the breast, trying to hold on to something that was, with each beat of their children's American hearts, slipping away.

Perhaps an uncle was teasing me, or I caught a snatch of conversation. I was running and stopped short near the stairs. "I'm never getting married," I announced. "I'm never having kids."

Maybe I'd said it before, but this time people heard. My mother took me aside. "Don't say that," she hissed. "You're too young to decide that, so don't."

But suddenly I knew what I'd said was absolutely true.

Sometimes a silencing succeeds. Pushing the unwanted thought deep into the body—for where else would it go?—we manage to bury it in the heaps of memories to be forgotten, wishes to be abandoned, skins to be shed. Even the most fervent dream of childhood can wither, shrivel into a husk that, when we later encounter it, surprises us in its frailty: *It seemed so important at the time!*

Other times, a thought or instinct, submerged, grows. And later its strength is a wonder to us, as it reveals itself: a secret drive that was propelling us all along to our destiny.

I did not press the issue with my parents; did not breach my wall to let them into the deep questionings going on within me. Instead I slathered on mortar and brick; and slowly, almost subliminally, a plan clarified itself in my mind. Its refrain was familiar, comforting. I would get out of here; I would show them.

The war I had felt in middle school was somehow, by the time I left high school, transmuted to a clash of civilizations within me. On one side was the family, with its "Indian" demands of duty, obedience, tradition. And what was tradition but memory made rigid, the self strapped into the path of previous selves, so that none should stray, none could be lost? Almost all of my cousins, even those born and raised in North America, were having arranged marriages. Some even spoke of it with romance in their voices.

But when I imagined marrying a stranger, becoming a wife and mother, I felt queasy. I wanted something more, though for a time I could not name that desire. My sexuality was a deep font within me, hidden, an underground stream whose currents were too swift and dark to dip into without a solid footing on free soil.

And certain layers of the conflict remained invisible to me: the construction of American adolescence as a time of experimentation and rebellion, for example, which could not be reconciled with my parents' idea of pre-adulthood as a time to take on increasing responsibilities and accept guidance that shaped one's future. What I felt was America's siren call of freedom, individual and sweet. I was seduced; I could hardly wait to be seduced.

I did not argue with my parents — not in general, and certainly not about dating or marriage. When a cousin was seeing a woman outside the community, I heard my parents' disapproval; I remember my father opining, perhaps theoretically, that the boy's mother always had the option of kicking him out. I did not need a specific threat directed at me to take this personally, to fear disownment, to know I needed to guard the secret of my future rebellion. It would stay safe behind my wall, at least until I was prepared to strike out on my own.

As high school rolled on, my plan took shape. Education would be my ticket out, as it had been for my parents, for a generation of the Third World's best and brightest. I wasn't quite sure what I would do with my freedom, but I knew distance was imperative. I bided my time, kept my grades high and my reputation sparkling clean, and applied to the university of my dreams. I was possessed of a classic emigrant's push–pull impulse to find a better life for myself.

When I look back on how I felt about my parents as a teenager, it is as if we were continents. I was America, they were India, and there were no direct flights, phone lines, e-mails. We spoke in telegrams, blue-and-white block letters, urgent, frantic, devastating.

Of course the dichotomy was false. They were not India; I was not America. I am Indian in body, tongue, to anyone I meet in the streets, and increasingly even in my spiritual inclinations. My parents are American in their politics, their optimism, their belief in the dream—for they came to this country at a time more open and hopeful than any I have known. We could also list the ways in which I could be called un-American and they un-Indian. And all such lists are unsatisfactory, for they do not describe us in the end, not even a little. We are not portioned out in percentages; we are whole beings. Indian, American, Fijian, queer, et cetera—whatever we are, we are simply, in the end, ourselves.

Yet the dichotomy persists, is somehow useful to someone. Even today, young people in our community feel the pull of *American* temptations versus *Indian* values: as if adolescents in India harbor no desires, face no decisions; as if American parents operate without moral principles; as if the young everywhere are not capable of valuing, only of being tempted. If oppression works by dividing us from one another, then surely a primary split is this generation gap. The children of immigrants, the so-called second generation, grow up with an experience so different from that of our parents—and are encouraged somehow to blame both our parents and ourselves for the conflicts that such difference necessarily engenders. Since as a child I had no theories of race, racism, or cultural assimilation, I blamed my parents for the conflict I felt between the worlds; and, too, I castigated myself—the bad daughter, the selfish and ungrateful child.

And yet, something in me insisted on plotting a path toward what I saw as, quite simply, freedom. Toward myself.

I was seventeen years old when I traveled the nearly three thousand miles from my home in Michigan to Stanford University. It felt like a migration as momentous as any my ancestors might have experienced, from the crusty boundaries of the old world to the vast, romanticized horizons of the new.

Stanford was red and gold, adobe and clay, a celebration of light. The dorms were co-ed and there were no curfews. "We trust you," my parents said as they dropped me off. I heard it as an implicit warning: *Don't let us down.* No other daughter in our community had been allowed to travel so far alone, they told me; they were progressive, they believed in education, for girls as much as for boys. To my parents the opportunities ahead of me were academic, career-boosting, intellectual. I knew that they were also sexual, and that I had better not get caught.

The distance between my campus and my parents was deeply reassuring. Before leaving Michigan, two girlfriends and I had been talking about what we would do once we reached the faraway paradise of university. One wanted to get drunk; one wanted to do mushrooms; and I wanted to lose my virginity.

Within the first week—before freshman orientation had ended—I invited a boy back to my room. We fumbled around awkwardly, and afterward, the smell of him still on my crisp new sheets, I called one of my high school friends to report, "I did it." I wept, but not with grief. My tears were one part relief, two parts jubilation. I felt as if I had shed a burden, as if I had tasted my first freedom. As a bonus, I hoped my forfeit would make me unmarriageable in Indian terms, whenever that time came.

Within a month, my father was in the hospital for a triple bypass operation on his heart. Suddenly I felt guilty; had I somehow, with my wild behavior—my secret betrayal—managed to physically break his heart? My rational mind tried to assure me he could not have known what I was doing; but the emotional entanglement between my parents' expectations and my own desires would take me years of practicing freedom to undo.

I slept around, and felt myself opening. I soon acquired a boyfriend, and when my parents visited for a weekend, my freshman dorm conspired to keep my secret. I discovered, in the arms of others, that I was not an ugly, shy loner of a girl. I could be beautiful, witty, brilliant, flirtatious, coy, sensual, myself. I discovered power, and the power of surrender. I drew new outlines of my moral life: respect, communication, honesty, but not chastity. And of my body: mine.

My parents' values came to seem increasingly foreign, unreasonable, even oppressive. I took feminist studies courses that provided a theoretical landscape for my feelings and gave me one way to understand the great divide: it wasn't India, or even my parents, but patriarchy that was attempting to regulate, neutralize, and shame me out of following the true thread of my desire. Feminism offered, too, a righteous outlet for my anger, and a political justification for my yearning to break free of the community patriarchs who called me Daughter and demanded their tea. I rejected the idea of marriage as the only proper housing for female sexuality. From there it seemed a small and logical step to a women-only sex life; as a movement slogan put it, "Feminism is the theory, lesbianism is the practice."

Of course, life is rarely as simple as it seems in theory to an eighteen-year-old. As soon as I declared myself a lesbian, I was beset by male suitors, one of whom became my next boyfriend. This sexuality business was, to say the least, confusing.

I believed, in those years, that to be a good Indian girl meant to live entirely without sexual desire; that my longing itself, let alone any action to fulfill it, made me bad, wrong, and un-Indian. My entire understanding of my culture was that transmitted by my parents, who in turn passed on what they had been taught, at a level they considered appropriate for a child; I did not learn about my father's erotic art until years later. Their version, steeped in duty and obedience and propriety, was of course only a fragment of Hinduism and of India itself, not a totality. But it was a dominant and authoritative, self-authorizing version.

My father quite literally wrote the book on being a good Hindu American child: a workbook for earning a Scouting merit badge in Hinduism, which he developed while my brother was a Cub Scout. It discussed sexuality—*kama*—as a canon, one of the four major elements of a Hindu life, if practiced strictly within marriage. Otherwise it described kama as an impediment to merit, a hindrance—not a sin exactly, not in the Judeo-Christian view of sin, but an obstacle to spiritual development, enlightenment, and being good.

This hegemonic view was one of my sole windows into "Indian culture," yet my body told me another truth. I have proofread multiple updates of this workbook over the years, filling it with the copyediting marks I learned from my high school journalism teacher, the first woman on whom I ever had a crush. It was no wonder I experienced a split self.

To understand myself better, I started going to a support group for "lesbian, bisexual, and questioning" women, led by the student health clinic's first openly lesbian therapist, whom I had carefully scoped out by writing a profile of her for the *Stanford Daily*. The group included a fellow *Daily* staff member; a woman who was so infatuated with one of the Indigo Girls that she traveled from city to city to cheer at their concerts; and a pretty, dark-haired medical student who asked me to dinner.

She had a car, so she picked me up at my dorm. "Oh, you dressed up," she commented as we embraced in the foyer. "You even wore pantyhose." I was embarrassed, and tugged at my short skirt. I had thought it was a date. But over dinner she told me about her tortured relationship with an on-again-off-again, currently-trying-to-work-it-out girlfriend.

Nevertheless, she came back to my dorm room afterward and, in the spirit of mutual support, asked if I would help her by mirroring the affirmations her therapist had prescribed. We sat cross-legged facing each other on my not-too-lumpy futon mattress, which lay on the floor and was covered with a colorful Mexican striped blanket I had purchased from one of the many vendors who filled the campus's main plaza on weekends.

"You are beautiful," she said, looking into my eyes.

"You are beautiful," I repeated dutifully. We were to maintain eye contact, as this would help her see her own reflection.

"You deserve love," she said.

"You deserve love," I repeated, shifting slightly on my seat.

"I love you," she said.

"I love you," I whispered. It was becoming very intense. I had never even kissed a girl, as I'd confessed to her earlier in the evening, yet here I was saying "I love you" — although the *I* and the *you* were both her, not me. Weren't they?

"Thank you," she said.

"Thank you," I said, which was funny, but neither of us laughed.

There was a pause. "You've never been kissed?" she asked.

No, I confirmed.

"Well — would you like a kiss?"

I nodded. It was a generous offer.

She leaned forward, still cross-legged on the floor, and pressed her lips to mine. They were pink, soft; pleasant. Then they were gone. I opened my eyes, not knowing when I had closed them.

"Thank you," I said again, feeling truly grateful; feeling one step closer to being who I wanted, or was meant, to become.

By late sophomore year I was describing myself as bisexual or lesbian to myself, to my friends, and to most of campus. I didn't mind my boyfriend, but I felt I was merely marking time with him until I figured out how to be with a woman. I had seen a therapist at the student health center, who reassured me I was normal; taken almost enough feminist studies classes for a minor; and helped found a feminist literary journal and our university's tame version of the radical organization Queer Nation.

All of this took place, not in secret exactly — I was wildly, recklessly, open about it on campus — but separate from my family, outside their domain. The two worlds, and who I was in each, became mutually exclusive. On visits home I was the good daughter, successful student, on track for my parents' version of the ideal life. On campus I was the radical bisexual lesbian feminist, writer, activist. I was so visible that I still run into strangers who know my name from those years; I counted the miles again, nearly three thousand, surely more than enough to protect me from my parents' gaze.

The construction of these two selves felt exhausting, necessary, and oddly familiar. In a way this secrecy, this silence, was merely an extension of my earlier splitting: home/school, Indian/American. Straight/queer: it seemed the only way to keep each aspect of myself safe — an illusion that, though it served me at the time, was bound to collapse. I don't know why I did not see the inevitable collision coming; perhaps I did, but thought or hoped I could control its timing. Or maybe the split self was the only trick I had; I believed it would work because it had been at work all my life.

For all my parents knew, I was spending my semesters earning A's and working as a student journalist at the *Stanford Daily*. This was also true, and earned me a summer internship at *Time* magazine in New York between my junior and senior years.

Nineteen years old, alone in Manhattan, I went to my first grown-up Queer Nation meeting and marched in my first gay pride parade, shouting slogans ("We're here, we're queer, get used to it!") alongside more than a hundred strangers in the radical Lesbian Avengers contingent. The atmosphere on the streets and in the city's gay neighborhood was electric, in a way that for previous generations it could not have been. In the wake of the AIDS epidemic, which had claimed gay men as its first victims, a fierce movement based on defining oneself by one's sexual identity had arisen in the United States in the 1980s. SILENCE = DEATH: I can still see the white-on-black lettering printed on T-shirts that seemed ubiquitous by the summer of 1991, when a miniature version of it adorned a button attached to my backpack. The words referred to both AIDS activism and our sexuality itself; and if silence meant death, then being and speaking out was the only way to live. OUT, LOUD, AND PROUD went another slogan: more T-shirts, more buttons, and huge roaring chants that we shouted in angry, exhilarating street demonstrations. Pride was to be the remedy for a history of shame. Because of AIDS, gay Americans like me, as our most ardent activists argued, could no longer afford the luxury of hiding, of assimilating. Coming out became an urgent political act, a statement of integrity, a life-and-death matter with real money at stake for AIDS treatment and research at a time when the federal government seemed content to let *us* die.

This *us,* like every *we* or *us* I have ever encountered, disturbed me even at the time, partial as it was. My friendly "lesbian, gay, bisexual, and questioning" community at Stanford had seemed racially mixed, with women of color as strong and visible leaders. But the mainstream queer world to which I had access through its institutions in Manhattan — a community center, free support groups and activist meetings, the big, organized Pride events—looked very white and often very male. Still, at a Pride party, I met a woman of color. Her skin was smooth and light brown, her accent bridged Puerto Rico and Yonkers, and she asked me to dance. When we were hot and sweating, we went out to the patio and kissed in the June night breeze. We made a date to see *Paris Is Burning*, the hot queer documentary that was earning rave reviews that summer.

Exiting the movie theater into the brightness of mid-evening, I felt aglow with anticipation. We stopped at my first gay bar; underage, I ordered a soft drink. Then we walked to the NYU apartment I was sharing with a dental student from Jamaica. My roommate was out. We went into my room, sat down on the twin bed. We were high above East Twenty-sixth Street, and from the window we could see the lights of Brooklyn.

"Do you know what two women do in bed?" my date asked me. She was older, and I had told her I was a "lesbian virgin."

I nodded, exuding what I hoped was confidence. I had no idea.

By the time she left, I did.

And I knew how I wanted to live the rest of my life.

I don't know where desire begins; whether it is with us from birth, latent as genes and destiny, or comes as gift and curse somewhere along the way. Whatever its roots, surely its particular expression in each lifetime is shaped by what touches us: culture, experience, relationships, history.

Had I come of age in a different time and place, perhaps I could not have named my desire. I might have suppressed it all my life; or married a man but engaged in furtive affairs with women; or chosen other routes of emigration from heterosexuality. Suicide, religious chastity, a lifetime of silence, or a subterranean and hidden sex life are some of the alternatives to Out, Loud, and Proud.

As I was coming out to myself, it was comforting to construct a narrative of childhood Otherness. The fact that I had never felt *normal* made radical queer politics all the more appealing. The norm was deeply flawed, not only about sexuality but at its core; we were right, and righteous, in raging against it with all our will. Queer theory, activism, and rage seemed to offer absolution for my childhood: I hadn't fit in because that safe suburban world was not worth fitting into; its values were corrupt and its hypocrisy ran deep. Liberation meant that I did not have to strive any longer to be one of that gang.

And yet, to migrate away from a community of migrants is to experience a particular kind of disorientation, a dual displacement. To free oneself from a family already in free-float means taking in a heady rush of air, the illusion of being an individual. One forgets the original nature of the longing, deep-rooted, almost atavistic, for clan, tribe, home.

A few weeks after my first lesbian affair, I was back home, sitting on the beige sectional sofa watching television with my parents. I was keeping the worlds separate as planets, trying not to let material from one atmosphere seep into the other, so my parents knew nothing of my summer adventures. Senior year was only a few days away; my mind was already in California.

My father stood up and turned off the TV. This was alarming because we had a remote control; in fact, it was in his hand. He set it down, then turned to look at me.

My mother said, "There's something we want to talk to you about."

"OK," I said, looking from one to the other with what I hoped was an innocent, or at least neutral, expression.

"This will be your last year in school," my father said, sitting down. "You've always known we would arrange your marriage. So it's time to start thinking about it."

"There's a boy in Toronto you've met," my mother began. "And that one in Florida . . ."

I started to cry.

"It's OK," said my mother. "When my parents brought it up, I cried too. We're just talking about it now. It won't happen until after you graduate."

She put her arms around me. I cried harder, my chest exploding in giant, noisy sobs that, combined with the inward pressure of her body, left me barely any room to breathe. I was trying to make myself stop, but sheer terror had set in.

One of them brought me a glass of water, a box of tissues. They exchanged glances, kept quiet, and waited until I had regained my composure, at least a little.

"Is there anything you want to tell us?" my father said.

· · ·

I did not want to tell them, not then. And even if I had, where could I begin?

Would I start by reminding them of the day I was fourteen years old, when I had first said the No, and they had not wanted to hear it?

Could I describe how that No had melted over the last three years into a Yes, the Yes of my deepest self, a Yes to an alternate world so wide and sunny it left me, often, afloat with joy and possibility?

Would I mention the *aha*'s from the feminist and lesbian books I'd been reading? The crushes and fantasies I'd suppressed and never acted on in high school, not wanting to risk my long-range plan? The secret money I'd been squirreling away against the day when I might be disowned?

I thought of my parents saying, *We trust you;* I thought of my last year of university, which would cost twenty thousand dollars, a sum I could not possibly afford on my own; I thought of the stories I'd heard of girls being forced into marriage, or sent abruptly to India, or kicked out of the house; and I kept mum.

I shook my head furiously. I sipped some water. I looked down into the glass. I sipped some more.

My parents exchanged looks.

"Well," my father said. "We were hoping you would be honest with us, but . . ."

In June, from Stanford, I had mailed a box of papers to my summer address in New York. Inside were books, a teddy bear, a binder of my writing. One issue of the campus feminist newspaper contained an essay I had written about my newfound bisexual/lesbian identity, explicit with details of my sex life. My journals noted sadly that my relationship with my parents was now "mainly financial."

Through a series of UPS mishaps, the box ended up at my parents' home in Michigan. It was tattered and torn; my parents had repacked it and forwarded it to me, without comment, over the summer. Now my father referred to it.

Some papers had "fallen out," he said. They had read them. Was it true?

I kept my eyes down as I nodded, mute and angry and afraid.

. . .

Dear Mummy and Pappa,

I want to tell you something . . . I am the same person I was before you read this letter . . .

I had written the lines two years earlier, a feminist studies class assignment in empathy, based on the premise that the personal is political: Write a letter to your parents coming out as gay. But my letter was real, and I had spent hours and nights agonizing over it. Long after that class ended, I was still struggling with how to tell my parents I was not the good Indian girl they had raised, the daughter who would become a wife and then a mother. I would break the link of generations. I would be what no one else in our family, in our whole community, had ever claimed to be. I would break their hearts—but I had neither the words nor the will to tell them this.

Whenever I had thought of coming out to my parents, I thought of every other South Asian family I knew: My schoolmates, mostly heterosexual, who snuck around on dates living in fear that someone would see them and report home. My parents' friends who forbade their son from seeing his white girlfriend and kept him on a short leash, checking the miles on his odometer to see that he drove only to and from his college. My cousin whose mother was so desperate to stop his love marriage that she sent away to South Africa for witch-doctor potions that she put in his food. I knew that, for my parents, the fact that I was having any sex at all would be as deep a calamity as my queerness.

But every time I thought of yielding to my parents' wishes, I thought again of the families I knew: husbands and wives who shared nothing but caste; women who ate last and served their men in every way; young girls sent into marriage barely knowing the rudiments of menstruation and pregnancy, let alone sexual pleasure. It was a vision shaped both by my experience and by white feminism, a vision that was, like much of what an adolescent knows, both wholly accurate and far too simple; but I could not, would not, fit myself back into it.

Now I no longer had to decide when and how to come out. In a way that fact was a relief, and in retrospect it certainly is; it might have taken me years otherwise. But I still did not know how to communicate across the gap between our worlds, which had become a chasm in the three years since I had left home. For the children of immigrants are also migrants; we cross the waters daily. Some of us become seasick. Others close our eyes and inhale the salt wind. Its fragrance is always bittersweet.

What they really wanted to know was why, and how could I, how dare I. Later they floated other explanations: it was California, it was America, it was my stubbornness. But that night they asked other questions.

Had I told anyone in the family, any of my cousins, or my friends in the local Indian community? No; that, at least, was a relief. My reputation and the family's remained intact, at least for now.

"What about AIDS?" said my mother.

"I know more about AIDS than you do," I said. I had gone to safe-sex workshops at school; I learned about condoms and dental dams and sharing bodily fluids. "I'm not a kid."

"You're an educated idiot," my father said, disgust and disappointment mixed in the lines of his face.

Then he had a question. "Bisexual—does that mean you sleep with boys *and* girls?"

"Yup," I said. I was angry too. "That's what it means."

My parents had already paid fall tuition, so I went back to school for one quarter; they made it clear they would not subsidize my "lifestyle" beyond that. We fought over the phone; I hung up on my mother and felt it was an act of liberation, even though I cried for days afterward. It was around this time that my parents learned that my brother, who was in university in New York, had been secretly dating Heidi for years.

I can see now that my parents, like most parents, deeply loved us and wanted only the best for us. They were not engaged in a lifelong conspiracy to suppress our true selves, as it sometimes seemed to my brother and me in our adolescent fury; really, they only wanted us to be happy. They believed our happiness would take the same shape as theirs: outward assimilation and material success in America, inward Indianness and a hewing to tradition in private life.

But just as education separated my parents from their own families, something separated my brother and me from our parents. Call it the Sexual Revolution, the Generation Gap, the United States of America— whatever it was, surely it deserved capital letters. Like our parents, we believed we were "choosing the best of both worlds." To them it seemed (as perhaps it seemed to their parents, before them) that we were abandoning their world entirely.

My mother wrote us both a letter, several pages long, which she photocopied, keeping the original in a secret place not even my father knew. In it she called us ungrateful and said she wished she had never had children. I sent home a couple of my poems about the beauty of lesbian love, trying to explain myself; she told me she didn't want to read that filth. My father tried to make peace, but the rest of us were having none of it.

In our misery, my brother and I grew closer than we ever had been. I took eighteen credits and graduated in December with a bachelor's in communication, Stanford's name for the department that included journalism. I didn't get my minor in feminist studies; I would have needed the rest of the year to write the required thesis.

It was the recession of 1991–92, and journalism jobs were scarce. I moved back home and sent out dozens of résumés. My mother's eyes were red and teary all the time, and probably mine were too. She took me to a gynecologist who tested me for hormonal abnormalities, to see if my sexual orientation could be cured by modern medicine. "Don't worry," the doctor said as she pulled my blood, "you look like a normal woman to me." I was oddly passive in my consent to this procedure, and relieved when the tests came back normal. Since I was still seeing my college boyfriend, the doctor also put me on the Pill.

At Christmas, for the first time since we had moved to America, my parents made no preparations. My brother and I went out and bought a fresh-cut tree, hauled the decorations out of the garage, and put them up ourselves. No one baked cookies. One afternoon my father and I were alone in the house.

"I thought I would help you invest your first paycheck," he said; after his heart surgery, he had decided to leave the academic pressure cooker and become an independent financial planner. "I never thought my own daughter would put it in a savings account for, what, two percent interest?"

He shook his head. He rested his elbows on the dining room table and lowered his chin into them.

For the first time he looked to me like an old man. I had seen him as an oppressor, but we were trapped in roles and fantasies of each other that had to be demolished before we could begin anew.

"I always thought of you as my princess," he said. "I imagined your wedding would be the happiest day of my life."

It was the first time I saw him cry.

My mother burned through her anger till it wore her out, when she gave up and tried to learn to accept. My father's peacemaking yielded results. I grew up; we all did. After those first months of arguments, we never talked much about my sexuality. Somehow we came to an uneasy truce, and began reaching across the divide.

A month or two after Christmas, when I found my first post-college journalism job and moved away, my mother packed me a spice box so I could keep the tastes of home, and sent occasional care packages of Divali sweets, spicy fried *puris*, and mango pickles. That spring my parents invited the boyfriend to their house. My father asked him if he intended to marry me. Poor guy—he explained that he had proposed to me, but I had refused on the grounds that I was a lesbian. Later my parents met my serious female partners, cordially, politely.

Once or twice a year my mother, on the telephone, would mention that so-and-so's parents were *inquiring* about me. "I told them, I don't think my daughter's interested," she'd say. A pause. "Right?" And that little speck of hope, the rise in her voice, made me want to cry.

"That's right," I would say—firmly, I hoped. And gently, I hoped.

A wall still stood between what I thought of as my real life and what I shared with my parents on visits home or on the phone. To avoid constant conflict, I felt a pressure to blend in again: to reassimilate with their community's values, to disappear my sexuality, to continue to look and act like the good Indian child of the Hinduism workbook, even if it was a façade.

And yet, as I met other lesbians and gay men of South Asian heritage, dozens and then hundreds, I began bit by bit to integrate my warring selves. Integration: as different a model from assimilation as junior high school is from adulthood. We organized workshops, discussion groups, conferences. Those of us who had survived our childhoods and adolescences by whitewashing, suppressing, and wishing away our cultural difference explored new ways to reclaim it. Those of us who had been told our queerness was a Western disease began to retrieve our own histories, unearthing millennia of evidence of same-sex relationships in ancient

South Asian cultures in stone, in text. And some of us began creating new texts, works of mythologized autobiography or poetry that spoke to the tension in our hearts. We took back or reinvented rituals; in 2002 I attended one of the first lesbian Hindu weddings in the United States, complete with holy fire and Sanskrit-muttering priest and a buffet banquet of delicious vegetarian fare.

Every queer South Asian conference featured an emotional session called Coming Out to Parents, or Relating to Our Families of Birth, or even *Dear Mummy & Pappa*. But the main purpose of our gatherings was often affirmation: to tell ourselves, against all assertions to the contrary, that we could be both Indian and lesbian, both Pakistani and gay, both Bangladeshi and bisexual; that we were neither traitors nor deviants nor heretics but merely humans trying to love. Among these peers, some of whom became close friends, I felt that perhaps I had found my own people—my home.

We continue to find one another. In 2007 I was thrilled to meet, at a conference, women who were overcoming great odds to organize and support lesbians in rural Gujarat, near my family's ancestral villages. From them I bought a poster, tricolor like India's flag, that proudly declares "Indian and Lesbian" in English, Hindi, and Gujarati. It hangs in my living room, framed and under glass like a precious artwork, or perhaps a mirror: totem, reminder, proof that I—we—exist.

I no longer wish to be Ann, or Marie, or even Gita. After half a lifetime of subtly Americanizing the pronunciation of my name, in the past year I have begun to say it the Gujarati way: Minal, *mee-nalr*. The vowels have a specific, rolling intonation; the final letter is a consonant that does not exist in English, somewhere in the borderland between *l* and *r*. Each time I say my name this way, I have the sensation of integrating language itself.

I have come to understand that queerness is a migration as momentous as any other, a journey from one world to the next. My earliest sense of alienation feels, now, like a source: a dual, twining root of both my queerness and my writing. For it is in such a splitting that the self becomes a constant observer, of both itself and others—first as a technology of survival, then as amusement, curiosity, habit, and finally for its own sake. And, observing, solitary, one cannot help developing ideas, critiques, leaps of explanation and imagination; narratives.

To write this book I traveled the world interviewing relatives, after more than a dozen years of keeping all my relations at arm's length. For one of my generation to be interested in the old-time ways and stories sometimes brought tears to my elders' eyes. It brought questions, too, including the ones I began dreading as soon as I bought my plane tickets: *When are you getting married?* followed shortly by *Why not?*

Mostly I evaded the questions with a simple "It's not for me." Repeated once or twice, it was usually enough. Sometimes I added a Gujarati saying, *Sukhi jiv dukh maa laakhe;* loosely translated, "Why throw a happy life into suffering?" and, usually, everyone laughed. Sometimes I resorted to my parents' well-worn excuse: I was busy with my work. On a couple of occasions I came out to relatives who I thought would understand, cousins and aunts to whom I could explain in English; I kept hoping the news would reach a key person who would tell everyone else, so that I would never have to come out again. But it seems I was unskilled in working the family gossip machine; and the truth is, I often passed up opportunities to out myself. Like any journalist I did not want to become the story I was reporting; I did not want my interviews to become focused on me. A combination of this desire, the language barrier, and simple cowardice stopped me. As a result, the questions continued.

In South Africa, a distant aunt took me on an after-dinner excursion to her sister's house, where no one spoke to me and I was not introduced. My aunt spent ten minutes chatting with her sister, and then we left. I gave the mysterious interlude no thought until another uncle asked if we had been there, if a certain young man was present. Without knowing it I had been up for marital consideration.

There are people in my extended family who will read for the first time here that I am a lesbian. They will think that they do not know any other gay people, that there have never been any in our community, and they will be wrong. They will think my parents' hearts must be broken, and they will be only partly right. There will be a minor conflagration perhaps, a worldwide ripple of gossip and conjecture and rumor, and any number of personal comments and questions so odd I will not know how to respond. And then it will pass, and the next community scandal will take over: someone swindling someone, or someone's wife running off with the pool boy.

Someday I expect that a cousin of a cousin, a distant niece or nephew, or a close one, will come up to me and say, *Me too.* Until then I suppose a certain kind of loneliness will persist, alleviated by the new family and community I have made and by the gifts that have come my way. Grace, joy, love, gratitude: these too are elements of my path. When I touch my lover's hand in the dark, I know what the goddess wrote for me.

On the trip I also became curious about my destiny, and sought out an astrologer in India. He and his family were renting the house where my father grew up, which my grandfather had built with the proceeds from Narseys back in 1937. The date was engraved on its façade; it was still the family homestead, though none of us had lived there for decades. Inside, old photographs of my ancestors hung from the moldings. I sat in the front room among them, before a dark wooden desk where the astrologer saw his clients.

He wore a patterned silk shirt, his tools laid out before him: eyeglasses, calculator, pen, datebook, ruled legal paper. More businesslike than mystical, his manner was somber and polite. He looked at the chart he had drawn up, based on my birth, and gave me bad news. The name I had been given was the exact opposite of my *raasi*, or name-horoscope, a factor that leads to rage and volatility. To repair it, I ought to go back to something like Gita.

Astrologically, I was stubborn by nature, he added. I had probably had great difficulty in my education and failed several times, but had eventually succeeded by the grace of god. Having missed the most auspicious window for marrying early in my twenties, I ought to hurry. Probably I would marry a pale-eyed man, and we would have many fights. Also many children, mostly boys.

I could make a lot of money on the black market. And I would do well to open a gas station.

Somehow, as I walked away from my fate, I managed not to laugh out loud. Perhaps my parents were right, at least about astrologers.

A year later, the last of my father's brothers in Fiji was preparing to emigrate. Cleaning house, he came across artifacts from my grandparents, including my first horoscope: the one commissioned by my grandmother when I was born. It arrived in the mail, and of course I could not resist. My father sat with me to translate.

On a red printed form under an etching of Ganesh, a seer in India had sketched out in blue ink the position of the stars at the time of my birth: 7:42 P.M. July 12, 1971, America. This was translated to Samvat year 2027, day 5 of the waning half of the month of Ashaad. I was born under the moon-sign of Kumbh, the word for a water pot, roughly equivalent to Aquarius in the Western zodiac. Based on the stars, the astronomer suggested five names for me: Saroj, Sashpu, Sudha, Gauri, and Gita. Mars was prominent in my chart, signifying a stubborn and difficult nature. My element was copper, and my footprint was auspicious.

I told my father I was curious what my destiny would have been if my parents had followed this horoscope. If I had been this girl named Gita. He blinked.

"But *dikraa*," he said—dear one, daughter—"your fate could not have been any different than it is." What is written, by the deity and based on one's own karma, is written.

I felt a slight choking in my throat, as by this I knew that, even if he disapproved or had trouble understanding, he accepted my life.

Every migrant constructs, or spends her life seeking, a new definition of home. For me it is a word with many edges, multifaceted as a crystal or a goddess of a thousand and one names, an infinity of arms. It is the queer planet where I live, filled with gay men and lesbian women, the tattooed and the pierced, sissy boys, butch girls, people born with indeterminate genitalia, women who pass as or identify as or have become men, drag queens, interracial couples of all genders. It is the hearts of my lovers and friends, the created family that all free queer people know, the one we construct far from our original homes: filled with joy and true acceptance, not merely grudging tolerance, a safe place to name and learn to fulfill our truest desires. In one sense this queer tribe is on the leading edge of society, language, and medical knowledge; yet in another, we are the most ancient sort of village, a way of organizing our needs and relationships—human life and its elements, all of its purposes.

Home too is again my first family, to whom the others might all be freaks, my mother's cooking and my father's ideas, the web of relations and traditions that surround us on holy days and in times of crisis or celebration. And it is the home that exists only inside me, which encompasses and unites all that is held together by my fragile skin, and which consists of a constant, prickly sensation of traveling between worlds that seem forever irreconcilable.

But perhaps this gap is itself the illusion.

In my mother's village in India, in a hut that seems to be located at the very center of the crossroads, lives a person born male, who never married and who refers to herself exclusively in the feminine. Gujarati is a gender-inflected language, in which even the simplest sentences reveal the speaker's sex, require a choice. Duliyaa, as she is called, lives with her mother and has never married. She seems to have a soft spot for children; the day we met, she was holding a small child, and she remembered my mother, who was seven years old the last time they had met. And they embraced warmly.

Far from any queer movement or urban politics, far from academic theories of gender, lives a possibility, a true heritage of tolerance and integration. Among a people who can and have absorbed so much, whose gods are many-limbed and multigendered, whose lives are filled with all manner of suffering, sexual identity is the least of it. I do not know how Duliyaa would "identify," were it even possible to translate and define the terms from my world—gay, queer, queen, transgender, transsexual, let alone the newer and more exotic "genderqueer" or the brilliantly cynical "genderfucked." All I know is that this tall, lanky, biologically male exterior holds a being who somehow, for more than sixty years, has quietly asserted, in a place as remote from radical gender politics as we can imagine, the truth of her own pure being.

Where are you from? asks the white woman at the bathhouse, March 2005.

It is a first, natural question.

Here, I say, *San Francisco.* I was born here, have lived here many years.

Oh? In her voice I hear a faint rise: disbelief, wonder, a set of questions she does not ask. Steam rises from our bodies in the cool city night, towels wrapped around us like layers of stories we aren't willing to release. The conversation moves on, but I am thinking of all the times I have faced this question—dozens? hundreds?—and how, even now, I feel I must defend or explain my answer. Often *San Francisco* is enough; but equally often, my questioner wants more. *No, I mean, where are you* really *from?*

I might list all the other places I have lived, from New Zealand to suburban Michigan to Silicon Valley—but none of these would give a clue as to either ethnicity or character. I find myself resisting the expected answer: *India.* For just as my questioner suspects by the looks of me that San Francisco is an oversimplification, that there must be more to the story, I know that India is too easy an answer. I could describe my parents' series of migrations, including Fiji, but I would have to go back another generation to match up a landscape with my phenotype: skin tone, hair, features. My extended family lives in nine countries at this writing; am I not in some way *from* all of these places? Within India, too, we have a deeper history than a simple region or village name. We are, if legend is to be believed, from royalty, from mud, and from fire.

But yes, India: a foreign country to me, the place where all four of my great-grandmothers bathed in lakes and streams, six yards of cotton wrapped around them for modesty. A hundred years ago they would not have conceived of a daughter stepping naked and free of shame into heated pools and saunas, with women of all the world's races for bathing companions. Puzzling over a question whose answer they knew in their bones.

And yet, as far as I travel from my family, I am never lost.

There are moments now when the wall, the one that grew up so strongly around me in childhood, seems to have dissolved entirely. Or I have absorbed it into myself; it is no longer made of brick, but of skin, and is perhaps no more than the boundary each of us has, our simple sense of self. It is a hard-won unity, not to live in compartmentalized fragments; easier sometimes to avoid explaining the rites and vocabularies of one tribe to the other. Yet the moments when I have felt truly integrated shine brighter than suns in my memory; I would not trade them for a princess's ransom.

It was only when I began traveling among my relatives for this book that I came to understand how each life is a tangle of push and pull; how each migration opens up future directions; and how my own journey, which I had come to believe and been made to feel was so unusual as to be selfish and freakish, was in fact continuous with a long heritage of moving from the known to the unknown, from tradition into modernity, from village India into a cosmopolitan world. In my interviews I found not only success stories but also secret shames, sometimes one buried within the other: illegal border crossings, whisperings of second wives and concubines, stories of abuse and survival, turn-off-the-tape-recorder moments that I knew I could not retell but that I absorbed nonetheless. As I unveil a piece of the vast silence about sexuality in order to tell my own story, I know these other secrets are the context.

Shame is bone-deep, says my reiki-shiatsu healer, as her brown hands massage my muscles, tense from typing. I close my eyes, and an image arises: a grid of fishbones under my skin. Interconnected, sharp-edged, like the history of all of the women in my family, the bones are flexible and nearly translucent. I try to describe this new spine, its compelling, almost mathematical beauty.

My name means fish, I tell her. Where am I from? This is my body, this is where I live.

part four: destiny

2001

Estimated size of the Indian diaspora: 11,510,644
Countries with more than 10,000 people of Indian origin: 47

1. USA
2. Saudi Arabia
3. England and Wales
4. South Africa
5. Canada
6. Mauritius
7. Trinidad and Tobago
8. Guyana
9. Fiji
10. Oman
11. Singapore
12. Kuwait
13. Réunion
14. Netherlands
15. Australia
16. Surinam
17. Qatar
18. Bahrain
19. Kenya
20. Yemen Arab Republic
21. United Arab Emirates
22. Tanganyika
23. Thailand
24. Italy
25. Portugal
26. France
27. Jamaica
28. Indonesia
29. New Zealand
30. Hong Kong
31. Israel
32. Guadeloupe
33. Philippines
34. Germany
35. Madagascar
36. Spain
37. Nigeria
38. Mozambique
39. Zimbabwe
40. Russia
41. Switzerland
42. Zambia
43. Libya
44. Uganda
45. Austria
46. Lebanon
47. Sweden

Vaasudeva kutumbukam.
The whole world is one family.
—Ancient Sanskrit mantra

*I*T IS OCTOBER and the women are dancing. All around the world we put on our long skirts and tight bodices, wrap ourselves in gauzy shawls, fasten jewels at our throats and bells around our ankles. We dance barefoot in temples, where we have temples; or community centers, high school gymnasiums, even bare fields. The dance is what remains the same: a sacred circle.

Garbaa, the word for the Gujarati folk dance, comes from a Sanskrit root, *grb,* for womb. Round and round we twirl to celebrate Navratri, the lunar festival of nine nights of dancing in honor of the goddess. I have danced the garbaa with my cousins at a newly erected temple in New Zealand, where Indians are running more and more corner stores ("dairies") and clustering together in new neighborhoods. In Fiji, I have danced it with my aunts at a temple whose walls slide away to let in the tropical night. I have swirled and sweated it with relatives and friends in London, New York, Toronto. And as a child in Michigan, I twirled round a fluorescent-lit multipurpose room in the Plymouth Cultural Center, whose hallways we shared with white-robed tae kwon do students and bulging ice hockey players.

Always it is the cusp of seasons: harvest, or planting. The soundtrack booms from live singers and musicians, or only a precious cassette tape (now CD or iPod) recorded (downloaded, bootlegged) from the old country. Always the oldest women cluster around the edges, on bleachers or folding chairs or the floor, gossiping or watching silently as they clutch knees and hips long past dancing. Every generation has its place, and gives way to the others. Middle-aged women form the outer ring, moving slowly to the 3/3 beat, clapping their hands three times: once at the earth, once at the waist, once at the sky. The circle advances, counterclockwise. In an inner ring, younger women and girls who are just becoming women show off fancier moves; wrists and hips swivel with a grace and vanity befitting their age, as if they know that this is their time on earth. At the very center, the littlest girls run around and groove to their own beats, wild foals dressed up for a few nights as princesses.

At midnight we chant the praise-song of prayer. We pass around a tray with the small flame whose grace we accept one by one; we make offerings of coins and bills; we share the sanctified food. Then we emerge sweating and sated, bundling up in winter coats to cross the tarred parking lot, or walking down hot dusty lanes to an ancestral home.

If diaspora is defined by the phenomenon of dispersal, then bringing together the stories of a diaspora may be a task as wisely undertaken as that of piecing Humpty Dumpty back together again. And trying to look into our diaspora's future, as I want to do in this last chapter, can feel like examining a cracked mirror. It can never be fused into smooth glass again; better, perhaps, to construct a mosaic.

But what is it that glues us together, across time and space? Each generation grapples with a new set of circumstances, inheriting some traditions and discarding others. The choices of what to change and what to continue are made not once and for all, but daily, yearly, life by life. What, then, is the fabric of the shared identity that seems to persist, though in places it frays? Is it still, after so many generations, India—or the memory of India?

INDIA

The first time I met Jaydeep, he was running, as if for his life.

This is the impression I will always have of him: desperate, determined, out of breath. In the dust and heat he was chasing our car, to guide us—the lost American relatives—to his house. Once indoors, he had barely caught his breath when he jumped up again and went to a corner of the single room that served as living room and bedroom for him, his parents, and his younger brother. From the cupboard he took out a folder, which he presented to my father. "I want to come to America," he said.

Jaydeep's mother is my cousin Bharati. Among my thirty-six first cousins, she and her brother are the only ones who remain in India. Their mother, Sarasvati, my mother's eldest sister, is the only one of my parents' eleven siblings who never migrated out of India. While Bharati's brother still lives near the ancestral villages, Bharati and her family have moved to Kalyaan, north of Mumbai (formerly Bombay).

To reach Kalyaan we had followed the massive above-ground water and sewage pipes that wound through the last choked suburbs of the city, past the failed utopia of New Bombay, past factories of handmade bricks drying in uneven red piles, past miles of diesel-colored weeds and children squatting by the roadside, past gated communities where overseas Indians spend their new U.S. dollars on private parking and swimming pools and views of the swamps where no slum-shacks can stand—and at last into a town. Our driver, who came with the rented car, stopped for a fifth time to ask directions. As he rolled down his window, a face pushed into the conditioned air.

"Why, it's Jaydeep!" said my mother, and the face grinned, a door opened, and he squeezed in next to me. My first impressions were: thin boy in thin shirt, head too big for body, age twelve to fourteen. Panting, he told us cheerfully, "I've been chasing you for ten minutes." He guided the driver back toward the one-room apartment we had missed, on the sandy lane whose name no one knew, in the unnumbered building with its back to the dry, wide stream. My father asked, "How are you? How old are you now?"

"Twenty-two," he answered. "Yesterday was my birthday. Here we are; park here."

We emerged from the car's tinted interior into the bright Indian sun, blinking. His mother stood at the entry to the sandy lane. It was almost noon.

Inside, Jaydeep perched on the edge of the bed where we were all sitting, and his legs trembled with nervous energy.

"Let them rest a little first, Jaydeep," his mother admonished, telling us, "He hardly slept."

So we sat awhile in the narrow room with its two windows, small and high, shuttered against the midday heat. A small television suspended from the ceiling transmitted a staticky color picture, though the sound was turned off. The walls were painted bright blue, and a fake cockroach climbed up one of them—the work of Jaydeep's brother, Pradeep, who was sixteen going on ten. A twin bed was pushed against each wall, and we sat on these, with a narrow coffee table between us.

The sons and their father, a thin, white-haired tailor, sat and talked with us as Bharati busied herself in the kitchen. It was the size of an American closet, with a few open shelves bearing pots and dishes, and a wood-eating contraption that sat on the floor and served as both oven and stove. Next to the kitchen were the bathrooms: one room housing a tiled pit toilet, the other a walled-off area with a tap, a bucket, and a drain, for bathing and for washing dishes or clothes. From this triangular area Bharati emerged shortly with a full meal of vegetables, rotli, rice, daal, and sweets.

Pradeep, who had an interest in cooking, had made the mattar paneer. My father complimented the dish and joked, "You'll be in America faster than your brother," and Jaydeep piped up, "I can cook too!"

"Only kidding," said my father, but Jaydeep was still talking: "I'll do anything, any kind of job—" As he spoke and we ate, every muscle in his wiry body seemed to be straining. I had the odd idea that he was making a great effort, in fact, not to fall to his knees and beg us for help.

I had never met Jaydeep's family, though I knew something of their story. Bharati's mother, my aunt Sarasvati, was named for the goddess of learning, but she did not finish even elementary school. Unlike my mother and the other children, Sarasvati grew up in India with neither parents nor siblings. As her father, Narotam, was struggling to gain a foothold in Fiji, Sarasvati was raised by her grandparents, was married at a young age, and became a mother of four. Eventually she and her family moved to the outskirts of Bombay, in the great rural-to-urban migration that was transforming, and was a result of the transformation of, India's postwar economy. But they remained poor; millions of other rural émigrés were packing the cities as well, driving down wages and clustering together in slumlike conditions. Sarasvati's husband wanted her to ask for money from her rich relatives overseas, and under duress she wrote let-

ters to her father in Fiji. My mother remembers one letter from Sarasvati's son arriving in the 1950s: *Ma has been burnt, please send money for
treatment.* The boy had drawn a rough sketch of her face showing how
the burn covered a third of it. Narotam did not know whether the story
was true or just another ploy for cash, but his heart was soft and he sent
money. For decades my mother remembered the sketch, one of the only
likenesses she ever saw of her eldest sister in their years apart. Sarasvati
died in 1982 of cancer. Twenty years later my mother had a chance to ask
her nephew about the burn, and learned for the first time that the sketch
was real: a kitchen accident.

Of Sarasvati's daughters, one migrated by marriage to Fiji and later
to New Zealand. Another lived in India most of her life while her husband worked as a tailor in Kuwait; by a most circuitous route of family
sponsorship, through their own daughter's in-laws, they arrived in the
United States in 2003. And Bharati inherited her mother's character, qualities I recognize from our grandmother: quiet temperament, gentle smile,
hard work, stoicism in the face of suffering. As we visited, Bharati was
caring for her ailing father-in-law, who lived nearby and in addition to
being so ill that he needed almost constant care was so ill-tempered that
he berated her for providing it. Bharati did not seem to resent her fate.

It is no coincidence, I think, that the poorest members of my family
are those who still live in India. They are not dirt poor; they work, they
eat, and they even manage to accumulate some money. Bharati's brother
had told us, for example, that after two decades of working for a chemical factory, he was glad to have saved up enough to pay for the wedding
of his daughter, who was just coming of age. They have small luxuries:
television, perhaps a telephone. But they lack the large ones that we in
the diaspora take as necessities: cars, computers, microwave ovens.

Nor do they have what some consider the greatest luxury of all: the
freedom to leave India. And it was this, we would learn, that Jaydeep
craved the most from us, his American kin. After lunch, the talk turned
at last to Jaydeep and his future plans.

Jaydeep was the fruit of his parents' hard work and his country's investment in education. He was the first in his family to finish high school; he
had a bachelor's degree in accounting and a master's in desktop publishing, and was completing a second master's course in business. He had just

found a job as a computer graphics technician for a small firm that etched images on glass for designer doorways and windows. He had hope.

He showed us the brochure he had been saving, advertising a scheme to migrate to the United States: an expensive course that would prepare students to take a certification exam in accounting. His smile was so broad and optimistic that it seemed to take over his jawline and light up the dim room.

My father, a financial planner, scanned the brochure and expressed skepticism. America had plenty of accountants, he said, and it was not a desired immigration category. Then, drawing on his long training as a professor, he delivered a somewhat pedantic discourse on the various ways to get to America.

The simplest, he said, was to have a lot of money and come on a business visa: ten thousand dollars, or half a million rupees. Of course, he noted, that would not apply. Jaydeep, with his dual degrees, was making two thousand rupees a month: fifty dollars.

Then there was illegal immigration, which my father could not recommend, and which in any case had become much more difficult since September 11, 2001. Next, sponsorship by an immediate relative—sibling or parent—which Jaydeep did not have. Three ways now remained: school, marriage, or work in a category that the United States desperately needed. Accounting was not one of these. Computers were, but the barriers to entry were high; he would need a job in hand from an American company, and those jobs were going to highly recruited graduates of the elite Indian Institutes of Technology, not people with correspondence-course degrees like Jaydeep.

My father ran down the list of options for Jaydeep, and shook his head as if discouraged. Perhaps Australia, he said. Perhaps New Zealand, where Jaydeep's aunt was living.

Perhaps Canada.

TORONTO

In the suburbs of Canada's largest metropolis, a cultural and economic capital whose multiculturalism is evident on nearly every block, my cousin Raju is living out, in effect, Jaydeep's dream. When his mother, Lila, my father's baby sister, had migrated to Canada, she was joining her husband, Mahendra, who had come a year earlier and found work. Raju was born in Fiji just two years earlier, in 1965; a Toronto-born sister and brother followed. But within a few years Mahendra was disabled in a car accident, and the young family found themselves on welfare. With little English or education, Lila found factory work. Eventually Mahendra recovered and became an insurance salesman, known to his customers as Mike. With two incomes and a series of loans, the family gradually eked its way back into the middle class.

From this background, their eldest son emerged with a singular determination. Raju is what I grew up calling him, but almost everyone else calls him Roger. His three-page corporate biography, titled "Roger Sholanki: A success story," begins:

> Growing up, Roger Sholanki was the type of child who possessed that certain drive and motivation that most kids didn't have. The type that walked to the corner store during lunch break to load up on candy, only to turn around and sell it for a decent profit to other kids around the schoolyard. Some call it the entrepreneurial spirit. Some may even call it greediness. But no matter what term you choose, **the bottom line is that Roger was born with the knack to make money.**

Roger loved fast cars, took up auto mechanics, and built go-karts, giving rides to neighborhood children "for twenty five cents a pop." In tenth grade, he failed a class in computers—but determined to try again. From the biography:

> After all, Einstein once failed math. As it happened, perseverance prevailed and Roger finished Grade 11 computers at the top of his class with an A+. Though this may seem to be a miniscule accomplishment in the grand scheme of things, it is a perfect illustration of his desire to succeed. *"If somebody tells me I can't do something, it just motivates me to show them how it's done,"* Roger explains. [Emphases in original]

While still in high school, he started building and selling computers. He enrolled in a local polytechnic university, graduated with a degree in computer science, and went to work for a large travel agency, developing software to help agents log transactions at the point of sale. Eventually, point-of-sale software would become his ticket to wealth. He took a series of corporate computer jobs throughout the personal-computer boom of the 1980s, spending nights and weekends on his own ventures; his first company resold hardware and software. By 1992, he had started his second company, a small consulting firm that earned contracts in the millions of dollars from some of Canada's largest corporations. By 1999, on his third venture, his point-of-sale software for cell phone providers was dominating the North American market. This, according to his official biography, "made Roger a financial success at the age of thirty-two." He then started a fourth company, took it public, and would eventually sell it to start yet another venture.

I interviewed Raju, whom I could never bring myself to call Roger, and his wife, Judy, in their "library," which featured burgundy leather sofas and dark, softly gleaming wood paneling. Like the homes of new-money tech entrepreneurs everywhere, their large suburban house was tastefully outfitted in neutral colors, with plenty of shiny new appliances, a chandelier in the foyer, and furnishings that might have been decorator-approved. Their two school-age children were well mannered and polite, and wore designer jeans. Judy, who had grown up in a large Indo-Trinidadian family in Toronto, was slim, flawlessly coiffed, and had a passion for shopping; she spent many of her afternoons at the mall. We talked about their marriage (an intercaste scandal within our family), their childhood in Canada (Judy remembered racism, with schoolyard bullies picking on Vietnamese "boat children"; Raju remembered being one of the bullies), and the experience of diaspora.

"So," I asked Raju, "do you feel more Indian, Canadian, or something in between?"

He paused before answering. "Actually," he said, "I feel American." Americans, he explained, were serious about making money, and so was he. "Basically my identity is, I'm a capitalist."

Hong Kong

It is this capitalist drive to succeed, rather than some nostalgic connection to India, that some theorists believe is the true connection among

citizens of the global Indian diaspora. As the United States dominates
the economy and popular culture of countries all over the globe, and as-
serts a greater and greater role as the world's sole superpower, perhaps
we are all flashy bits of the American mirror, more starred-and-striped
than we know. Or perhaps the American dream is only one manifesta-
tion of a kind of economic success that my relatives have been pursuing
for more than a century: the Fijian dream, the South African dream, the
Australian dream, the Hong Kong dream.

As diaspora entrepreneurs go, Raju/Roger, the self-made man, is far
less typical than my third cousin Hemesh, in Hong Kong. I interviewed
him in his firm's upstairs office—Chhiba Trading, named for his great-
grandfather, who was my grandfather Narotam's uncle. Hemesh was
working long hours running the modest import-export business, taking
regular business trips to factories in China whose goods he shipped out
of the world's busiest port in Hong Kong. He was not an individualist;
rather, he was proud of carrying on a family tradition.

Hemesh's father, Harilal, had come to Hong Kong in 1970. The move
was a natural outgrowth of his family's booming business in Fiji. For
years Harilal and his three brothers had been buying textiles, toys, cos-
tume jewelry, sewing machines, transistor radios, and more from Japan,
Taiwan, mainland China, and Hong Kong, then reselling the goods to retailers in Fiji and other nearby islands. Such import-export was profitable, but the commissions could kill you: five percent to the agent in
Asia, five percent to the agent in the Pacific, and soon your profit margin
was halved, or worse. Harilal was already making frequent trips to Asia,
to inspect and buy the latest electronics and household goods, when the
family decided to try cutting out at least one middleman by opening up
a shop in Hong Kong.

At first, Harilal's primary customer was the family firm in Suva. A
handful of other Khatri shopkeepers had hit upon the same strategy; in
Hong Kong's crowded real-estate market, they settled for tiny bachelor
apartments and small offices with minimal staffs. They tried to ship
goods immediately; when they had to store them, they rented space instead of buying warehouses. They worked twelve-hour days and hired
bilingual locals to negotiate with Chinese factory owners for the best
deals. Once they had set up shop, they sent for their families.

Hemesh and the other children learned Gujarati at home, Cantonese in the streets, and English in their British-run private schools. Business was good, and Harilal opened an office in Taiwan, then one in Bangkok. The Indians were a tiny minority; an exact count was hard to come by because of their highly transitory nature, but India's embassy in the mid-1990s estimated 23,000 people of Indian origin living in Hong Kong. Despite this tiny number, relative to the island's population of six million, Indian businessmen were estimated to account for nine percent of the international trade. The Khatri community at its peak in the 1980s comprised about eighty people, including young Hemesh.

Hemesh left Hong Kong for a year to study business in London, then returned to the family firm, which he called "the best school for business." He began making sales trips to Fiji with suitcases full of samples. Then, after Fiji's 1987 coups and the resulting economic decline, all of the "Hong-Kong-walas," as the Khatris in Hong Kong called themselves, were forced to look for other markets. One became "king of Nepal," another specialized in the Middle East, and so on. Working hard to coexist while trading in essentially the same industry, they carved out niches for themselves. Of course, conflicts were inevitable: families quarreled over tricky business deals and perceived social snubs, and one man was ostracized for taking two Chinese concubines. But overall, they remained a tight-knit clan bound by a common culture. To allow for both cordiality and survival within the tiny community, they maintained the gentlemen's agreement not to compete with one another. Hemesh and his father ended up developing the trade in Africa.

For a time, Africa took Hemesh away from home six months out of the year. Business only grew better. Khatri families came and went, creating a kind of temporary community that was, in some ways, a reflection of the nature of Hong Kong itself. When Harilal and his peers had first arrived on the island in the 1960s and early 1970s, it was a British colony under ninety-nine-year lease from China. The turnover date of 1998, when communist China would take over capitalist Hong Kong, had seemed sufficiently distant. Who knew; perhaps Britain would buy the colony outright, or China would lose the Cold War. Anything was possible, and certainly not worth worrying about so far in advance.

But by the mid-1990s, each week seemed to bring new turnover rumors: The communists would nationalize all private enterprise; no, they would respect private enterprise. The government would evict non-Chinese; no, it would open up the immense China market. The Indians would become stateless; no, they would be given British passports; no, they would have to go home to Fiji or India.

Amid the uncertainty, some traders left Hong Kong. They took their families back to Fiji or moved on to a third country; they shut down their businesses or sold them to others in the community. Hemesh and his family decided to stay. In the end, the Chinese takeover of Hong Kong meant only two concrete changes in their lives: they managed to obtain British passports, and their children had to learn written Chinese alongside English in school.

Life in Hong Kong is all vertical, all about ascent. Its citizens live like birds, perched in the air high above the city. Even at the Central Library, where I went to look up statistics and histories of Indians in the colony, people stood in neat lines to enter the elevator, as if we were traveling up the Empire State Building instead of to the ninth-floor reference desk. One can buy anything in Hong Kong—a three-thousand-dollar Louis Vuitton purse at the most sumptuous of luxury malls, or a three-dollar version of the same item in the alley behind. Ensconced in small high-rise apartments packed with multiple generations of family members, my Hong Kong relatives seemed to have perfected the art of feathering their nests with all manner of comforts while also being always ready to fly.

When I interviewed Hemesh, he was confident that the turnover had posed no problems for businessmen. But another threat was presenting itself: the emergence of Chinese capitalism. For a century, China's insularity and British efficiency had given Hong Kong traders a virtual monopoly on importing goods into China and exporting the products of Chinese factories to the world. Now China was opening up, as was evident a short boat ride away from Hong Kong, in the new city of Shenzhen. Once a tract of shrimp and litchi farms, Shenzhen had been transformed into a giant experiment with capitalism: a "free enterprise zone" with thousands of garment factories, silicon chip manufacturers, high-rise buildings, and, somewhat incongruously, three sprawling theme parks for tourists. International buyers no longer needed Hong Kong; they could now deal directly with factory owners in Shenzhen and other designated Chinese centers of industry. They could cut out the middleman.

And then there was, for the Khatris, a social change. Once home to perhaps twenty-five families, enough to hold an annual festival and organize a soccer league for the men, Hong Kong by 2001 had only four Khatri families. I had met all of them at a Divali party at Hemesh's place the night before our interview; they barely filled the apartment. Some of the children were growing up with Chinese accents and almost no contact with their ancestral traditions. In the tiny apartments that are the lot of all but the wealthiest Hong Kongers, the Khatris' sense of isolation was growing. Hong Kong no longer felt like a frontier; it felt like exile. It was, for many of those who could manage it, time to move on.

Chhiba Trading remains a remote outpost of our diaspora, tucked into a dead-end lane of shops displaying dried herbs and cheap leather goods. Within a few years of our interview, Hemesh had taken his family to Australia, though his father remained in Hong Kong to keep up the office. On the day I interviewed Hemesh there, several staff members, all Chinese, worked quietly at their desks. Hemesh explained that although he was fluent in Cantonese, most Chinese factory owners preferred to deal with other Chinese, so he employed some local "translators." On his desk were piles of papers and several varieties of batteries. He noticed my glance, and said, "These are for export to Africa." Oh? "Very cheap, but they only last a few hours. For Africa price matters more than quality. You couldn't sell these in America, but for Africa, they are the only ones."

I asked a few more questions about the trade, and he warmed to his subject. Every three to four months he had to tour the African continent, checking on customers and the market, trying to collect payments amid the constant currency devaluations. Goods from China—not just batteries but cloth, household items, and anything else—were perfect because they could be provided as cheaply as Africans could afford to buy. "The thing about items going to Africa is, they will never sell in Europe or the States. Because for one thing they'll never pass the quality control; I mean, the example is the battery. If you want the price of a battery like this" — he held one up — "the first thing they'll ask you in China is, How long do you want it to run? And I can get you a battery at a price which says that if you run it continuously on this tape recorder" — he pointed to my hand-held machine — "it will run for only fifteen minutes. What is the value of that? In America you wouldn't even pay fifteen cents for a fifteen-minute battery, you'd go and complain that it didn't even work. In Africa, who's going to see about a complaint? You can sell them in bulk, so it works out."

I looked at my tape recorder, and the pile of batteries on the desk, and the calm black eyes of the businessman-cousin in front of me: a series of reflective surfaces, tiny mirrors whose messages I could not decipher.

South Africa

If Hemesh was trading with Africans at a cool and businesslike distance, my relatives in South Africa were encountering them up close, particularly since the end of apartheid. That intimacy has led them to numerous responses: racism, tension, fear, rage, emigration, attempts at re-segregation — and in some cases, compassion and hope.

Outside Johannesburg, I met up with my second cousin Praveena. A single mother since her husband's suicide just after their daughter was born, Praveena is just a few years older than I am. I stayed with her family for a couple of days, and we were able to talk easily. Praveena was living with her parents, brother, and four-year-old daughter in Lenasia — "Land of the Asians," a formerly Indian-only suburb that, like the rest of the new South Africa, was in a period of transition. Many Indians were moving "up" to the formerly white areas. Black and "coloured" (South Africa's term for mixed-race) people were likewise moving "up" to the Indian areas. Most Indians were not pleased by these newcomers.

Lenasia looked to me like any suburb in America, but with more barbed wire; security was one of South Africa's fastest-growing industries. Everyone I met was concerned about the growing crime rate. Everyone had experienced or heard of crimes that were shocking in their brutality, even allowing for some exaggeration: street muggings, carjackings, home break-ins, multiple rape-murders of whole families. While Indians had welcomed the end of apartheid, many were somewhere between ambivalent and fearful about black-majority rule.

In this volatile environment, Praveena was a teacher in the integrating public-school system. The position made her, de facto, one of the people trying to bridge the racial divides that had been enforced in South Africa for generations. She took me on a visit to her school, where the staff remained almost all Indian but where the student body now included Indian, black, and "coloured" — but no white — children.

Y. Chengalroyen, the school's principal, sat down with me for one class period and gave me an overview of what was happening in the school system. One problem, he said, was that people who were active in the anti-apartheid struggle had been given important posts overseeing public education, pushing out skilled career educators. These activists seemed to be modeling their administration on the U.S. public-school system, with erratic results.

Another, more immediate issue was that Indians were moving their children out to schools in white areas or to private schools, where they paid up to 8,000 rand ($800) per year in tuition. His high school was functioning on less than 600 rand ($60) per pupil per year. "Indians are not prepared to uplift the schools in their own areas," he complained. Into the vacuum came black and "coloured" students, from areas whose schools were even worse off. He was allocated one staff member per thirty-five students, which included the principal and deputy principal.

Chengalroyen bore no nostalgia for apartheid; he had been an activist himself, involved in the early days of the national teachers' union, and a leader in the movement to protest a history curriculum that included little but the mythologizing tales of white settlers. But he was frustrated by the scope of the challenge. "Parents have become desperate to send their children to good schools," he acknowledged. "Our teachers are not very relaxed."

At 8 A.M. the morning assembly opened, and the students chanted in unison: "Let God be in my head, and in my understanding; let God be in my eyes, and in my looking . . ." While the other teachers huddled together and talked under an awning, Praveena walked up and down the neat rows of her students, saying good morning. Her students were mostly "matriculates," meaning that they were in their last year; she taught biology, physics, chemistry, and mathematics. At 8:10, she unlocked her classroom door, and the chattering students filed in. By American standards, they seemed polite and well behaved, most saying "Good morning, ma'am" as they entered. Praveena launched into a lesson on vectors and polygons, scrawling problems and diagrams on the board: "A spider in search of food crawls 2 meters on a bearing of 225 degrees, then 3 meters on a bearing of 270 degrees, 2 meters on a bearing of 315 degrees," and so on for several more steps; "Determine the resultant displacement of the spider." Sitting in the teacher's chair near the front, I tried to solve the problem, then gave up. Instead I watched the class: "coloured" girls with light skin and fine features, darker African girls with hairstyles that would not have been out of place in the latest rap videos, Muslim girls wearing black headscarves, and Hindu girls with henna highlights and eyeglasses. The boys were less varied in their hairdos, and everyone wore the school's uniform, gray with accents of red and white. The students seemed to have grouped themselves by race in their seating choices, but in my quick survey, I could detect no hostile currents among them; they seemed attentive and focused on learning. By 8:30 A.M., Praveena had chalk on the scarf of her salwar kameez.

In third period, she taught physics. "In your opinion you're doing work," she started off, "but scientifically, you're doing *nothing*." This was a prelude to explaining that "Work is done when a Force is applied to a Mass, and the object moves in the direction of the Force." Heads bent over papers; pencils were raised. She described Newton's second law, then concluded, "You're only doing Work if a Force causes a Mass to be displaced." There were forty-eight students in the class, and when she asked them to break into small groups to solve a problem together, chaos ensued. She had to shout to regain their attention. By 11 A.M., Praveena was exhausted—and she had three more classes to teach.

On Saturdays and Sundays she also taught, all day, giving private lessons in her family's garage to students who could pay for extra tutoring. At first only Indians came; then, as the schools integrated, other students asked if they could also come. She told me, "At first I was guilty, but then my heart told me, you mustn't be so ugly. They are children too, and I am a teacher. And I'm so glad I took them, they are lovely children, they want to learn so much."

By the end of each day, chalk dust forms a sort of Milky Way across

Praveena's blouse. The moral force of the anti-apartheid resistance has caused a great displacement; now, for the Indians as for other South Africans, there is work to be done.

NEW JERSEY

Praveena and her family were planning to stay in South Africa—while I was there, they were looking to buy a bigger house—but many of their relations and peers had chosen emigration. At a Starbucks on Astor Place in lower Manhattan, I met my father's cousin's son Nainesh, who was in his first year as a biology major at New York University. We rode the train back to the New Jersey suburbs where his family had lived since 1995. Before that they had spent ten years in Toronto, and before that, in an infancy he cannot remember, they were in South Africa. His grandfather was the eldest brother of my paternal grandmother, Kaashi. The great-grandfather we shared, Ramjee Govind, had first traveled to South Africa in 1899.

Nainesh was now nineteen, and when I told him the subject of my book, he said, "That's so boring—I can't think of anything interesting about our family, not one thing." At home, his brother Vimal, a year younger, was more interested, or more tactful: "I'd like to read that book, I can't wait." Their youngest brother, Amit, only thirteen, said nothing at all. They invited me to join them on an excursion to see *American Desi,* an independent feature film that had just come out about the second-generation Indo-American experience, along with other members of the Kshatriya (Khatri) Youth Association of New Jersey. Both brothers had served a term as president of the caste-based group, despite being only half-Khatri. Their parents had had one of the first "love marriages" in our family, after meeting in a Hindu youth group in South Africa.

"I joined every club I could," Nainesh said by way of explanation of his involvement in KYA. When they moved from Toronto to New Jersey, Nainesh was thirteen. At school white youths taunted the brothers with racist comments. New Jersey's Indian population was growing steadily, and the backlash was fierce; the state had seen a rash of unsolved hate crimes in the late 1980s, committed by an anonymous group who called themselves the Dotbusters and took as their target the bindi, or "dot," that Hindu women wear on their foreheads.

KYA gave both boys a forum in which they quickly became leaders, though a few parents murmured about the bad influence; the boys were mixed-caste and were rumored to be wild and even (gasp) to date. Lean and tall, in black leather bomber jackets, they towered over the rest of the youth group. With their slightly rakish good looks, they stood out like young James Deans or Matt Dillons in a cluster of sheltered suburbanites.

At the theater, a red neon sign on the parking structure identified our destination only as CINE_AS. Once a Regal Cinemas franchisee, the multiplex now featured all Indian movies all the time, mostly Bollywood megastar musicals. It was Saturday night, and the theater was full.

Onscreen, the main character, Kris (Krishnagopal) Reddy, drove away from his suburban New Jersey home toward college vowing, "This year's going to be very different!"

"*Mein bhi*," said Nainesh loudly — Hindi for "Me too" — eliciting a round of laughs from his friends. When another character in the movie, Salim, kissed a huge poster of the voluptuous Bollywood star Rekha, the audience laughed and Nainesh said aloud, "What's wrong with doing that? I do that." When Salim opined that Indian girls in the United States can't cook, Nainesh blurted out, "He's got a good point." And at the first shot of the long-haired, light-skinned heroine, Nainesh moaned in appreciation: "Aah."

Afterward, as everyone clustered in the lobby to say their goodbyes or make plans for the rest of the night, Nainesh waxed enthusiastic: "That movie was totally about my life, I could identify with everything!" At a diner with those KYA members old enough or free enough to stay out late, Nainesh said he identified strongly with the term "ABCD," which stands for "American-Born Confused Desi," *desi* meaning Indian — a self-mocking label that hints at the difficulties of forging a new identity in the United States.

Middlesex County, New Jersey, where we went to see the movie, is home to one of the highest concentrations of people of Indian origin in the United States. And since the United States is now the country outside South Asia with the most Indians in the world, Nainesh and his peers might be said to be living at the epicenter of the diaspora.

One might look to them, then, for a hint at its future: a people almost wholly identified with their new country, but still drawn to form connections to those of the same background. For this next generation of the diaspora, the lands settled by their ancestors are but distant homelands. India herself is not within their, or perhaps even their parents', living memory.

INDIA

My first clear memories are of India, vivid and colorful, like a handful of snapshots. Because I was four, my sense of chronology still loose, these images float like snippets of film: close-up on my own hand, lifting toward my mouth, hot fried nuts from a cone bought on the street. Across the way, a small girl, perhaps my age or a bit older, is starving. Her bones are thin, her eyes sunken and lined with kohl. She, her mother, and a baby sit on the sidewalk, begging—they are desperately poor, and I become desperate to help. I walk to her and give her my food.

My mother tells me that every day we stayed at that hotel, the Taj on the waterfront in Bombay, I gave that girl whatever food or money I was allowed to give away.

And somehow, in memory, this is connected with the story of Jaydeep: a need too big to fill, the desire and futility of the effort to help.

After we left Kalyaan that first afternoon, I kept thinking about the options we had laid out for him. Becoming a student was possible but unaffordable; he was willing, eager even, to work, but a student visa would not let him support himself. Marriage would be easiest in terms of paperwork, but it would be next to impossible to find an American citizen from our community willing to marry a tiny man from a poor family; girls with green cards had so many other options. A work visa seemed out of reach, particularly given the sudden bursting of the Internet economy's bubble; the trend now was toward outsourcing and "reverse migration," with H-1B holders going home and Indo-American entrepreneurs heading back to the subcontinent to make their money. The United States was no longer rolling out the welcome mat for educated immigrants as it had for my parents' generation, so many of whom ended up Americans almost by accident. Coming to America now seemed like a Gordian knot of laws and policies, and as I lay in bed trying to untangle it, I knew Jaydeep would also be lying awake.

. . .

When my research took me back to Mumbai alone, I decided to visit Jaydeep and his family again. In a bookstore I looked for a belated birthday gift, something that might help or encourage Jaydeep in his ambitions; perhaps something American. My eye fell on a small paperback: Dale Carnegie's *How to Win Friends and Influence People*. I had it wrapped.

At the house in Kalyaan I ate another meal with them, and asked to interview Jaydeep for the record.

"Why do you want to go to America?" I asked.

"That is big question!"

"Yeah."

"I make lots and lots of money," he said.

"Mmm. Anything else?"

"And my ambition is one of the billionaire person in the world."

"And you think that's easier in America than anywhere else?"

"That's easier *only* in America!"

"Only America, not India or Australia or somewhere else?"

"American style is also one of the best preferences of my life. That is also important, American style."

"Style meaning what?"

"The way to talk, and . . . longs buildings . . ."

He had seen America's tall buildings on the BBC news. Whenever he bought a local newspaper, he would look at the currency exchange rate for American dollars. He memorized the names of states and cities. And in cybercafés he would pay twenty rupees an hour for time to browse websites for stories and pictures of America, degree programs, and advice on how to migrate.

Studies of voluntary migration have shown that it is rarely either the wealthiest or the poorest of any society who migrate. The rich are doing fine and have little incentive to uproot themselves, while the most desperate generally lack both resources and stamina for the journey. Somewhere in between are those who have access to information about the other world and can see the gap between their own lives and the dream. In terms of the old push–pull model of migration, India's problems— population, pollution, corruption, poverty—are overwhelming; the push factors for emigration are as strong as ever. And as global television (*Friends, The Bold and the Beautiful*) and free trade (Domino's Pizza,

Tommy Hilfiger) sell the tastes and pleasures of American lifestyles, the pull is growing as well. Added to that are the dot-com successes returning home from the gold rush, for holiday, telling tales of overnight fortunes "over there." From the viewpoint of Jaydeep and others like him, the other side must have seemed a magical world, as indeed its marketers meant it to seem. And so it was America — not Australia or New Zealand or even Canada — that fired Jaydeep's imagination.

On our first visit, Jaydeep had bought an "American" cake to celebrate his birthday with us. Perhaps he intended the shared ritual, re-created from American television, as an auspicious way to inaugurate his American connection. But there were no candles, and we neither sang — it not seeming to be the tradition — nor ate, being afraid that the cream filling, unrefrigerated for hours, would distress our sensitive American stomachs.

After my second visit to Jaydeep's home, I had a vague dream. I was in a crowd of people, searching, waiting, pushing. We were all struggling and straining, though for a time I could not have said why. Then I saw — I was searching for a space on a ship. The ship that would leave Mumbai.

A few days later I boarded that airship, of course. For me and for anyone with an American passport, borders sometimes seem entirely arbitrary: imaginary lines etched on a globe, painted stripes to be stepped over as lightly as crossing the street. It is easy to forget that for others they are all but impregnable.

I think of myself as a small child leaving India, after only a brief visit, with India on my tongue: salty *bor* fruit pickled in vinegar, thick dark honey on rotli, words. And leaving my parents as a teenager, not pausing to look behind; but returning, with however much difficulty, each time. Perhaps we in the diaspora are always leaving India, or that part of India, real or imagined, which lives in our souls, memories, skins. And this constant journeying separates us, irrevocably, from those who do not or cannot leave.

After returning home, I stayed in touch with Jaydeep for a while. His e-mails were affectionate; he asked each time for my blessings, and spoke of me as a second mother — a notion that made me so uncomfortable I did not respond for a few days to each e-mail, and then did not remark on that reference. I supposed his gushing language was simply an effort to translate the affection already contained in our mother tongue, and my discomfort an American aversion to too much intimacy. After all, the Gujarati word for mother's sister or female cousin, *maasi*, contains the word *maa*, mother. We wrote back and forth, but there were gaps; sometimes I could not understand his English, nor he mine.

Eventually, perhaps when I proved impotent as a gateway to America, his messages took an aggressive turn. "You come and eat my food, I hope my interview helpful," he wrote bitterly. Then they became abusive, and I stopped writing back. His last e-mail to me was so furious that it was barely coherent.

Looking back at the notes of our first meeting, reading through the advice we gave him, I can see how useless and evasive we must have seemed. I feel sympathy for his dilemma, and along with it, sorrow: for the basic inequality between us, for his clear sense of betrayal. The implicit promise of my American presence in his life, my friendliness and empathy, was that I could help him, too, to become an American. That I cannot is a matter for legitimate frustration, even rage.

And his story reminds me that as migrants, the crime of abandonment never quite leaves us. Migration song is not only the melody line of the ones who leave; it is also the deep blue undertones of those who, unwilling, remain. The story of the not-diaspora, the ones we leave behind and who watch our accumulations with a mixture of envy and rage, is ever present, whether we choose to see it or not. And so the homeland is, perhaps, where we come to weep; to see what we were and might have been; to have our hearts broken, again and again.

LONDON

Five weeks after leaving Jaydeep, I was at another birthday party.

Traveling from India to England, it had occurred to me that I was reversing the journey of the first Englishmen to land in Surat. In the four centuries since, the differences between the two countries have eroded somewhat; bureaucracies in South Asia are dominated by the English language, while London's best food is cooked by South Asian immigrants. I landed in Finchley, a tidy suburb north of London; there, as it happened, my cousin's daughter Minal was turning sweet sixteen.

Where Jaydeep's mock-Western birthday party had struck me as ad hoc and slightly sad, Minal's was warm and filled with the simple luxuries that we in the West are used to taking for granted. The cake, picked up at a bakery, was of the right size and shape for a birthday, and unquestionably safe to eat; the electricity did not flicker out as we gathered around it; there were candles to be blown out and wished over. Gathered around the dinner table were a suitable party: the birthday girl and her sister; their parents; uncle, aunt, and cousins who lived down the road; a school friend; me, the visitor; and her grandmother, my father's eldest sister, Kamla, known as Kamu.

Aunt Kamu was seventy-five and had lived in London more than four decades. Born and raised in India, except for a brief stint in Fiji, she had been betrothed in infancy. India's new laws barring child marriage meant that the actual wedding waited until she was eighteen. Soon afterward her father arranged for her husband, Vallabh, to migrate to Suva and work at Narseys. Vallabh traveled to Fiji twice on the four-year stints allowed by migration laws of the time, eventually obtaining a British Commonwealth passport. With that, he decided to try his luck in London.

Kamu joined him in 1961 with their two sons. At first she found England terribly cold and gloomy; with little education and no English, everything was difficult to navigate. A third son and then a daughter were born. London was expensive, and no one was eager to rent a decent house to an immigrant family of six. They made do in a drafty apartment. And then the eldest boy, Harish, came down with leukemia.

Through the nightmare of shuttling him through public hospitals, trying to understand the doctors' questions and instructions, Kamu held her family together. She and her husband donated blood, were evicted from one apartment and moved into another, somehow kept the other children fed and clothed; and when despite everything Harish died, she vowed to learn English. *That* part of the ordeal, at least, would never happen again.

Minal's father, Chandraprakash, or Chando, was the second son. Now, so many years later, everyone thinks of him as the oldest brother, but he says he will always think of himself as the middle son. He and the youngest brother, Mukesh, eventually married and started their own families. They stayed with their parents for many years, until at last the house where they grew up started feeling far too small. Then Chando moved his family out, a few blocks away, and Mukesh and his family stayed. They still get together at least once a week for meals, and the children come and go easily from one home to the other. For years they ran a tailoring factory with industrial-grade sewing and cutting machines in their basement. Now Mukesh works as an accountant, and Chando runs a card shop; these enterprises, combined with savvy real-estate investments made by their father, enable them to live comfortably.

At Minal's birthday party I gave her a wire sculpture of our name that I had bought a couple of days earlier from a street vendor outside the Tate Gallery. I tried to give her some money, too, in a card; after all, I had stayed with the family a whole month while I researched diaspora history at the British Library. But Aunt Kamu made me take it back; then, after some haggling, we settled for a lesser amount.

Later, as we sprawled out on their parents' big bed, I interviewed Minal and her sister about their lives growing up in London. Sumita, or Sumi, was two years older, about to enter university; Minal was in her second year of high school.

Because Minal and I have the same name, I couldn't help comparing. Although I am more than twice her age, we have some similarities: both raised in English-speaking countries, we speak Gujarati with an accent and wear jeans and T-shirts a good deal of the time. These traits alone separate us from many of our relatives.

But in other ways, our experiences are completely different. Where I grew up as an invisible minority far away from any extended family, Minal and her sister have lived all their lives in an extensive network of community surrounded by cousins, aunts, uncles, and grandparents. Owing to a completely different racial and colonial history, South Asians are one of Britain's most visible minorities. That, combined with the forces of globalization in recent years, means that South Asia is represented in the politics and popular culture around Minal to a degree I never experienced. A new Andrew Lloyd Webber musical with a Bollywood spin was about to premiere; the department store Selfridges was holding a month-long Bollywood-themed sale; and there was no shortage of groceries, restaurants, community resources, or role models. In teenage-girl-world, this meant, for example, that Minal and Sumi had crushes on Bollywood heroes whose posters adorned their bedroom walls. The sisters' tastes differed—Minal favored Hrithik Roshan, the gray-eyed star, while Sumi preferred long-haired bad boy Bobby Deol—but all of their icons of both male and female beauty came from Hindi films that streamed into their home at any hour of the day, thanks to satellite television. A generation earlier, the only access to such narratives had been by scratchy VHS, copied over and over, then rented from Indian stores or passed from household to household; theaters in the big Indian areas had shown Indian films, but not up in Finchley, a middle-class suburb of London. Now CDs and DVDs, Zee TV, MTV Asia, and MP3s bring the latest Indian popular culture to every diasporan who desires and can afford it. From Hong Kong (where the broadcasts originate) to Fiji (where they are recorded and then cut free of advertising for local rebroadcast), from London to South Africa to North America, my relatives follow the same soap operas and game shows and breathlessly await the latest releases of their favorite stars, all the while claiming that television is not so important to them. Minal's grandmother, my aunt, has learned in her seventies to program the VCR so that she never misses an episode of her favorite shows, though the shows do not matter to her at all, she says.

On a personal level, the cultural and demographic shifts also meant that Minal and Sumi grew up enjoying a clique of school friends who, like them, are second- or third-generation British Asians. They had instant-message access to their cousins both locally and globally, and could spend hours chatting online and trading jokes with one another. An estimated 1,200 Khatris were living in the London area in 2001, and their annual functions had outgrown the town hall of the heavily Indian district of Wembley.

While Minal's parents' social life was Indian, then, so was her own. Technology and a community of peers gave her access not to an ancestral India—fossilized, irrelevant, and tradition-bound—but to a living and wildly modern sense of Indianness, a youth culture with roots in both the diaspora and a subcontinent that was itself rapidly westernizing. For a Khatri community talent show, Minal and Sumi choreographed a dance routine for their younger cousins and friends to a popular Hindi film song. Sumi also performed in a garbaa, while Minal won first prize in snooker. The selves they formed in this climate seemed enviably integrated, and their reality was so different that I had to suspend my act of imagining myself in the other Minal's adolescence. The whole sensation was simply too foreign to me.

In a measure of just how different, I asked a serious question, applying in a way my own litmus test of alienation: Had they ever thought about *not* having arranged marriages?

The sisters looked at each other. Sure, they said, it would be nice to marry for love; but they couldn't imagine breaking their parents' hearts like that.

And yet they were wholly comfortable being, and identifying as, British. "When the British ran India, no one starved," their grandmother was fond of saying. Spending my days in the India Office of the British Library, reading of Great Britain's conquest and sometimes brutal treatment of India and Indians—I was reviewing famine logs, records of the salt march, Gandhi's campaigns in South Africa, and so on—I felt a kind of disturbance at being in the belly of the imperial beast. Some days it was as if I could see clearly how the fine monuments and buildings of central London, the world-class collections of art and knowledge, the entire sleek infrastructure from the high-speed subway to the smoothly gliding elevators in every building, all of the continuing fruits of empire, had been undergirded by the sweat and blood of millions in the colonies. "Without the British, none of us would be here," Minal's father told me —and included me in the statement, too, since, as he pointed out, without the British there would have been no Indians in Fiji, and without Fiji our grandparents could have never afforded to send my father to the United States to study.

Minal's grandfather Vallabh had decided many years ago that, since they were in a new country, they should change a little. Every Sunday, he decreed, instead of flat, round rotli with dinner, they would have English bread. He has long since passed away, but the family still follows the tradition. Six nights a week, rotli; on the seventh, bread.

On one of my last afternoons in London, my cousin Mukesh, Minal and Sumi's uncle, took me on a guided tour of London. He is a few years older than I, born and raised in London, married with two children, and we had talked easily during my month-long visit about family, politics, and the politics of the family. Our afternoon tour took us past Trafalgar Square, where demonstrators were staging a peace protest against the new war in Afghanistan. I confessed that I had marched in such protests back home, and we both sympathized with the cause of peace. His progressive outlook, though not unusual for a British Asian of his generation—raised under Margaret Thatcher's xenophobic policies, targeted by a racist white movement—was such a novelty in our family that I felt more comfortable at his home than I had anywhere else in my travels. Perhaps, too, I had learned after many months of traveling among relatives to settle in, to relax in the presence of my relations, to be less on edge and less afraid of judgments and vulnerability. Though I did not come out to Mukesh, I wondered if he had guessed or heard; in any case, he let slip that he had a lesbian school friend.

In that simple conversation, I realized what a relief it was to be able to integrate the various sides of my persona; not to feel like a freak within my clan because of my progressive views. And on my next airplane ride I had a sensation I had not felt during the entire eight months or so of my overseas travels. It was that particular brand of loneliness called homesickness—not for America, to which I was returning, but for the home I had just left behind.

IOWA

It is hard to think of any place more quintessentially American than Ames, Iowa. A town of thirty thousand surrounded by cornfields, Ames is home to the Iowa State University Cyclones and to a tiny, three-leaf branch of my family tree: my aunt Tara and her two sons, Dhiren and Nilesh.

I traveled to Ames for Dhiren's wedding to Alana Ho, a Vietnamese American woman whom he met when she cut his hair at the local JCPenney. Obviously it was a "love marriage," not arranged.

On the wedding Saturday, my cousin was nervous, but these were no typical premarital jitters. He and Alana had dated for six years, braving their parents' disapproval and tears, to reach this moment. His anxiety now was about the schedule.

This was actually Day Three of a four-day celebration involving four languages and four hundred guests. The procession would kick off a fifteen-hour marathon of events: Hindu wedding ceremony (in Sanskrit and Gujarati), Indian lunch, Vietnamese ancestor rites, Catholic mass (in Vietnamese and English), photo session, Chinese banquet reception.

To pull it off, everything had to happen precisely as scheduled — not, as Dhiren had emphasized to his mother over and over again, on "Indian Standard Time."

For his mother, Tara, the weekend was also a balancing act: between the wishes of her own conservative relatives and those of her American-born son and his in-laws. If each and every rite was not performed correctly for her eldest son, her family would be disappointed, and the gods might not properly bless the marriage. But if she didn't comply with the tight schedule, Dhiren would be furious.

So Tara compromised, keeping all the ceremonies but asking the priest to perform a short version wherever possible. The ritual chants were in the dead language of Sanskrit, anyway; to this Gujarati-speaking family, they might as well be in Greek. Or Vietnamese.

Days One and Two had been filled with preliminary ceremonies. Everything had gone smoothly enough, unless you counted the cheese platters that didn't show up, the missed plane connection that delayed the opening ceremonies for four and a half hours, the chill rain that pushed outdoor rituals into the family room, and the fact that Tara had forgotten to book a priest for Day One. It wasn't bad, considering the inevitable chaos of a Hindu wedding — in which events are determined not by written etiquette or the word of a religious authority, but by heated discussions among a family's elders.

Here, the experts were numerous. They included Tara's father, who in 1929 had migrated from India to Fiji, becoming a successful businessman and patriarch of a large family. These days, he spent most of his waking hours maintaining a continuous flow of Scotch and whiskey through his eighty-four-year-old veins.

Pouring the drinks was Tara's older brother, Mahen, who with his wife, Manjula, had flown in from Hong Kong. They had lived there thirty-five years, as long as Tara had lived in Ames, but Manjula still wore a sari every day, neatly pressed and draped. Rounding out the maternal relatives were Tara's three sisters, the younger from California, the older two from Canada. Between them, Tara's siblings had married ten of their own children to an assortment of Indian and non-Indian spouses — making them experts on the minutiae of marriage rites.

Uncles, aunts, and cousins from Fiji, South Carolina, and other exotic locations were also in attendance, along with a number of former national table tennis champions—close friends of the groom, who was the No. 1 table tennis (not Ping-Pong) player in the country when he was nine years old, and spent his high school years at the U.S. Olympic training camp in Boulder, Colorado, preparing for the Olympics with the U.S. national team. Dhiren's first coach had been his father, Champak, who had learned to play table tennis on the ship voyage from Fiji to America in 1963. My own parents, from California, also were on hand and saw themselves as chief counselors, since they had planned and survived my brother's Hindu-Catholic wedding.

Finally, there was our aunt Pushpa, who could not attend but who, as the groom's senior relative on his father's side, sent fax after fax from her home in Fiji. How many coconuts would be needed for the rituals? Could ordinary lawn clippings be substituted for the sacred *kusha* grass traditionally used as an offering? Which times of day were astrologically most auspicious for each rite? These and other pressing questions were raised, then answered, by Pushpa's faxes.

If Dhiren's father, Champak, had been present, Dhiren would have relied on him to turn some of the chaos into order. But Champ, as almost everyone in Ames called him, had died less than a year earlier, victim of a massive Father's Day heart attack. Most of the people assembled for the wedding had come to Champ's funeral, crowding into the same downstairs family room where now his photograph sat on the mantel, garlanded with silk flowers. Below it, a festive red banner and symbols drawn with felt-tip markers honored the family goddess, seeking her blessings for the new couple.

Religious taboo prevented Dhiren's mother, Tara, a new widow, from participating in many of the ceremonies; my parents stood in for Dhiren's, sitting with him at the ritual altar. From time to time, each of them looked up at Champ's photograph, and Dhiren often seemed to be gritting his teeth to keep from crying. At the end of the second day's prayers, when Dhiren bowed to each of his deceased ancestors in turn, Tara broke down and wept, and so did her sons; then, quietly, so did the rest of us. The wedding festivities, like the fresh paint and new white carpeting in the family room, could not cover over a grief that was still raw.

On the morning of Day Three, the procession departed at 8:30 A.M. —right on time, according to the handwritten schedule that Nilesh had photocopied for all family members (with the note, "BTW, God told me this is how it's going to be . . ."). The *jaan* was an institution stretching back centuries. Every one of Dhiren's forefathers had taken the ritual step with his right foot out of the house and then, at the end of the journey, stepped with his right foot into the wedding canopy with its sacred fire. When bride and groom circled the flames four times, they were married in the eyes of Agni, the Hindu god of fire and ritual. Our grandparents had walked around the wedding fire as children, back in India early in the century; our parents had done so in Fiji in the 1960s; and our generation was reenacting these rites all over the world, with a constant remixing of authenticity and innovation.

Traditionally the jaan had been a singing, dancing parade along dusty village streets. But in Iowa, it was a motorcade of a dozen cars driving past newly planted cornfields, the sprouts just an inch or two high. In the parking lot of the Comfort Suites motel, owned by a Gujarati family friend, Dhiren broke a clay pot with his foot, and Alana's mother accepted him into the banquet hall. He took a seat next to the priest under a four-pillar canopy, jerry-built from plumbers' pipes that had been spray-painted gold and decorated with pink flowers. Instead of a fire, a candle sat at the center, a compromise between the demands of the fire god and the hotel's fire code.

By 11:30 A.M., when "The Wedding MUST end (Indian, that is)" according to Nilesh's schedule, the wedding did end (Indian, that is). The flame was circled and extinguished, the audience applauded, and lunch was served as the groomsmen dashed into a hotel suite to change into tuxedos for the Christian wedding.

Dhiren did not smile at the Hindu wedding, nor during the Vietnamese ceremony in which his mother reluctantly accepted a whole roasted pig with yellow lilies in its ears from Alana's parents, and certainly not at the mass when his relatives had to be shushed by the priest. He did force a smile for the seemingly endless photo sessions, and when at the reception the guests clinked their glasses, American-style, he also smiled as he leaned over to kiss his bride—on the cheek, respecting the modesty of both of their cultures.

Here again was the tightrope that Dhiren and Alana had been walking for months: how to balance their own modern sensibilities with two

different sets of old-country values. Even the menu for the wedding banquet had been a scuffle, ending in a compromise between Indian and
Vietnamese palates: Chinese food, with oversize martini glasses full of
red chili paste for those needing a little extra kick. Giant crab legs, noodles, spicy green beans, beef, and chicken joined a selection of vegetarian Indian leftovers from lunch, for the purists.

Finally, when the day was almost over, and the scheduling most definitely was, and Dhiren had had a couple of glasses of Scotch, a genuine
smile came onto his lips and stayed there. As the DJ called the first dance,
to Jim Brickman's "Valentine," Dhiren and Alana stood under purple,
green, and yellow disco lights. Smoke from dry ice rose into the glow,
and soap bubbles floated out of a bubble machine—a scene straight from
the fantasies of the bride's teenage sisters, who had planned this portion
of the evening. At the other end of the ballroom, Tara and my mother
handed out favors to the guests: traditional Indian sweets in foil boxes.
The disco ball spun and ABBA's "Dancing Queen" came on. Then the
aunts in saris, the Iowa friends, the young cousins already being eyed by
the matchmakers all came together on the dance floor, shaking their
limbs to rhythms as suitably diverse as Cyndi Lauper, Lauryn Hill,
bhangra, salsa, and Vietnamese pop. The party was, all of a sudden, hip
and cosmopolitan, a scene that could have been taking place in Mumbai,
Hong Kong, New York. As Dhiren's friend Jaime, a Venezuelan table
tennis player turned Internet entrepreneur, quipped, "I can't believe this
is Ames!" And as Nilesh's schedule said, capping the day, "Reception—
Let the good times Roll! . . . thank god, right?"

Only in the diaspora.

Everything was put into a small photo album to be circulated back to
Aunt Pushpa and our other relations around the world, except for the
presentation of the sacrilegious pig.

FIJI

In Suva, I stayed a few nights with Aunt Pushpa's family, where I learned
her folk remedies. To treat a cold, boil a nugget each of copper, silver,
and gold in a pot and stand over it, breathing in the steam. For pinkeye,
sweep seven fresh mango leaves over the affected eye seven times, then
tie them in a bunch where no one, especially the patient, will look at

them. As they dry, the pinkeye will heal. If no mango leaves are available, Aunt Pushpa told me, you can substitute seven cloves of garlic.

The traditions my parents had left behind as superstition and old wives' tales, I found interesting, humorous, and enjoyable. Pushpa and her husband lived in a house on a hill with their younger son and his family, but the son had put in emigration papers and was waiting to hear from New Zealand and Australia. He had found himself afraid of native Fijians ever since the coup and the ensuing increase in violent crime; he feared letting his children near them. He and his wife were both accountants, so they were sure to be approved. Within a year he hoped to emigrate.

In Fiji I also stayed with my father's youngest brother and his wife, and with various cousins of my parents. It was politic to dole out my time among the families, an arrangement that also allowed me to interview people in a leisurely way. In every house there were empty rooms and cupboards, plenty of extra pillows. "I cried when we sold the beds," one aunt told me. Her sons were already in Australia; she and her husband were just waiting out the months until their papers came through and they could join them. In many homes only the older people were left, the young people having taken jobs abroad. Nearly every day of my visit I heard of another relative who was applying, or had been approved, or had already started to pack, to move overseas. I had arrived at the very moment of migration, when the old country empties out and a society will be re-created, reinvented, in new lands.

In a time of great change, such as the past century has seen, each life also contains a moment that comes to stand for the transition from the old world to the new. I have looked for this moment of migration in every life, and in my own, until I begin to believe I can see them all, shimmering, a string of lit buoys in the dark sea of history—each light leading to the next, so that the tracing of many lives takes on both a luminosity and a kind of causality, which is the law of karma. As I write, I find that each story takes on a personal quality; that is, I begin to take each of my ancestors' lives personally, almost as if I am looking in their lives for what made me, and looking ahead to what I will make: finding a place for myself in the stream, in this most intimate history. I am reweaving the threads, reassembling what has seemed ruptured by time, geography, temperament, quarrel, or neglect, gaps in memory and in the historical record through which our stories, being small ones, might so easily slip and disappear.

But perhaps our stories are not so small after all. For even as I write this, I see the whole sweep of history, the epic of my people, and here too is what I want to say: The real story of our diaspora began long, long ago, and continues past the end of these pages. It is being written by every computer programmer in Silicon Valley and contract laborer in Kuwait, even now; every new wife stopping to barter in a foreign market, to search among the strange fruits and vegetables for some familiar flavor, even now; every schoolchild feeling all eyes upon her as she pronounces the jewel of her name in her ancestors' accent, before she has lost it for good, even now.

The moment of migration is not singular, of course, but part of the string of moments, as the universe is composed (it seems now) of strings, each looped to the next in inextricable continuity. Rupture the strings, and you create a black hole. A journey is only a place to start the story; the human story. And we migrants are not merely curiosities and wonders, but humans after all; if we stand out in the throng, it is only because the storyteller chooses our moment, our string. The trajectory of light has crossed us, illumined us—as a thread seems, in the proper angle of sunset, to burn.

MICHIGAN

In the Hindu temple that he helped raise, in the midwestern town where my family spent its formative American years, my father celebrated his sixty-fifth birthday in April 2007 among seventy or eighty of his closest friends. Relatives drove up from Toronto and Iowa, and others from around the world telephoned their congratulations: from Texas, Fiji, New Zealand, Australia, Hong Kong, London. In southeastern Michigan, the mini-community of mostly Gujarati engineers and other professionals for which my parents had served as a kind of glue for twenty years coalesced again. The food was spicy and familiar, catered by one of the now-abundant Indian restaurants that dot a landscape where once we made long pilgrimages to distant suburbs to find a single spice shop. As with most areas of the country, Michigan is no longer as homogeneous as it once was; Indians have been the largest single immigrant group to the Detroit suburbs in recent years, with the latest census showing 54,000 people of South Asian origin making their home in the state.

In the 1980s, when my father's Apple IIe computer was brand-new and his hope that his children would marry within the caste was intact, he compiled a directory of the Khatris of North America. The families numbered a couple of hundred, and most cooperated by providing complete listings, including their children's birth dates — which everyone knew was not only for curiosity but also for ease of matching. Although the community was spread out, such a census was a project that one organized man could conquer in his spare time. It took him perhaps six months, and the resulting booklet was thirty-two pages in neat dot-matrix columns.

Today, hundreds of families of our clan live all over the North American continent; there are Khatri societies from Modesto to New Jersey, from Houston to Toronto. Each one holds annual talent shows, picnics, holy-day feasts, and summer barbecues featuring whiskey and curried lamb. No print directory has been compiled; it would be an unwieldy and fast-changing enterprise.

And as the number of "mixed" marriages grows, there is the difficulty of defining who "counts." At least one Khatri association has held a public debate on whether girls who marry outside the caste should continue to be invited to social events or, upon their deaths, be sent funeral wreaths from the caste association. This debate is intricately wound with the story of our people today, a people far from one home and trying to make another. What were once considered isolated and shameful "family problems" have been identified as a trend, one that is snowballing forward, despite fierce efforts to preserve the old ways. Even for those who stand up to rant against mixed marriages, each discussion is a step forward. It is through such conversations that culture changes. What was once unthinkable becomes, slowly and bitterly but surely, part of the common experience. A taboo devolves — like overcooked vegetables, business scandals, too-bright saris, or too-dark skin — into a topic of gossip. Each "first" — the first *American* wife, the first *American* husband — implies and makes way for others to come.

I am also a first. As far as I know, I am the only lesbian, and the only writer, in the recorded history of our clan. It is only now that the circumstances conducive to my existence have come into being.

And perhaps for that, I must thank my great-grandfather, who gave up the art of prophecy for the art of trade. In our family, he was the first to leave the homeland; the first swerve on the map toward infinite destinations.

Marrying and procreating beyond one's circle of birth is not, of course, unique to our community. The 2000 U.S. Census counted Americans of mixed race for the first time, and found 6.8 million of them, with a large percentage of those being children—quite remarkable for a nation where segregation and anti-miscegenation laws existed within living memory, and where many immigrant communities work to hew strongly to their own. Among these new multiracial Americans are my three nieces, who dressed up for my father's birthday festivities in new salwar kameez made of bright flowing synthetic fabric adorned with sequins and gold trim. Their parents, whose marriage was so groundbreaking, are no longer the only mixed-race couple in our family, and the children do not seem destined to be the confused pariahs that the elder generations once feared they would be.

Rather, with their soft brown curls and creamy-to-olive skin, Zoë, Ava, and Téa were the darlings of the crowd—easily stealing the spotlight from the birthday celebrant, who could not have been more glad. At age five, Zoë adores both Dora the Explorer and the Hindu monkey god Hanuman; she loves both the grandfather who taught her the University of Michigan fight song and the one who tells her long stories drawn from the great Indian epics. She is also old enough to explore her identity, coming up with such apparently spontaneous formations as "I'm Indian, and Ava and Téa are Indian, and Daddy's Indian, but Mama's not Indian —right?" along with "I'm a girl, Mama's a girl, Daddy's a boy, Ava's a girl, Téa's a girl . . . Grandpa, do you have a penis?"

Diaspora is nothing if not an endless series of questions. May they proliferate.

HOME

Another Navratri approaches; the air cools; the moon is new. I am spending this year home in San Francisco, so I can plan to go with my mother and with friends to dance the garbaa for nine nights, or at least a few.

Our options are plentiful in the nearby bedroom communities of Silicon Valley, where the Indian population has tripled in the last two decades. We might go to the temple in Fremont, to the college gymnasium in Hayward, or even to the massive Oakland Coliseum, where Indo-Americans pack the house to dance to traditional tunes belted out by a famous singer from Gujarat; she is known for wearing masculine attire, and news articles note coyly that she is always accompanied by her female "best friend," who has been traveling with her since high school. Having set out to write the stories of relatives scattered around the world, to uncover our humble histories, I find myself dancing.

As the garbaa speeds up, the cut mirrors that decorate our skirts scatter the light: swirl of dancers and audience, children, men, old people, teenagers; deities perched on altars, carved or sculpted, garlanded in gold and flowers; a moonless sky full of stars. If we could track one tiny mirror's journey, all that it reflects and refracts, we might see the world entire.

At night we dream of circles, spinning, the earth tilting under our feet.

CHRONOLOGY

ca. 961–1242   Solanki (Chaulukya) dynasty rules northwestern India

1607   First British East India Company ship lands in India, at Surat

1765   Naanji, earliest paternal ancestor recorded by family genealogist

Aug. 1, 1834   Slavery abolished in British Empire

Sept. 9, 1834   Beginning of Indian indenture: thirty-six men sign agreement in Calcutta to become laborers in Mauritius

1857   Indian Mutiny; Queen Victoria takes over rule of India from British East India Company and proclaims "equal and impartial protection of the law" for Indians as British subjects

1874   British take possession of Fiji

1893   Mohandas Gandhi travels to South Africa, begins to agitate for rights of Indians as subjects of British Empire

1902   British win Anglo-Boer War in South Africa

1905   GANDA KAPITAN, my paternal great-great-uncle, travels to South Africa

1909   MOTIRAM NARSEY, my paternal great-grandfather, travels to Fiji

1911   M. Narsey & Co. opens its doors in Suva, Fiji

1912   G. C. Kapitan Vegetarian Restaurant opens its doors in Durban, South Africa

1914   Gandhi leaves South Africa and returns to India, where he will work for independence

1916   British India ends indenture system, phasing it out by 1920

1917   United States bars South Asian immigrants

1918–19   Worldwide flu epidemic kills millions, including Motiram Narsey

1922   Ratanji Narsey, Motiram's eldest son, my paternal grandfather, migrates to Fiji

1923   U.S. Supreme Court rules that South Asians, although "Caucasian," are not "white" and are therefore ineligible for U.S. citizenship

1930   Gandhi leads salt march to protest British rule of India

1931   **NAROTAM CHHAGAN**, my maternal grandfather, travels to Fiji

1946   Motiram Narsey's brothers retire to India; Ratanji Narsey takes over M. Narsey & Co. operations in Fiji

1946–49   United Nations holds sessions and debates on situation of Indians in South Africa

1947   India and Pakistan become independent nations

1948   Apartheid government elected to power in South Africa

1949   Riots in Durban, South Africa

1950   **RANCHHOD HAZRAT**, my father's brother, travels to Fiji

1952   Ratanji Narsey and others establish Merchants Club in Fiji, a drinking club for Gujarati businessmen

1953–56   M. Narsey & Co. becomes Narseys Ltd., first nonwhite company to receive license to sell liquor in Fiji

1963   Duty-free boom begins in Fiji

         BHUPENDRA HAJRATWALA, my father, travels to United States along with Champak Narotam, my mother's brother

1965   United States begins to allow significant Asian immigration

1967   **BHANU NAROTAM** marries Bhupendra Hajratwala and travels to United States

1969   New Narseys building completed in Suva

1970   Fiji wins independence; Indians make up more than 50 percent of population

         Ratanji Narsey dies in Tokyo airport; company leadership passes to his eldest son, my uncle Chiman Narsey

1971   **MINAL HAJRATWALA** born; family migrates to New Zealand

1972   Dictator Idi Amin expels Indians from Uganda

1978   Hajratwalas migrate to United States again

1981   Narseys has 110 employees, six retail divisions, two joint ventures, two factories, and more than one million shares held by family members

1987   Two military coups in Fiji; economic sanctions; Fiji Indians begin to emigrate

1988   **RANCHHOD HAZRAT**, my father's brother, moves with his family to Australia

1989–90   Indo-American hotel and motel owners organize to battle discrimination

1990   United States institutes "Diversity Visa Act," a.k.a. immigration lottery

1992   G. C. Kapitan & Son Vegetarian Restaurant ceases operations in South Africa

1994   Narseys department store closes in Fiji

1995   South Africa holds first post-apartheid elections

1997   British hand over Hong Kong to China upon conclusion of ninety-nine-year lease

1999   **MALA KUMAR**, my mother's niece, and her family move from Fiji to Los Angeles after winning immigration lottery

2000   Military coup in Fiji; Indian emigration increases

        3,391 U.S. households have a South Asian head of household and a same-gender partner, according to *Trikone* magazine's analysis of census data

2001   11.5 million people of Indian origin living abroad, according to Indian government

2009   19 million to 30 million people of Indian origin living abroad, according to unofficial estimates

NOTES

PAGE

EPIGRAPH

xvii　*On the sixth night Vidhaataa:* While textual references cite Vidhaataa as a god (one face of the masculine deity Brahma), many Hindus worship Vidhaataa as a goddess. I have followed this grass-roots practice.

PAGE

1. WATER

1　*The Solanki dynasty:* Transliteration creates a diversity of spellings. Various sources call this dynasty by the name Chaulakya or Chalukya, tracing the etymology to *challu,* the palm of the deity's hand, where they were formed (Tod, *Annals and Antiquities,* p. 112; and the 1896 *Gazetteer of the Bombay Presidency,* p. 156). Sholanki is another modern variation. As for other names cited in this chapter: Mulraaj is found in the texts as Mularaj and Mularaja, and seems to come from *mula,* root, and *raajaa,* king. Chaamundaa (also Camunda, Chamunda) seems to take her name from two buffalo demons she killed, named Chanda and Munda. Tod lists the other fire-pit (*Agnikunda*) tribes as Rathod, Parmar, and Chohan—all common surnames in our Khatri community of the five villages.

4　*Vadodara is:* The population and relative size of Vadodara—known in the days of the British as Baroda—are drawn from the "Index of Primacy" table, based on the 2001 census, at the website of the Urban Development and Urban Housing Department, Government of Gujarat (www.udd.gujarat.gov.in/udd/urb _scn.htm).

　　an honorary parade: Photographic engraving, San Francisco Public Library "India" photo file, unsourced image dated February 5, 1876.

5　*"emaciated body":* David Kinsley, *Hindu Goddesses* (Berkeley: University of California Press, 1988), p. 148.

7　*Vishnu's sixth incarnation:* The listed number and order of Vishnu's incarnations vary, even among ancient authorities; Dipavali and Bebek Debroy's summary English translation of the *Agni Purana* (New Delhi: Books for All, 1991) lists Parasurama as the sixth. The story of the slaughter of the Kshatriyas twenty-one times is contained in the Mahabharata, the great Hindu war epic.

The creation of new warriors from the fire pit is told in various lesser scriptures known collectively as the Puranas.

9   *an old Gujarati text*: Raobahadur Govindabhai Hathibhai Desai, ed., *Vadodaraa Raajya-Praantik Sarava Sangraha* [Survey of the Baroda State, Baroda District] (Baroda: Lohana Mitra Steam Printing Press, 1921), pp. 25–29.

10   *invaders from Bombay*: Tod, *Annals and Antiquities*.
     "Scythian mercenaries": A. H. Bingley, *Handbook on Rajputs* (1899; reprint New Delhi: Asian Educational Services, 1986), p. 111.

11   *In every wedding*: I supplement my own viewing of the Mulraaj ritual with two written descriptions, both contained in booklets self-published by community members: "Our Kshatriya Samskaras, I—Srimant" by my parents, Bhanu and Bhupendra Hajratwala (Pleasanton, Calif., 2007), and "An Indepth Study of Gotarej" by Venilal A. Khatri and Prabhat C. Kapadia (Lautoka, Fiji, 1997). The latter attempts to explain the tradition thus: "In the olden days when wedding processions used to take place, it required the services of soldiers or security people to protect them from bandits etc. This has remained in the psyche of the people . . . [O]ne could say that the couple's life may have obstacles now and then; thus protection may be required from society or any other worldly cause" (p. 25).
     11.5 million: *Report of the High Level Committee on the Indian Diaspora,* 2002. See the note at the beginning of Part I below for an explanation of how I have calculated this and other estimates of the size of the diaspora.

12   *nostalgia was a diagnosed condition*: Joy and Peter Brain, "Nostalgia and Alligator Bite—Morbidity and Mortality Among Indian Migrants to Natal, 1884–1911," *South African Medical Journal* 65 (January 21, 1984): 98–102.

PART ONE: "COOLIES"

15   Various methods have been used over the past two centuries to calculate the size of India's diaspora. The numbers I cite on the opening pages for Parts I, II, III, and IV, while not directly comparable to one another, represent the best information available in each time period. The 1900 figures, from a report to the British House of Commons titled *Restrictions upon British Indian Subjects in British Colonies and Dependencies,* can be considered quite accurate in representing the size of the population of those who left India via the indenture system; they do not count "passenger" Indians, who formed a fairly small group relative to the whole. From 1916 to 1947, after indenture voyages ended, the primary source is the British Empire, which relied on its governors abroad to report or estimate their local figures. The data sets are flawed, as censuses in the colonies were irregular; also, some surveys collected data worldwide, while others counted only British possessions. After 1947, there is a gap in official information until independent India's first comprehensive effort at measuring its diaspora, in 2001. Nongovernmental organizations and scholars attempted to fill the gap. Sources are marked in the notes for each set of numbers given. Readers interested in the figures from which I drew these cumulative numbers may wish to review the complete data at the following website: www.minalhajratwala.com/statistics.

2. CLOTH

To reconstruct the history of M. Narsey & Co. in this chapter, as well as of the Narseys firm in Chapter 5, I relied on four written sources: (1) For 1900–1945, Kamal Kant Prasad's unpublished dissertation. (2) For official minutes and filings during the 1953–97 period, the Narseys Ltd. file at the government Registrar of Companies, Suva, which I viewed there in November 2001. (3) For a narrative summary of the company's history until 1981, an unpublished scholarly paper written by my cousin Kiran C. Narsey while a student that includes details furnished by his own father (now deceased), who was then the patriarch of the company. (4) For insight into the company's final years, from January 1991 onward, copies of correspondence and meeting minutes kindly provided to me by Jiten M. Narsey. Where these accounts differed in matters of fact, I have relied on the written documents in the order listed above. Interpretation of the facts is, of course, mine.

19   *"What is Fiji?"*: The recruiter is quoted in the memoirs of Totaram Sanadhya, *My Twenty-one Years*, pp. 33–35.

20   *Casting about for a practical solution*: Abolition of slavery was "the first great impetus" for Indian indenture, says an official history included in the 1910 *Report of the Committee on Emigration from India to the Crown Colonies and Protectorates:* "Indian indentured immigration has rendered invaluable service to those of our Colonies in which, on the emancipation of the negro slaves, the sugar industry was threatened with ruin . . ." (p. 21). Tinker's *A New System of Slavery* includes a comprehensive treatment of the economic relationship between slavery and indenture in the empire.
    The Indians signed up for: Lal, *Crossing the Kala Pani*, pp. 6–7.

21   *Eventually 1.5 million*: Tinker, *New System of Slavery*.

22   *Excavated from*: Calico Museum of Textiles, *Textile Trade*.
    Four millennia ago: Chaudhuri, *Trade and Civilisation*.
    the Gypsies trekked north: Angus Fraser, *The Gypsies* (Oxford: Blackwell, 1992), notes the similarities between Romany and northern Indian languages, although the provenance of these peoples is, of course, not definitive. He also cites Heinrich Grellman, a German ethnographer and historical linguist writing in 1787, who reached "the tentative conclusion that the closest affinity was with the Surat dialect (i.e. Gujarati)," and theorizes that the Gypsies were members of the Kshatriya or warrior caste who fled defeats in the eighth and twelfth centuries. But he admits that this notion "will hardly endear itself to the more sceptical reader" (pp. 15–22, 196).
    Muslim traders built boats: Chaudhuri, *Trade and Civilisation*.
    "The sun never sets": Henry Lytton Bulwer (Lord Dalling) and Evelyn Ashley, *The Life of Henry John Temple, Viscount Palmerston: With Selections from His Correspondence* (London: Richard Bentley & Son, 1874), 3:121. Lord Palmerston was secretary of state for foreign affairs at the time of this speech before the House of Commons on March 1, 1843.

23   *Founded as a minor port*: Janaki, *Some Aspects*, chap. 3.

23   *Under Muslim rule*: Das Gupta, *Indian Merchants*, p. 20.

Each March, four ships: Ogilby, *Asia, the First Part*, p. 223.

Muslims from Gujarat traversed: Janaki, *Gujarat as the Arabs Knew It.*

Company ships: Historians use various dates for the beginning of the British presence in Surat. The first British East India Company expedition to reach Surat landed in November 1607. In 1609 the British established a small settlement; in 1611 they obtained permission to trade. The company's factors were allowed to establish a warehouse and offices (known as a "factory") in 1613. Fragmentary journals from these voyages are housed at the British Library's India Office and catalogued in the "List of Marine Records of the Late East India Company, Introduction" (1896). Unfortunately, the journal pages that would have referred to the first landing have been lost.

The Portuguese and the Dutch: A New General Collection, pp. 346–47.

John Ovington, chaplain: A Voyage to Surat, pp. 130–31.

the list of items traded at Surat: Janaki, *Some Aspects;* and Ogilby, *Asia, the First Part*, p. 215.

24   *"Portugefes, Arabians, Perfians"*: Ogilby, *Asia, the First Part*, p. 211.

"fwallows all the Gold": Ibid., p. 222.

In London the craze: Calico Museum of Textiles, *Textile Trade.*

Parliamentarians fretted: Janaki, *Some Aspects*, chap. 3.

"the clamour reached": Ibid.

And the city was plagued: Das Gupta, *Indian Merchants*, p. 7.

25   *"As a class they are said to be"*: Surat District Gazetteer, 1877, quoted in R. K. Patil, *Gold and Silver Thread Industry of Surat: A Socio-Economic Survey* (Surat: Chunilal Gandhi Vidyabhavan Studies No. 6, 1956).

Few were educated: Choksey, *Economic Life*, p. 227.

Navsari was more cosmopolitan: Census of India, 1941.

As hub of its subdistrict: Baroda Administrative Report 1908–09 and 1909–10.

In Motiram's time, the region: Census of India, 1931. Map.

26   *six hundred liquor shops*: Baroda Administrative Report 1908–09, p. 21.

a single high school: Ibid., p. 131.

The maharaja: Sayaji Rao III, the *gaikwad*, or ruler, of the princely state of Baroda from 1874 to 1939, was considered one of the more humane and liberal of the "native rulers," even sympathizing with the Indian nationalist movement. James, *Raj*, p. 337.

His annual report: Baroda Administrative Report 1908–09 and 1909–10.

One weaver could: Doug Peacock, *Cotton Times* (www.cottontimes.co.uk).

27   *As late as 1866*: Calico Museum of Textiles, *Textile Trade.*

three-quarters of the cloth: Choksey, *Economic Life*, p. 226.

In 1900, three million acres: These figures are for the Bombay Presidency, which encompassed British Gujarat and more. Ibid.

The British-controlled portion: Ibid.

28   *Thousands in the region*: Ibid., p. 170.

Historians used to speak: E. G. Ravenstein first formulated the push–pull principle, though he did not use the term, in a pair of articles published in 1885 and 1889 titled "The Laws of Migration" (*Journal of the Royal Statistical Society* 46:167–235 and 52:241–305).

29 *Then in 1901*: Prasad, "The Gujaratis of Fiji," pp. 25–27.

In 1908: Ibid., p. 27. The date of Motiram's arrival may be disputed. Prasad's account, based on passport applications, says Motiram was the second Khatri to arrive in Fiji, first traveling in 1909, and that he visited India in 1916. By this timeline, the first Khatri in Fiji would have been Narotam Karsandas; I am indebted to his descendant Ranjit Solanki, my cousin's husband, who kindly pointed me to a brief reference that eventually led me to Prasad's dissertation. Kiran Narsey's family history, however, says Motiram Narsey arrived in 1907, then returned home for a visit in 1909 after two years. These are not necessarily contradictory, as passports became mandatory only in 1907: Motiram could have traveled early that year without a passport, then visited India in 1909 and returned to Fiji with his first passport. However, Prasad also attributes his date to a July 1974 interview with the late Jayanti Badshah, who was Motiram's sister's son and a Narseys partner.

30 *"anxiously thrust away"*: Anonymous, "Calcutta, the City of Palaces," *Harper's New Monthly Magazine*, February 1867, p. 299.

Ships laden with: Parts of modern Malaysia were then known as the Straits Settlements and Federated Malay Colonies; modern Guyana was then British Guiana. What we know as South Africa consisted of four separate entities; of these, only the Colony of Natal imported indentured workers from India, although many of these workers made their way to the Transvaal colony. *Report of the Committee on Indian Emigration*, 1910.

a typical cargo: From 1907 to 1913, two to three indenture ships arrived in Fiji per year, each carrying 758 to 1,131 people. *Report of the Deputation*, 1922, "Appendix 1: Immigration and Repatriation, Numerical List of Ships."

A contemporary contract: Fiji Royal Gazette, 1910.

eleven to eighteen weeks: Lal, *Crossing the Kala Pani*, p. 9.

suicide or meningitis: Report of the Committee, 1910, p. 162.

31 *Steaming in toward Fiji*: Mrs. J. J. McHugh, "Recollections of Early Suva," in *Transactions and Proceedings of the Fiji Society*, pp. 210–14.

But the ship veered: Colman Wall, "Historical Notes on Suva," *Domodomo: A Scholarly Journal of the Fiji Museum*, 1996, p. 28.

From there they could: Ibid.

31 *In the harbor*: Postcard of Suva Harbour, 1895.

"When we arrived in Fiji": This quote, attributed to a 1911 arrival, is from Ali, *Plantation to Politics*, p. 6.

Of the three thousand: Prasad, "The Gujaratis of Fiji," p. 30.

32 *This "tragic episode"*: "The Conquest of the Fijians," in *What Then Must We Do?*, translated by Aylmer Maude (1886; reprint Devon, UK: Green Books, 1991).

ended in 1874: Ali, *Plantation to Politics*, p. 3.

It was an early British governor: Lal, "Labouring Men," p. 27.

32   *Fresh from postings*: T. A. Donnelly, M. Quanchi, G.J.A. Kerr, *Fiji in the Pacific: A History and Geography of Fiji*, fourth edition (Milton, Australia: Jacaranda, 1994), p. 48.

In 1879, the first: Ali, *Plantation to Politics*, p. 14.

33   *An English guidebook*: Schütz, *Suva: A History and Guide*.

Indians made up nearly a third: McNeill and Lal, *Report to the Government of India*.

exports had tripled: Testimony of Fiji magistrate Robert Malcolm Booth, April 26, 1909, contained in *Report of the Committee on Emigration, Part 2, Minutes of Evidence*, 1910, p. 62.

The year that Motiram arrived: Schütz, *Suva: A History and Guide*, p. 25.

"served in truly oriental style": Ibid., p. 29.

Suva boasted: Mrs. J. J. McHugh, "Recollections of Early Suva," in *Transactions and Proceedings of the Fiji Society*, pp. 210–14.

Walter Horne & Co. Ltd.: *Fiji Times and Herald*, Feb. 13, 1919, p. 5.

36   *A hitching post*: Prasad, "The Gujaratis of Fiji," p. 187.

A few yards away: Sir Henry Scott, "The Development of Suva," in *Transactions and Proceedings of the Fiji Society*, pp. 15–20.

37   *"Conditions were bad"*: Choksey, *Economic Life*.

"The Narsey business": Prasad, "The Gujaratis of Fiji," p. 189.

38   *In the Fiji census*: McNeill and Lal, *Report to the Government of India*, p. 260.

39   *In the* Fiji Times and Herald: January 3, 1919, p. 2.

In 1918, a ship: This occurred in what was then called Western Samoa, now simply Samoa, not to be confused with the nearby American Samoa. Michael Field, "NZ Apologises for Colonial Blunders," Agence France-Presse, June 3, 2002.

PAGE   3. BREAD

For the status of Indians in South Africa and the Gujarati Indians' response, I drew primarily on the government documents listed in the bibliography; issues of *Indian Opinion*, the newspaper published by Gandhi's movement in South Africa; Gandhi's memoir *Satyagraha in South Africa;* and contemporaneous histories including Joshi's *The Tyranny of Colour* (1942) and Naicker's *A Historical Synopsis* (ca. 1945). Three recent histories provided additional detail: Freund, *Insiders and Outsiders;* Bhana and Brain, *Setting Down Roots;* and Huttenback, *Gandhi in South Africa*, which was particularly useful for its detailed timeline of laws and restrictions. Kalpana Hiralal kindly provided me with parts of her dissertation, "Indian Family Businesses in the Natal Economy, 1890–1950" (University of Natal, Pietermaritzburg, 2000), which informed my understanding of the Gujaratis of Grey Street.

I use the contemporary term "Afrikaners" throughout this chapter to refer to the dominant white group in South Africa, even during the colonial period when they were known, sometimes proudly and sometimes with derision, as the Boers. Insight into Afrikaner politics was provided by sources including O'Meara's *Forty Lost Years* and Calpin's *At Last We Have Got Our Country Back*.

"To deny yourself": Jan Hennop, March 4, 2001.

44 *"There were, say"*: Indian Opinion, December 2, 1905, pp. 812–13.

45 *The first whites settled*: Leonard Thompson, *A History of South Africa*, revised edition (New Haven: Yale University Press, 1995), pp. 33–36.

"The fate of the Colony": Quoted in Huttenback, *Gandhi in South Africa*, p. 4.

46 *"The ordinary Coolie"*: Ibid., p. 16.

"There is probably not": Ibid., p. 19.

47 *The census taker warned*: Census of the Colony of Natal, April 1904, pp. 25–26.

"As the steamers sailed": Indian Opinion, December 2, 1905, pp. 812–13.

48 *At the port leading to*: The shortest way to reach Johannesburg was to disembark at Delagoa Bay, in modern Mozambique, and then travel inland by train.

"The whole subject is": Huttenback, *Gandhi in South Africa*, p. 69, quoting a Colonial Office minute dated June 17, 1897.

Trade with India: James, *Raj*, p. 365.

By 1901: Restrictions upon British Indian Subjects, 1900.

49 *"entirely satisfactory"*: Ibid.

50 *One shipmaster locked*: Indian Opinion, November 11–18, 1905, pp. 764, 778.

And officials confiscated: Bhana and Brain, *Setting Down Roots*, pp. 130–36.

"a second-rate Bombay": Indian Opinion, December 30, 1905, p. 875. My description of Durban and its Grey Street area early in the century also draws from Tichmann's *Gandhi Sites in Durban*; Badsha's *Imperial Ghetto*; and *The Official Guide to Durban with Map*, 1926–27 edition, published by the Durban Publicity Association.

51 *"black matter in the wrong place"*: Quoted in Huttenback, *Gandhi in South Africa*, p. 244.

52 *three thousand indentured*: Indian Opinion supplement, February 18, 1905.

"on the smell of an oil rag": The origin of this phrase is uncertain, but it is repeatedly found in written and oral texts of the time. Huttenback, in *Gandhi in South Africa*, cites one of the earliest instances, an article in the *Rhodesia Herald*, June 4, 1898, which says that Indians are "filthy dirty, and with their uncleanly habits may at any time sow the seeds of deadly epidemic. They live upon what may be termed the smell of an oiled rag, and the result is that in certain branches of business they dislocated trade by cutting-down prices, to the detriment of the legitimate trader" (p. 237).

52 *By 1908, the licensing bureau*: Huttenback, *Gandhi in South Africa*, p. 246.

53 *el capitán*: Newspaper profile of Ranchhod Kapitan contained in Kapitan family file, Old Courthouse Museum, Durban.

55 *at a courtyard fountain*: Meer, *Portrait of Indian South Africans*, p. 188.

"a religion that recognizes polygamy": Cape Supreme Court, vol. 81, case no. 319.

"I then awoke": Satyagraha in South Africa, p. 33.

56 *At 113 Grey Street*: Bridglal Pachai, "Aliens in the Political Hierarchy," in Pachai, *South Africa's Indians*, p. 21.

It became "shameful": Satyagraha in South Africa, p. 68.

57 *Three in five were born*: Dhupelia-Mesthrie, *From Cane Fields to Freedom*, p. 13.

In keeping with the times: Meer, *Portrait of Indian South Africans*, p. 190.

58 *Aboobaker Mansions*: named for Aboobaker Amod, elsewhere spelled Abu-bakr. According to Dhupelia-Mesthrie, Amod was the first "passenger" Indian in South Africa and the first to receive a license to trade in West Street.
As black Africans entered: University of Natal, *Durban Housing Survey*, p. 21.

59 *a 1944 planning map*: Racial zoning map titled "Proposals Recommended by the Provincial Post-War Works and Reconstruction Commission, 1944," included in University of Natal, *Durban Housing Survey*.
The date of this change: South Africa's Group Areas Amendment Act, Act 57 of 1957, gave the executive branch the power to create proclamations that would levy a £200 fine or impose two years of imprisonment on a person found guilty of "attending any place of public entertainment or partaking of any refreshment at a place where refreshments are served" in a segregated area. Proclamation No. 333, of November 1, 1957, imposed the law nationwide, effectively segregating most restaurants and other public spaces. (*Survey of Race Relations, 1956–57*, pp. 27–29.) However, a similar restriction had already been in effect in Durban, as locals date the bunny chow's invention to the 1940s or earlier.

60 *To aid white family farms*: Details of bread policies and pricing throughout this section are from official histories contained in two South African government documents: the *Report of the Commission of Inquiry into the Government's Bread Subsidy Scheme* by a commission chaired by F. J. Davin (September 1985), and *Evaluating the Deregulation Process: Wheat to Bread Value Chain* by the Section 7 Committee of the National Agricultural Marketing Council (December 1999).

61 *"Vote for white bread"*: O'Meara, *Forty Lost Years*, p. 19.
Back in 1912: *Indian Opinion*, January 13, 1912, p. 15.

62 *The glossy twenty-eight-page mini-magazine*: Durban City Council and the Durban Joint Wards Committee, *The Indian in Natal: Is He the Victim of Oppression?*
South Africa, with its 266,000: UK, India Office, "Review of Important Events Relating to or Affecting Indians," 1944 and 1945.
As the list of countries grew: UK, India Office, "Indians Overseas: A Guide to Source Materials."

63 *"pariah capitalism"*: This term was coined by the German sociologist and economist Max Weber (1864–1920), who appropriated a term that originally referred to an "untouchable" group of southern India (the Parai or Paraiyar people). Weber employed it to describe his problematic but influential theory of the Jews' role in European capitalism; he argued that the Jewish or "pariah" model represented a premodern, prerational version of capitalism, whereas modern and rational capitalism has its roots in Protestantism. Some argue that the "pariah capitalism" term is more properly restricted to a despised, rather than middleman, merchant community. It seems clear to me that the Indians of South Africa were both, to a varying degree.
"We hold ourselves bound": "Proclamation by the Queen in Council, to the Princes, Chiefs, and People of India," *Calcutta Gazette*, Nov. 1, 1858. Reprinted in *The Government of India: Being a Digest of the Statute Law Relating Thereto*,

with Historical Introduction and Illustrative Documents by Sir Courtenay Ilbert (Oxford: Clarendon Press, 1898), pp. 571–74.

64 *blue-and-white telegrams*: UK, India Office, "Representations from Indian Associations in South Africa."
the United Nations: India, "Question of the Treatment of Indians."

65 *"The dark shadow"*: Yusuf Dadoo, *South Africa—on the Road to Fascism* (London: India League, November 1948), pamphlet.

67 *"the descendants of some"*: *Satyagraha in South Africa*, p. 8.
"most humiliating": Bhana and Pachai, *A Documentary History*, p. 32.

68 *"As some of our Indian children"*: *Indian Opinion*, May 18, 1912.
When the Natal Native Congress: A. J. van Wyk, "'Roses and Rue': Public Opinion in Natal, 1910–1915," in Pachai, *South Africa's Indians*, p. 123.
In 1939, answering: *The Collected Works of Mahatma Gandhi*, 74:507.
By contrast, Jawaharlal Nehru: "The Condition of Indians Abroad" (July 12, 1939), in *Selected Works of Jawaharlal Nehru* (Calcutta: Orient Longman, 1982).

69 *It came at five o'clock*: For reconstruction of the riots, I have relied on the following sources: (1) Webb and Kirkwood, *The Durban Riots and After,* published by the reliable South African Institute of Race Relations in the year of the event; overheard dialogue during the violence is taken from their well-reported account. (2) Newspaper accounts of the riots published in the *Natal Mercury,* January 13–27, 1949. (3) Arun Gandhi, who recounts his firsthand experiences in his memoir, *A Patch of White.* Additionally, Kogila Moodley's "The Ambivalence of Survival Politics in Indian-African Relations," in Pachai, *South Africa's Indians,* informed my understanding of the riots and the factors that led up to them.

70 *"masses of irritable human beings"*: *Report of the Judicial Commission on Native Affairs in Durban,* chaired by F. N. Broome, June 1949.

71 *The Grey Street merchants*: Surat Hindu Association of Durban, "Platinum Jubilee" commemorative publication, 1982.
A contemporary report: Webb and Kirkwood, *The Durban Riots and After.* By contrast, official reports attributed 34 deaths to the Watts uprising of 1965, 43 deaths to the Detroit violence in 1967, and 53 deaths to the Rodney King riots in Los Angeles in 1992.

78 *Grey Street was "frozen"*: Maasdorp and Pillay, in *Urban Relocation,* argue that the racial restrictions artificially retarded Grey Street's economic development: "The continued postponement of the final group areas declaration, together with uncertainty as to the outcome, generally discouraged investment and made it difficult to obtain bonds and loans. Owners tended to neglect the maintenance of their properties, and the area became increasingly shabby" (p. 182).

79 *Despite the white perceptions*: As late as 1971–72, a survey of a sample of Durban voters showed 56 percent of Afrikaans-speaking citizens, and 30 percent of English-speaking citizens, agreeing that "the Indians can never really fit into the South African community." Lawrence Schlemmer, *Privilege, Prejudice and Parties: A Study of Patterns of Political Motivation Among White Voters in Durban* (Johannesburg: SAIRR, 1973).

79   *In the* Natal Mercury: "Death of Mr. G. Kapitan," February 5, 1972.

81   *more than a million Indians:* As of 2001, the number of people of Indian origin living in the east and south African countries of Kenya, Uganda, Tanzania, Mozambique, Zimbabwe, and South Africa was estimated at 1.26 million, according to the Indian government's *Report of the High Level Committee on the Indian Diaspora.*

PART TWO: SUBJECTS

83   Figures are drawn from "Review of Important Events Relating to or Affecting Indians," 1944–45. This annual report compiled by the India Office accounted only for British possessions and therefore left out the two Dutch territories with large Indian populations. This is the first set of figures presented here that unites all the regions of South Africa statistically, although they had been politically united in 1910.

4. SALT

For the chronology of the 1930 salt march in this chapter, I drew primarily on Gandhi's day-by-day reports and speeches, as contained in his *Collected Works* (cited as *CWMG*). Additional context was provided by Weber, *On the Salt March,* and Tewari, *Sabarmati to Dandi.*

85   *"Instead of a common riot":* Gazetteer of India, Gujarat State, Surat District (1962), p. 187.

89   *From the script:* John Briley, "Gandhi" (1982).

91   *The decline of Gandevi's weaving:* Census of India, 1931, pp. 289–90.

92   *"furiously thinking":* CWMG, 48:366.

93   *"the State can reach":* CWMG, 48:532.

A massive infrastructure: Gazetteer of Bombay City and Island (1909), p. 459. For a narrative of one man's quest to find the remnants of the thorny hedge designed to stop contraband salt, see Roy Moxham, *The Great Hedge of India* (New York: Carroll & Graf, 2001).

"The illegality is": CWMG, 48:366.

94   *Nine thousand gathered:* Weber, *On the Salt March,* p. 320.

Navsari's population: Census of India, 1931.

95   *counterfeit, machine-made versions:* Gandhi refers to the problem of fake khaadi several times in his correspondence, articles, and speeches during the Dandi period, and also met with mill owners to try to stop production of the fake-homemade cloth; see, for example, *CWMG*, 49:21, 49:22, and 49:94.

"Sweets, even if prepared": CWMG, 48:416.

"We shall have to use water": CWMG, 49:5.

the nineteen-point code: CWMG, 48:354.

96   *"Dandi itself has a tragic":* CWMG, 49:120.

"the war against salt tax": CWMG, 49:25.

At mass demonstrations: Weber, *On the Salt March,* p. 391.

"Suddenly, at a word": Miller's article is quoted in ibid., pp. 444–45.

98 *"rendering . . . unconscious"*: *The Black Regime at Dharasana*. This booklet was published by the secretary of the Gujarat Provincial Congress Committee, Gandhi's organization, shortly after the events described.

Bertrand Russell, for example: "Mahatma Gandhi," *Atlantic Monthly*, December 1952.

99 *By 1933, so many*: Waiz, *Indians Abroad Directory*.

100 *fifth on the list*: Ibid.

Fiji's afternoon newspaper reported: *Fiji Times and Herald*, September 3, 1931.

tons of sugar: Lal, *Broken Waves*, p. 62.

101 *"There are certain undesirable"*: Gillion, *The Fiji Indians*, pp. 115–17.

M. Narsey & Co. spearheaded: Prasad, "The Gujaratis of Fiji."

102 *"Better is one's own"*: *Bhagavad Geeta*, 3:19, translated by Prabha Duneja (Delhi: Govindram Hasanand, 1998).

104 *The final British count*: "Review of Important Events Relating to or Affecting Indians," 1944–45.

the three-striped flag: CWMG, 47:426.

108 *"stick of light"*: CWMG, 49:120.

PAGE   5. STORY

In addition to the sources listed under the Chapter 2 notes, this chapter also drew from my own interviews with family members conducted in 2000–2002; I am grateful to all who candidly discussed the company with me. Jayesh V. Khatri kindly lent me his only copy of his unpublished master's thesis, which provided important context about the duty-free market. Jiten T. Narsey, now a senior partner with the architectural firm Larsen, Holtom, Maybin & Associates of Suva, which designed the Narseys building in the 1960s, provided copies of blueprints and discussed the building, as well as other key Fiji buildings and the Navsari houses, in detail with me. Mahendra Gokal provided an account of the origins of the Narhari Electronics partnership. Jiten T. Narsey and Bhanu Hajratwala described for me the scene when cruise ships landed in Suva in the 1960s. Over one Coca-Cola and three whiskey-and-sodas, Uttam Narsey gave me a tour and history of the Merchants Club—which is now open to both sexes.

111 *"It is almost impossible to like"*: Michener (New York: Random House, 1951), p. 123.

116 *2,500, or three percent*: Prasad, "The Gujaratis of Fiji," p. 105.

132 *The Universal Eng.-Guj.*: By Shantilal Sarabhai Oza (Bombay: R. R. Sheth, 1940).

134 *When the government published*: Department of Lands, Mines and Surveys, Government of Fiji, *Colony Street Directory*, 1963.

144 *"white Australia"*: For this policy and its impact on Indians, I have drawn from Marie M. de Lepervanche, *Indians in a White Australia* (Sydney: George Allen, 1984), and Laksiri Jayasuriya and Kee Pookong, *The Asianisation of Australia? Some Facts About the Myths* (Melbourne: Melbourne University Press, 1999).

145 *In New Zealand, change*: For a review of policy as it related to Indians, see Bennett, *Asian Students in New Zealand*, and Ongley, "Immigration, Employment and Ethnic Relations."

146 *nearly forty thousand*: Chetty and Prasad, *Fiji's Emigration*, p. 10.

PART THREE: CITIZENS

151 The estimated size of the diaspora in 1984 and the list of countries are drawn from I. J. Bahadur Singh, ed., *Indians in South Asia* (New Delhi: Sterling/India International Centre, 1984), "Appendix I: Table on Distribution of Indians Overseas."

6. BRAINS

"Brain-drain" material is drawn from various sources. The compendium edited by Adams, *The Brain Drain*, provided a diversity of contemporary views, including the epigraph to this chapter. I also relied on U.S. government reports cited in the bibliography; McKnight, *Scientists Abroad;* Newland, *International Migration;* Niland, *The Asian Engineering Brain Drain;* Herbert G. Grubel and Anthony Scott, *The Brain Drain: Determinants, Measurement and Welfare Effects* (Waterloo, Ontario: Wilfrid Laurier University Press, 1977); Kamal Nayan Kabra, *Political Economy of Brain Drain: Reverse Technology Transfer* (New Delhi: Arnold-Heinemann Publishers, 1976); and Sharon Stanton Russell and Michael S. Teitelbaum, *International Migration and International Trade*, World Bank Discussion Papers No. 160 (Washington, D.C.: World Bank, 1992). For Nehru's science policy, including direct quotations included in this chapter, see Nanda, *Science and Technology in India.*

156 *"Brains go"*: Quoted in V. M. Dandekar, "India," in Adams, *The Brain Drain.*

158 *She skipped grade two*: I have taken the liberty of translating the academic years of the British educational system, which are counted as "standards" one through six followed by "forms" one through six, into the system of "grades" familiar to the North American reader. In both cases the total is twelve years of education prior to high school graduation.

172 *on the site of a large detention camp*: The first Indian Institute of Technology was founded in 1950 on the site of Hijli Detention Camp. "Institute History," IIT Kharagpur (www.iitkgp.ac.in/institute/history.php).

183 *most of the rest were visiting*: Melendy, *Asians in America*, p. 244.

184 *Enrolled at first*: Ibid., p. 185.

To their new bosses: Ibid., pp. 226–28.

never exceeding one thousand: Ibid., p. 186.

Japanese scientists: Roger Daniels, *The Politics of Prejudice: The Anti-Japanese Movement in California and the Struggle for Japanese Exclusion* (Berkeley: University of California Press, 1977), p. 33.

CROWD NUMBERING 500: *Morning Reveille and Evening American* (Bellingham, Wash.), Thursday morning, September 5, 1907.

185 *In 1913, California's Alien Land Law*: Chan, *Asian Americans*, p. 195.

"the most undesirable": *California and the Oriental*, p. 101.

In 1923, the Supreme Court: *U.S. v. Bhagat Singh Thind*, decided by the U.S. Supreme Court on February 19, 1923; unanimous opinion written by Justice George Sutherland.

Students, however: Under section 4(e) of the 1924 immigration law, alien students were considered "nonquota immigrants" who could be admitted without regard to national quotas. Under section 214(f) of the 1952 law, they were reclassified as "nonimmigrants" and given a special visa that was valid for the length of their studies. *I&N Reporter* 1, no. 3 (January 1953).

During the 1920s: Melendy, *Asians in America*, p. 205.

186 *In 1944, the Senate*: Ibid., p. 235.

105 Chinese immigrants each year: Kitano and Daniels, *Asian Americans*, p. 16.

It took two more years: Inder Singh (president of the Global Organization of People of Indian Origin International), "Long Struggle Marked Battle for U.S. Citizenship," *India-West*, June 30, 2006, pp. A4–A6.

At last, in 1946: Daniels, "History of Indian Immigration to the United States," p. 235.

Quietly, Congress authorized: *I&N Reporter* 19, no. 1 (July 1970): 1, and *I&N Reporter* 5, no. 1 (July 1956).

U.S. psychiatric hospitals: Adams, *The Brain Drain*, p. 236.

187 *"it became American policy"*: Paul Ritterband, "Law, Policy, and Behavior: Educational Exchange Policy and Student Migration," *American Journal of Sociology* 76, no. 1 (July 1970): 71–82.

America's class of foreign students: *I&N Reporter* 12, no. 2 (October 1964), Table 3: "Nonimmigrant Aliens Admitted, by Class of Admission."

188 *Just a few months earlier*: *I&N Reporter* 11, no. 1 (July 1962): 8.

This was another recent change: Ibid.

193 *in October 1962, a minor adjustment*: Public Law 87-855, Oct. 24, 1962.

Since 1946, one hundred: Brinley Thomas, "'Modern' Migration," in Adams, *The Brain Drain*.

194 *immediately tripled*: Asian scientists and engineers with green cards numbered 498 in 1962, and 1,406 in 1963, according to a WHO study. Alfonso Mejia, Helena Pizurki, and Erica Royston, Division of Health Manpower Development of the World Health Organization, *Foreign Medical Graduates: The Case of the United States* (Lexington, Mass.: Lexington Books, 1980), p. 7.

"Send me your trained": The poem is quoted in Patricio R. Mamot, *Foreign Medical Graduates in America* (Springfield, Ill.: Charles C. Thomas, 1974), p. 13.

198 *That act had been*: Public Law 414, Chapter 477, Section 201; 66 Stat., p. 175.

as measured by the census of 1920: As a result of this provision, of the roughly 154,000 quota visas that the 1952 act made available each year after 1952, the vast majority (125,000) went to northern and western Europe. A further 24,000 went to southern and eastern Europe. (Western Hemisphere immigrants were not subject to quotas.) Note that I have referred to the act's "quota areas" as "countries," although certain territories and non-nations also received quota allocations. *I&N Reporter* 4, no. 1 (July 1955): 6.

199 *"urgently needed"*: *I&N Reporter* 4, no. 1 (July 1955): 7.

203 *The latest census*: Melendy, *Asians in America*, p. 256.

206 *"The Immigration Service official"*: *I&N Reporter* 19, no. 1 (July 1970): 6.

On October 3, 1965: Melendy, *Asians in America*, p. 41.

"This bill that we will sign today": Audio of Johnson's comments re-aired in "1965 Immigration Law Changed Face of America," *All Things Considered*, National Public Radio, May 9, 2006.

207   *In fact, the act*: In addition to the law itself, the following *I&N Reporter* articles provided context and details of the act's impact: Robert B. Lindsey, "The Act of October 3, 1965," 14, no. 4 (April 1966): 103–4, 111–15; Helen F. Eckerson, "Recent Immigration to the United States," 15, no. 1 (July 1966): 19–20; and John J. Murray, "Labor Certification . . . for Third and Sixth Preference Aliens and Nonpreference Cases," 15, no. 4 (April 1967): 50–52.

      "unexpected side effects": *I&N Reporter* 17, no. 1 (July 1968): 1–3.

215   *China and India accounted for*: National Science Foundation, *Scientists, Engineers*, p. 43.

      according to the most reliable figure: A U.N. analysis of the 100,262 foreign students who were living in the United States in 1967 estimated that 70 percent came from Less Developed Countries. Report of the U.N. Secretary General, *Outflow of Trained Personnel from the LDCs*, November 5, 1968.

      The representative from Dahomey: Adams, *The Brain Drain*, pp. 7–12.

216   *A 1967 bibliography*: McKnight, *Scientists Abroad*, p. 50.

      over 90 percent: Adams, *The Brain Drain*, pp. 1–8.

      "While with one hand": Quoted in ibid., p. 608.

      "There is the gravest ground": McKnight, *Scientists Abroad*, p. 22.

      "seemed more concerned": Adams, *The Brain Drain*, pp. 234–35.

217   *A survey of Indian students*: Niland, *The Asian Engineering Brain Drain*.

227   *That semester, nearly five thousand*: From July to December 1967, 4,729 dependents of foreign students were admitted to the United States. *I&N Reporter* 17, no. 4 (April 1969): 59.

228   *Located in a cluster*: For the history of the Finkbine Park barracks, see Bob Hibbs, "Saturday Postcard 212: The Fine Arts at Iowa," *Iowa City Press Citizen*, September 20, 2003.

231   *"friendship and cooperation"*: *I&N Reporter* 19, no. 1 (July 1970): 3.

233   *Within the year, so many*: *I&N Reporter* 17, no. 1 (July 1968): 1–3, and *I&N Reporter* 17, no. 3 (January 1969): 38.

      "We are in the international market": U.S. House subcommittee, *Brain Drain: A Study of the Persistent Issue*, p. 36.

      India had just: *I&N Reporter* 17, no. 1 (July 1968): 2.

239   *he fit the typical profile*: Figures in this paragraph are from National Science Foundation, *Scientists, Engineers*, pp. vi, 6–7.

      This eightfold increase: *I&N Reporter* 19, no. 4 (April 1971): 52.

      one in four "aliens": *I&N Reporter* 19, no. 2 (October 1970): 23.

240   *California was not one of the eight*: *I&N Reporter* 16, no. 2 (October 1967): 37–40.

241   *By long policy and practice, New Zealand*: See source notes for Chapter 5.

243   Spice Is the Variety: *Otago Daily Times*, June 20, 1978, p. 15.

247   *"In India, cars are not"*: V. M. Dandekar, "India," in Adams, *The Brain Drain*.

      "If the neighbours": Nem Kumar Jain, *Science and Scientists in India (Vedic to Modern)* (Delhi: Indian Book Gallery, 1982), p. 65.

      "lack of appreciation of their work": *New York Times*, July 24, 1966. Quoted in Adams, *The Brain Drain*.

      600,000 graduates: Adams, *The Brain Drain*, p. 90.

median pay of about 300 rupees: Census of India, 1961, Monograph No. 1.

249 *"cumulative inertia"*: Mathematical model developed by Dr. Robert McGinnis of Cornell, cited in *Mobility of PhD's Before and After the Doctorate, with Associated Economic and Educational Characteristics of States,* Career Patterns Report No. 3 prepared for the National Institutes of Health by the Research Division, Office of Scientific Personnel, National Research Council (Washington, D.C.: National Academy of Sciences, 1971), p. 197.

250 *Indian doctors in Michigan*: The American Association of Physicians from India, subsequently renamed the American Association of Physicians of Indian Origin, formed "after a fireside discussion in Detroit Michigan in 1982," according to its official history.

252 *Indian community in Michigan*: The migration of Indian engineers to the auto industry was not accidental; in 1923, Henry Ford began recruiting engineering students from India who were attending the University of California to work in his factories at a daily wage of $5. Ford's offer was strategic, offering the students a solution to the higher nonresident tuition fees they suddenly had to pay because of the U.S. Supreme Court ruling that year making Indians ineligible for citizenship on the grounds that they were not "white." Within three years, more than a hundred Indian students had entered the Ford training program, according to reports filed by British consulate staff who tracked the activities of British Indians in the United States. "Indians Overseas. Ford Motor Works, Detroit, U.S.A. Training of British Indians" (correspondence file, Economic and Overseas Department, India Office, British Library IOR/L/E/7/1459).

"almost 80 percent": Portes and Rumbaut, *Immigrant America,* p. 19.

7. SHELTER

259 *During the ritual*: Bhanu and Bhupendra Hajratwala, *Our Kshatriya Samskaras: 1. Simant* (California: North American Hindu Association, 2007).

268 *"She was always attentive"*: Prabhati Mukherjee, *Hindu Women: Narrative Models,* revised edition (Calcutta: Orient Longman, 1994), pp. 13–14.

269 *"the first person to get up"*: Ibid., p. 28.

Daughter, wife, widow: See, for example, the Laws of Manu 5:149, "In her childhood [a girl] should be under the will of her father; in [her] youth, of [her] husband; her husband being dead, of her sons; a woman should never enjoy her own will." Translated by Thadani, in *Sakhiyani,* p. 54.

273 *high proportion of Indian wives*: See, for example, R. Aaron et al., "Suicides in Young People in Rural Southern India," *Lancet* 363, no. 9415: 1117–18.

275 *The* Modern Combined: Shantilal Sarabhai Oza and Ramanbhai G. Bhatt (Mumbai: R. R. Sheth, 2001).

276 *by 1996*: Fiji Islands Bureau of Statistics, *1996 Fiji Census of Population and Housing Analytical Report: Part 1, Demographic Characteristics,* 1998.

277 *55,000 lucky winners*: The number of winners and other regulations governing the lottery have changed since its inception in 1986. The provisions governing Madhukant's application were contained in Section 131, Diversity Immigrants, of the Immigration Act of 1990 (Public Law 649, passed by the 101st Congress,

2nd session, on November 29, 1990). For important context, I drew on news accounts in various periodicals including the *Boston Irish Reporter* and the *New York Amsterdam News*, both of which tracked developments regularly for their readers. The following articles (listed chronologically) provided details included here: Karlyn Barker, "U.S. Lottery Will Award 20,000 Visas in 1989–90," *Washington Post*, March 2, 1989; Mae M. Cheng, "The New New Yorkers: The Luck of the Draw," *Newsday*, January 15, 1997; "Diversity Lottery Program to Give 55,000 Green Cards," *New York Amsterdam News*, January 24, 1997; "Stakes Are High in U.S. Visa Lottery," *Boston Irish Reporter*, March 1, 1997; Richard Springer, "Indians Jump to Third Place in Immigration to U.S.," *India-West*, May 2, 1997, front page; and William Branigin, "House Republican Wants Immigration Policy to Favor the Educated," *Washington Post*, April 22, 1998.

279 *In West Africa*: Sierra Leone News Archives, February 1997 (www.sierra-leone.org /Archives/slnews0297.pdf).
Ireland's ambassador was reportedly: Mark Krikorian, "Lucky Visas," *Washington Post*, March 14, 1996.

283 *They had twenty thousand hotels*: Turkel, "From Ragas to Riches," part 1.

284 *By 1963, a social scientist*: Jain, *The Gujaratis of San Francisco*.

285 *President Eisenhower signed*: David A. Pfeiffer, "Ike's Interstates at 50: Anniversary of the Highway System Recalls Eisenhower's Role as Catalyst," *Prologue*, quarterly journal of the National Archives and Records Administration, 38, no. 2 (Summer 2006).

286 *Half a dozen motel property brokers told*: Scott, "Indians Snap Up Small Motels."
self-insuring and loaning funds to one another: Turkel, "From Ragas to Riches," part 2.
Justice Department launched: Scott, "Indians Snap Up Small Motels."
Days Inn conducted: Interview with Ramesh Gokal, 2001.

287 *"nearly every exit"*: "Indian Immigrants Prosper as Owners of Motels," Associated Press, June 22, 1985.

293 Saalo gaando chhe: *Saalo* literally means "brother-in-law" — that is, your sister's husband — and is a curse word because it implies that the speaker has slept with your sister. As there is no English equivalent, I have approximated the word as "bastard." *Gaando:* Crazy. *Chhe:* Is.

PAGE   8. BODY

297 *"To assimilate means"*: Adrienne Rich, "Resisting Amnesia: History and Personal Life (1983)," in *Blood, Bread, and Poetry* (New York: W. W. Norton, 1986), p. 142.

304 *most segregated*: U.S. Census Bureau, *Racial and Ethnic Residential Segregation in the United States: 1980–2000*, Series CENSR-3, 2002 (www.census.gov/hhes /www/housing/housing_patterns/papertoc.html).

305 *A canal had opened*: Township of Canton, *Canton Sesquicentennial Commemorative Book, 1834–1984*, June 1984.
In 1834 this particular stop was named: "Historic Canton," Canton Historical Society, last updated September 9, 2007 (www.cantonhistoricalsociety.org).
As the "Sweet Corn Capital": Roy R. Schultz, *Canton Area, the Sweet Corn Capi-*

tol of Michigan: An Era in Cantons History [*sic*], undated pamphlet published by the Canton Historical Society.

306 *The region had lost 87,500 jobs*: SEMCOG, *Economic Development*, p. 4.

311 *the Census Bureau counted*: Susan Koshy, "Category Crisis: South Asian Americans and the Questions of Race and Ethnicity," *Diaspora* 7, no. 3 (Winter 1998): 294.

"inconspicuous" and "rapidly assimilated": Portes and Rumbaut, *Immigrant America*, p. 19.

Rarely did the researchers find: Of the 27,803 Indians who immigrated in 1987, 10 percent went to New York, 8 percent to Chicago, and 4 percent to Los Angeles, with the remaining 78 percent settling in other destinations. This was the complete opposite of many other immigrant communities at the time; 77 percent of Cubans, for example, went to Miami. Ibid., p. 38.

most educated, most professional: According to an analysis of 1980 census data on immigrants, those from India had the highest level of educational attainment (66.2 percent had four years or more of college, versus 6.2 percent of the U.S. population as a whole) and were the most likely to be working in professions (48.8 percent of adults over age twenty-five, versus 12.3 percent of U.S. adults). Ibid., pp. 60–70.

313 *Before 1808, Native Americans*: "The Treaties," Chippewa Ottawa Resource Authority (www.1836cora.org/treaties.html).

314 *"into several numbered townships"*: Diane Follmer Wilson, *Cornerstones: A History of Canton Township Families* (Canton, Mich.: Canton Historical Society, 1988).

A few years later, the NAACP: Riddle, "Race and Reaction."

315 *A map published*: Reproduced in ibid.

"Residential construction": Charter Township of Canton, *Future Land Use Plan*.

At the same time, Detroit: Ray Suarez, *The Old Neighborhood: What We Lost in the Great Suburban Migration, 1966–1999* (New York: Free Press, 1999), p. 248.

The Census Bureau ordered: Charter Township of Canton, *Future Land Use Plan*.

Our white brick house: Ibid.

Our elementary schools: Ching-li Wang, *Population Change in Michigan: 1980–1984*, State of Michigan, Department of Management and Budget, November 1985.

318 *"It's because of motherfuckers"*: Zia, *Asian American Dreams*, chap. 3.

In southeastern Michigan: SEMCOG, *Community Profiles in Southeast Michigan, 1980 Census*.

324 *"Feminism is the theory"*: This phrase is traditionally attributed to author and activist Ti-Grace Atkinson, although its provenance and accuracy are debated.

327 *the split self*: In employing this metaphor to describe my response to the traumas of my migration(s), I do not mean to co-opt or minimize the suffering of those who experience clinical split-personality and/or schizophrenic conditions. For a treatment of migration trauma's possible causal relationship to such conditions, see Elizabeth Cantor-Graae and Jean-Paul Selten, "Schizophrenia and Migration: A Meta-Analysis and Review," *American Journal of Psychiatry*, no. 162

(2005): 12–24; and for schizophrenia among South Asian women migrants in particular, the work of Dr. Dinesh Bhugra, dean of the Royal College of Psychiatrists and professor of mental health and cultural diversity at the Institute of Psychiatry in London. Additionally, the theorist Vijay Prashad makes an interesting connection between such split thinking among U.S. Indians (the split being, in his conception, a moral home life versus an immoral external engagement with capitalism) and the *girmit* experience, in *The Karma of Brown Folk* (Minneapolis: University of Minnesota Press, 2000), pp. 104–5.

328 *Exiting the movie theater*: I am grateful to the editors of *Contours of the Heart: South Asians Map North America* (New York: Asian American Writers Workshop, 1996) for publishing an early poem from which this passage is drawn.

334 *unearthing millennia of evidence*: See, for example, Thadani, *Sakhiyani;* and Ruth Vanita and Saleem Kidwai, eds., *Same-Sex Love in India: Readings from Literature and History* (London: St. Martin's, 2000). I first learned of these and other resources via *Trikone* magazine (www.trikone.org). For a critical view of the limits of such history, as well as a brief survey of queer South Asian organizing in the 1980s and mid-1990s, see Nayan Shah, "Sexuality, Identity, and the Uses of History," in *Q&A: Queer in Asian America,* edited by D. Eng and A. Home (Philadelphia: Temple University Press, 1998).

PART FOUR: DESTINY

348 *bringing together the stories*: My thinking on this challenge was informed by these words by the scholar Eleni Coundouriotis: "A diaspora becomes intelligible at the moment when a communal identity re-emerges from fragmentation. The narrative of diaspora is always working against the etymology of the word 'diaspora,' which signifies dispersion." *Diaspora: A Journal of Transnational Studies* 10, no. 1 (Spring 2001): 37.

354 *It is this capitalist drive*: See, for example, Joel Kotkin, *Tribes: How Race, Religion, and Identity Determine Success in the New Global Economy* (New York: Random House, 1993), chap. 7, "The Greater India."

356 *The Indians were a tiny*: White, *Turbans and Traders.*

363 *Middlesex County, New Jersey*: For a book-length treatment of the Middlesex County phenomenon, see Kalita, *Suburban Sahibs.*

365 *Studies of voluntary migration*: See, for example, Portes and Rumbaut, *Immigrant America*, pp. 10–13.

378 *largest single immigrant group*: SEMCOG, *Patterns of Diversity.*

380 *The 2000 U.S. Census counted*: Nicholas A. Jones and Amy Symens Smith, "The Two or More Races Population: 2000," Census 2000 Brief, November 2001 (www.census.gov/prod/2001pubs/c2kbr01-6.pdf).

SELECTED BIBLIOGRAPHY

Of the rich body of work on the diaspora that is now available, I list below those sources from which I drew directly, sorted so that readers seeking further information about particular countries can easily find the relevant works. Titles listed in the "General" category cover more than one country or address some aspect of the diaspora as a whole. Sources listed below are generally those to which I refer multiple times. Sources cited only once appear in full in the Notes section. *HMSO*, below, stands for His/Her Majesty's Stationery Office, the primary publisher of British government documents.

In addition, the following newspapers provided valuable contemporary accounts: in Fiji, the *Fiji Times* and the *Fiji Times and Herald*; in India, *Navajivan*; and in South Africa, the *Indian Opinion*, the *Natal Witness*, and the *Natal Mercury*. Specific editions are cited in the Notes.

GENERAL

Adams, Walter, ed. *The Brain Drain*. Papers presented at international conference on the "brain drain" at Lausanne, Switzerland, August 1967. New York: Macmillan, 1968.

Chaudhuri, K. N. *Trade and Civilisation in the Indian Ocean: An Economic History from the Rise of Islam to 1750*. Cambridge: Cambridge University Press, 1985.

Christopher, A. J. *The British Empire at Its Zenith*. New York: Croom Helm, 1988.

Colombo Plan Bureau. *Special Topic, Brain Drain: Country Papers, the Working Paper and the Report of the Special Topic Committee*. Prepared for annual meeting of committee implementing the 1962 Colombo Plan for Co-operative Economic Development in South and South-east Asia, held October–November 1972, New Delhi. Colombo, Sri Lanka: Colombo Plan Bureau, 1971.

Gandhi, Mohandas Karamchand. *An Autobiography; or, The Story of My Experiments with Truth.* Translated by Mahadev Desai. Ahmedabad: Navajivan Publishing House, 1927.

———. *The Collected Works of Mahatma Gandhi.* 98 volumes. Ahmedabad: Navajivan Trust, 1970. Abbreviated as *CWMG* in the Notes. Although I consulted paper volumes, this resource is now available online (www.gandhiserve.org/cwmg/cwmg.html).

Gish, Oscar. *Doctor Migration and Brain Drain: The Impact of the International Demand for Doctors on Health Services in Developing Countries.* Occasional Papers on Social Administration, Number 43. London: Social Administration Research Trust, 1971.

Gupta, Anirudha, ed. *Indians Abroad, Asia and Africa: Report of an International Seminar.* Proceedings of an April 1969 seminar held in New Delhi by the Indian Council for Africa and the Indian Council for Cultural Relations. New Delhi: Indian Council for Africa, 1971.

Guy, John. *Woven Cargoes: Indian Textiles in the East.* London: Thames and Hudson, 1998.

India. Ministry of External Affairs. Non Resident Indians & Persons of Indian Origin Division. *Report of the High Level Committee on the Indian Diaspora.* New Delhi: Government of India, January 8, 2002 (www.indian diaspora.nic.in/diasporapdf/part1-est.pdf).

Jain, Ravindra K. *Indian Communities Abroad: Themes and Literature.* New Delhi: Manohar, 1993.

McKnight, Allan D. *Scientists Abroad: A Study of the International Movement of Persons in Science and Technology.* Paris: United Nations Educational, Scientific and Cultural Organization, 1971.

Muthanna, I. M. *People of India in North America (United States, Canada, W. Indies and Fiji).* Bangalore: Lotus Printers, 1982.

Newland, Kathleen. *International Migration: The Search for Work.* Worldwatch Paper 33. Washington, D.C.: Worldwatch Institute, November 1979.

Tinker, Hugh. *The Banyan Tree: Overseas Emigrants from India, Pakistan and Bangladesh.* Oxford: Oxford University Press, 1977.

———. *A New System of Slavery: The Export of Indian Labour Overseas, 1830–1920.* Oxford: Oxford University Press, 1974.

———. *Separate and Unequal: India and the Indians in the British Commonwealth, 1920–1950.* Vancouver: University of British Columbia Press, 1976.

United Kingdom, Colonial Office. *Report of the Committee on Emigration from India to the Crown Colonies and Protectorates.* London: HMSO, 1910.

———. *Restrictions upon British Indian Subjects in British Colonies and Dependencies.* Includes census. London: HMSO, December 7, 1900.

United Kingdom, India Office. "Colonies Committee. Main file." 1922–25. British Library IOR/L/E/7/1319.

———. "Indians Overseas: A Guide to Source Materials in the India Office Records, for the Study of Indian Emigration, 1830–1950." By Timothy N. Thomas, 1985.

———. "Review of Important Events Relating to or Affecting Indians in Different Parts of the British Empire." Series of annual reports, 1936–46. British Library IOR/L/PJ/8/184.

Waiz, S. A. *Indians Abroad Directory.* Bombay: Imperial Indian Citizenship Association, 1933.

FIJI

Ali, Ahmed. *Plantation to Politics: Studies on Fiji Indians.* Suva: University of the South Pacific, 1980.

Bhasin, K. D. *Report on Economic and Commercial Conditions in Fiji Islands for the Year 1957.* Office of the Commissioner for the Government of India in Fiji. New Delhi: Ministry of Commerce and Industry, 1957.

Chetty, Nand Kishor, and Satendra Prasad. *Fiji's Emigration: An Examination of Contemporary Trends and Issues.* Demographic Report No. 4. Suva: University of the South Pacific/U.N. Population Fund, 1993.

Colpani, Satya. *Beyond the Black Waters: A Memoir of Sir Sathi Narain.* Suva: University of the South Pacific, 1996.

Coulter, John Wesley. *The Drama of Fiji: A Contemporary History.* Rutland, Vt.: Charles E. Tuttle, 1967.

———. *Fiji: Little India of the Pacific.* Chicago: University of Chicago Press, 1942.

Fiji, Legislative Council. *Annual Report on Indian Immigration to, Indian Emigration from, and Indentured Indian Immigrants in the Colony for the Year 1910.* June 16, 1911. National Archives of Fiji, Suva.

Fiji Society of Science and Industry. *Transactions and Proceedings of the Fiji Society of Science and Industry for the Years 1940 to 1944.* Vol. 4 (December 1953).

Gillion, K. L. *The Fiji Indians: Challenge to European Dominance, 1920–1946.* Canberra: Australian National University Press, 1977.

————. *Fiji's Indian Migrants: A History to the End of Indenture in 1920*. Oxford: Oxford University Press, 1976.

Khatri, Jayesh V. "Duty Free Shop Responses to a Declining Market in Fiji." Master's thesis, University of the South Pacific, 1995.

Lal, Brij V. *Broken Waves: A History of the Fiji Islands in the Twentieth Century.* Honolulu: University of Hawaii Press, 1992.

————, ed. *Crossing the Kala Pani: A Documentary History of Indian Indenture in Fiji.* Canberra: Division of Pacific and Asian History, Australian National University, 1998.

————. "Labouring Men and Nothing More: Some Problems of Indian Indenture in Fiji." In *Indentured Labour in the British Empire, 1834–1920*, edited by Kay Saunders. London: Croom Helm, 1984.

Lambert, S. M. *East Indian and Fijian in Fiji: Their Changing Numerical Relation.* Special Publication 32. Honolulu: Bernice P. Bishop Museum, 1938.

Mayer, Adrian C. *Peasants in the Pacific: A Study of Fiji Indian Rural Society.* Berkeley: University of California Press, 1973.

McNeill, James, and Chimman Lal. *Report to the Government of India on the Conditions of Indian Immigrants in Four British Colonies and Surinam. Part II: Surinam, Jamaica, Fiji, and General Remarks.* London: HMSO, 1915.

Nandan, Satendra. *The Wounded Sea.* Sydney: Simon and Schuster, 1991.

Narsey, Kiran C. "Historical Development of a Local Firm: A Case Study of Narseys Ltd." Unpublished, courtesy of the author, June 1981.

Prasad, Kamal Kant. "The Gujaratis of Fiji, 1900–1945: A Study of an Indian Immigrant Trader Community." PhD dissertation, University of British Columbia, 1978.

Sanadhya, Totaram. *My Twenty-one Years in the Fiji Islands; and, The Story of the Haunted Line.* Translated and edited by John Dunham Kelly and Uttra Kumari Singh. Suva: Fiji Museum, 1991.

Schütz, Albert J. *Suva: A History and Guide.* Sydney: Pacific Publications, 1978.

United Kingdom, India Office. *Report of the Deputation of the Government of India to Fiji, Strictly Confidential.* Simla, India: Government Central Press, September 1922. British Library, IOR/L/E/7/1276.

HONG KONG

Indian Chamber of Commerce, Hong Kong. *Annual Report.* 1962–68, 1975, 1981–83.

White, Barbara-Sue. *Turbans and Traders: Hong Kong's Indian Communities.* Hong Kong: Oxford University Press, 1994.

INDIA

Baroda Administrative Report. 1908–09 and 1909–10. Bombay: Times Press, 1910–11.

Bose, Ashish. *India's Billion Plus People: 2001 Census Highlights, Methodology and Media Coverage.* New Delhi: B. R. Publishing, 2001.

Bühler, G. *Eleven Land-Grants of the Chaulukyas of Anhilvad: A Contribution to the History of Gujarat.* Bombay: Education Society's Press, 1877.

Calico Museum of Textiles. *Textile Trade of India with the Outside World, 15th–19th Century.* 2nd edition. Ahmedabad: D. S. Mehta/Sarabhai Foundation, 1999.

Census of India, 1931. Vol. 19, *Baroda,* Part 1, *Report.* Compiled by Satya V. Mukerjea, Census Commissioner of the Baroda State. Bombay: Times of India Press, 1932.

Census of India, 1961, Monograph No. 1, Scientific and Technical Personnel. Compiled by K. Ray for the Council of Scientific and Industrial Research, Office of the Registrar General. New Delhi: Ministry of Home Affairs, 1965.

Choksey, R. D. *Economic Life in the Bombay Gujarat, 1800–1939.* New York: Asia Publishing House, 1968.

Das Gupta, Ashin. *Indian Merchants and the Decline of Surat, 1700–1750.* South Asian Institute, University of Heidelberg. Wiesbaden, Germany: Franz Steiner Verlag, 1979.

Gahlot, Sukhvir Singh. *Castes and Tribes of Rajastan.* Jodhpur: Jain Brothers, 1989.

Gazetteer of Bombay City and Island. Vol. 2. Bombay: Times Press, 1909.

Gazetteer of the Bombay Presidency. Vol. 2, Part 1, *History of Gujarat.* Bombay: Government Central Press, 1896.

Gazetteer of India. Vol. 2, *Maharashtra State, Greater Bombay District.* Revised edition. Bombay: Government Central Press, 1987.

Gazetteer of India, Gujarat State, Surat District. Edited by M. R. Palande. 2nd revised edition. Ahmedabad: Government Printing Stationery and Publications, 1962.

Gujarat Provincial Congress Committee. *The Black Regime at Dharasana: A Brief Survey of the "Dharasana Raid."* Ahmedabad: Navajivan Press, 1930.

James, Lawrence. *Raj: The Making and Unmaking of British India.* New York: St. Martin's, 1998.

Janaki, Vengalil A. *Gujarat as the Arabs Knew It: A Study in Historical Geography.* Baroda: University of Baroda Press, 1969.

————. *Some Aspects of the Historical Geography of Surat.* Geography Research Paper Series No. 7. Baroda: University of Baroda Press, 1974.

Majumdar, Asoke Kumar. *Chaulukyas of Gujarat: A Survey of the History and Culture of Gujarat from the Middle of the Tenth to the End of the Thirteenth Century.* Bombay: Bharatiya Vidya Bhavan, 1956. (This is also the source of the Abdul Qadir Badauni quote that appears at the end of my introductory "Note on the Text.")

Nanda, B. R., ed. *Science and Technology in India.* New Delhi: Nehru Memorial Museum and Library/Vikas Publishing House, 1977.

Ogilby, John. *Asia, the First Part, Being An Accurate Description of Persia, And the Several Provinces thereof. The Vast Empire of the Great Mogol, And other Parts of India: And their Several Kingdoms and Regions.* London: His Majesty's Cosmographer, 1673.

Ovington, John. *A Voyage to Surat in the Year 1689.* Originally published in 1696; reprinted as *Ovington's Voyage to Surat,* edited by H. G. Rawlinson. London: Oxford University Press, 1929.

Tewari, Jyotsna. *Sabarmati to Dandi: Gandhi's Non-violent March and the Raj.* Delhi: Raj Publications, 1995.

Thadani, Giti. *Sakhiyani: Lesbian Desire in Ancient and Modern India.* London: Cassell, 1996.

Tod, James. *Annals and Antiquities of Rajasthan or the Central and Western Rajput States of India, Volume I.* Originally published in 1829; republished in an edition edited by William Crooke. London: Oxford University Press, 1920.

Voyages to the South-East and East Indies. Vol. 1 of "A New General Collection of Voyages and Travels, Consisting of the Most Esteemed Relations which have Hitherto been Published in any Language." London: Thomas Astley, 1745.

Weber, Thomas. *On the Salt March: The Historiography of Gandhi's March to Dandi.* New Delhi: HarperCollins, 1998.

NEW ZEALAND

Bennett, Neville. *Asian Students in New Zealand.* Institute of Policy Studies/Asia 2000 Foundation Series. Wellington: Victoria University, 1998.

New Zealand, Population and Demography Division of Statistics. *New Zealand Now: Asian New Zealanders.* Wellington: Statistics New Zealand/Te Tari Tatau, 1995.

Ongley, Patrick. "Immigration, Employment and Ethnic Relations." In *Nga Patai: Racism and Ethnic Relations in Aotearoa/New Zealand,* edited by Paul Spoonley, David Pearson, and Cluny Macpherson. Palmerston North, N.Z.: Dunmore, 1996.

SOUTH AFRICA

Badsha, Omar. *Imperial Ghetto: Ways of Seeing in a South African City.* Social Identities South Africa Series. Cape Town: South Africa History Online, 2001.

Bhana, Surendra. *Gandhi's Legacy: The Natal Indian Congress, 1894–1994.* Pietermaritzburg: University of Natal Press, 1997.

Bhana, Surendra, and Joy Brain. *Setting Down Roots: Indian Migrants in South Africa, 1860–1911.* Johannesburg: Witwatersrand University Press, 1990.

Bhana, Surendra, and Bridglal Pachai. *A Documentary History of Indian South Africans, 1860–1982.* Stanford, Calif.: Hoover Institution Press, 1984.

Bramdaw, Dhanee, ed. *The South African Indian Who's Who and Commercial Directory.* Pietermaritzburg: Natal Witness, 1935/1939.

Calpin, G. H. *At Last We Have Got Our Country Back.* Cape Town: Buren, 1969.

Census of the Colony of Natal, April 1904. Pietermaritzburg: Government Printers, 1905.

Dhupelia-Mesthrie, Uma. *From Cane Fields to Freedom: A Chronicle of Indian South African Life.* Durban: Kwela, 2000.

Ebr.-Vally, Rehana. *Kala Pani: Caste and Colour in South Africa.* Cape Town: Kwela, 2001.

Freund, Bill. *Insiders and Outsiders: The Indian Working Class of Durban, 1910–1990.* Portsmouth, N.H.: Heinemann, 1995.

Gandhi, Arun. *A Patch of White.* Bombay: Thacker, 1969.

Gandhi, Mohandas Karamchand. *Satyagraha in South Africa.* Translated by Valji Govindji Desai. Ahmedabad: Navajivan Trust, 1928.

Hey, P. D. *The Rise of the Natal Indian Elite.* Funded by the National Council for Social Research. Pietermaritzburg: Natal Witness, 1961.

Huttenback, Robert A. *Gandhi in South Africa: British Imperialism and the Indian Question, 1860–1914.* Ithaca, N.Y.: Cornell University Press, 1971.

India, Department of External Affairs and Commonwealth Relations. "Question of the Treatment of Indians in South Africa Before the United Nations Organisation." Part I: Proceedings of the Nineteenth Meeting of the General Committee of the First Session of the General Assembly,

Held on the 24th October 1946. Part II: Speeches Made at, and the Proceedings of, the Meetings of the Joint First and Sixth Committees of the First Session of the General Assembly, Held in November 1946. Simla, India: Government of India, 1947.

India, Information Services. *Treatment of Indians in South Africa: Recent Developments.* Washington, D.C.: Government of India, 1947.

Joshi, P. S. *The Tyranny of Colour: A Study of the Indian Problem in South Africa.* Self-published. Durban, 1942.

Kajee, A. I., P. R. Pather, and A. Christopher. *Treatment of Indians in South Africa: A Memorandum of Facts.* Cape Town: South African Indian Congress, 1946.

Kumar, P. Pratap. *Hindus in South Africa: Their Traditions and Beliefs.* Durban: University of Durban-Westville, 2000.

Kuper, Leo, Hilstan Watts, and Ronald Davies. *Durban: A Study in Racial Ecology.* London: Jonathan Cape, 1958.

Maasdorp, Gavin, and Nesen Pillay. *Urban Relocation and Racial Segregation: The Case of Indian South Africans.* Durban: Department of Economics, University of Natal, 1977.

Meer, Fatima. *Portrait of Indian South Africans.* Durban: Avon House, 1961.

Naicker, G. M. *A Historical Synopsis of the Indian Question in South Africa.* Durban: Anti-Segregation Council, 1945[?].

O'Meara, Dan. *Forty Lost Years: The Apartheid State and the Politics of the National Party, 1948–1994.* Athens: Ohio University Press, 1996.

Pachai, Bridglal. *The International Aspects of the South African Indian Question, 1860–1971.* Cape Town: C. Struik, 1971.

———, ed. *South Africa's Indians: The Evolution of a Minority.* Washington, D.C.: University Press of America, 1979.

Ramamurthi, T. G. *Apartheid and Indian South Africans: A Study of the Role of Ethnic Indians in the Struggle Against Apartheid in South Africa.* New Delhi: Reliance, 1995.

Schrire, Robert, ed. *Malan to De Klerk: Leadership in the Apartheid State.* New York: St. Martin's Press, 1994.

South African Institute of Race Relations. *Indian Life and Labour in Natal.* New Africa Pamphlet No. 23. Survey conducted by Raymond Burrows. Johannesburg: SAIRR, 1952.

———. *A Survey of Race Relations, 1948–1949.* Johannesburg: SAIRR, 1950.

———. *A Survey of Race Relations in South Africa, 1956–1957.* Johannesburg: SAIRR, 1958.

Tichmann, Paul. *Gandhi Sites in Durban.* Durban: Local History Museums, 1998.

Webb, Maurice, and Kenneth Kirkwood. *The Durban Riots and After.* Johannesburg: SAIRR, 1949.

Webb, Maurice, and V. Sirkari Naidoo. *The Indian—Citizen or Subject?* Pamphlet, reprinted from *Race Relations Journal* 14, no. 1. Johannesburg: SAIRR, 1947.

Union of South Africa. *Report of the Asiatic Inquiry Commission.* Cape Town: Government Printers, 1921.

United Kingdom, India Office. "Indians in Natal: Main file 1901–1925." British Library, IOR/L/E/7/1274.

———. "Representations from Indian Associations in South Africa (related to Land Act), 1943–44." File of telegrams and other correspondence. British Library, IOR/L/E/8/300.

University of Natal, Department of Economics. *The Durban Housing Survey: A Study of Housing in a Multi-Racial Community.* Natal Regional Survey Additional Report No. 2. Pietermaritzburg: University of Natal Press, 1952.

UNITED STATES

Barringer, Herbert, Robert W. Gardner, and Michael J. Levin. *Asians and Pacific Islanders in the United States.* National Committee for Research on the 1980 Census. New York: Russell Sage Foundation, 1993.

Bhakta, Govind B. *Patels: A Gujarati Community History in the United States.* Los Angeles: UCLA Asian American Studies Center Press, 2002.

California, State Board of Control. *California and the Oriental: Japanese, Chinese, and Hindus.* Report to Gov. Wm. D. Stephens, June 19, 1920.

Chan, Sucheng. *Asian Americans: An Interpretive History.* Immigrant Heritage of America Series. Boston: Twayne, 1991.

Charter Township of Canton, Wayne County, Michigan. *Future Land Use Plan.* Written January 1976 by Impact (Improved Planning Action); adopted by the Canton Township Planning Commission on April 20, 1976.

Daniels, Roger. "History of Indian Immigration to the United States: An Interpretive Essay." New York: Asia Society, 1989.

Espiritu, Yen Le. *Asian American Panethnicity: Bridging Institutions and Identities.* Philadelphia: Temple University Press, 1992.

Hudson, Samuel. *Michigan's Tenth Largest: A History of the Plymouth-Canton Community School District (1830–1986).* Plymouth: School District, 1997.

Jain, Usha R. *The Gujaratis of San Francisco.* New York: AMS Press, 1989.

Kalita, S. Mitra. *Suburban Sahibs: Three Immigrant Families and Their Passage from India to America.* New Brunswick, N.J.: Rutgers University Press, 2005.

Kitano, Harry H. L., and Roger Daniels. *Asian Americans: Emerging Minorities.* 2nd edition. Englewood Cliffs, N.J.: Prentice Hall, 1995.

Melendy, Brett H. *Asians in America: Filipinos, Koreans, and East Indians.* Boston: Twayne, 1977.

Niland, John R. *The Asian Engineering Brain Drain: A Study of International Relocation into the United States from India, China, Korea, Thailand and Japan.* Lexington, Mass.: Heath Lexington, 1970.

Portes, Alejandro, and Rubén G. Rumbaut. *Immigrant America: A Portrait.* Berkeley: University of California Press, 1990.

Riddle, David. "Race and Reaction in Warren, Michigan, 1971–1974: *Bradley v. Milliken* and the Cross-District Busing Controversy." *Michigan Historical Review* 26, no. 2 (Fall 2000): 1–50.

Saran, Parmatma. *The Asian Indian Experience in the United States.* Cambridge, Mass.: Schenkman, 1985.

Scott, Gale. "Indians Snap Up Small Motels; Immigration Probe Under Way." *Washington Post,* May 7, 1979.

Southeast Michigan Council of Governments. *Community Profiles in Southeast Michigan, 1980 Census.* Vol. 1, *Macomb, Oakland, and Wayne Counties.* Detroit: SEMCOG, 1981.

———. *Economic Development in Southeast Michigan: A Profile and Inventory.* Detroit: SEMCOG, June 1980.

———. *Patterns of Diversity and Change in Southeast Michigan.* Detroit: SEMCOG, August 1994.

Takaki, Ronald. *Strangers from a Different Shore: A History of Asian Americans.* Boston: Little, Brown, 1989.

Turkel, Stanley. "From Ragas to Riches: A Wonderful American Immigrant Success Story." *HotelInteractive.com.* Part 1, May 2, 2006 (www.hotel interactive.com/index.asp?page_id=5000&article_id=5847). Part 2, June 1, 2006 (www.hotelinteractive.com/index.asp?page_id=5000&article_id =5920).

Ueda, Reed. *Postwar Immigrant America: A Social History.* Boston: Bedford/St. Martin's, 1994.

United States, Department of Justice, Immigration and Naturalization Service. *I&N Reporter,* volumes 1–19 (July 1952–April 1971).

United States, House of Representatives, Committee on Foreign Affairs, Sub-committee on National Security Policy and Scientific Developments. *Brain Drain: A Study of the Persistent Issue of International Scientific Mobility*. Washington, D.C.: Congressional Research Service, Library of Congress, September 1974.

United States, National Science Foundation. *Scientists, Engineers, and Physicians from Abroad: Trends Through Fiscal Year 1970*. Surveys of Science Resources Series. Washington, D.C.: National Science Foundation, 1972.

Yamato, Alexander, Soo-Young Chin, Wendy L. Ng, and Joel Franks. *Asian Americans in the United States*. Vol. 1. Dubuque, Iowa: Kendall/Hunt, 1993.

Zia, Helen. *Asian American Dreams: The Emergence of an American People*. New York: Farrar, Straus and Giroux, 2000.

INTERVIEWS

I am grateful to those family members, and a few others, who agreed to be interviewed for this book. Not all of their stories ended up in the manuscript, but all contributed to the whole. Most interviews were conducted in person in 2001–02, with a few subsequent in-person and phone interviews.

In Australia: Ashok Narsey, Hemant and Dipika Hazrat, Hemlata Kumar, Kaushaliya Kumar, Manjula Hazrat, Mukesh and Alka Hazrat, (late) Ranchhod Hazrat.

In Canada: Damayanti and Dhiraj Motiram, Jaisri Khatri, (late) Kanchan Gowri, Lila Sholanki, Neena Sen, Roger (Raju) and Judy Sholanki, Uttam and Vanita Morriswala.

In Fiji: (late) Bhagwan Gokal, Brijlal Kapadia, Jagmohan Narsey, Jiten M. Narsey, Jiten T. Narsey, Lili Narsey, Mahendra and Panna Hazratwala, Pratibha Kumar-Aniawala, Pushpa Vrajlal, R. I. Kapadia, Ratilal and Dhangauri Narsey, Tara Gopaldas, Thakor ("Tom") Narsey, Uttam Narsey, Venilal Narsey.

In Hong Kong: Hemesh Chhiba, Mahendra Gokal.

In India: Amrat Khatri, Bimal Barot, Harish Kapadia, Jaswant Kapadia, Jaydeep Parmar, (late) Jekisan Narsai Chohan.

In New Zealand: (late) Manilal Narsey, Pravin and Laxmi Narsey, Rama Khatri.

In South Africa: Bina Nagar, Gangaram Ramjee, Harilal Ramjee, Mahendra Kapitan, Praveena Ramjee, Renuka Kooverjee, Savita Nagar, Veena Kapitan.

In the United Kingdom: Anil Hazratwala, Chandraprakash Khatri, Harilal Narsai, Kamlaben Khatri, Minal Khatri, Mukesh Khatri, Sumita Khatri, Rajnikant Khatri, Shashikant Khatri.

In the United States: Bhanu Hajratwala, Bharti Damudar, Bhupendra Hajratwala, Dhiren Narotam, Kokila Kalidas, Mala and Madhukant Kumar, Moti Dullabh, Nainesh Ramjee, Nayan Hajratwala and Heidi Naasko, Ramesh Gokal, Tara Narotam, Vinay Kumar, Vrajlal Ramjee.

FAMILY TREES

KEY

============ means marriage

Male main character of a chapter in BOLD SMALL CAPS

Female main character of a chapter in *BOLD ITALIC SMALL CAPS*

Male names in roman

Female names in *italic*

maternal

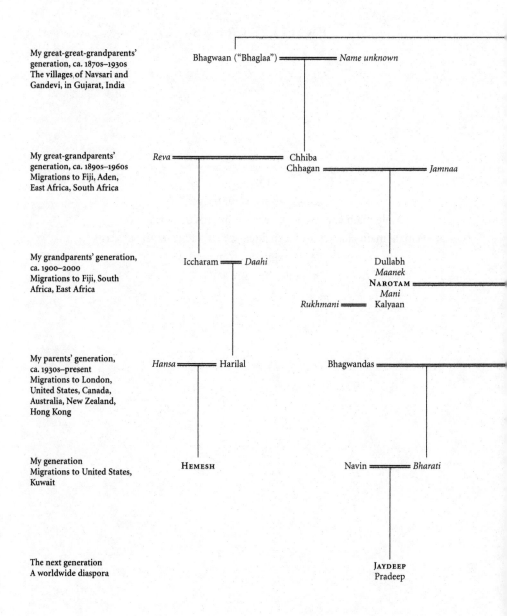

My great-great-grandparents' generation, ca. 1870s–1930s
The villages of Navsari and Gandevi, in Gujarat, India

Bhagwaan ("Bhaglaa") ══════ *Name unknown*

My great-grandparents' generation, ca. 1890s–1960s
Migrations to Fiji, Aden, East Africa, South Africa

Reva ══════ Chhiba
Chhagan ══════ *Jamnaa*

My grandparents' generation, ca. 1900–2000
Migrations to Fiji, South Africa, East Africa

Iccharam ══ *Daahi*

Dullabh
Maanek
NAROTAM ══════
Mani
Rukhmani ══ Kalyaan

My parents' generation, ca. 1930s–present
Migrations to London, United States, Canada, Australia, New Zealand, Hong Kong

Hansa ══ Harilal

Bhagwandas ══════

My generation
Migrations to United States, Kuwait

HEMESH

Navin ══════ *Bharati*

The next generation
A worldwide diaspora

JAYDEEP
Pradeep

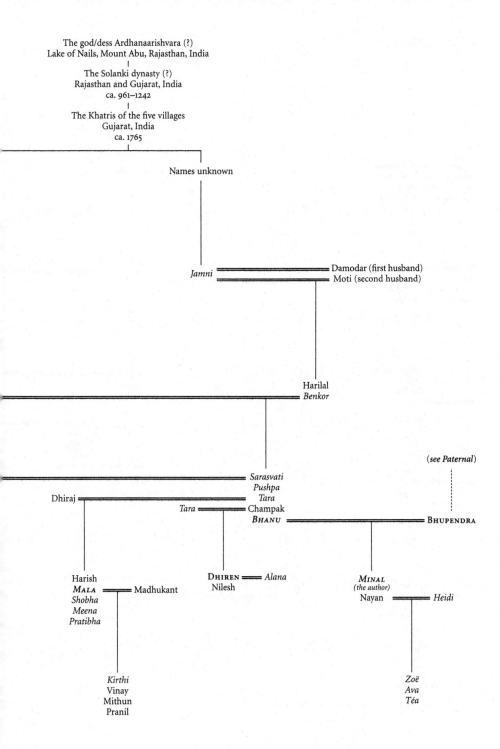

The god/dess Ardhanaarishvara (?)
Lake of Nails, Mount Abu, Rajasthan, India

The Solanki dynasty (?)
Rajasthan and Gujarat, India
ca. 961–1242

The Khatris of the five villages
Gujarat, India
ca. 1765

Names unknown

Jamni ═══ Damodar (first husband)
═══ Moti (second husband)

Harilal
Benkor

(*see Paternal*)

Sarasvati
Pushpa
Tara
Dhiraj ═══ *Tara* ═══ Champak
BHANU ═══ BHUPENDRA

Harish
MALA ═══ Madhukant
Shobha
Meena
Pratibha

DHIREN ═══ *Alana*
Nilesh

MINAL
(*the author*)
Nayan ═══ *Heidi*

Kirthi
Vinay
Mithun
Pranil

Zoë
Ava
Téa

419

paternal

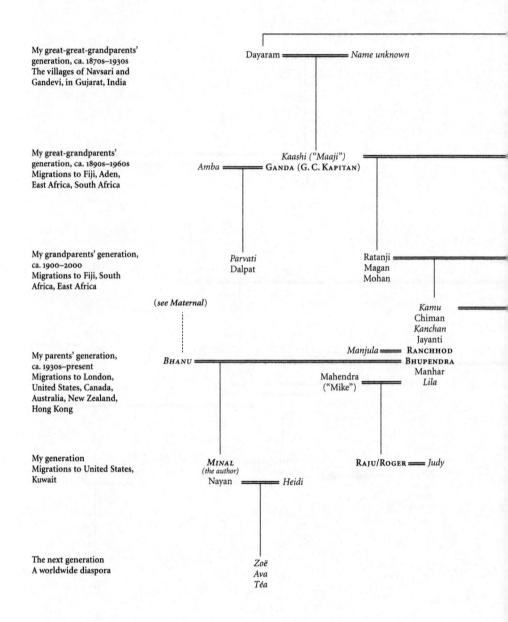

My great-great-grandparents' generation, ca. 1870s–1930s
The villages of Navsari and Gandevi, in Gujarat, India

Dayaram ══════ Name unknown

My great-grandparents' generation, ca. 1890s–1960s
Migrations to Fiji, Aden, East Africa, South Africa

Kaashi ("Maaji")
Amba ══════ GANDA (G. C. KAPITAN)

My grandparents' generation, ca. 1900–2000
Migrations to Fiji, South Africa, East Africa

Parvati
Dalpat

Ratanji
Magan
Mohan

(see Maternal)

Kamu
Chiman
Kanchan
Jayanti

My parents' generation, ca. 1930s–present
Migrations to London, United States, Canada, Australia, New Zealand, Hong Kong

BHANU ══════

Manjula ══════ RANCHHOD
BHUPENDRA
Manhar
Lila

Mahendra ("Mike") ══════

My generation
Migrations to United States, Kuwait

MINAL
(the author)
Nayan ══════ Heidi

RAJU/ROGER ══════ Judy

The next generation
A worldwide diaspora

Zoë
Ava
Téa

420

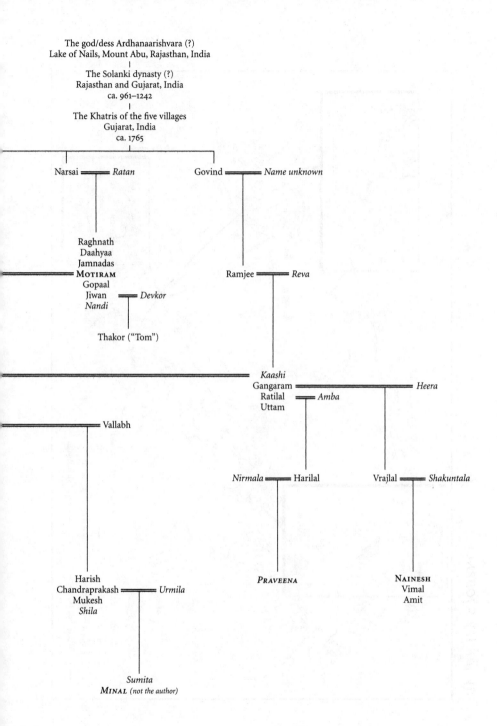

The god/dess Ardhanaarishvara (?)
Lake of Nails, Mount Abu, Rajasthan, India

The Solanki dynasty (?)
Rajasthan and Gujarat, India
ca. 961–1242

The Khatris of the five villages
Gujarat, India
ca. 1765

Narsai ═══ *Ratan*   Govind ═══ *Name unknown*

Raghnath
Daahyaa
Jamnadas
MOTIRAM   Ramjee ═══ *Reva*
Gopaal
Jiwan ═══ *Devkor*
Nandi

Thakor ("Tom")

Kaashi
Gangaram ═══ *Heera*
Ratilal ═══ *Amba*
Uttam

Vallabh

Nirmala ═══ Harilal   Vrajlal ═══ *Shakuntala*

Harish
Chandraprakash ═══ *Urmila*   **PRAVEENA**   **NAINESH**
Mukesh   Vimal
Shila   Amit

Sumita
MINAL (not the author)

421

my family's journey

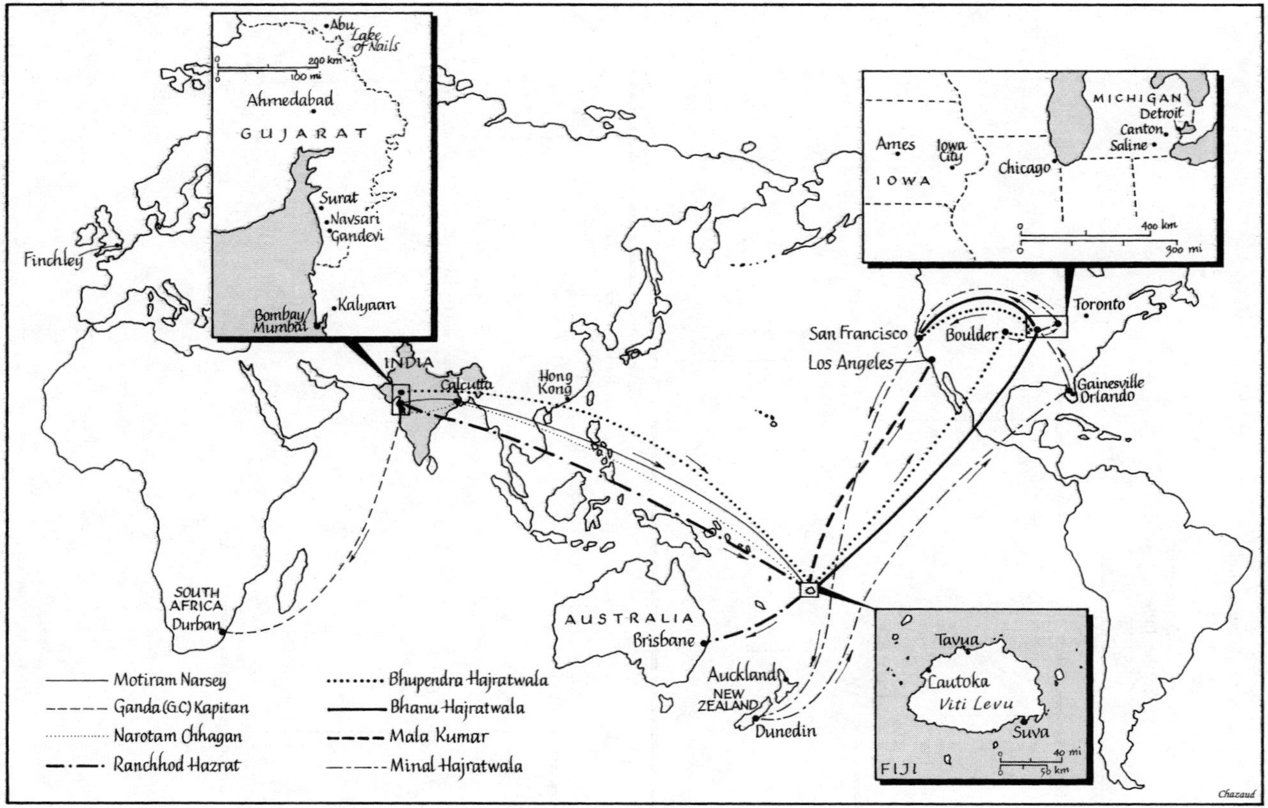

INDEX